Macroeconomics Under Flexible Exchange Rates

LSE Handbooks in Economics Series

This series is designed to present new work across the discipline of theoretical and applied economics. Written at a level suitable for advanced students and professional economists it will draw attention to new areas of economic enquiry, areas of contention and debate and the reporting of new research findings. The series will call on the expertise of one of the foremost groups of economists in the world and the authors will be drawn from a wide international base.

The Economics of Training
P. Chapman
The Econometric Analysis of Times Series
A. C. Harvey
Public Enterprise Economics (2nd edn)
R. Rees
Informal Economic Activity
J. J. Thomas

LSE Handbooks in Economics Series

Macroeconomics Under Flexible Exchange Rates

Manfred Gärtner

Department of Economics, University of St Gallen

HARVESTER WHEATSHEAF

New York London Toronto Sydney Tokyo Singapore

First published 1993 by
Prentice Hall/Harvester Wheatsheaf
Campus 400, Maylands Avenue
Hemel Hempstead
Hertfordshire, HP2 7EZ
A division of
Simon & Schuster International Group

Typeset in 10/12 pt Times by Vision Typesetting, Manchester

Printed and bound in Great Britain by
T. J. International Ltd.

British Library Cataloguing in Publication Data

A catalogue record for this book is available from the British Library

ISBN 0-7450-1326-0 (hbk)
ISBN 0-7450-1327-9 (pbk)

---

4 5 98 97 96

To David, Lou, Chris, Dennis, and Kai

Contents

Preface

This book focuses on theory. A concomitant discussion of relevant empirical work might well have doubled the volume of this text. Despite its focus on theory, though, it is an applied book in the sense that the models discussed tackle macroeconomic problems which have been challenging open economies ever since the collapse of the last worldwide system of fixed exchange rates established under the treaty of Bretton Woods. To underscore this link between theory and reality, theoretical developments are frequently motivated as responses to hitherto unexplained real-world phenomena.

The book is intended for use by advanced undergraduate students or as an introductory text during the first graduate year, where it may bridge the huge gap between standard textbook analyses and the level of articles in learned journals. It should also prove useful for professional economists in business, organizations, or government agencies at the national or international level, who are required to keep on top of theoretical developments in this field. Ideally, readers should already have been exposed to macroeconomic theory at an intermediate level. However, something less than this might do as well. As an example, much of the book has been used successfully with fourth year political science students majoring in international relations. Some previous exposure to open economy macroeconomics at an introductory level – as characterized by the Mundell–Fleming model – is also assumed. Even this is not an indispensable condition, however, as the essentials of the Mundell–Fleming model under flexible exchange rates are reviewed in the first chapter. This review is rather compact, however, and a complete novice would certainly have to consult some introductory macro text where this sort of open economy problem is dealt with at a slower pace.

The presumed mathematical skills are rather modest, even though leafing through the book for the first time may convey a different impression. Straightforward algebraic manipulations and elementary rates of differentiation will carry the reader through most of the mathematical analyses. On a few occasions experience with difference and differential equations will help. Three extremely useful formal tools of a less basic nature are introduced in the form of easy-to-use recipes as they are needed. These are the implicit function rule, which facilitates comparative-static analyses of general function models, the concept of phase diagrams, which provides ready insights into the stability of nonlinear differential equation systems, and a method for solving rational expectations models.

Beginning in the second chapter, the reader is guided through what has been achieved in the field of flexible exchange rate macroeconomics during the past two decades. While the book's emphasis on the macroeconomic disequilibrium approach to the exchange rate certainly reflects my own preference, all other landmark models and approaches find their proper place as well: the monetarist approach, currency substitution, the portfolio balance approach, equilibrium exchange rates, as well as topics such as bubbles or the peso problem. The book is capped off by a (lengthy) concluding chapter on political-economic issues under flexible exchange rates.

The models covered in this book are very much what any expert in this field would select. Nevertheless, the following features (should) make the book a unique text in its field:

1. *Compact introduction of models.* Whenever the discussion turns to a new model, or returns to a model which was introduced in a previous chapter, all equations making up the model are given in one structured context. This renders each model easy to take in at a glance and provides a convenient point of reference.

2. *Multi-method discussion of major models.* All major models are discussed *verbally*, on an intuitive basis, then given a careful *formal analysis*, and are finally explained *graphically*. Whenever this kind of separation appeared unduly awkward, graphical accounts of the central mechanisms feature prominently in the discussion.

3. *Step-by-step derivation of results.* The book makes every effort not to leave out any relevant step during the analytical derivation of results. It differs from journal articles and many other textbooks in that a conscious attempt is made not to frustrate students with remarks such as 'standard manipulations yield' or 'as the reader can easily convince himself'. Instead, how to arrive at the desired result is shown in a *step-by-step* fashion, even though this means repetition and there is the risk of occasionally boring readers with a more advanced background.

4. *Extensive use of graphical analysis.* The book very much presents the state of the art on flexible exchange rate macroeconomics in pictures. Even to readers who are daunted by mathematical methods, *some 100 carefully*

conceived figures provide access to what research on flexible exchange rates has accomplished and what it currently discusses.

5. *How to do research.* Readers are encouraged to not only acquire a passive understanding of the models emphasized in the book, but also to learn how to put them into practice on new problems. With this in mind, the monetary approach to the exchange rate is not discussed merely in a standard textbook setting, as are the other models. In addition, many issues of a more advanced nature are carefully analyzed, such as supply shocks, structural goods markets, stochastic money supply processes, learning processes when expectations are not rational, technology and preference shocks, rational bubbles, and more. Readers preferring or requiring less depth may skip these sections without necessarily encountering problems in subsequent chapters.

6. *Worked problems.* Throughout the book students are confronted with inserts containing problems. Their prime purpose is not to review or control the understanding of previous material, but to lure readers into waters not covered by the text. A detailed discussion of problems raised is given at the end of each chapter.

Instants of frustration inevitably occur while working on a project such as this. Now that the book is complete it is my pleasure to express my gratitude to those who have helped in its preparation, having shared both the dull times and the fun. Several people stand out. Eva Leemann, who did an excellent job of transcribing several versions of the quite demanding manuscript, some of them from dictaphone, while insisting in her unique Swiss way that English was not one of her strong points at all. Friederike Pohlenz has developed outstanding expertise while creating most of the graphs on her PC. The vast majority of the figures was produced in Micrografx's CHARISMA 2.1 and transferred directly to film – for those who may be curious. Guido Boller checked most of the text for language errors and saved me from quite a number of blunders. He, Benedikt Braumann, Monika Bütler, and Klaus Wellershoff also commented extensively on a first draft of Chapter 9. Many thanks to all of them, and also to my students who worked with previous drafts of the material covered in this book. They too drew my attention to dozens of errors and provided many useful suggestions for improvements.

Manfred Gärtner
University of St Gallen, Switzerland

July 1992

Models

Chapter 1

Open-economy macroeconomics: introduction and outline

During the past two decades industrial countries have had to battle with a whole series of economic problems:

- Exploding oil prices followed by surges in unemployment.
- Lasting or recurring inflation.
- The accumulation of massive debtor or lender positions at the international level.
- Abrupt and often irreversible changes in international competiveness.
- The renaissance and growing importance of protectionism in new forms.

The extent to which economic policy has succeeded in fighting these problems can only be understood when projected against the background of a highly integrated world economy with steadily intensifying flows of capital and goods. This insight is already dominating US macroeconomics textbooks aiming at the American market, as students are confronted at an early stage with the special problems of open economies. All the more, analyzing macroeconomic issues in an open economy setting becomes a *must* for all other countries.

No analysis of complex problems can do without abstraction. Economists have chosen to analyze international economic relations in three distinct areas. Each of these areas focuses on a comprehensible number of aspects considered relevant for specific issues, while ignoring others. The three areas of analysis are (1) the description and analysis of national and international institutions; (2) the 'pure' analysis of international trade (focusing on what goes on behind the veil of money); and (3) monetary macroeconomics of open economies.

1. *The description and economic analysis of institutions* is of central importance. Only the existence of specific institutions or contractual

agreements renders international economic relations a subject of scientific analysis in its own right:

- The observed low mobility of labour and (decreasingly so) of capital between countries is at the core of orthodox explanations of international trade, which proceed from the assumption of different factor endowments. Low factor mobility, however, is not primarily due to things like transport costs, risk aversion or strong regional ties. Instead, major causes are institutional barriers erected on the borders, such as overt or concealed immigration quotas or hindrances to capital flows.
- By definition, exchange rate movements can only generate cycles and trends in relative prices as long as countries insist on having their own currencies and do not fix the exchange rate in one way or other. Even if exchange rates are fixed, the need for a field called open-economy macroeconomics continues to exist as long as the institutional restrictions on factor mobility mentioned above are not removed. Not until a common currency and common goods and factor markets exist, as envisaged by the European Community for the 1990s, will the problems associated with international economic relations within that area 'degenerate' to the structural problems which we also encounter in closed economies. It would feel kind of awkward, anyway, to speak of *international* economic relations when addressing problems that occur within the European Community characterized by common labour, goods, and capital markets, monetary union, harmonization of taxes, and the delegation of further political powers to the electoral bodies in Brussels or Strasbourg.

All this signals the importance of national and, in particular, international institutions such as the GATT, the OECD, the World Bank or the International Monetary Fund. It makes it crucial to be familiar with the relevant institutions, to analyze their economic importance, to look for new and, from an economic perspective, better institutions and to develop political–economic explanations of when and why institutions come and go and how they can be improved.

2. *The pure theory of international trade* looks at incentive structures which the veil of money may sometimes blur or hide. These incentive structures determine which goods are exchanged internationally and in what amounts. They determine the terms at which goods are traded, how tariffs or other protectionist instruments in the short and in the long run bear on the state of the economy, on growth or on distribution, etc. A central characteristic of the pure theory of international trade is that it looks at pure barter economies, which excludes, by definition, the

possibility of balance of payments problems and methodologically calls for a widespread use of microeconomic concepts of analysis.

3. *The monetary analysis of open economies*, by contrast, focuses on macroeconomic issues and is a key building block of modern macroeconomics. Accordingly, the monetary analysis of international economic relations differs from the pure theory of international trade not only in respect to the subject of analysis, but also as regards the methods involved. However, to the extent that economists succeed in their necessary efforts to provide an improved microfoundation of macroeconomics, these methodological differences are being blurred. Quite recently, **hysteresis** is becoming a catchword in international economics, referring to the possibility that temporary deteriorations in one country's competitive position may have a lasting impact on trade patterns and market shares. Both the issues involved there and the methods employed place hysteresis on the border-line between the pure theory of international trade and monetary macroeconomics of the open economy.

1.1 The balance of payments

Monetary macroeconomics of the *open* economy differs from monetary analysis of the closed economy by taking into consideration the flow of goods, services and capital between home and abroad. Countries keep track of these transactions in their **balance of payments** (BP), which is subdivided into the **current-account** (CA) balance, the **capital-account** (CP) balance and the **official reserve account** (OR) balance.[1]

$$BP = CA + CP + OR = 0 \tag{1.1}$$

Table 1.1 gives a crude breakdown of the balance of payments for the G-5 countries. Probably the most important point to note is that any transaction recorded in the balance of payments requires the sale or the

Table 1.1 Balance of payments in G-5 countries, 1990, billions of dollars

	France	*Germany*	*Japan*	*UK*	*USA*
Current account balance (CA)	−9.9	46.8	35.9	−24.6	−92.2
Balance on goods and services	[0.3]	[69.5]	[41.4]	[−15.8]	[−69.8]
Merchandise trade balance	(−14.0)	(71.6)	(63.6)	(−32.5)	(−108.1)
Invisible trade balance	(14.3)	(−2.0)	(−22.2)	(16.7)	(38.3)
Unilateral transfers	[−9.9]	[−22.7]	[−5.5]	[−8.8]	[−22.4]
Capital account balance (CP)	21.7	−41.3	−42.5	23.4	63.7
Official reserve account balance (OR)	−11.8	−5.5	6.6	1.2	28.5

Source: International Monetary Fund, International Financial Statistics, data tape.

purchase of foreign currency. Therefore, when the balance of payments is in equilibrium, the foreign exchange market is in equilibrium as well.

Equation (1.1) states that, in a general sense, the balance of payments is always in equilibrium. This is due to the fact that each transaction is recorded on the debit side and on the credit side of an account. When people talk about balance of payments deficits or surpluses, they always refer to some subaccount of the balance of payments.

Put simply, the official reserve account tracks changes in the central bank's foreign currency holdings. A positive (negative) value signals that the central bank has been a net buyer (seller) in the foreign exchange market, and the private sector, whose transactions are recorded in the current account and in the capital account, is a net seller (buyer):

$$-OR = CA + CP \tag{1.2}$$

The *negative* of the official reserve account balance, $-OR$, is sometimes called the **official settlements balance**. While it is usually used as a barometer of balance of payments disequilibria, it also indicates to what extent the central bank has intervened in and thus distorted the price in the foreign exchange market. Under a system of flexible exchange rates the central bank completely abstains from the foreign exchange market. It is axiomatic that $OR = 0$, and the balance of payments can register neither a deficit nor a surplus:

$$CA + CP = 0 \tag{1.3}$$

A look at the official reserve account balances in Table 1.1 makes the point that equation (1.3) states a property of an ideal system of flexible exchange rates which major industrial countries did not quite reach in 1990.

While accounting definitions plus the complete abstention of the central bank from the foreign exchange markets under flexible exchange rates equilibrate the balance of payments by definition, the balance of payments cannot be ignored in macroeconomic analyses of open economies under flexible exchange rates. There are two major reasons for this.

1. The balance of payments equilibrium described in (1.3) can be accomplished in many different ways: by a current account deficit and an equivalent surplus in the capital account; by a current account surplus and an equivalent deficit in the capital account; or by both the current account and the capital account being in equilibrium. Therefore, what goes on in the various accounts making up the balance of payments equilibrium may have important consequences for economic growth and the long-run development of foreign debt.

2. In a way, our balance of payments equation $CA + CP = 0$ resembles the *ex post* identity $S = I$ in the national accounts of a closed economy. While

the balance of payments is always in equilibrium *ex post*, the more interesting question for economists is whether the balance of payments is in equilibrium *ex ante*. This is the case if no unplanned or, given the present set of parameters, unwanted transactions are being conducted. This cannot possibly be determined by looking at the statistical data alone. Rather, we must develop an *economic understanding* of the transactions tracked in the current account and in the capital account. Pertinent attempts to explain net exports and net capital flows bring familiar macroeconomic variables into focus, such as aggregate income, the price level, interest rates, both at home and abroad, exchange rates and exchange rate expectations. A balance of payments equilibrium, and thus, by the same token, an equilibrium in the foreign exchange market, in principle can be achieved by an unlimited number of combinations of those economic variables. Luckily, the number of possibilities is reduced by the fact that the money market and the domestic goods market call for certain relationships between macroeconomic variables. An analysis of economic problems linked to the balance of payments, therefore, cannot be conducted by means of an isolated look at the balance of payments. Rather, the balance of payments must be embedded into a complete model of the macroeconomy. In this context exchange rate theory finds its proper role in macroeconomics.

1.2 The goods market, the money market and the foreign exchange market

The pioneering macroeconomic analyses of open economies under flexible (and fixed) exchange rates are due to Mundell (1963) and Fleming (1962). Even today the Mundell–Fleming model offers some useful answers to elementary questions regarding the open economy. What is more, recent theoretical developments as discussed in Chapters 2–4 have their roots in this earlier approach. The following discussion of the Mundell–Fleming model is rather concise, assuming some familiarity with the model on the part of the reader.[2] This section will also give the opportunity to introduce some key concepts.

1.2.1 Formal presentation of equilibria

The Mundell–Fleming model picks up on the Keynesian IS–LM model for the closed economy, and adds those relationships considered relevant for the open economy. Just what those building blocks are can be seen from Model 1.1.

Model 1.1
The Mundell–Fleming model

1 Goods market

$Y+RQ=C+I+G+X$		goods market equilibrium	(1.4)
$C=C(Y)$	$0<C_Y<1$	consumption	(1.5)
$I=I(i)$	$I_i<0$	investment	(1.6)
$Q=Q(Y,R)$	$Q_Y>0; Q_R<0$	imports	(1.7)
$X=X(Y^*,R)$	$X_{Y^*}>0; X_R>0$	exports	(1.8)

2 Money market

$\frac{M^d}{P}=L(Y,i)$	$L_Y>0; L_i<0$	money demand	(1.9)
$M^s=M^d=M$		money market equilibrium	(1.10)

3 Foreign exchange market

$BP=CA+CP=0$		balance of payments	(1.11)
$CA=PX-EP^*Q$		current account	(1.12)
$CP=K[i-i^*-E(\dot{e})]$	$K_i=-K_{i^*}=-K_{E(\dot{e})}>0$	capital account	(1.13)

Notes: The signs or magnitudes of (partial) derivatives with respect to the subscript are given next to the behavioural equations. Variables are defined as follows:

Y	domestic national income	M^d	money demand
Q	imports	M^s	money supply
C	consumption	M	money
I	investment	i	nominal interest rate
G	government spending	BP	balance of payments
X	exports	CA	current account
R	real exchange rate ($\equiv EP^*/P$)	CP	capital account
E	exchange rate	i^*	foreign interest rate
P	domestic price level	$E(\dot{e})$	expected depreciation
P^*	foreign price level	Y^*	foreign national income

The IS schedule

Equations (1.4)–(1.8) describe the goods market in the open economy in the Keynesian tradition. Equation (1.4) is the familiar equilibrium condition. In equilibrium, planned expenditure for domestic goods by domestic residents and by foreigners must equal domestic output plus imports (turned into its domestic goods equivalent by multiplication with the real exchange rate). Behavioural equations (1.5)–(1.8) postulate behavioural functions explaining consumption, investment, imports and exports in general terms. After substituting (1.5)–(1.8) into the equilibrium condition (1.4), therefore, the traditional IS schedule does not give the interest rate as an explicit function of aggregate income, but instead as an *implicit* function hidden in the relation under certain conditions.[3]

$$I(i)-Y+C(Y)+G+X(Y^*,R)-RQ(Y,R)=F(i,Y,G,Y^*,R)=0 \quad (1.14)$$

These conditions are being met here. We obtain the slope of the hidden IS schedule by computing the total differential of (1.14), holding exogenous variables constant[4] and solving for $\partial i/\partial Y$. Another, more direct way to obtain the slope is by applying the **implicit function rule**.[5] This rule states that if (1.14) implies a function $i=f(Y)$, we have

$$\frac{\partial i}{\partial Y}=-\frac{F_Y}{F_i}=-\frac{C_Y-RQ_Y-1}{I_i}<0 \quad (1.15)$$

Equation (1.15) says that our implicit IS schedule possesses a negative slope. In economic terms the IS curve answers the question of what interest rate is required to make sure that individuals plan to demand a given supply of domestically produced goods. The left-hand side of equation (1.4) is the total supply of goods on the home market, including imports. The right-hand side gives desired demand, including exports. Imports Q are expressed in an equivalent number of domestically produced goods by multiplication with the real exchange rate R, the terms of trade between domestically and foreign produced goods.

Of course, the market-clearing interest rate indicated by the IS curve changes as soon as exogenous variables change. How such exogenous changes shift the IS curve is also easily obtained by applying the implicit function rule:

$$\frac{\partial i}{\partial G}=-\frac{F_G}{F_i}=-\frac{1}{I_i}>0 \quad (1.16)$$

$$\frac{\partial i}{\partial Y^*}=-\frac{F_{Y^*}}{F_i}=-\frac{X_{Y^*}}{I_i}>0 \quad (1.17)$$

$$\frac{\partial i}{\partial R}=-\frac{F_R}{F_i}=-\frac{X_R-Q-RQ_R}{I_i}>0 \quad (1.18)$$

An increase in government expenditure, an increase in aggregate income abroad and – if the Marshall–Lerner condition holds (this states the requirements for a depreciation to improve the current account – see the discussion of the J-curve effect on p. 23) – a real depreciation of the domestic currency all stimulate the demand for domestically produced goods and shift the IS curve upwards.

The LM schedule

According to equations (1.9) and (1.10) the relation

$$\frac{M}{P}-L(Y,i)=\tilde{L}(Y,i,P,M)=0 \tag{1.19}$$

implies an LM curve. This equilibrium condition for the money market possesses the slope

$$\frac{\partial i}{\partial Y}=-\frac{\tilde{L}_Y}{\tilde{L}_i}=-\frac{-L_Y}{-L_i}>0 \tag{1.20}$$

A money supply increase shifts the LM curve downward, since for a given level of income the opportunity costs of holding money, that is, interest rates, must fall to induce individuals to demand the additional supply of liquidity:

$$\frac{\partial i}{\partial M}=-\frac{\tilde{L}_M}{\tilde{L}_i}=-\frac{1/P}{-L_i}<0 \tag{1.21}$$

The opposite effect obtains if the price level rises, thus reducing the real-money supply:

$$\frac{\partial i}{\partial P}=-\frac{\tilde{L}_P}{\tilde{L}_i}=-\frac{-M/P^2}{-L_i}>0 \tag{1.22}$$

A movement of the exchange rate has no impact on the position of the LM curve, since from equation (1.19) we obtain $\partial i/\partial E=0$.

The FE schedule

As the final building block of the Mundell–Fleming model, equation (1.11) defines the balance of payments equilibrium. Under flexible exchange rates, when central banks abstain from the foreign exchanges, this can be considered the equilibrium condition for the foreign exchange market. Henceforth we will refer to this equilibrium condition as the FE schedule.[6] The exchange rate gives the amount of domestic currency one has to pay for one unit of foreign currency. So a *rising* exchange rate indicates that the domestic currency is *losing* value – it *depreciates*. This needs special mention because it runs against intuition. It follows from the simple fact that if the exchange rate goes up one has to pay more domestic currency to acquire one unit of foreign currency. So one unit of domestic currency buys less. Domestic currency has lost value.

Demand for domestic currency arises either from the export of goods and services or from capital imports. In both cases foreigners have to acquire domestic currency – in order to purchase goods in the first case and in order to acquire domestic bonds in the second case. On the other hand, imports of goods and capital exports always generate an additional supply of domestic currency. Thus the foreign exchange market only clears if the balance of payments is in equilibrium.

Under a system of flexible exchange rates the balance of payments comprises the current account (equation (1.12)) – expressed in domestic currency – and the capital account (that is, the net flow of *private* capital). Equation (1.13) 'explains' the capital account. It postulates that capital moves to wherever expected yields are higher. Domestic bond yields equal the domestic interest rate. The expected yields of foreign bonds equal the foreign interest rate plus expected depreciation of the domestic currency, which implies an equivalent appreciation of the foreign currency. Inflation differentials do not bear on relative yields as long as individuals always intend to spend their wealth eventually at home. Then domestic inflation reduces the real value of both investments to the same extent, and can therefore be neglected. Inflation abroad is not relevant either, since we are interested in the purchasing power of the home currency.[7]

Substitution of (1.12) and (1.13) into (1.11) and making use of (1.7) and (1.8) yields

$$PX(Y^*, R) - EP^*Q(Y, R) + K[i - i^* - E(\dot{e})] = 0 \tag{1.23}$$

This **equilibrium schedule for the foreign exchange market** possesses the slope

$$\frac{\partial i}{\partial Y} = -\frac{-EP^*Q_Y}{K_i} > 0 \tag{1.24}$$

The foreign exchange market only remains in equilibrium if, *ceteris paribus*, an increase in aggregate income, which deteriorates the current account, is being compensated for by rising interest rates, which make domestic bonds more attractive and improve the capital account.

Figure 1.1 shows the equilibrium schedules for the three markets comprising the Mundell–Fleming model of the open economy in the i/Y plane. Given the assumptions employed, the IS schedule has a negative slope, while both the LM and the FE schedules have positive slopes. Which of the two latter schedules is steeper must remain open and eventually depends on how mobile capital is across borders. Actually, the depicted case of a positively sloped FE curve does not hold generally. Rather, under certain quite plausible assumptions concerning the relationship between capital mobility and balance of payments equilibrium, the two interesting special cases of a horizontal and of a vertical FE curve exist. The following remarks are intended to clarify this.

The role of capital mobility

If the balance of payments equation (1.23) can be considered the equilibrium condition for the foreign exchange market, then the markets

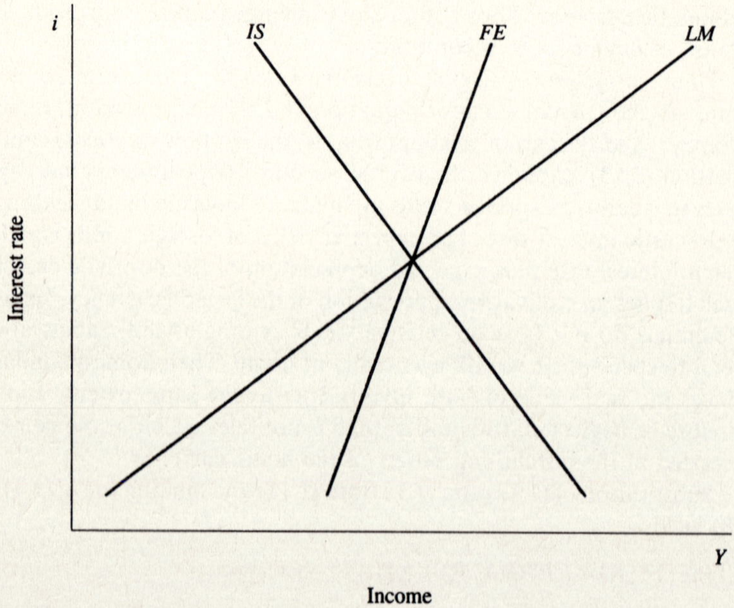

Figure 1.1 Market equilibrium schedules in the Mundell–Fleming model when capital mobility is very low

behind the current account and the capital account must provide the supply of and the demand for foreign exchange. Thus the steady *flow* of (more or less perishable) goods and services, which are monitored in the current account, determines how much currency is supplied and demanded. On the other hand, changes in the *stocks* of foreign assets, which are included in the capital account, also induce supplies of and demands for currencies. Which of the two, the current account or the capital account, responds more strongly to parameter changes eventually determines the price in the foreign exchange market, the exchange rate. For this reason exchange rate theories are called **flow models** if the *flows* of goods and services traced by the current account determine the exchange rate in the first place. **Stock models** of the exchange rate postulate that changes in the *stock* of assets, surveyed in the capital account, are the key determinant of the exchange rate (see Figure 1.10 on page 28).

The remaining chapters of this book will demonstrate that modern theories of exchange rate determination focus on the capital account (and therefore on stocks), sometimes exclusively. In this context the terms **mobility** and **substitutability** of assets are of central importance. A brief discussion of these terms may, therefore, prove useful.

Foreign and domestic assets are **perfect substitutes** only if both are evaluated solely on the basis of their expected returns. Minimal differences would draw the entire investment capital into the asset which offers higher expected returns. Given this, the foreign exchange market can only be in equilibrium if domestic bonds offer the same expected yields as foreign bonds:

$$i = i^* + E(\dot{e})$$

This equilibrium condition is known as **uncovered**, or open, **interest parity**. It only holds if market participants are **risk-neutral**. Since the effective yield of a foreign asset is always influenced by the unpredictable development of the exchange rate, foreign assets are riskier than domestic assets, which offer a fixed interest payment. In order to make risk-averse investors indifferent between domestic and foreign assets, foreign assets have to pay a **risk premium** (RP).[8] This turns the equilibrium condition into

$$i = i^* + E(\dot{e}) + RP$$

The extent to which domestic and foreign assets are substitutes therefore determines equilibrium in the international asset market.

Another term which is sometimes used as a synonym for perfect substitutability is **perfect mobility of capital**. Table 1.2 shows how the two terms are related.

Capital can only be considered perfectly mobile if it can be moved into the preferred form of investment any time without delay and in the desired amount. The columns of Table 1.2 distinguish between perfect and imperfect substitutability, the rows between perfect and imperfect capital mobility. Of the four cases which are logically possible, the south-west case has to be excluded since perfect mobility of capital is a necessary condition for perfect substitutability.[9] A foreign asset can never be a perfect substitute for some domestic asset unless tied-up funds can be repatriated at any time.

On the other hand, it is certainly possible that capital is perfectly mobile, while foreign and domestic assets are nevertheless imperfect substitutes.[10] It has been stated above that another important precondition for perfect substitutability is risk neutrality of the individuals involved. Table 1.2 shows how substitutability and capital mobility bear on the short- and long-run market responses to a displacement from equilibrium. The degree of substitutability determines whether the long-run *equilibrium* contains a risk premium or not. The extent to which capital is mobile determines how *quickly* the long-run equilibrium value is approached. If capital is perfectly mobile, the market clears instantaneously, and short- and long-run responses are identical. When both mobility and substitutability are less than perfect, however, the market needs time to adjust to its new long-run equilibrium.

Table 1.2 Asset market equilibrium at different degrees of capital mobility and substitutability

		Substitutability			
		perfect		not perfect	
Capital mobility	*perfect*	short run	long run	short run	long run
		$i=i^*+E(\dot{e})$	$i=i^*+E(\dot{e})$	$i=i^*+E(\dot{e})+RP$	$i=i^*+E(\dot{e})+RP$
	not perfect	short run	long run	short run	long run
		not possible		$i\neq i^*+E(\dot{e})+RP$	$i=i^*+E(\dot{e})+RP$

Notes: Here i is the nominal return in the home currency and $i^*+E(\dot{e})$ the expected nominal return in the foreign currency. RP is the risk premium.

For the remainder of this chapter we postulate risk neutrality. The terms mobility and substitutability of capital may then conveniently be used as synonyms.

Interpretation of equations (1.23) and (1.24) in the light of the above arguments reveals that when we computed the positive slope of the FE curve as (1.24) (repeated here for convenience)

$$\frac{\partial i}{\partial Y} = -\frac{-EP^*Q_Y}{K_i} > 0 \tag{1.24}$$

we implicitly postulated imperfect mobility of capital, that is, a positive but finite value for K_i.

When capital is perfectly mobile, uncovered interest parity holds continuously exactly because minimal differences between expected yields at home and abroad immediately trigger unlimited flows of capital. In other words, the reaction of the capital account to changes of the interest rate is *infinitely large*. Perfect capital mobility is thus characterized by $K_i \to \infty$. In this case we have, according to equation (1.24),

$$\frac{\partial i}{\partial Y} = 0 \tag{1.24'}$$

If exchange rate expectations are stationary, that is, $E(\dot{e}) = 0$, the capital account and, by the same token, the balance of payments can only be in equilibrium if the domestic and the foreign interest rates are identical.[11] In this case the FE curve is *horizontal* (Figure 1.2, *FE″*). The exchange rate is exclusively determined by the desired stocks of domestic and foreign assets. Flows of goods and services are irrelevant.

At the other extreme, if, say due to strictly enforced capital controls, capital is completely immobile and cannot respond to changes of the interest rate differential at all, we have $K_i = 0$, and, as a consequence,

$$\frac{\partial i}{\partial Y} \to \infty \tag{1.24''}$$

Ceteris paribus, the balance of payments is only in equilibrium for one particular level of aggregate income. There is no trade-off against changes of the interest rate differential. The FE curve is vertical (Figure 1.2, *FE*). Changes of the exchange rate exclusively reflect changes in the flow of goods and services.

FE′ depicts the general case, which we had already postulated in Figure 1.1, where capital is mobile to a limited extent and both flows and stocks determine the exchange rate.

On the FE curves depicted in Figure 1.2 the foreign exchange market is in equilibrium or, at the same time, the balance of payments is in

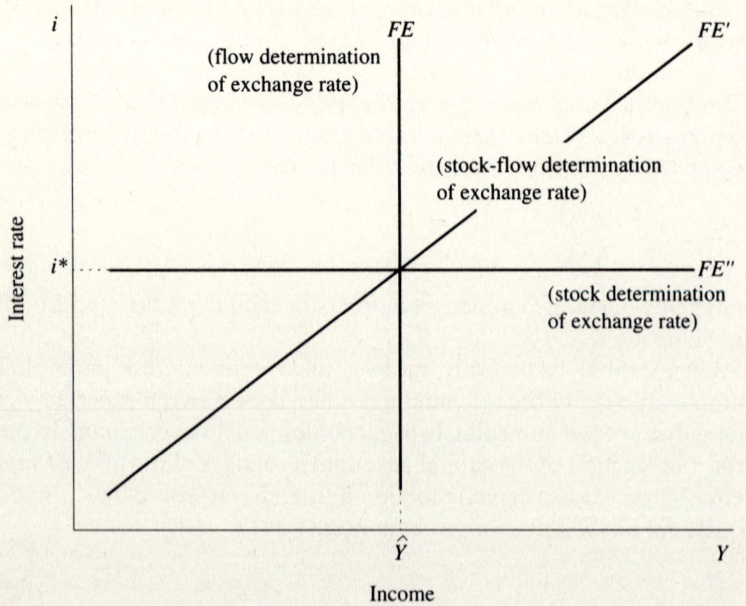

Figure 1.2 Equilibrium schedules for the foreign exchange market when capital mobility is perfect (*FE''*), imperfect (*FE'*) and absent (*FE*)

equilibrium. Each movement away from the FE curve generates an *incipient* balance of payments and foreign exchange market disequilibrium. However, this is immediately counterbalanced by a movement of the exchange rate to a new market-clearing value. Thus a disequilibrium cannot really come into existence. In the case *FE''*, the area above the FE curve characterizes an *incipient surplus*. This implies an incipient excess demand for domestic currency, which is immediately eliminated by an appreciation. In the area below the FE curve there is an incipient balance of payments deficit which triggers a depreciation of the home currency.

While so far we have simply characterized it as the balance of payments equilibrium condition, the FE curve deserves some closer scrutiny; in particular, in the present case of perfect capital mobility. As has already been stated in note 11, the balance of payments is in equilibrium if, and only if, we are on the FE curve. The capital account may be balanced on the FE curve, but this must not happen. If it were balanced at all points on the FE curve, the current account would also be balanced at all points. This is not possible, however. Prices are exogenous by assumption. The exchange rate does not change as long as the foreign exchange market remains in equilibrium; but aggregate income and imports grow as we move to the right *on* the FE curve. Thus, for a given exchange rate only *one* point on the

FE curve exists which balances both the current account and the capital account.

The apparent puzzle is solved by noting that when expected yields at home and abroad are equal, investors are completely indifferent between putting their money in domestic or foreign assets. As long as we remain *on* the FE curve, the international capital market is prepared to finance any deficit or surplus in the current account. The asset market is always in equilibrium, though the capital account may not be balanced. This renders it possible that, while we move to the left on the FE curve, increasing deficits in the capital account are observed, though domestic and foreign bond yields remain identical. Of course, this property only holds for a constant real exchange rate. If we move on the FE curve while or because, for example, the exchange rate changes simultaneously, the reactions of the current account need reappraisal, since now two variables change which affect the current account in opposite directions. We will return to this point below.

The results obtained for the case of complete capital mobility also apply in the case of a positively sloped FE curve: the area to the north in Figure 1.2 characterizes an incipient balance of payments surplus; the area to the south an incipient deficit. *Ceteris paribus*, as we move north-east on the FE curve, the current account deteriorates and the capital account improves.

When capital is completely immobile the FE curve is vertical above the single level of aggregate income, $\hat{Y}$, which equilibrates the balance of payments. This very income level at the same time balances the current account, given that capital flows are entirely prohibited or *must* balance by regulation. If capital immobility, however, only means that capital flows cannot respond to changes in the interest differential, a current account disequilibrium may be associated with $\hat{Y}$. To the left of the FE curve in Figure 1.2 the balance of payments tends to be in surplus and the exchange rate falls. The opposite applies to the right of the FE curve.

The position of the FE curve depends on all those parameters which have an influence on the current account through import and export demand, and on those which determine the comparative attractiveness of foreign investments. Parameters belonging to the first group are foreign income Y^* and the real exchange rate R. An increase of Y^* has a negative impact on the position of the curve:

$$\frac{\partial i}{\partial Y^*} = -\frac{PX_{Y^*}}{K_i} < 0 \qquad (1.25)$$

Thus the FE curve shifts downward if foreign income rises. This is because the implied improvement of the current account and of the balance of payments has to be compensated for by an interest rate reduction which worsens the capital account.

The effect of a real depreciation on the position of the schedule is uncertain. Assume that the real depreciation results from a depreciation of the nominal exchange rate with constant domestic and foreign price levels: then, when differentiating the FE schedule implied in equation (1.23) with respect to E, we obtain

$$\frac{\partial i}{\partial E} = -\frac{PX_E - EP^*Q_E - P^*Q}{K_i} \tag{1.26}$$

Recall the definition $R \equiv EP^*/P$, which shows that since X and Q depend on the real exchange rate R, they also depend on the nominal exchange rate E.[12] Whether a devaluation shifts the FE curve upward or downward is determined by the sign of the numerator on the right-hand side of (1.26), that is, by whether the current account improves or not. A look at the three channels through which a depreciation affects exports and imports, expressed in domestic currency, reveals that the current account must not necessarily improve:

1. A depreciation makes domestic goods cheaper abroad, thus increasing export demand ($X_E > 0$). With P being constant, domestic currency income from exports increases as well and, accordingly, the current account improves.
2. A depreciation raises domestic currency prices for imports, decreasing the volume demanded ($Q_E < 0$). *Ceteris paribus*, this also improves the current account.
3. A depreciation makes the home country pay more for any remaining imports. As a consequence, the current account deteriorates, *ceteris paribus*.

Combining the effects described as channels 1, 2 and 3, the depreciation does not improve the current account under all conditions. It is improved only if the quantity reactions occurring through channels 1 and 2 outweigh the price effect occurring through channel 3. The exact circumstances under which a devaluation improves the current account of the devaluating country are known as the **Marshall–Lerner condition**.

In deriving this condition, we begin by noting that the response of the current account to a devaluation is given by the numerator on the right-hand side of equation (1.26). So we are looking for the condition under which

$$P\frac{\partial X}{\partial E} - EP^*\frac{\partial Q}{\partial E} - P^*Q > 0 \tag{1.27}$$

To keep the analysis simple, let the economy initially be in a long-run equilibrium in which **purchasing power parity** holds and the current account is balanced. The purchasing-power parity hypothesis says that a given basket of goods costs the same amount abroad as it does at home:

$$P = EP^* \tag{1.28}$$

Given (1.28), a current-account equilibrium implies $X = Q$. Expanding the first term in equation (1.27) by X and making use of $P = EP^*$, we obtain

$$XP^* \frac{\partial X}{X} \frac{E}{\partial E} - EP^* \frac{\partial Q}{\partial E} - P^*Q > 0 \tag{1.27'}$$

After expanding the middle term on the left-hand side of (1.27′) by Q and substituting the first X in the left-hand term by Q (since $X = Q$) we may pull out P^*Q to obtain

$$P^*Q\left(\frac{\partial X}{X} \frac{E}{\partial E} - \frac{\partial Q}{Q} \frac{E}{\partial E} - 1\right) > 0 \tag{1.27''}$$

Since $P^*Q > 0$, a devaluation improves an (initially balanced) current account if, and only if, the expression given in parentheses is positive. Denoting the exchange rate elasticity[13] of the demand for exports by ε_E^X and the exchange rate elasticity of the demand for imports by ε_E^Q, the expression given in parentheses turns into the familiar form of the Marshall–Lerner condition,

$$\varepsilon_E^X - \varepsilon_E^Q > 1 \tag{1.29}$$

or, since ε_E^Q is negative,

$$|\varepsilon_E^X| + |\varepsilon_E^Q| > 1 \tag{1.29'}$$

The exchange rate elasticities of export and import demand must, in absolute terms, add up to more than 1 in order to compensate for the rise in import prices caused by a depreciation.

It should be emphasized that the Marshall–Lerner condition is derived under the assumption that the elasticity of the supply of goods at home and abroad is infinitely large.[14] This is needed to justify the assumption that both price levels remain constant, no matter what amount of domestic and foreign goods is produced, and implies the assumption of unemployment in the Keynesian tradition.

The foreign interest rate i^* and expected depreciation $E(\dot{e})$ both affect the position of the FE curve because of the role which these variables play in the determination of the capital account. Applying the implicit function rule, we obtain

$$\frac{\partial i}{\partial i^*} = -\frac{K_{i^*}}{K_i} = 1 \tag{1.30}$$

An increase in the foreign interest rate calls for an equivalent increase in the domestic interest rate if domestic assets are to maintain their comparative attractiveness in order to keep the balance of payments in equilibrium.

The same argument applies to a change in expected depreciation. A rise of expected depreciation has the same effect on the expected yield of foreign assets as a rise in i^*. It does not come as a surprise, therefore, that we obtain

$$\frac{\partial i}{\partial E(\dot{e})} = -\frac{K_{E(\dot{e})}}{K_i} = 1 \tag{1.31}$$

Rising depreciation expectations hence move the FE schedule upward.

1.2.2 Graphical presentation and analysis of the model

The acquired knowledge of the three markets of the Mundell–Fleming model and of how parameter changes affect market equilibria should put us in a position to analyze the comparative-static properties of the model. We will settle for a graphical analysis of the model and distinguish between the cases of perfect and of less than perfect mobility of capital. This should enable readers to analyze the case of completely immobile capital on their own.

Perfect capital mobility

Figure 1.3 illustrates the consequences of a fiscal expansion by means of an increase in government spending. The initial consequence of an increase in government spending is a shift of the IS curve to the right to IS'. This disturbs the initial macroeconomic equilibrium in B. If this were a closed economy, the short-run effect of this stimulation would be to increase both the nominal interest rate and aggregate output, moving the equilibrium to B''. The partial crowding-out of private demand by government spending via an interest rate increase cannot occur in an open economy with perfect capital mobility, however. Here we should actually move along the FE curve to B'. This in turn would generate an excess demand for money which only an interest rate increase could eliminate.

Thus any attempted movement from B to the right or to the north-east in Figure 1.3 would drive the interest rate up and produce an excess demand for domestic currency. With a continuously cleared foreign exchange market, however, no excess demand is ever really observed. Rather, it is immediately and completely eliminated by an appreciation. This worsens the competitive position of the home country, and exports fall because of the comparative increase of prices for domestic products. This shifts the IS curve to the left until it is back in its initial position, IS.

The result is that under flexible exchange rates a fiscal stimulation does not affect aggregate income in the long run. Whether any effect is observed

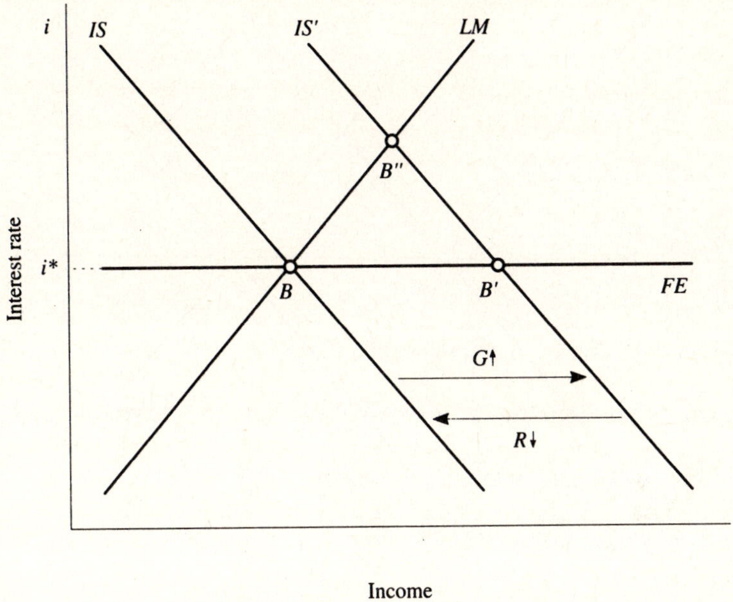

Figure 1.3 Fiscal expansion under flexible exchange rates and perfect capital mobility

at all depends on how quickly movements of the interest rate eliminate money market disequilibria. With a perfectly flexible interest rate the money market is in permanent equilibrium – just like the balance of payments. Following an increase in government spending, the economy always remains in *B*. Only the goods market moves into a temporary position of excess demand, since its equilibrium locus is shifted to *IS'*. As the domestic currency appreciates in nominal and real terms, this excess demand is eliminated. If we allow for temporary disequilibria in the money market as well, the fiscal expansion shifts our economy on the FE curve to the right (into *B'*) and then, as the real exchange rate *R* falls, back into *B*. In this case we observe a *transitory* increase in aggregate income.

The preceding analysis of the effects of a fiscal expansion may serve to demonstrate that any results of how the current account changes while we move on the FE curve only hold under *ceteris paribus* conditions. Note that if the current account was in equilibrium in *B before* the fiscal expansion it must be in deficit in *B after* a fiscal expansion. This is because the exchange rate has fallen and, thus, with income being the same as before, net exports are smaller. This is to show that we can observe two different balance of payments situations in the very same point on the FE curve, if a variable has *changed* which has been assumed constant when constructing the curve.

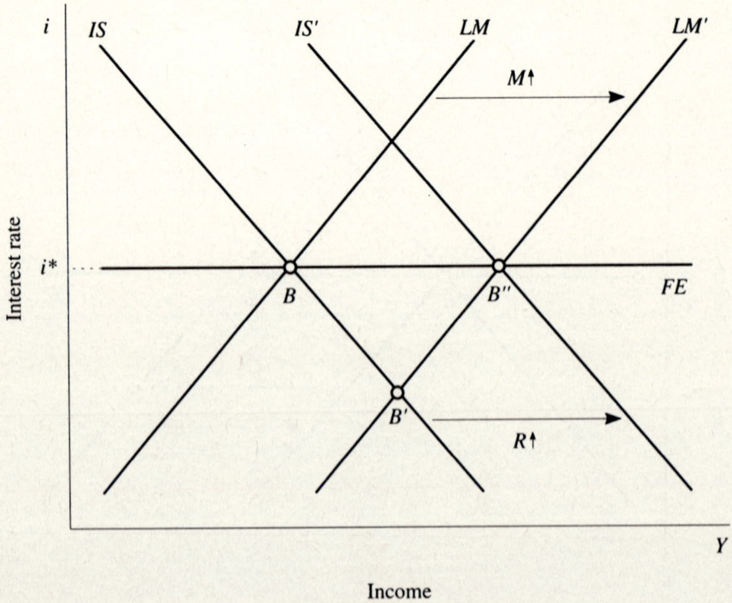

Figure 1.4 Monetary expansion under flexible exchange rates and perfect capital mobility

Next we derive the consequences of a money supply increase under flexible exchange rates (Figure 1.4). A money supply increase shifts the LM curve to the right into the position LM'. This produces an incipient excess supply of real balances in B and, hence, an incipient fall of the interest rate. To prevent the interest rate from actually falling, the foreign exchange market responds by depreciating the domestic currency. This moves the IS curve to the right into IS', where it intersects LM' on FE. In passing we may note that the current account *improves* as we move from B to B''. This contradicts the *ceteris paribus* result derived above. It is due to the fact that while moving from B to B'' the real exchange rate has risen, and this has dominated the partial negative effect of the increase of aggregate income on the current account.

To sum up: given the assumptions of the Mundell–Fleming model, a money supply increase raises aggregate income in the long run.

Imperfect capital mobility

If capital is mobile, though not perfectly so, a balance of payments equilibrium pertains for all combinations of i and Y which lie on a curve with positive slope. This FE curve may be steeper or flatter than the LM

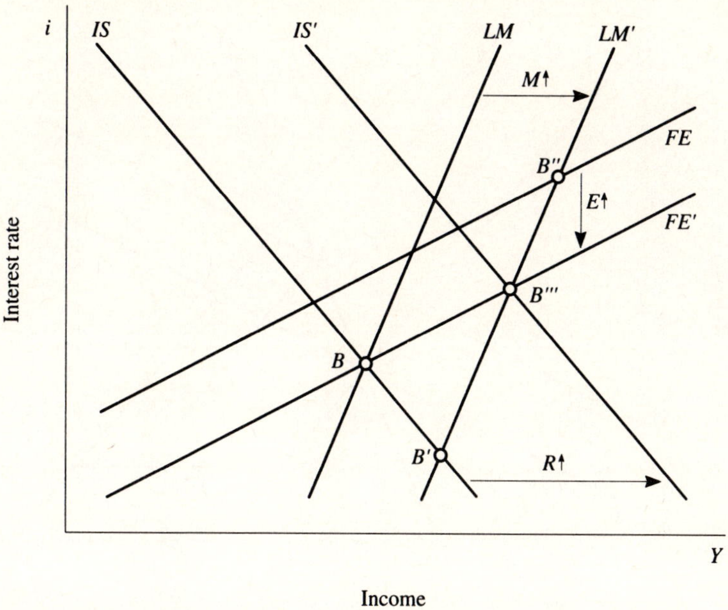

Figure 1.5 Monetary expansion under flexible exchange rates and imperfect capital mobility

curve. Since the consequences of a money supply increase are the same in both cases, we turn to this policy measure first (Figure 1.5). If capital mobility is less than perfect, policy measures not only have potential effects on the positions of the equilibrium curves for the goods market and the money market, but shift the FE curve as well. This does not decisively affect the consequences of monetary expansion, but will bear on our analysis of fiscal policy below.

As we have demonstrated above, whether the Marshall–Lerner condition holds determines whether a depreciation shifts the FE curve upward or down. If the Marshall–Lerner condition is being met (see equation (1.29′), a devaluation improves the current account and, as a consequence, either aggregate income must rise and/or the interest rate must fall in order to compensate for this. This shifts the balance of payments equilibrium condition down to the right on Figure 1.5.

Now if the money supply is increased under flexible exchange rates, this shifts *LM* to *LM′*. The incipient excess liquidity puts a downward pressure on the interest rate, generating an incipient excess demand for foreign currency and thus causes the domestic currency to depreciate. This shifts both the goods market equilibrium schedule (from *IS* to *IS′*) and the

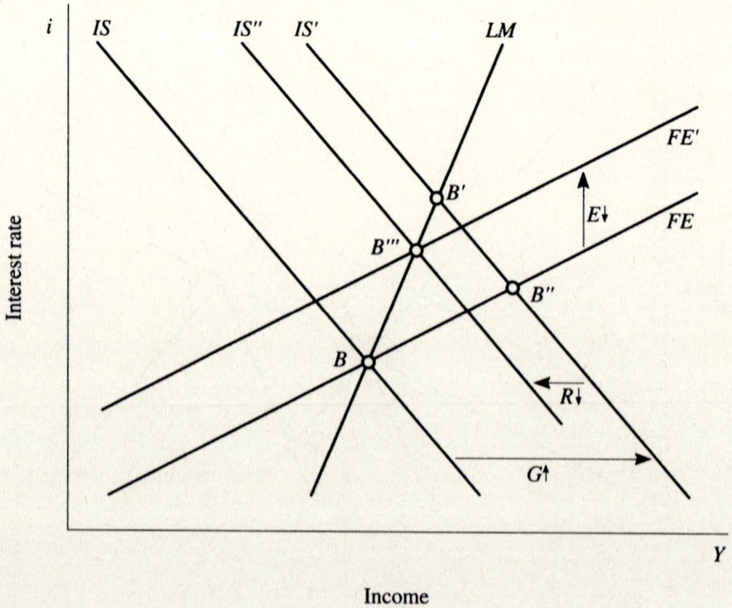

Figure 1.6 Fiscal expansion under flexible exchange rates and high capital mobility

balance of payments equilibrium schedule (from *FE* to *FE'*). The new long-run equilibrium is established at *B'''*, where aggregate income is at a permanently higher level.

Turning to an analysis of the consequences of increasing government spending, two cases must be distinguished. Assume for now that capital mobility is relatively high, which makes the FE curve *flatter* than the LM curve (see Figure 1.6). Increased government spending initially shifts the IS curve to *IS'*. This puts an upward pressure on domestic interest rates. In a closed economy, without the constraint of a balance of payments equilibrium condition, the interest rate would actually rise to the value associated with *B'*. In our open economy the domestic currency appreciates, which works against the interest rate increase. The appreciation reduces net exports and moves the IS curve back to the left in Figure 1.6. Since the balance of payments equilibrium schedule moves upward at the same time, the new overall equilibrium obtains at *B'''*, before the IS curve is back in its original position. Thus, when capital mobility is less than perfect, there is no complete crowding-out of foreign demand. Hence, whether fiscal policy affects aggregate output under flexible exchange rates eventually depends on whether domestic and foreign assets are perfect substitutes or not.

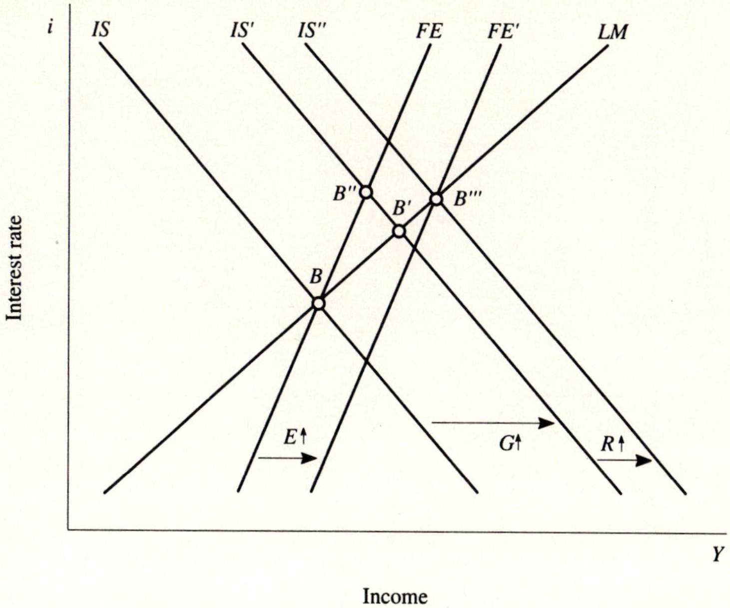

Figure 1.7 Fiscal expansion under flexible exchange rates and low capital mobility

If capital mobility is comparatively low, the FE curve is steeper than the LM curve (see Figure 1.7). Now, for a given change of income, the interest rate increase required to bring the balance of payments back into equilibrium is higher than the interest rate increase required to bring the money market back into equilibrium. Thus, if we move on the LM curve in a north-easterly direction towards *B'* on Figure 1.7, the balance of payment worsens. The exchange rate rises, net exports improve, the IS curve moves further to the right. At the same time the depreciation shifts the FE curve down. The new long-run equilibrium obtains at *B'''*. This replicates the result obtained above for the case of comparatively high capital mobility, namely that fiscal policy may work even under flexible exchange rates, if domestic and foreign assets are imperfect substitutes.

The J curve

So far we have assumed the Marshall–Lerner condition to hold, that is, that a devaluation improves the current account. From an empirical perspective this is a plausible assumption – but only in the long run. Initially, following a devaluation the current account may quite well deteriorate before the effects stressed by the Marshall–Lerner condition become strong enough to

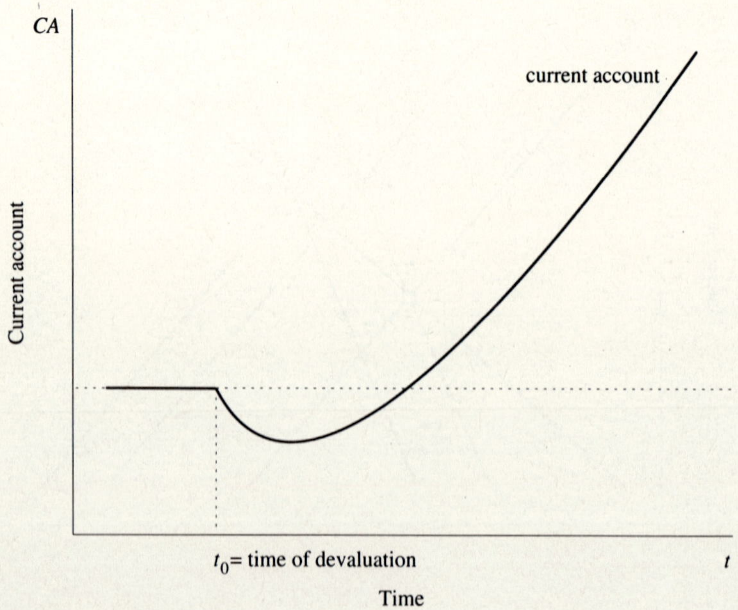

Figure 1.8 Sketch of the J-curve effect

improve the current account. Since a graphical sketch of this development of the current account after a devaluation resembles the letter J, it is generally referred to as the **J-curve effect** (see Figure 1.8).

The J-curve effect may be described by reference to the current account, as stated in equation (1.12), and its reaction to a devaluation. The Mundell–Fleming model considers domestic and foreign prices exogenous variables. This is justified if the domestic economy is small and underemployed. Under a more general perspective which includes the possibility of full employment, this assumption must be dropped. Nevertheless, we may continue to keep the foreign price level fixed if the home country is small. Given this more general set of assumptions, differentiating the current account with respect to the exchange rate gives

$$\frac{\partial CA}{\partial E} = PX_E + P_E X - EP^* Q_E - P^* Q \tag{1.32}$$

A depreciation affects the current account via three channels: the first exists by definition and hence works without delay; the second needs some time; and the third may produce noticeable results only with considerable delay. Following a devaluation, the current account may not be expected to improve before the medium run, after import and export *volumes* have changed in response to new relative prices.

1. *Immediate response*. Immediately after the devaluation, importers and exporters are stuck in contracts which they entered before the devaluation. *Prices and volumes are fixed* at their pre-devaluation levels. Hence, we may postulate $X_E = P_E = Q_E = 0$. Inserting this into (1.32), we see that a devaluation by one currency unit *worsens* the current account by P^*Q, since more domestic currency has to be paid for imports being fixed in volume and in foreign currency prices. This effect does not occur, of course, if contracts fix import prices in domestic currency. But this is the exception rather than the rule.

2. *Medium-run response*. New contracts fixed after the devaluation will reflect that relative prices have changed in favour of domestic products. Denote pre-devaluation values of variables by the subscript 0, and post-devaluation values by the subscript 1: then relative prices before the devaluation were $R_0 = E_0P^*/P_0$, and after the devaluation they are $R_1 = E_1P^*/P_0 > R_0$. After this change of relative prices, demand shifts from foreign goods towards domestically produced goods, thus $X_E > 0$ and $Q_E < 0$. This response of import and export volumes may be observed quite soon after a devaluation, but in certain circumstances may not show its full effect until several years have passed.[15] As soon as this effect begins to materialize, the current account improves relative to the bottom point of the J pattern, and, once the Marshall–Lerner condition is being met, compared to the original situation.

3. *Long-run response*. In the long run, which we denote by the subscript 2, the increased demand for domestic products cannot leave prices unaffected, unless we continue to experience an extreme situation of underemployment. If the price elasticity of the domestic goods supply is finite, higher export volumes are only supplied at higher prices. This continues to improve the current account. However, it also takes a bite out of the competitive advantage gained by the devaluation. This *real* appreciation of the domestic currency again triggers delayed responses of export and import *volumes*; now, however, in the opposite direction, which worsens the current account.

In its absolute form the purchasing-power parity hypothesis postulates the law of one price on international markets. Given this, we would expect the real exchange rate to return eventually to its initial equilibrium value. With the exchange rate being fixed at E_1 and the foreign price level being exogenous, this implies that the percentage increase of domestic prices eventually matches the initial percentage increase of the exchange rate, so that $R_2 = E_1P^*/P_2 = R_0$. This means that a *nominal* devaluation cannot affect the current account in the long run.

The US experience of the 1980s (see Figure 1.9) provides a good real-world illustration of the J-curve effect. It also provides a good starting point for a discussion of advanced issues related to the J-curve hypothesis.

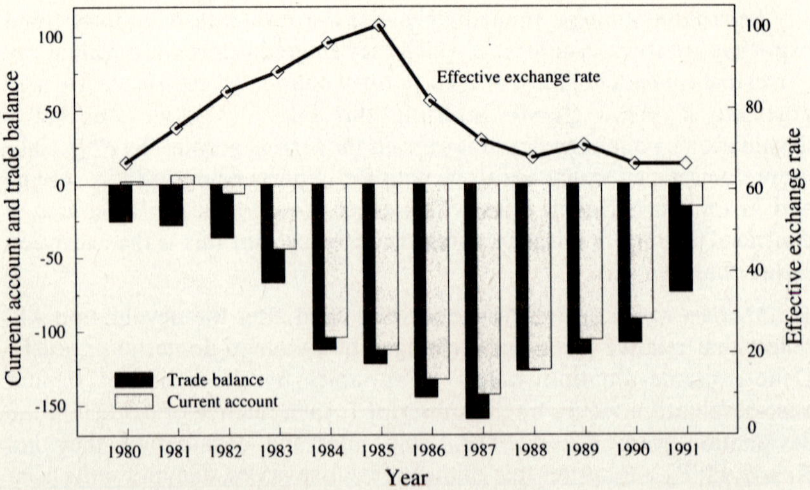

Figure 1.9 Empirical illustration of the J-curve effect for the United States based on current-account and effective exchange rate data 1980–91 (Source: International Financial Statistics)

From 1980 to 1985 the effective exchange rate[16] of the US dollar versus other major currencies dramatically increased for five years in a row. While the US current account was more-or-less balanced before the dollar began to soar, the first-year effect of the dollar improvement in 1981 was an *improvement* of the current account – just as the J-curve hypothesis suggests. Further dollar appreciations in 1982 and later brought the current account into deficit. As the dollar began to depreciate drastically in 1986 the current account continued to deteriorate for another two years before signs of improvement began to show in 1988. The still extremely high current account deficit in 1990 is all the more surprising as in this year the effective exchange rate of the dollar was even below its 1980 level.

While the characteristics of the data presented in Figure 1.9 are roughly in line with the J-curve hypothesis, two points deserve mention.

1. The initial improvement of the current account in 1981 was very small indeed. While this justifies doubts regarding the quantitative importance of the J-curve effect, it is relatively easily explained in the case of the United States. It has been noted above that, even in theory, the immediate perverse reaction of the current account can only occur if import prices are fixed in the foreign currency. The country in the world for which this holds to a smaller extent than for other countries is probably the United States. More than any other currency, the dollar serves as the unit of account in international transactions.

2. Despite the massive depreciation of the dollar after 1985 the current account has for a long time stubbornly refused to improve.[17] There could be more behind this than the conventional J-curve effect. Possibly, the extraordinarily pronounced and long-lasting overvaluation of the dollar between 1981 and 1985 has shattered and reorganized structures in the world markets so deeply that a return of the real exchange rate to its former value is not enough to reestablish original structures. Five years of massive dollar overvaluation gave foreign competitors of American companies sufficient time and incentives to enter the American market and to drive American companies out of markets in third countries. This cannot be undone by an elimination of the dollar overvaluation alone. In this context, drawing on an earlier discussion in labour market economics, international economists have begun to look into the phenomenon of **hysteresis** in international trade.[18] Hysteresis is 'what is left behind', and refers to the structural dimension of current-account disequilibria. Analyzing its relevance and implication is of great interest to monetary macroeconomics; but it cannot do without drawing on results and models from the pure theory of international trade.

1.3 Outline of the book

The Mundell–Fleming model, which we have briefly recapitulated in the second section of this introductory chapter, is an early example of today's dominating view that the exchange rate primarily reflects desired wealth portfolios of individuals, and is thus determined in the *capital account*. The *current account* (and the flows of goods and services recorded in it) plays a rather modest role in modern approaches. Rather than having any short-run effect, the current account is used to derive long-run tendencies from the impact of current-account disequilibria on domestic wealth.

Figure 1.10 provides an overview of the macroeconomic exchange rate models presented in this book and puts them into perspective. Characteristic assumptions or features are listed below each approach, along with the respective chapter(s) where they are dealt with.

At the core of all modern approaches is the proposition that exchange rate determination is dominated by the demand for assets at home and abroad as listed in the capital account. The **monetary approach** assumes (1) that foreign money is no substitute for domestic money (foreigners do not hold domestic money, domestic residents do not hold foreign money), and (2) that interest-bearing assets at home and abroad are perfect substitutes. The **portfolio balance approach**, discussed in Chapter 7, drops the assumption of domestic and foreign assets being perfect substitutes. **Currency substitution models** are presented in Chapter 6. In contrast to the

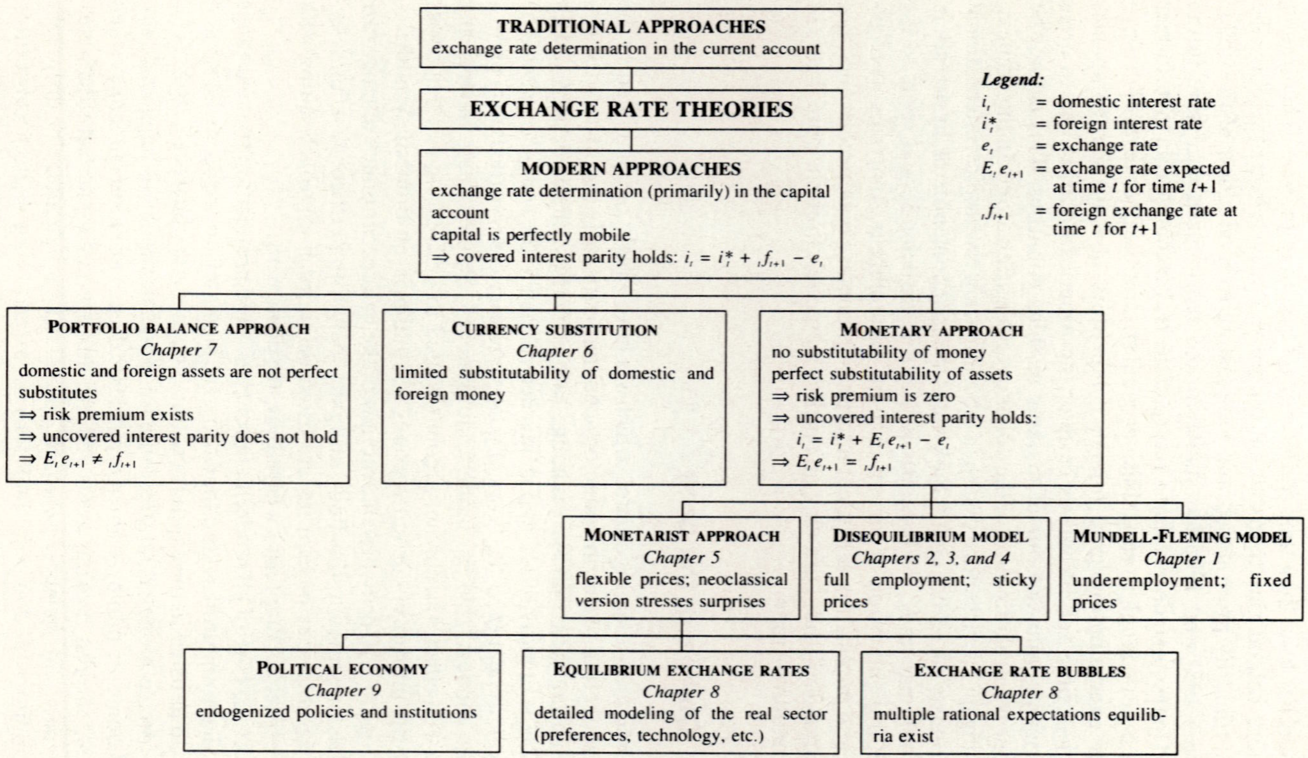

Figure 1.10 Outline of the book

other models, they assume that to some extent foreign money may be used as a substitute for domestic money by domestic residents.

Approaches also differ with respect to the postulated flexibility of goods prices. In principle, the assumption of fixed goods prices, sticky goods prices and perfectly flexible goods prices can be combined with any conceivable assumption about the substitutability of money or assets. This book analyzes the consequences of different degrees of goods prices flexibility in a systematic fashion only in the context of the monetary approach. The assumption of perfectly fixed goods prices and, hence, underemployed production factors, with which we have worked in the present chapter, lead us to the **Mundell–Fleming model**. Note, however, that in the context of this model we have also analyzed the cases of limited and of completely absent capital mobility. Given this, it would not be completely out of place to subsume the former variant of the Mundell–Fleming model under the heading 'portfolio balance approach'. This could be justified in formal terms if we reduce the portfolio balance approach to the assumption of less than perfect substitutability of capital. As regards contents, however, it would not really do justice to the portfolio balance approach. Contrary to what we did in the context of the Mundell–Fleming model, the portfolio balance approach does not just introduce imperfect capital mobility by postulating a finite interest elasticity of the capital account. Rather, the portfolio balance approach models the demands for all available assets in explicit terms, and the required equilibrium conditions on each individual market.

At the centre of the book is the **macroeconomic disequilibrium approach to the exchange rate** as introduced by Dornbusch (1976) (Chapters 2, 3 and 4). This approach postulates a fully employed economy with sticky prices, that is, prices which are fixed in the short run and flexible in the long run. This model also serves as a vehicle for an extensive analysis of questions related to expectations formation.

The **monetarist exchange rate model** postulates completely flexible prices which keep the goods market in permanent equilibrium. Chapter 5 introduces and discusses this approach, along with a modified version called the **neoclassical exchange rate model**.

In addition to a very concise glimpse at the state of the art of empirical research on exchange rates, Chapter 8 introduces two recent developments in exchange rate theory. Both are introduced in the context of the monetarist approach to the exchange rate, though their central insights may be introduced into other exchange rate models as well.

Equilibrium exchange rate models cease to represent the real part of the economy in an *ad hoc* fashion without explicit microfoundation, as monetary approaches to the exchange rate do. If Figure 1.10 nevertheless subsumes these models under the category of *monetarist approaches* this is because the textbook equilibrium exchange rate model adopts the monetary part of the monetarist exchange rate model. The equilibrium exchange rate models emphasize that changes of the nominal and real exchange rate may be equilibrium responses to changes of consumer preferences and to productivity shocks.

The **theory of exchange rate bubbles** (and, in a related way, the so-called **peso problem**) addresses uncertain exchange rate expectations in a new way. Uncertainty does not come in the form of stochastic disturbances with an expected value of zero, which overlay exchange rate movements. Rather, investors see a number of quite different but nevertheless feasible development paths. If, for example, two possible paths are believed to exist, one of which is the return to the equilibrium value and the other is an accelerating movement away from equilibrium, investors may rationally stick to holding the currency which appreciates away from equilibrium. The condition is that the accelerating and rationally foreseen appreciation exactly compensates for the expected loss that would occur if the exchange rate returned to its equilibrium value.

The final chapter shifts focus by adding elements from public choice and the modern theory of economic policy. It discusses how utility maximization of policymakers, interest groups and voters may influence the course of an open economy in the short run and in the long run. Such considerations from political economy could be added to any exchange rate model discussed in the book. Here the so-called neoclassical exchange rate model, a close relative of the monetarist model, provides the economic background.

NOTES

1. Accounting conventions may differ substantially between countries. The terminology adopted here is that of the US Department of Commerce.
2. These days the Mundell–Fleming model is part of almost any macroeconomics textbook and of any introduction to international economics. Particularly well suited for self study are, for example, Branson (1989: Ch. 17), Dernburg (1989: Part II), Dornbusch and Fischer (1990: Ch. 6) and Mankiw (1992: Ch. 13).
3. Given that the partial derivatives F_i and F_Y exist, and F_Y is nonzero at a point satisfying $F(i, Y, G, Y^*, R)=0$, then an implicitly defined function $i=f(Y)$, that is, an IS curve, exists in the neighbourhood of the point under consideration. Both conditions are met in the present context, since $F_i=I_i$ and $F_Y=-I+C_Y-RQ_Y<0$. A more precise and a more general statement of the **implicit function theorem** addressed here is given in Chiang (1984: 206).
4. For now – and whenever we graph the model in the i/Y plane – the real exchange rate R is assumed constant, though it is actually an endogenous variable. This spares us the probably not very illuminating attempt to draw the model in three dimensions, with i, Y and R on the axes, by means of IS, LM and, FE *planes*.

5. The implicit function rule is discussed in Chiang (1984: 208).
6. The FE curve derives its name from the fact that it combines all points at which the foreign exchange market clears.
7. Of course, this statement only holds under *ceteris paribus* conditions. If increasing inflation abroad results in rising appreciation expectations, foreign inflation becomes a relevant variable, of course – however, only in the form of an instrument for depreciation expectations.
8. The risk premium requested for holding a particular asset is an endogenous variable. For example, it may depend on the share of the asset under consideration in total wealth. Typically, for a small share the requested risk premium is very small – in gambling it is even negative. When shares approach 100 per cent of total wealth the risk premium may become infinitely large.
9. In other words, perfect capital mobility is a *necessary* condition for perfect substitutability.
10. Thus, perfect capital mobility is a necessary, but *not a sufficient*, condition for perfect substitutability.
11. To be more precise: given the assumptions employed here, $i=i^*$ is a *necessary* condition for balance of payments equilibrium, and a *sufficient* one. For a balanced capital account the condition $i=i^*$ is *necessary* but *not sufficient*. We will return to this issue shortly.
12. Application of the chain rule yields:

$$X_E=\frac{\partial X}{\partial R}\frac{\partial R}{\partial E}=X_R\frac{P^*}{P}$$

13. Remember: an elasticity measures the percentage rate of change of a variable in response to a 1 per cent increase of some other variable.

    Strictly speaking, the Marshall–Lerner condition should be cast in terms of price elasticities instead of exchange rate elasticities. In doing this, the price is always expressed in terms of domestic currency. From the perspective of Germany the dollar price elasticity of export demand is $\varepsilon^X_{1/E}=-\varepsilon^X_E$, and instead of corresponding to (1.29′) the Marshall–Lerner condition reads $-\varepsilon^X_{1/E}-\varepsilon^Q_E>1$.
14. The condition for the general case of *finite* supply elasticities is known as the **Robinson condition**. Define the mark price elasticities of German export supply as η^X_E and the dollar price elasticity of the supply of American import goods on the German market as $\eta^Q_{1/E}$. Then the Robinson condition for a normal response of the current account is

$$1+\varepsilon^X_{1/E}+\varepsilon^Q_E<(1+\eta^X_E+\eta^Q_{1/E})\frac{\varepsilon^X_{1/E}\varepsilon^Q_E}{\eta^X_E\eta^Q_{1/E}}$$

    Derivations of this condition can be found in Niehans (1984: 70ff.), who calls it the Bircherdike condition, or in Takayama (1977: 268–70).
15. A well-known example for small price elasticities in the short run, but quite large ones in the long run, are imports of crude oil.
16. The effective exchange rate of the dollar computed by the International Monetary Fund is a weighted average of the reciprocal values of bilateral exchange rates of the dollar *vis-à-vis* other currencies. If this index rises, the dollar *appreciates*.
17. The current-account figure for 1991 is misleading, since it is heavily influenced by payments of foreign governments to the United States after the Gulf War.

The balance of trade, which does not suffer from this bias, reports continuing large deficits.

18. See Baldwin (1988). On the history of the term hysteresis and its meaning in economics see Cross and Allan (1988).

REFERENCES

Baldwin, Richard (1988) 'Hysteresis in import prices: The beachhead effect', *The American Economic Review* 78, (4), 773–85.

Branson, William H. (1989) *Macroeconomic Theory and Policy*, 3rd edn, New York: Harper & Row.

Chiang, Alpha C. (1984) *Fundamental Methods of Mathematical Economics*, 3rd edn, Singapore: McGraw-Hill.

Cross, Rod and Andrew Allan (1988) 'On the history of hysteresis', in Rod Cross (ed.) *Unemployment, Hysteresis and the Natural Rate Hypothesis*, Oxford: Basil Blackwell, 26–38.

Dernburg, Thomas F. (1989) *Global Macroeconomics*, New York: Harper & Row.

Dornbusch, Rudiger and Stanley Fischer (1990) *Macroeconomics*, 5th edn, New York: McGraw-Hill.

Fleming, J. Marcus (1962) 'Domestic financial policies under fixed and under floating exchange rates', *IMF Staff Papers* 3, 369–80.

Mankiw, N. Gregory (1992) *Macroeconomics*, New York: Worth.

Mundell, Robert A. (1963) 'Capital mobility and stabilization policy under fixed and flexible exchange rates', *Canadian Journal of Economics and Political Science* 78, 475–85.

Niehans, Jürg (1984) *International Monetary Economics*, Oxford: Phillip Allan.

Takayama, Akira (1977) *International Trade*, New York: Holt, Rinehart & Winston.

Chapter 2

Sticky prices and the asset market approach to the exchange rate

The Mundell–Fleming model introduced in Chapter 1 permits a smooth transition from the IS–LM model for closed economies to the analysis of open economies, under both fixed and flexible exchange rates. Of course, the model possesses all the weaknesses common among Keynesian textbook models:

1. National income is uniquely determined by aggregate demand. This can only be justified as long as unemployment exists in Keynesian tradition.
2. The price level is fixed. This too can at best be justified as a first approximation when unemployment exists.
3. The return on interest-bearing investments abroad is set equal to the foreign interest rate. This implicitly assumes stationary exchange rate expectations (agents always believe that the exchange rate will remain at its current level).

Recent research in monetary macroeconomics with flexible exchange rates has replaced these criticized assumptions with more realistic ones. The result is a very versatile model which, on the one hand, clearly exhibits some characteristics of the Mundell–Fleming model, yet, on the other hand, contains modern concepts such as rational expectations. Also it explicitly models the development of variables over time. Hence, it is not limited to a comparison of stationary-state equilibria as the Mundell–Fleming model is. Instead, it can precisely trace the adjustment path from one equilibrium to another.

The model referred to was introduced by Dornbusch in 1976 and is occasionally called the **macroeconomic disequilibrium approach to the exchange rate**. It will play a central role in this book, mainly because of its versatility and its outstanding importance for pertinent research, but also because of its simplicity, which qualifies it as a textbook model. Most of the material presented in the remaining chapters of the book will only be of benefit to those readers with a profound understanding of the Dornbusch model. We therefore proceed to develop this model graphically, verbally and mathematically in a slightly simplified version.[1]

2.1 The Dornbusch model (simplified version)

The formal structure of our basic model is presented in Model 2.1. The small open economy is composed of three markets. Here the attribute 'small' means that changes within this economy will affect neither world market prices nor the world interest rate. The attribute 'open' signals that the economy is linked to international goods and capital markets. Let us begin with an interpretation of the structural equations for the three markets.

Model 2.1
Dornbusch model (simplified version)

1 Goods market		
$\dot{p}=\pi(y^d-y)$	Phillips curve	(2.1)
$y^d=\delta(e-p)+\gamma y+g$	aggregate demand	(2.2)
2 Money market		
$m^d=p+\phi y-\lambda i$	money demand	(2.3)
$m^s=m^d=m$	money market equilibrium	(2.4)
3 International asset market		
$i=i^*+E(\dot{e})$	asset market equilibrium	(2.5)
$E(\dot{e})=\theta(\bar{e}-e)$	expectations formation	(2.6)

Notes: Lower-case variables are in natural logarithms, an exception being the interest rate. A dot indicates the change of the respective variable over time. Greek letters denote positive parameters. $E(.)$ is the expectations operator. Variables are defined as follows:

$\dot{p}$	domestic inflation rate	i	domestic interest rate
y^d	aggregate demand for domestic goods	m	domestic money
y	aggregate supply of domestic goods (exogenous)	i^*	foreign interest rate (exogenous)
e	exchange rate	$\dot{e}$	rate of depreciation
p	domestic price level	$\bar{e}$	equilibrium exchange rate
g	government expenditure	m^s	domestic money supply
		m^d	domestic money demand

2.1.1 The goods market

On the goods market desired demand for goods y^d faces an exogenous supply of goods y. The latter is assumed to represent full employment output. Goods prices are **sticky**. They do respond to market disequilibria with a factor π, but not fast enough to eliminate those disequilibria instantly. The neoclassical case of perfectly flexible prices and, thus, permanent goods market equilibrium $y^d = y$ results as $\pi \to \infty$. For $\pi = 0$ the price level would be completely rigid – a rather senseless assumption in a fully employed economy.

The price reaction function (2.1) is a Phillips curve without inflation expectations on the right-hand side. This may be justified with the argument that we are modelling so-called stationary economies which do not experience continuing inflation. The inclusion of an expected inflation term in (2.1) has no consequences for the short- and long-run properties of the model in the case of an *unexpected* shock. However, since the medium-run properties and the short-run responses of the model to *expected* shocks are indeed different when inflation expectations are included, a number of scholars have augmented equation (2.1) by inflation expectations, thus expanding the Dornbusch model.[2]

Equation (2.2′) describes the determinants of aggregate demand y^d. The first term represents net exports which depend on the real exchange rate $e-p$.[3] The term γy – which is held constant in our present full-employment context – stands for income-dependent demand for domestic goods, in particular private consumption. The variable g is a fiscal portmanteau variable: it comprises both government expenditures and demand stimulated by tax policies. Contrary to the Dornbusch model, the dependence of private investment on the interest rate is not considered here. This renders the model a lot more transparent, without qualitatively changing its major implications. Besides that, empirical evidence for the dependence of private investment on interest rates is much harder to find than empirical support for the other determinants of aggregate demand.

2.1.2 The money market

According to equation (2.4), the money market is permanently in equilibrium. Supply and demand shocks are immediately intercepted by a perfectly flexible interest rate. Equation (2.3) is a logarithmic equation which results from taking the natural logarithm on both sides of a conventional money demand function of the form $M^d/P = Y^{\phi} exp(-\lambda i)$. This is a fairly standard relationship which postulates that real-money demand depends on aggregate income and the nominal interest rate.

2.1.3 The international asset market

The equilibrium condition supplied for the international asset market is based on the assumption that domestic and foreign assets are perfect substitutes, which can only be the case if there is perfect capital mobility. As we have discussed at some length in Chapter 1, this means that the balance of payments can only be in equilibrium if asset returns at home equal expected asset returns abroad. This is exactly what equation (2.5) states and is known as **uncovered interest parity**. Equation (2.5) also states that the return for domestic assets equals the domestic interest rate. The expected return for foreign assets equals the foreign interest rate i^* plus the expected rate of depreciation $E(\dot{e})$ of the domestic currency (which is identical to the expected appreciation of the foreign currency).[4]

Equation (2.6) is a plausible hypothesis for expectations formation, though it may be regarded as arbitrary for the time being. Market participants believe that the exchange rate moves asymptotically towards its equilibrium value $\bar{e}$. Later on we will study the question of whether or not this type of **adaptive expectations** formation produces systematic forecast errors.

2.1.4 Graphical analysis

Now that we are familiar with the structure of the model, we may proceed to analyze the reactions of the endogenous variables, the interest rate, the exchange rate and the price level, to exogenous shocks or policy measures. The mere fact that goods market disequilibria are possible because of sticky prices justifies the supposition that short-run reactions of our model will be clearly different from those appearing in the long run. Drawing on Figure 2.1, we begin with the graphical and verbal analysis of the model. The results derived here will be substantiated and generalized by means of mathematical analyses below.

The goods market is depicted in the first quadrant. In accordance with Keynesian models, the locus of goods market equilibria is denoted by IS. Its slope of 1 results from the goods market equations (2.1) and (2.2′). Substitution of (2.2′) into (2.1) and employing the equilibrium condition $\dot{p}=0$ (which implies $y^d=y$)[5] results (after solving for p) in

$$p=e+\frac{g}{\delta}-\frac{(1-\gamma)y}{\delta} \tag{2.7}$$

In order to maintain a given equilibrium in the goods market, the exchange rate and the price level must move in perfect harmony. If the exchange rate rises by 5 per cent, the price level must do the same.

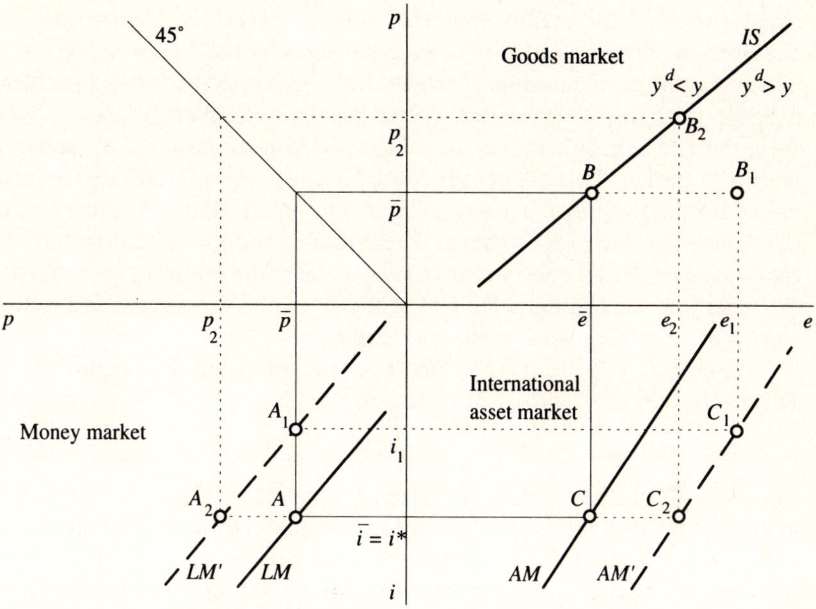

Figure 2.1 Graphical representation of a simplified version of the Dornbusch (1976) model of flexible exchange rates

Accordingly, for a given level of government demand there exists exactly *one* real exchange rate at which aggregate demand equals exogenous aggregate supply.

If we start from any equilibrium point on the IS schedule and raise the price level p while holding the exchange rate e constant, this makes domestic goods more expensive compared to foreign goods. This dampens demand for domestic goods, and the resulting excess-supply situation causes the price level to fall. Analogously, the area below the IS schedule represents excess-demand situations. From any point in this area the price level rises.

The LM schedule depicted in the third quadrant is obtained by substituting (2.4) into (2.3) and solving for i:

$$i = \frac{1}{\lambda}(p - m + \phi y) \tag{2.8}$$

The LM schedule indicates all combinations of p and i for which actors exactly demand the given nominal money supply. If the price level rises, the real money supply will fall. In order for money demand to decline as well, the opportunity cost of holding real balances, measured by the interest rate i, must rise. Since the interest rate is perfectly flexible, demand will always equal supply. This means that the money market is permanently in equilibrium, signifying also that we are *always on the LM schedule*.

Any equilibrium schedule is drawn for a given set of those variables, exogenous or not, that are not written on the axes. If the money supply rises, the LM schedule moves, as we can see from equation (2.8), upward and/or to the left. This happens because for any given interest rate the now larger nominal supply of money will only be demanded if it is reduced by a rising price level to exactly the same real-money supply that existed before the expansion. For a constant price level, a declining interest rate could do the same job. Accordingly, the LM schedule moves downward and to the right when the supply of goods y is expanded.

Equations (2.5) and (2.6) describe the asset market equilibrium. Substitution of (2.6) into (2.5) results in

$$i = i^* + \theta(\bar{e} - e) \tag{2.9}$$

Equation (2.9) shows that for given exogenous values i^* and $\bar{e}$ the international asset market may be in equilibrium for different combinations of the domestic interest rate and the exchange rate. With its negative slope, the straight line AM visualizes the information contained in equation (2.9) that the asset market can only remain in equilibrium if a rising interest rate is accompanied by a falling exchange rate and vice versa. The economic rationalization for this is as follows: the asset market equilibrium requires that domestic returns equal expected foreign returns. If the domestic interest rate and, therefore, the return for domestic assets increase, the expected return for foreign assets must increase as well. For a given foreign interest rate i^* this can only be accomplished if investors expect not only interest income from an investment abroad, but in addition gains from an appreciation of the foreign currency (which is a depreciation of the domestic currency). According to the exchange rate expectations formation hypothesis (2.6), the domestic currency is only then expected to depreciate for a given equilibrium exchange rate $\bar{e}$ if the exchange rate first drops *below* the equilibrium exchange rate, that is, if it *ap*preciates. Since the exchange rate is a 'fast' variable, just like the interest rate, incipient disequilibria are eliminated instantly and the asset market is kept in equilibrium *permanently*. Our small open economy, therefore, is always on the AM curve.

The long-run equilibrium values of the endogenous variables $\bar{e}$, $\bar{p}$ and $\bar{i}$ are determined by the relevant exogenous data, the policy variables, behavioural parameters and variables determined abroad. Contrary to current values, equilibrium values not only have to equilibrate supply and demand in the money market and in the asset market, but also in the goods market. A balanced goods market leaves the price level constant. Hence, with the monetary sector in permanent equilibrium, the interest rate and the exchange rate cannot change. Since $e = \bar{e}$ in long-run equilibrium, it follows from equation (2.9) that $i = i^*$. As a starting point for the analysis presented in the subsequent paragraphs, Figure 2.1 depicts an initial equilibrium in which all endogenous variables equal their long-run equilibrium values $\bar{e}$, $\bar{p}$ and i^*.

A money supply increase shifts the LM schedule to LM', throwing the economy off its initial equilibrium.

2.1.5 The long run

We begin by analyzing how the economy adjusts to the money supply increase in the long run. *In the long run* the domestic interest rate equals the foreign interest rate i^*. Since aggregate income is also fixed, we see from the money market equilibrium condition that the initial excess supply of money can only be removed by an increase of the price level which exactly matches the money supply increase. The long-run money market equilibrium thus shifts horizontally from A to A_2. Since money and the price level have increased proportionally, the quantity theory of money turns out to be a long-run property of our model.

On the goods market, equilibrium is only restored if the real exchange rate, $e - p$, returns to its initial value $\bar{e} - \bar{p}$. Since the price level has risen to p_2, the exchange rate must rise proportionally to e_2. The goods market equilibrium shifts from B to B_2.

The new equilibrium exchange rate e_2 provides for stationary exchange rate expectations.[6] Thus the asset market is now in a long-run equilibrium at C_2 with e_2 and i^*. The point C_2 is on a new asset market equilibrium schedule AM', the position of which is determined by the equilibrium exchange rate, as can be seen from equation (2.9).

2.1.6 The short run (impact effect)

Following a nominal money supply increase, the real money supply can only gradually return to its previous value, via a proportional increase of the price level. This is because equation (2.1) assumes prices to be sticky, that is, to respond slowly. Because of this price stickiness, horizontal movements in the money market quadrant are impossible in the short run. Thus we define the short run as the period of time that elapses before the price level starts to react. As long as the price level does not react and remains at $\bar{p}$, only a lowering of the domestic interest rate can stimulate money demand to rise up to increased real-money supply. Since the interest rate is perfectly flexible, it immediately drops to i_1 because this value will equilibrate the money market in A_1. With the domestic interest rate now being below the foreign interest rate, asset market equilibrium requires that this be compensated for by an expected appreciation of the domestic currency. For such expectations to develop the exchange rate must rise, not only to its new long-run equilibrium value e_2, but beyond that to e_1. According to equation (2.6), at e_1 individuals have appreciation expectations in the amount of $\theta(e_2 - e_1)$. The phenomenon described, that the exchange rate in the short run rises beyond the value needed to maintain a long-run equilibrium, is called **overshooting**.

2.1.7 Transition from the short to the long run

The motor propelling the transition from the short-term reaction to long-run equilibrium in B_2 is the disequilibrated goods market. In B_1 the demand for net exports exceeds its initial equilibrium value, thus creating an excess demand for domestic goods. This leads to rising prices, which reduces the real-money supply and drives the domestic interest rate up slowly. This gradually reduces the domestic interest deficit (compared to the foreign interest rate) and permits the exchange rate to move back towards its equilibrium value.

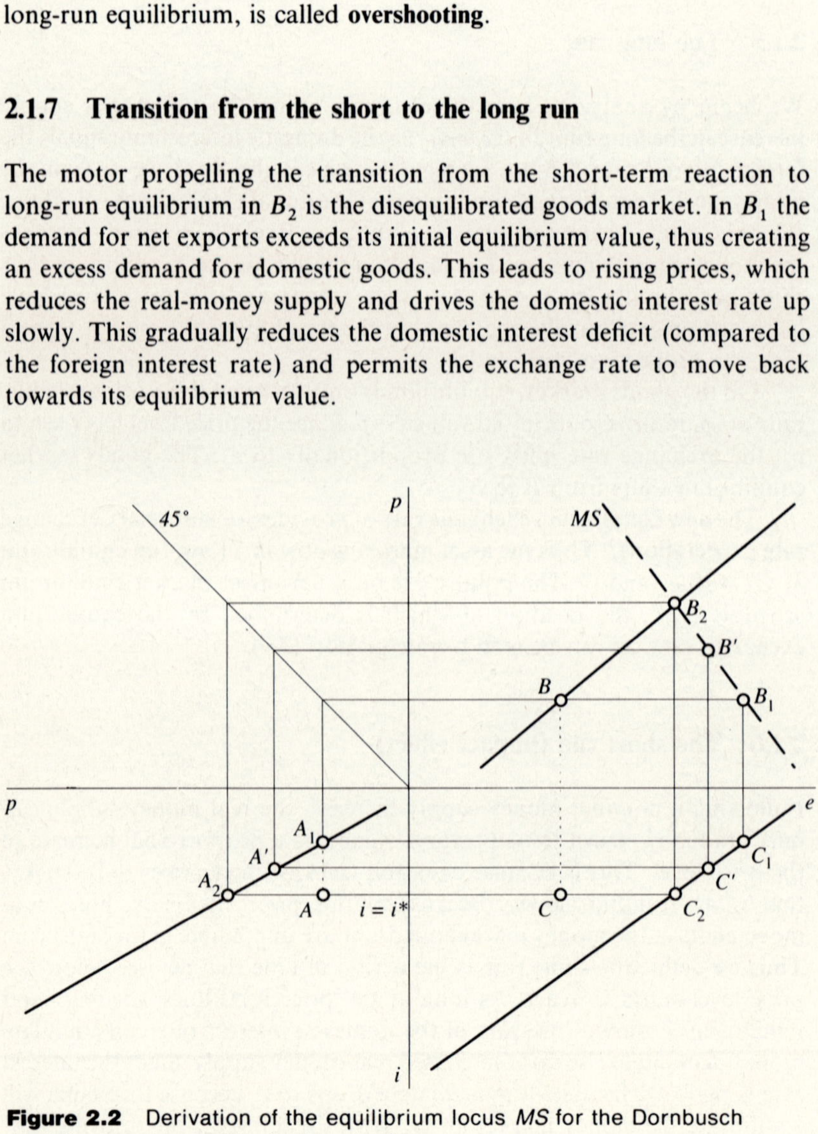

Figure 2.2 Derivation of the equilibrium locus *MS* for the Dornbusch model's monetary sector in the *p*/*e* plane

Figure 2.2 illustrates this adjustment process by depicting the first move on the goods market from B_1 to B', on the money market from A_1 to A' and on the asset market from C_1 to C'. Since in B' goods demand still exceeds goods supply, prices will continue to rise along with continuing appreciation of the exchange rate due to the money market and asset market effects described above. The real exchange rate continues on its path to a long-run goods market equilibrium until B_2 is reached (moving the money market to A_2 and the asset market to C_2).

2.1.8 Alternative presentation of money and asset market equilibria

B_1, B_2 and B' (in Figure 2.2) all show combinations of prices and exchange rates which permit simultaneous equilibrium in the money market and in the asset market. It is easy to generalize this and argue by the same token that any points on the broken line MS would have these same properties. Any point on MS is a potential equilibrium in the monetary sector of our model economy, which comprises the money and the asset market. This allows for a more compact graphical presentation of the model. The three building blocks of our model – the goods markets, the money market and the asset market – can thus be depicted in a single quadrant. The only disadvantage we have to put up with is the fact that the graph no longer shows movements of the interest rate.

The position of the MS schedule depends on the very same factors which determine the positions of the LM and the AM schedules. For example, if the LM schedule moves northwest in Figure 2.2 because of an expansion of the money supply, which at the same time moves the CA schedule down and to the right due to the increase of the equilibrium exchange rate, simultaneous equilibrium in both markets of the monetary sector, *ceteris paribus*, requires a higher exchange rate. This means that a money supply increase shifts the MS schedule to the right. Exchange rate overshooting can now be depicted as in Figure 2.3.

Assume our economy is in long-run equilibrium in B, with IS being the goods market equilibrium schedule and MS depicting possible equilibria in the monetary sector. If the money supply now expands unexpectedly and permanently, MS shift to MS'. Since the monetary sector is assumed to be in permanent equilibrium, the economy must immediately move to a point on MS' after the money supply increase. This new temporary equilibrium can only be in B_1 since the price level is sticky, which means constant in the short run. In B_1 the exchange rate is at e_1, exceeding its long-run equilibrium value $\bar{e}'$. Hence it overshoots. As soon as the price level begins to rise, the exchange rate simultaneously declines again and we move along MS' to B'.

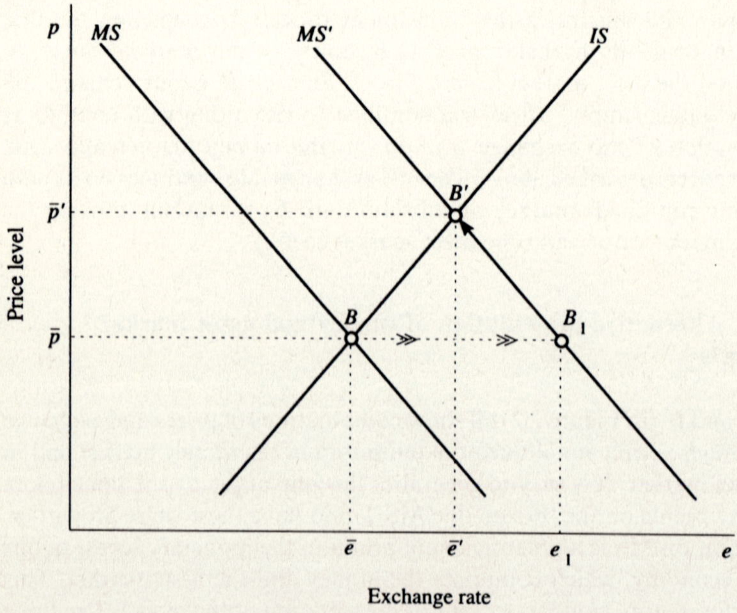

Figure 2.3 A concise representation of short- and long-run responses in the simplified Dornbusch model

2.1.9 Formal analysis of the model

The *goods market* is in equilibrium when demand equals supply ($y^d = y$). In this situation the price level is stable, and from (2.1) and (2.2′) we obtain

$$p = e + \frac{g}{\delta} - \frac{(1-\gamma)y}{\delta} \tag{2.7}$$

Goods market equilibrium only obtains for a specific real exchange rate. This particular rate may result from an unlimited number of combinations of p and e. As shown above, all these combinations may be represented by a straight line with a slope of 1 in the p/e plane (see Figure 2.3, for example).

The money market and the asset market are the building blocks of the *monetary sector*. In order to obtain the equilibrium condition for the entire monetary sector, we have to combine the known equilibrium conditions for the two constituent markets. Substituting (2.6) into (2.5), the result into (2.3) and making use of (2.4) yields

$$m - p = \phi y - \lambda i^* - \lambda\theta(\bar{e} - e) \tag{2.10}$$

or, after solving for p,

$$p=m-\phi y+\lambda i^*+\lambda\theta(\bar{e}-e) \tag{2.11}$$

Thus on the equilibrium locus for the monetary sector (MS curve) an inverse relationship exists between the price level and the exchange rate. Points off this equilibrium locus are not feasible, since 'prices' in the monetary sector – that is, the interest rate and the exchange rate – are fast variables, which immediately respond to any disturbance (that is, shifts of the MS schedule), thus keeping the monetary sector in permanent equilibrium.

The *slope* of the MS schedule, $-\lambda\theta$, is determined by two parameters: the speed θ at which agents expect the exchange rate to adjust to its equilibrium value; and $-\lambda$, the semi-interest elasticity of the demand for money.[7] The smaller these parameters are, the flatter is the MS schedule. Apart from the slope of the MS schedule, both parameters also determine the *position* of the MS schedule, along with $\bar{e}$ and the exogenous variables m, y and i^*. Before we can make any precise statements, however, we first have to analyze how the exogenous variables affect the equilibrium exchange rate.

Setting $e=\bar{e}$ in (2.11) yields

$$\bar{p}=m-\phi y+\lambda i^* \tag{2.12}$$

which shows that the price level is determined by monetary factors in the long run. Inserting (2.12) into (2.7), we obtain an expression for the equilibrium exchange rate:

$$\begin{aligned}\bar{e}&=m-\phi y+\lambda i^*-\frac{g}{\delta}+\frac{(1-\gamma)y}{\delta} \\ &=\bar{p}-\frac{g}{\delta}+\frac{(1-\gamma)y}{\delta}\end{aligned} \tag{2.13}$$

Thus in the long run purchasing-power parity and the quantity theory of money hold,

$$\mathrm{d}\bar{e}/\mathrm{d}\bar{p}=\mathrm{d}\bar{p}/\mathrm{d}m=\mathrm{d}\bar{e}/\mathrm{d}m=1 \tag{2.14}$$

though only partially, of course, that is, after changes in the monetary sphere. This is because in the long run the real exchange rate

$$\bar{e}-\bar{p}=\frac{-g+(1-\gamma)y}{\delta} \tag{2.15}$$

also responds to supply-side disturbances and to fiscal policy measures.

The IS curve (2.7) is a long-run equilibrium locus and may be ignored for short-run considerations. Thus the impact response of the exchange rate results from (2.11), the equilibrium locus of the monetary sector, which is also binding in the short run. Solving (2.11) for e results in

$$e=\bar{e}+\frac{m-p-\phi y}{\lambda\theta}+\frac{i^*}{\theta} \tag{2.16}$$

The short-run reactions of the exchange rate are obtained by differentiating (2.16) with respect to the variable under consideration, keeping the price level p constant. The impact effect of a money supply increase on the exchange rate is thus

$$\begin{aligned}\mathrm{d}e/\mathrm{d}m&=\mathrm{d}\bar{e}/\mathrm{d}m+\frac{1}{\lambda\theta}\\&=1+\frac{1}{\lambda\theta}>1\end{aligned}$$

In the short run, before prices have time to react, the exchange rate will rise more than the money supply and thus more than is necessary to bring the exchange rate to its long-run equilibrium. *The exchange rate overshoots.*

After the initial overshooting of the exchange rate the economy begins to adjust to its new long-run equilibrium. During this process the price level moves as prescribed by the Phillips curve resulting from equations (2.1) and (2.2′):

$$\dot{p}=\pi[\delta(e-p)-(1-\gamma)y+g] \tag{2.17}$$

Since (2.15) implies

$$(1-\gamma)y-g=\delta(\bar{e}-\bar{p})$$

equation (2.17) may be rewritten as

$$\dot{p}=\pi[\delta(e-\bar{e})-\delta(p-\bar{p})] \tag{2.18}$$

Substitution of (2.12) into (2.16) yields

$$e-\bar{e}=\frac{1}{\lambda\theta}(\bar{p}-p) \tag{2.19}$$

and after substituting (2.19) into (2.18), we finally obtain

$$\dot{p}=-\pi\left(\frac{\delta}{\lambda\theta}+\delta\right)(p-\bar{p})=-v(p-\bar{p}) \tag{2.20}$$

Equation (2.20) casts the price movement observed after the initial shock into the form of a linear first-order differential equation with constant coefficients and constant inhomogeneity. The solution of this equation is[8]

$$p(t)=\bar{p}+[p(0)-\bar{p}]\exp(-vt) \tag{2.21}$$

where $p(0)$ is the price level observed during the impact period, in period 0 – that is, while the exchange rate overshoots – and $\exp(-vt) \equiv e^{-vt}$.[9]

Because of $v > 0, \exp(-vt)$ falls towards 0 as t increases, and the price level converges to its long-run equilibrium value. Upon substitution of (2.21) into (2.19), we obtain

$$e(t) = \bar{e} - \frac{1}{\lambda\theta}[p(0) - \bar{p}]\exp(-vt) \tag{2.22}$$

Since (2.19) holds at any point in time, and, hence also at time $t = 0$, (2.22) may be rewritten as

$$e(t) = \bar{e} + [e(0) - \bar{e}]\exp(-vt) \tag{2.23}$$

Hence, following a disturbance, the exchange rate also moves asymptotically towards its equilibrium value. As can be seen, the price level and the exchange rate even adjust to their respective equilibrium values with the same speed. The speed at which an initial disequilibrium is eliminated depends on the adjustment coefficient v, or since in (2.20) we had defined

$$v = \pi\left(\frac{\delta}{\lambda\theta} + \delta\right) \tag{2.24}$$

on the four parameters π, δ, λ and θ. The speed of adjustment is higher, the faster prices increase in situations of excess demand, and the stronger the demand for goods responds to changes of the real exchange rate. The effect of the parameters of the monetary sector, the semi-interest elasticity of the demand for money λ, and the *expected* speed of adjustment of the exchange rate to its equilibrium value, denoted by θ, is less straightforward. The smaller those parameters are, the quicker the economy moves towards equilibrium. It would be premature, however, to conclude from this that λ and θ should be as small as possible. Recall that we have demonstrated above that following a monetary disturbance the exchange rate overshoots its equilibrium value by $1/(\lambda\theta)$, that is, it overshoots the more, the smaller λ and/or θ are.

Thus small values of λ or θ have a double and – if we prefer to see the economy in equilibrium – ambivalent effect. With small values of these parameters, a monetary disturbance moves the economy further away from its equilibrium value, while at the same time increasing the speed at which it moves back towards equilibrium.[10]

2.1.10 Summary

The preceding sections contain a simple model of a small open economy, the central *assumptions* of which are as follows:

1. The economy is in full employment.
2. Fluctuations in goods demand only result in price movements, not in output movements.
3. Goods prices are sticky: that is, they need time to react to and absorb demand fluctuations.
4. The interest rate and the exchange rate are perfectly flexible, so that the money market and the asset market are both in permanent equilibrium.

Major *results* derived from an analysis of the model are as follows:

1. In the long run the money supply determines the price level, as claimed by the quantity theory of money.
2. On an international level, purchasing-power parity holds in the long run. That means that after all variables have adjusted, the exchange rate reflects domestic and foreign price levels.
3. In the short run the exchange rate responds more strongly than will eventually be necessary to maintain overall equilibrium. The reason for this *overshooting* is the stickiness of prices. Stickiness initially restricts prices from making their required contribution to overall adjustment.

2.2 Are exchange rate expectations rational?

If the central message of the Dornbusch model – flexible exchange rates fluctuate more than the fundamental variables which determine equilibrium – were the result of an arbitrary exchange rate expectations formation hypothesis, this would greatly reduce the relevance of this message. This provokes the question of how reasonable the expectations formation hypothesis postulated by equation (2.6) may actually be.

Differentiating (2.23) with respect to time t, we obtain

$$\dot{e} = -v[e(0) - \bar{e}]\exp(-vt) \tag{2.25}$$

Making use of (2.23), equation (2.25) may be rewritten as

$$\dot{e} = -v(e - \bar{e}) \tag{2.26}$$

A comparison of (2.6) and (2.26) reveals that agents expect the exchange rate to converge towards equilibrium and that this actually does happen. This certainly speaks in favour of expectations formation hypothesis (2.6). It requires, however, that market participants know the equilibrium exchange rate. According to (2.13), quite a number of parameters must be known in order to determine $\bar{e}$ precisely. When $\bar{e}$ is

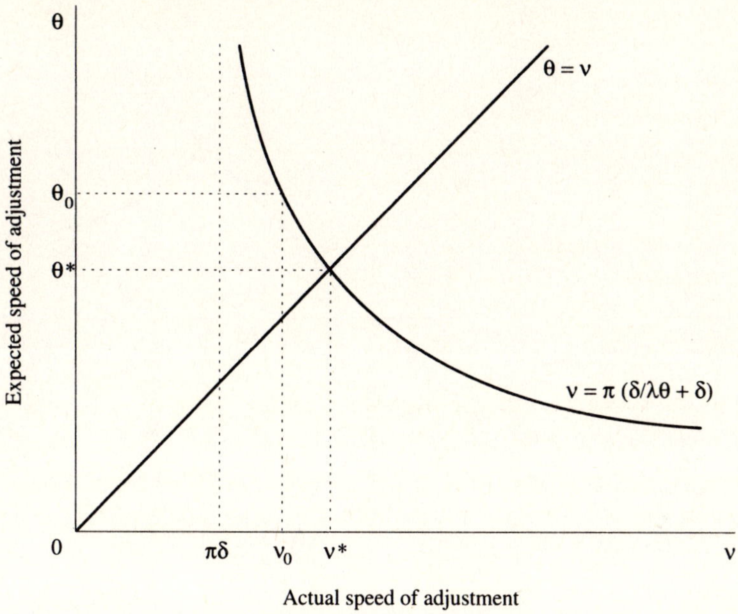

Figure 2.4 Actual and expected speeds of adjustment of the exchange rate to equilibrium

known, this still does not guarantee that the exchange rate will move towards equilibrium at the exact speed expected by the market. In particular, note a peculiar property of (2.24): the faster the market *expects* the exchange rate to converge towards its equilibrium value, the slower the exchange rate actually converges.

Figure 2.4 depicts this inverse relationship between the expected and the actual rate of convergence in the form of a hyperbola. The locus of consistent expectations $[\dot{e}=E(\dot{e})]$ is the 45° line. The point of intersection between this consistency condition and the hyperbola determines $\theta^*=v^*$, the value of θ for which $\theta^*(\bar{e}-e)=\dot{e}$. If the market expects convergence at a faster rate, for example θ_0, the exchange rate converges at the noticeably slower rate v_0 towards equilibrium.

θ^* may be computed from (2.24) by requiring $v=\theta$. Substituting results in

$$\theta^2-\pi\delta\theta-\pi\delta/\lambda=0$$

The two solutions of this quadratic equation are

$$\theta^*_{1,2}=\pi\delta/2\pm[\pi^2\delta^2/4+\pi\delta/\lambda]^{1/2} \tag{2.27}$$

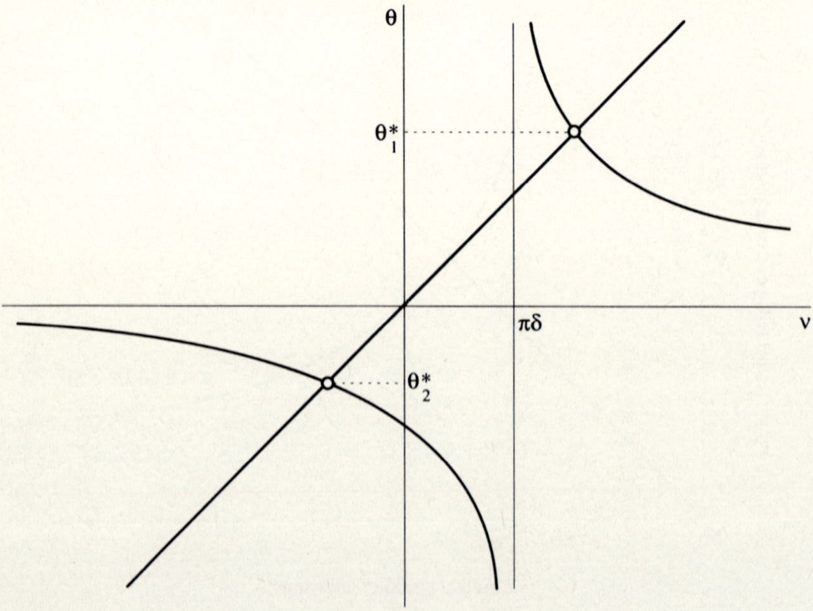

Figure 2.5 Stable and unstable solutions if perfect foresight is compatible with adaptive expectations

$\theta_1^* > 0$ corresponds to the value derived in Figure 2.4 and guarantees the stability of the model with perfect foresight. Since we excluded the possibility $\theta < 0$ – the market believes that the exchange rate will move further and further away from $\bar{e}$ – for economic reasons, our graphical analysis overlooked the fact that equation (2.24) has a second branch (see Figure 2.5).

The point of intersection of this second branch of the hyperbola with the $\theta = v$ line determines a second solution $\theta_2^* < 0$. In this case the market expects an existing disequilibrium of the exchange rate to grow continuously by a factor of $-\theta_2^*$ and this actually turns out to be the case.

The macroeconomic implications of the assumption that agents form depreciation expectations on the basis of $\theta = \theta_2^* < 0$ may be represented graphically. Substituting the definition of the equilibrium exchange rate (2.13) into the MS curve (2.11) we obtain:

$$p = -\lambda\theta e + (1+\lambda\theta)m - \left(\phi + \phi\lambda\theta - \frac{\lambda\theta}{\delta} + \frac{\lambda\theta\gamma}{\delta}\right)y + (1+\lambda\theta)\lambda i^* - \frac{\lambda\theta g}{\delta} \qquad (2.11')$$

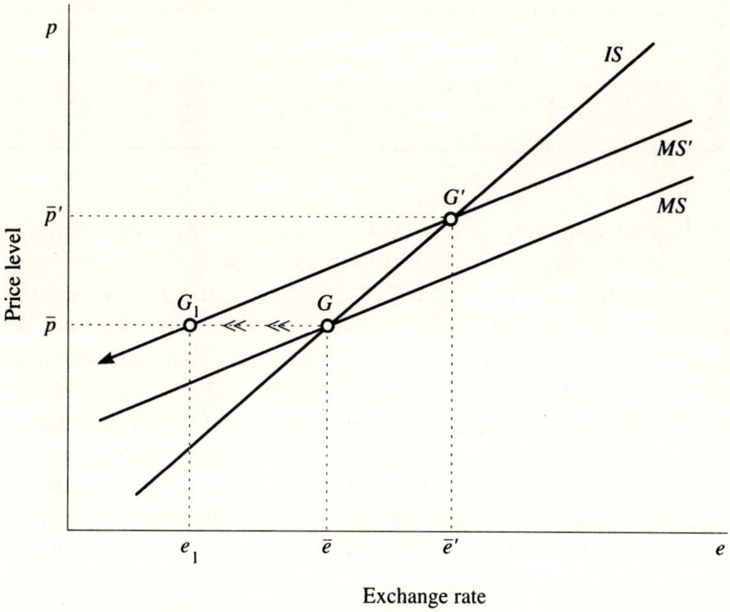

Figure 2.6 Developments under the assumption that perfect foresight implies that actors expect the exchange rate to move further and further away from equilibrium

Since we want to examine the consequences of an expansion of the money supply, we are only interested in the coefficients of e and m. Because of $-\lambda\theta > 0$ the MS curve now has a positive slope. Assume now $0 < -\lambda\theta < 1$, which means that the MS curve is flatter than the IS curve. Since our assumption also implies $1 + \lambda\theta > 0$, a money supply increase shifts the MS curve upwards. As Figure 2.6 illustrates, $\bar{e}$ and $\bar{p}$ increase. The exchange rate instantaneously appreciates to a point where the generated appreciation expectations (because of $\theta_2^* < 0$!) compensate for the deficit of the domestic interest rate compared to the foreign interest rate. Following the impact response, the exchange rate and the price level fall continuously (and, in the case of the exchange rate, expectedly so) and move further and further away from their respected 'equilibrium values'.

With this we have derived a rather discomforting result. Given a set of structural parameters, whether our model economy is stable or not only depends on whether agents expect it to be stable or not. If agents are convinced that an expansion in the money supply will lead to deflation and demand deficits, then exactly this will happen as the money supply is expanded. A tightening of the money supply, on the other hand, would trigger a hyperinflation, corresponding exactly to expectations.

PROBLEM 2.1

Discuss short-run, medium-run and long-run consequences of an expansion of the money supply for the case where $-\lambda\theta > 1$.

It may be argued, of course, that, according to experience, hyperinflations or accelerating deflations can only carry on for a limited period of time. If an unstable development were to begin, because it is expected by the economy, sooner or later political, but also economic, reactions would begin which would bring the unstable development to a halt: international capital controls, currency reforms, fixing the exchange rate, the use of foreign money for transactions at home and so on. If this is actually the case, however, and if agents can foresee this, they cannot possibly believe from the outset that the exchange rate will move forever further and further away from its (unstable) equilibrium value. But then the only remaining perfect foresight path which moves the economy along the MS schedule to a new long-run equilibrium after an unexpected shock is $\theta = \theta_1^* = v$.

2.3 Learning when expectations are not rational

As we have seen above, perfect foresight requires a great deal of information:[11]

1. The correct speed of adjustment θ_1^* can only be calculated when π, δ and λ are known.
2. Calculation of the equilibrium exchange rate $\bar{e}$ even requires the knowledge of ϕ, λ, δ, γ, m, y, i^* and g.

It is certainly legitimate to doubt whether individuals possess all that knowledge and are able to perform all the required calculations (including finding the solutions of a quadratic equation) in order to obtain θ^* and $\bar{e}$. If it was possible to show that simple learning schemes eventually make individuals act *as if* they could compute the true values of θ^* and $\bar{e}$, the assumption of perfect foresight would certainly sound a good deal less odd.

Assume an initial situation in which individuals are able to compute the equilibrium exchange rate $\bar{e}$ correctly, but expect an unrealistically fast return of the exchange rate to equilibrium after a disturbance ($\theta > \theta_1^*$). As a reference path, Figure 2.7 shows how, under perfect foresight, the exchange rate would adjust from one equilibrium G to a new one G' via G_1. If θ exceeds θ_1^*, the MS schedule rotates around G'. Since this schedule's slope is $-\lambda\theta$, the curve becomes steeper. The adjustment from G to G' now

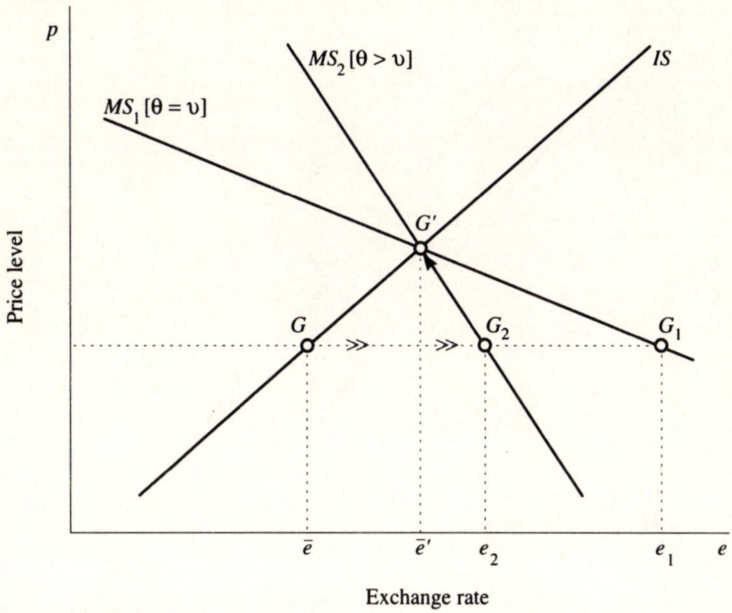

Figure 2.7 Development under the assumption that actors anticipate an unrealistically quick convergence of the exchange rate to its correctly perceived equilibrium value

proceeds via G_2 and – as long as θ remains unchanged – along the MS_2 schedule. It is unlikely, however, that rational actors would keep θ constant throughout the adjustment process. Because of $\theta > \theta_1^*$, we have $v < \theta$. In other words, along MS_2 the exchange rate never moves towards its equilibrium as quickly as expected. If individuals are smart enough to learn from systematic errors, they will sooner or later reduce θ, bringing it closer to its perfect foresight value θ_1^*. Thus the slope of the MS curve will probably start to become smaller while the adjustment process still lasts. Whether the time required for the adjustment to a *single* disturbance suffices to move the MS curve to MS_1 depends on how quickly individuals learn from systematic mistakes. In any case, repeated disturbances would eventually bring θ to θ_1^*.

Let us now change the scenario. Assume that individuals expect the correct adjustment speed ($\theta = \theta_1^*$) but are not able correctly to compute the equilibrium exchange rate (see Figure 2.8). In order to obtain a reference point and keep the arguments simple, let the initial equilibrium be G, in which $\bar{e}$ is seen correctly. Assumc now that individuals are led to believe that the equilibrium exchange rate has shifted from $\bar{e}$ to $\bar{e}'$, though it actually has not. Since individuals believe this without a valid reason, no

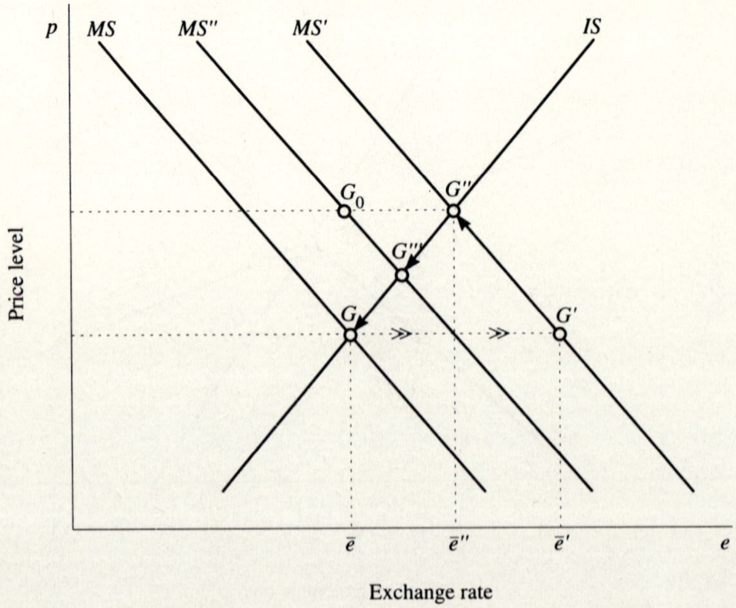

Figure 2.8 Development under the assumption that actors misperceive the equilibrium exchange rate

single exogenous parameter has changed. The price level is sticky and cannot respond immediately. As a consequence, the interest rate also remains unchanged and still corresponds to the foreign interest rate. For the international capital market to remain in equilibrium, the market must *not* expect the exchange rate to change. Therefore the exchange rate must jump to its new perceived equilibrium value $\bar{e}'$ immediately (see equation (2.11)). This argument should also clarify why the MS schedule exactly shifts into the position *MS*′.

Though the exchange rate should be in equilibrium in *G*′, it will begin to fall. This, of course, is due to the excess demand for domestic goods which exists in *G*′, causing goods prices to rise and real balances to fall, thus pushing the domestic interest rate up, and this finally calls for expectations of depreciation. These gradually build up as the economy moves along *MS*′ towards *G*″. In *G*″ the goods market is back to equilibrium. Therefore the price level and the exchange rate might settle down. However, there remains a great discrepancy between the expected and the actual exchange rate: on the one hand, the exchange rate is stationary at $\bar{e}''$; on the other hand, agents believe the equilibrium exchange rate to be $\bar{e}'$ and the exchange rate to move in this direction. In this situation agents will sooner or later have to realize that $\bar{e}'$ may not be the correct equilibrium exchange rate. It seems reasonable now to consider $\bar{e}''$ as the equilibrium exchange rate. This moves the MS schedule to MS'', moving the economy to G'''.[12] By the same token, however, the economy will not remain in G''' either. Continuous learning by the economic agents will cause the perceived equilibrium exchange rate to decline steadily, moving the MS schedule further to the left in Figure 2.8, until finally G is reached, where the equilibrium exchange rate is perceived correctly.

2.4 Perfect foresight

We now turn to analyze an expanded basic model under the explicit assumption of perfect foresight. This is worthwhile for several reasons:

1. Up to now we have demonstrated that $E(\dot{e})=\theta(\bar{e}-e)$ corresponds to perfect foresight if θ is picked correctly. However, this does not justify the reverse conclusion that perfect foresight must imply $E(\dot{e})=\theta^*(\bar{e}-e)$!
2. In later parts of this book we will turn to scenarios in which $E(\dot{e})=\theta(\bar{e}-e)$ is no longer compatible with perfect foresight. This is why it seems reasonable to introduce perfect foresight $[E(\dot{e})=\dot{e}]$ directly into our simple basic model.
3. Having introduced perfect foresight directly, we may use a by now familiar model to introduce the reader to the qualitative analysis of differential equations systems by means of phase diagrams. This rather simple method produces insights into the main dynamic characteristics of a model, without having to go to the trouble of solving the model quantitatively.

Due to the direct implementation of perfect foresight instead of adaptive expectations, the Dornbusch model's structure changes slightly, as shown in Model 2.2.

■ **Model 2.2**
Model with perfect foresight

1 Goods market

$\dot{p}=\pi(y^d-y)$	Phillips curve	(2.1)
$y^d=\delta(e-p)+\gamma y+g$	aggregate demand	(2.2′)

2 Money market

$m^d=p+\phi y-\lambda i$	money demand	(2.3)
$m^s=m^d=m$	money market equilibrium	(2.4)

3 International asset market

$i = i^* + E(\dot{e})$	asset market equilibrium	(2.5)
$E(\dot{e}) = \dot{e}$	perfect foresight	(2.6′)

Notes: The notes of the Dornbusch model (Model 2.1) apply. Variables are defined as follows:

- $\dot{p}$ domestic inflation rate
- y^d aggregate demand for domestic goods
- y aggregate supply of domestic goods (exogenous)
- e exchange rate
- p domestic price level
- g government expenditure
- i domestic interest rate
- m domestic money
- i^* foreign interest rate (exogenous)
- $\dot{e}$ rate of devaluation
- $\bar{e}$ equilibrium exchange rate
- $\dot{m}$ money supply growth rate

Formally, the new model variant can be written in a compact first-order differential equations system in two variables:

$$\dot{p} = \pi[\delta(e-p) - (1-\gamma)y + g] \tag{2.28}$$

$$\dot{e} = \frac{1}{\lambda}(p + \phi y - m) - i^* \tag{2.29}$$

The first equation explaining price movement has already been encountered previously in this chapter. It simply results from collecting goods market equations (2.1) and (2.2′). The second equation is a new one: it results from successively substituting (2.3), (2.5) and (2.6′) into the money market equilibrium condition (2.4).

Systems of equations are often cast in the form of matrix equations. In this form the model would look like this:

$$\begin{bmatrix} \dot{p} \\ \dot{e} \end{bmatrix} = \begin{bmatrix} -\pi\delta & \pi\delta \\ 1/\lambda & 0 \end{bmatrix} \begin{bmatrix} p \\ e \end{bmatrix} + \begin{bmatrix} \pi[g-(1-\gamma)y] \\ (\phi y - m)/\lambda - i^* \end{bmatrix} \tag{2.30}$$

This system of autonomous[13] first-order linear differential equations can be solved analytically, though with a certain effort. We will do without an explicit solution, using the model instead as an example to demonstrate the useful method of analyzing differential equations systems qualitatively by means of phase diagrams. This method too, however, will require a few calculations.

PROBLEM 2.2

Consider matrix equation (2.30). Derive the dynamic properties of the underlying system of differential equations mathematically. What is the economic meaning of the derived condition for stability?

In a first step, those conditions must be found under which the endogenous variables e and p no longer change. When discussing the graphical presentation of the model, we will refer to these conditions as **demarcation lines**. Setting $\dot{p}=0$ in equation (2.28) and solving for p, we obtain the first demarcation line:

$$p=e+\frac{g}{\delta}-\frac{(1-\gamma)y}{\delta} \tag{2.31}$$

Of course, this equation is identical with the goods market equilibrium schedule (2.7) and has unity slope. Setting $\dot{e}=0$ in equation (2.29) results in

$$p=m-\phi y+\lambda i^* \tag{2.32}$$

This is a horizontal line which intersects the ordinate at the equilibrium price level $\bar{p}$.

The $\dot{p}=0$ and the $\dot{e}=0$ curves are called demarcation lines because they divide the phase space (for example, the p/e plane) into four distinct regions for which the directions into which the endogenous variables p and e move can clearly be determined (see Figure 2.9). In order to find out into which direction the exchange rate moves in the area above the $\dot{e}=0$ demarcation line, we have to differentiate (2.29) with respect to p. This yields

$$\mathrm{d}\dot{e}/\mathrm{d}p=1/\lambda>0$$

If we now start from any point on the $\dot{e}=0$ line and move vertically upwards, $\dot{e}$ becomes positive. A positive rate of depreciation means that the exchange rate rises, moving us to the right. According to analogous reasoning, the exchange rate falls in the area below the $\dot{e}=0$ curve. In Figure 2.9 these insights are documented by means of horizontal arrows pointing to the right and to the left, respectively.

The movement of the price level to the right and to the left of the $\dot{p}=0$ schedule becomes obvious if we differentiate (2.28) with respect to e.[14] We do obtain

$$\mathrm{d}\dot{p}/\mathrm{d}e=\pi\delta>0$$

To the right of the demarcation line in Figure 2.9 the price level increases, in the area to the left it falls. These tendencies are documented by means of vertical arrows. Only at the point of intersection between both demarcation lines are both the price level and the exchange rate constant. At any other point either e or p changes, or both do. The general dynamic pattern is visualized by means of so-called **streamlines**.[15] The resulting picture may be summarized as follows:

1. There exists a line and only one line on which the system will move towards equilibrium after a disturbance under perfect foresight. This line is identical to the MS schedule employed above.

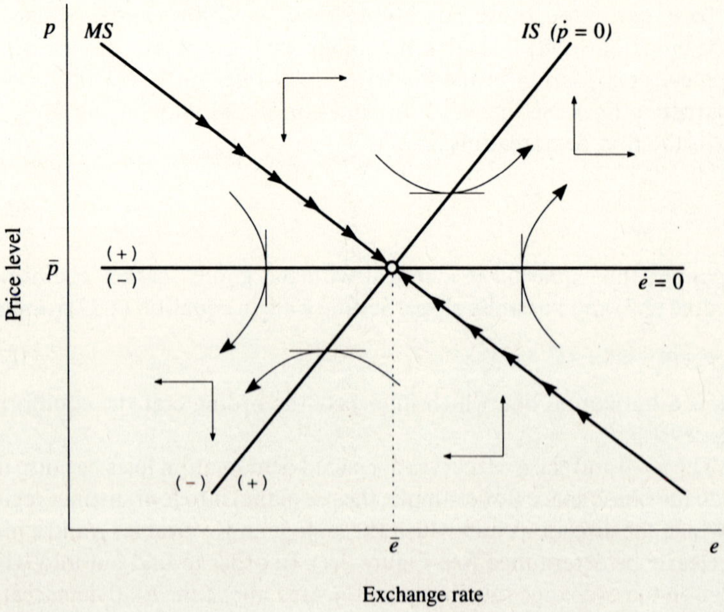

Figure 2.9 Presentation of dynamic characteristics by means of a phase diagram

2. Every point above the MS schedule eventually leads to continuing depeciation and price increases.

3. Every point below the MS schedule eventually leads to continuing appreciation and deflation.

Hence stability only exists when agents believe that the exchange rate always adjusts along *MS* towards its new equilibrium. This is a case of so-called **saddle path stability**. Following a shift of the MS curve, the exchange rate immediately jumps to its appropriate value on the new MS curve. Other expectations can also be compatible with the actual development, but will result in an unstable model. Analogously to the argument advanced above, it could be argued that individuals foresee the instability of perfect foresight paths and that experience tells them that brake mechanisms exogenous to the model will eventually stop an accelerating movement away from equilibrium. Hence the only feasible perfect foresight path is the one along the MS schedule.

It should be noted that saddle path stability, the possibility of both stable and unstable developments, is frequently encountered in deterministic models under perfect foresight or in stochastic models under rational expectations.[16]

> **PROBLEM 2.3**
> Compare the dynamics under perfect foresight depicted in Figure 2.9 to the paths depicted in Figures 2.3 and 2.6. Are the results compatible with each other?

2.5 Answers to the problems

Problem 2.1

The problem may be approached from two angles.

1. The coefficient $-\lambda\theta$ denotes the slope of the MS curve. The MS curve is steeper than the IS curve if $-\lambda\theta > 1$. According to (2.11′) $dp/dm = 1 + \lambda\theta$, which means that the money supply increase shifts the MS curve *downwards* if $-\lambda\theta > 1$ (see Figure 2.10).

Thus a money supply increase would move the long-run equilibrium point from G to G', which implies conventional comparative-static effects

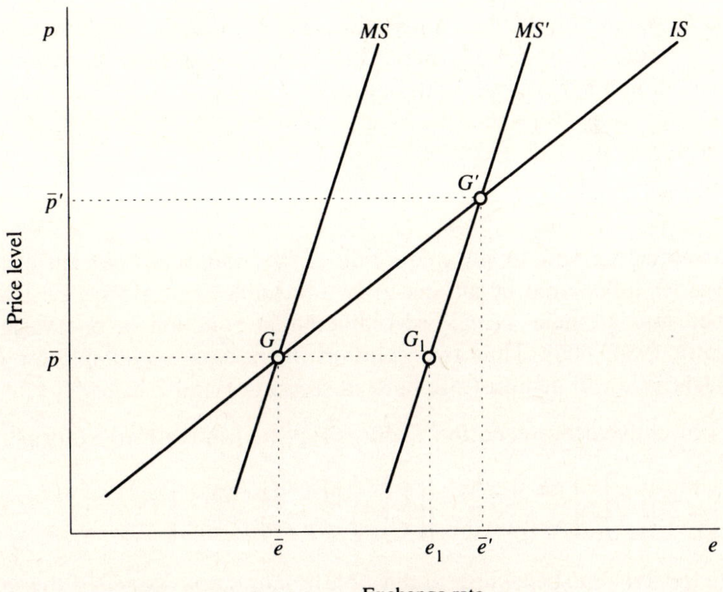

Figure 2.10 Short- and long-run responses when $-\lambda\theta > 1$

for the price level and the exchange rate. During the impact period the exchange rate would jump from $\bar{e}$ to e_1 and thus would not overshoot.

The medium-term dynamics appears puzzling. Since $e_1 < \bar{e}'$, under perfect foresight the exchange rate should move further and further away from its equilibrium value (recall that we assume $\theta < 0$). In order not to violate the equilibrium conditions for the monetary sector, this has to be achieved by moving down the MS′ curve, which implies falling prices. Since G_1 is in the area below the IS curve, where there is an excess demand for domestic goods, the price level actually should rise (equation (2.1)). So something appears to be wrong with our 'solution'.

2. We may now pose the question whether the postulated case $-\lambda\theta > 1$ can actually occur (of course, we might or should have started the analysis with this question). In fact, it can be shown that $-\lambda\theta < 1$. If this is true, it follows from (2.27)

$$\lambda\theta = \pi\delta\lambda/2 - \lambda(\pi^2\delta^2/4 + \pi\delta/4)^{1/2} > -1$$

Dividing both sides by λ and rearranging terms gives

$$1/\lambda + \pi\delta/2 > [\pi^2\delta^2/4 + \pi\delta/\lambda]^{1/2}$$

Raising both sides to the power of 2 we obtain

$$1/\lambda^2 + \pi\delta/\lambda + \pi^2\delta^2/4 > \pi^2\delta^2/4 + \pi\delta/\lambda$$

Thus the condition $-\lambda\theta < 1$ must always hold, that is, *the MS curve is always flatter than the IS curve*. Problem 2.1 assumed a parameter constellation which cannot really occur!

Problem 2.2

Before deciding how to solve equation (2.30), note that a system of two *first*-order differential equations in two variables can always be transformed into a single *second*-order differential equation in one variable (Chiang 1984: 606). Thus two solution methods are available for our problem. We will demonstrate both in sections 1 and 2 below:

1. For convenience equation (2.30) is repeated in rearranged form:

$$\begin{bmatrix} 1 & 0 \\ 0 & 1 \end{bmatrix} \begin{bmatrix} \dot{p} \\ \dot{e} \end{bmatrix} + \begin{bmatrix} \pi\delta & -\pi\delta \\ -1/\lambda & 0 \end{bmatrix} \begin{bmatrix} p \\ e \end{bmatrix} = \begin{bmatrix} \pi[g-(1-\gamma)y] \\ (\phi y - m)/\lambda - i^* \end{bmatrix}$$

Since the dynamic behaviour of this non-homogeneous system is the same as for the corresponding homogeneous system (in which the vector of constant terms equals zero), we analyze the latter. Starting with the trial solutions for the complimentary functions $p_c = q\exp(rt)$ and $e_c = n\exp(rt)$, where r denotes the characteristic roots, $p_c \equiv p - \bar{p}$, $e_c \equiv e - \bar{e}$, and q and n are arbitrary constants, we obtain

$$\begin{bmatrix} 1 & 0 \\ 0 & 1 \end{bmatrix} \begin{bmatrix} q \\ n \end{bmatrix} r\exp(rt) + \begin{bmatrix} \pi\delta & -\pi\delta \\ -1/\lambda & 0 \end{bmatrix} \begin{bmatrix} q \\ n \end{bmatrix} \exp(rt) = 0$$

Dividing both sides by exp(rt) and collecting terms yields

$$\left\{ r \begin{bmatrix} 1 & 0 \\ 0 & 1 \end{bmatrix} \begin{bmatrix} \pi\delta & -\pi\delta \\ -1/\lambda & 0 \end{bmatrix} \right\} \begin{bmatrix} q \\ n \end{bmatrix} = 0$$

A non-trivial solution calls for the determinant of the matrix in braces to be zero, that is:

$$\begin{vmatrix} r + \pi\delta & -\pi\delta \\ -1/\lambda & r \end{vmatrix} = r^2 + \pi\delta r - \frac{\pi\delta}{\lambda} = 0$$

The solution to this quadratic equation,

$$r_{1,2} = \frac{-\pi\delta \pm \sqrt{\pi^2\delta^2 + 4\pi\delta/\lambda}}{2}$$

gives two distinct real roots, $r_1 > 0$ and $r_2 < 0$. Substituting this into the above trial solutions we obtain the complementary functions

$$p_c = q_1\exp(r_1 t) + q_2\exp(r_2 t)$$
$$e_c = n_1\exp(r_1 t) + n_2\exp(r_2 t)$$

Since $r_1 > 0$, the model is inherently unstable. It would only be stable if $n_1 = q_1 = 0$ restricted the first term on the right-hand side to zero.

2. Substituting (2.2′) into (2.1) yields

$$\dot{p} = \pi\delta(e - p) + \pi g - \pi(1 - \gamma)\bar{y} \tag{2.33}$$

Combining equations (2.3), (2.4), (2.5) and (2.6′) gives

$$p = m - \phi y + \lambda Ri^* + \lambda\dot{e} \tag{2.34}$$

or, after differentiating with respect to time,

$$\dot{p} = \lambda\ddot{e} \tag{2.35}$$

Inserting (2.35) and (2.34) into (2.33) gives, after rearranging terms,

$$\ddot{e} + \pi\delta\dot{e} - \frac{\pi\delta}{\lambda}e = -\frac{\pi\delta}{\lambda}(m - \phi y + \lambda i^*) + \frac{\pi}{\lambda}[g - (1 - \gamma)y]$$

from which we obtain the same characteristic roots as obtained from the above differential-equations system:

$$r_{1,2}=\frac{-\pi\delta\pm\sqrt{\pi^2\delta^2+4\pi\delta/\lambda}}{2}$$

The general behaviour of the exchange rate is given by the equilibrium exchange rate plus the complementary function:

$$e=\bar{e}+e_c$$

Writing out the solution obtained for the complementary function, this becomes

$$e=\bar{e}+A_1\exp(r_1t)+A_2\exp(r_2t) \tag{2.36}$$

Given that $r_1>0$, the exchange rate only converges towards equilibrium if $A_1=0$.

3. To determine what the stability condition $A_1=0$ really means, we have to determine A_1. Differentiation of (2.36) with respect to time gives

$$\dot{e}=r_1A_1\exp(r_1t)+r_2A_2\exp(r_2t) \tag{2.37}$$

Evaluation of (2.36) at time 0 gives

$$e(0)=\bar{e}+A_1+A_2 \tag{2.36'}$$

Evaluation of (2.37) at time 0 gives

$$\dot{e}(0)=r_1A_1+r_2A_2 \tag{2.37'}$$

Solving (2.36′) for A_2 and inserting into (2.37′) gives

$$\dot{e}(0)=(r_1-r_2)A_1+r_2[e(0)-\bar{e}] \tag{2.38}$$

For $A_1=0$ we must require

$$\dot{e}(0)=r_2[e(0)-\bar{e}] \tag{2.39}$$

Substitution of (2.6′), (2.5), and (2.4) into (2.3), noting $\bar{p}=m-\phi y+\lambda i$ and evaluating at time 0 gives

$$\dot{e}(0)=\frac{1}{\lambda}[p(0)-\bar{p}] \tag{2.40}$$

Substituting (2.39) into (2.40) and solving for $p(0)$ yields

$$p(0)=\bar{e}+\lambda r_2[e(0)-\bar{e}] \tag{2.41}$$

Equation (2.41) is the point on the MS curve (2.11) at time 0 if $r_2=-\theta$. Comparing the solution for r_2 obtained above with (2.27), we see that $r_2=-\theta$ under perfect foresight. Hence, (2.39) simply says that our perfect foresight version is stable if we initially are on the MS curve which applies under perfect foresight.

Problem 2.3

Figure 2.3 shows the consequences of a money supply increase under the general assumption that the economy expects the exchange rate to converge to long-run equilibrium $[E(\dot{e})=\theta(\bar{e}-e)]$. Figure 2.4 shows that only one such value for θ, $\theta=v$, and thus only one particular slope of the MS curve is compatible with perfect foresight. This MS curve is identical with the stable adjustment path depicted in Figure 2.9. Besides that, Figure 2.9 suggests an unlimited number of other developments which are compatible with perfect foresight. Figure 2.3 shows only one such path. This follows from the fact that we have demonstrated $E(\dot{e})=\theta^*(\bar{e}-e) \rightarrow E(\dot{e})=\dot{e}$, but that the opposite conclusion does not hold: $E(\dot{e})=\dot{e} \nrightarrow E(\dot{e})=\theta^*(\bar{e}-e)$. Obviously, an unlimited number of expectations formation schemes are compatible with perfect foresight; however, all except one render the model unstable. To sum this up, we may state that Figures 2.3 and 2.9 are based on two distinct models postulating fundamentally different expectations formation schemes. The common denominator of both models is the version presented in Figure 2.7 with $MS_1[\theta=v]$.

APPENDIX

This appendix offers two things: the first part recapitulates the simplified Dornbusch model and its key implications, condensed into a one-page format. The second part discusses the original Dornbusch model. This is done out of a desire for completeness, and to satisfy student curiosity about what our simplication may have done to the original model.

The simplified Dornbusch model in a nutshell

In a nutshell the display shown in Figure 2.11 summarizes some of the more important insights of the macroeconomic disequilibrium approach to the exchange rate introduced earlier in this chapter. The left-hand column presents and explains the structural building blocks of the model. The centre column demonstrates how to arrive at equilibrium conditions for the real sector and the monetary sector, and depicts these conditions graphically. Finally, the right-hand column draws sectoral equilibria together to yield overall equilibrium values. The shaded section demonstrates how exchange rate overshooting results from sticky prices. Photocopied and used as a page marker in Chapters 2, 3, and 4 this summary may prove a useful source of reference and, if so desired, help to drum in this most important of the models discussed in the book.

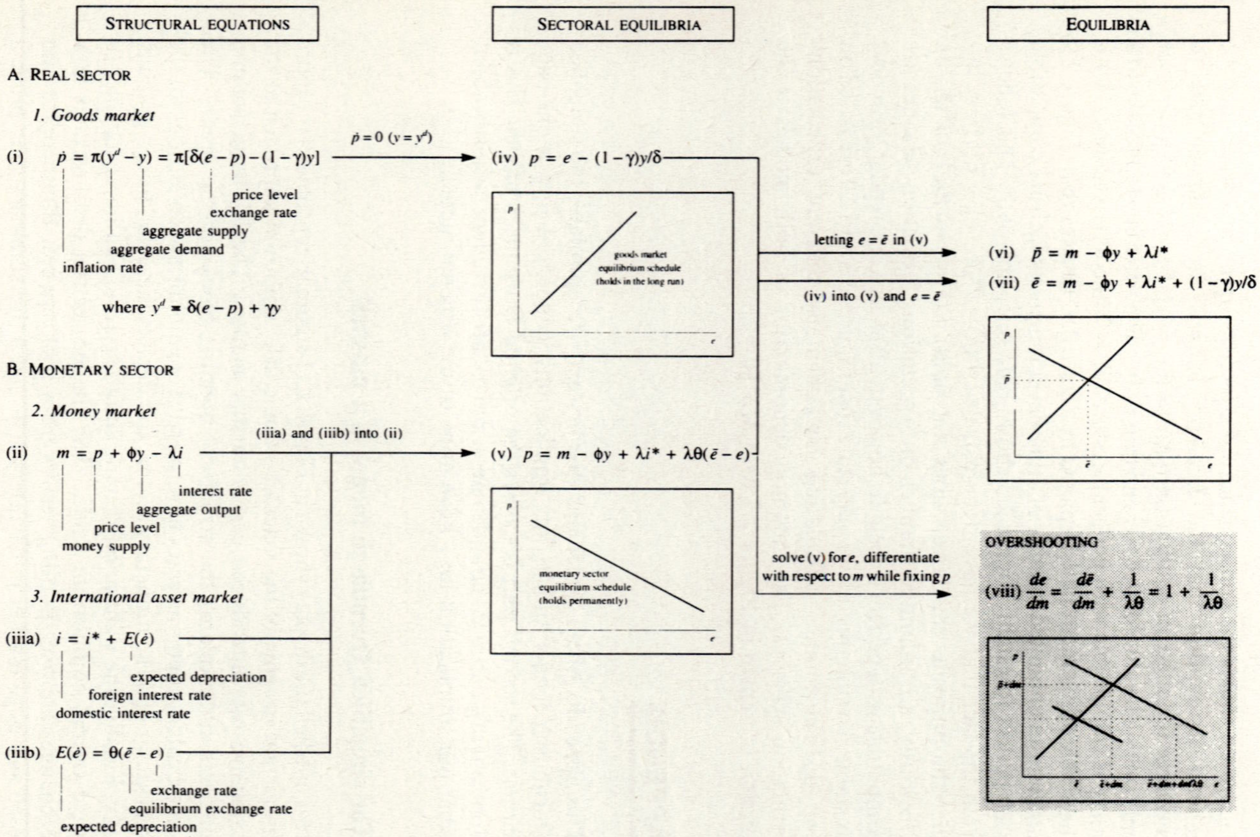

Figure 2.11 The simplified Dornbusch model in a nutshell

Dornbusch pure

Model 2.3 is the one advanced in Dornbusch (1976). The one aspect in which this model differs from the simplified version, which we analyzed in some detail in this chapter, is that aggregate demand depends on one more variable, namely the interest rate. Note that this provides a second link between the goods market and the monetary sector. The following points should be obvious without substantiation by formal analysis.

1. The modification only affects the goods market. The permanently binding equilibrium condition for the monetary sector is exactly the same as in the simplified version. Hence, since the impact response of the exchange rate to a money supply increase is determined by the equilibrium condition for the monetary sector alone, overshooting is exactly the same as in the simplified model.

2. Due to the two links between the goods market and the monetary sector, equilibria for the goods market are no longer unique. In the long

■ **Model 2.3**
Dornbusch model (original version)

1 Goods market

$\dot{p}=\pi(y^d-y)$	Phillips curve	(2.1)
$y^d=\delta(e-p)+\gamma y-\sigma i+g$	aggregate demand	(2.2)

2 Money market

$m^d=p+\phi y-\lambda i$	money demand	(2.3)
$m^s=m^d=m$	money market equilibrium	(2.4)

3 International asset market

$i=i^*+E(\dot{e})$	asset market equilibrium	(2.5)
$E(\dot{e})=\theta(\bar{e}-e)$	expectations formation	(2.6)

Notes: Lower-case variables are in natural logarithms, an exception being the interest rate. A dot indicates the change of the respective variable over time. Greek letters denote positive parameters. $E(.)$ is the expectations operator. Variables are defined as follows:

$\dot{p}$	domestic inflation rate	i	domestic interest rate
y^d	aggregate demand for domestic goods	m	domestic money
y	aggregate supply of domestic goods (exogenous)	i^*	foreign interest rate (exogenous)
e	exchange rate	$\dot{e}$	rate of depreciation
p	domestic price level	$\bar{e}$	equilibrium exchange rate
g	government expenditure	m^s	domestic money supply
		m^d	domestic money demand

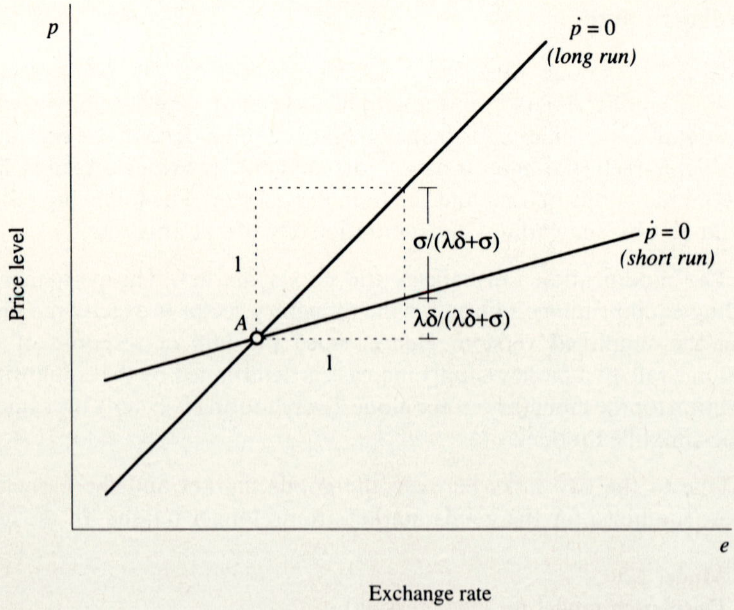

Figure 2.12 Real sector equilibrium conditions in the short and in the long run

run, when the domestic interest rate equals the foreign interest rate, $\dot{p}=0$ and substitution of (2.2) into (2.1) yields

$$p=e-\frac{(1-\gamma)y}{\delta}+\frac{g}{\delta}-\frac{\sigma i^*}{\delta} \tag{2.7$'$}$$

As in the simplified model, equation (2.7′) may be graphed as a straight line with unity slope, implying a constant real exchange rate.

In the short run the home interest rate may differ from the foreign one. Hence a variety of combinations between real exchange rates and interest rates exists, which equilibrate demand and supply in the goods market. This short-run goods market equilibrium is obtained by letting the interest rate in (2.7′) differ from the foreign interest rate. Then solve the money market equations (2.3) and (2.4) for the interest rate, and substitute the resulting equation into (2.7′). This yields

$$p=\frac{\lambda\delta}{\lambda\delta+\sigma}e+\frac{\sigma}{\lambda\delta+\sigma}m-\frac{\lambda(1-\gamma)+\sigma\phi}{\lambda\delta+\sigma}y+\frac{\lambda}{\lambda\delta+\sigma}g \tag{2.8$'$}$$

The short-run goods market equilibrium schedule is flatter than the long-run equilibrium schedule (see Figure 2.12). This is because in the short

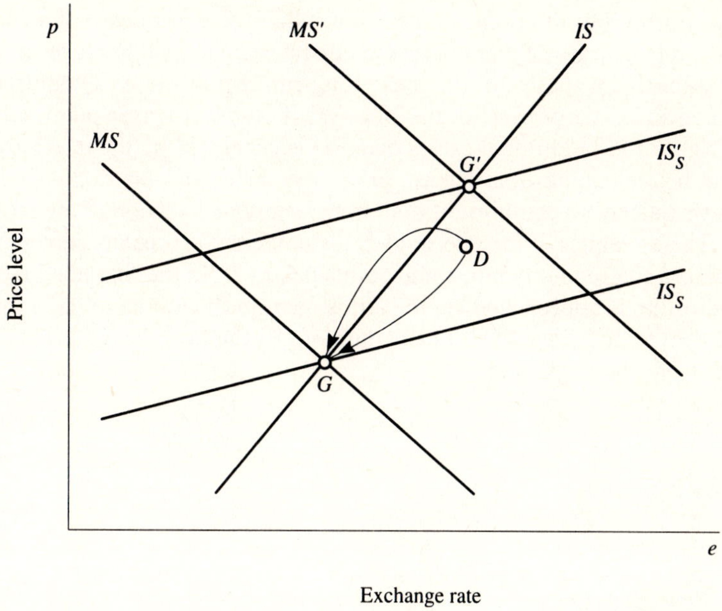

Figure 2.13 Equilibrium schedules in the pure Dornbusch model after a money supply increase

run a real depreciation (which raises desired demand) may partly be compensated for by an increase of the domestic interest rate (which reduces desired demand). Assume that from some point A on the long-run IS curve the exchange rate rises by 1 per cent: in the long run this would call for an equiproportionate increase of the price level in order to restore goods market equilibrium; in the short run the price level must only increase by $\lambda\delta/(\lambda\delta+\sigma)$ per cent. While this only reduces desired demand by $\lambda\delta^2/(\lambda\delta+\sigma)$ per cent, it also increases the interest rate by $\delta/(\lambda\delta+\sigma)$ per cent, which dampens demand by another $\delta\sigma/(\lambda\delta+\sigma)$ per cent. Both these direct and indirect consequences of the price increase add up to a reduction of desired demand by δ per cent. This exactly offsets the δ per cent demand increase caused by a 1 per cent devaluation.

By equating (2.7′) and (2.8′) we obtain the exchange rate at which both schedules intersect. Collecting terms and solving for e yields

$$\bar{e}=m-\phi y+\frac{1-\gamma}{\delta}y-\frac{g}{\delta}+\left(\lambda+\frac{\sigma}{\delta}\right)i^* \qquad (2.9')$$

which is the equilibrium exchange rate of the pure Dornbusch model.

Figure 2.13 shows how the short-run goods market equilibrium schedule shifts as the money supply increases, so as to pass through the new long-run equilibrium point. It also shows that the dependence of demand on the interest rate neither affects the impact effect in qualitative terms nor the adjustment path to the new long-run equilibrium. Quantitative differences exist, however, for the following reasons: at a given point, say, to the right of IS, additional excess demand is generated by the interest rate being below equilibrium. Hence, prices rise faster and the exchange rate adjusts quicker to equilibrium than in the simplified version of the model.

The dynamics of the two models also differs if erroneous perceptions displaced the economy into some point such as *D*. In the simplified model equilibrium is approached via the adjustment path with an initially rising and then falling price level. In the pure model the price level starts to fall right from the beginning.

NOTES

1. To simplify matters, we assume the demand for domestic goods to be independent of interest rates. See also Dornbusch (1987) and Frenkel and Rodriguez (1982).
2. See, for example, Buiter and Miller (1981), Bhandari and Turnovsky (1982) or Mussa (1982).
3. We have already defined the real exchange rate as EP^*/P in the previous chapter. When taking the natural logarithm we arrive at $\ln E + \ln P^* - \ln P \equiv e + p^* - p$. Setting the exogenous foreign price level $P^* = 1$, which implies $\ln P^* = p^* = 0$, the log of the real exchange rate becomes $e - p$.
4. Equation (2.5) is a common simplification of the equilibrium schedule for the international capital market, which is not very precise, however. While a unit of currency deposited at home will achieve a yield corresponding exactly to the domestic interest rate, the expected yield of the same investment abroad is $i^* + E(\dot{e}) + E(\dot{e})i^*$. It is composed of the interest payment, the expected return from foreign appreciation on the amount invested, and the expected return from appreciation on the negotiated interest payment. Thus the exact equilibrium condition is

   $$i = i^* + E(\dot{e}) + E(\dot{e})i^*$$

   Since the last term is very small under normal interest rates and exchange rate movements, it can be neglected within the context of macroeconomic models.
5. Because of this IS schedule's characteristic of showing those combinations of prices and the exchange rate which no longer change the price level, we may call it the $\dot{p} = 0$ schedule.
6. The expectation that the exchange rate will not change is called a stationary expectation.
7. An elasticity indicates the percentage change of one variable when another variable is raised by 1 per cent. The coefficient relating the natural logarithms of two variables is an elasticity. Thus, in equation (2.3) – the money demand schedule – the coefficient ϕ denotes the income elasticity of money demand. Since $-\lambda$ shows the relationship between the logarithm of a variable (m) and an absolute variable (i), this coefficient is called a semi-elasticity.

8. See, for example, Chiang (1984: Ch. 14) or Gandolfo (1980: Part 2, Chs 1 and 2).
9. We will do without the type of expression seen on the right-hand side in this identity, since e, usually denoting the Euler constant, is already being used for the logarithm of the exchange rate.
10. We will arrive at a similar result below when we examine the effects of an *announced* expansion of the money supply.
11. In the present context we call expectations irrational when upcoming changes of the exchange rate are systematically – that is, persistently in the same fashion – over- or underestimated.
12. Whether the movement from G'' to G''' directly proceeds along the IS schedule, or whether it moves, with a temporarily overshooting exchange rate, via G_0 along MS'', depends on whether conceptions of the equilibrium exchange rate move slowly or rapidly from $\bar{e}'$ to $\bar{e}''$.
13. We speak of an autonomous system when the coefficients remain constant as time moves on. See Chiang (1984: Chs 14, 15 and 18).
14. Calculating $d\dot{p}/dp = -\pi\delta$ instead would lead to exactly the same conclusions.
15. Other common expressions for streamlines are phase paths or phase trajectories.
16. In *deterministic* models there are, next to the explicit structural dependences, no other, random influences that are not explained by the underlying theory. If all agents are familiar with the model and the development of the exogenous variables, this will allow for *perfect foresight* on their part, such as $E(p_t) = p_t$ in discrete time. *Stochastic* models allow for the possibility of random influences in the same manner as is required in econometrics. Since, by definition, random influences cannot be predicted, even knowledge of both the model and all exogenous variables will not allow for perfect predictions. However, if available information is used in a manner that avoids systematic mistakes, we speak of *rational expectations*. In the example presented above this results in $E(p_t) = p_t + \varepsilon_t$, where ε is a random variable with an expected value of zero.

REFERENCES

Bhandari, Jagdeep S. and Stephen J. Turnovsky (1982) 'Alternative monetary policies in an inflationary equilibrium model of the open economy', *Weltwirtschaftliches Archiv* 118, 1–18.

Buiter, Willem H. and M. H. Miller (1981) 'Monetary policy and international competitiveness: The problem of adjustment', *Oxford Economic Papers* 33, 143–75.

Chiang, Alpha C. (1984) *Fundamental Methods of Mathematical Economics*, 3rd edn, Singapore: McGraw-Hill.

Dornbusch, Rudiger (1976) 'Expectations and exchange rate dynamics', *Journal of Political Economy* 84, 1167–76.

Dornbusch, Rudiger (1987) 'Exchange rate economics: 1986', *Economic Journal* 97, 1–18.

Frenkel, Jacob A. and Carlos A. Rodriguez (1982) 'Exchange rate dynamics and the overshooting hypothesis', *IMF Staff Papers* 29, 1–30.

Gandolfo, Giancarlo (1980) *Economic Dynamics: Methods and models*, 2nd edn, Amsterdam: North-Holland.

Mussa, Michael (1982) 'A model of exchange rate dynamics', *Journal of Political Economy* 90, 74–104.

Chapter 3

The robustness of the overshooting phenomenon

The central message of the macroeconomic disequilibrium approach to the exchange rate is as follows: exchange rates are more volatile than the fundamental variables which determine the exchange rate in the *long run*. This statement was derived and discussed in Chapter 2 in the context of a money supply increase. While this message of the Dornbusch model may have been an overall characteristic of flexible exchange rates for the past two decades, it is not difficult to find counterexamples: exchange rates do not always respond as strongly as the preceding move of fundamental variables will require in the long run; sometimes they may not respond at all, or even initially move in the wrong direction.

Such empirical observations may raise doubts about the Dornbusch model's potential to explain the real world. If it were possible, though, to demonstrate that overshooting is not an absolutely necessary feature of the Dornbusch model, but merely a possibility, this would significantly increase the model's potential to explain exchange rate movements since 1973. The following three sections will address exactly this question of how robust the overshooting result is with respect to small but reasonable modifications of the model. We will discover the following:

1. Whether the exchange rate overshoots or not crucially depends on the *type of disturbance* which causes the exchange rate to move.
2. If we *drop the assumption that domestic and foreign assets are perfect substitutes*, the exchange rate may, but must not, overshoot any longer.
3. Among others, the impact response of the exchange rate crucially depends on the *conclusions* drawn by individuals with regard to the *future course of monetary policy*.

3.1 Consequences of a supply shock

We begin by examining price and exchange rate reactions to a sudden surge in aggregate supply. Let us postulate a one-time and permanent increase in full-employment output, y. The resulting change of the equilibrium exchange rate is obtained by differentiating (from Chapter 2)

$$\bar{e}=m-\phi y+\lambda i^{*}-\frac{g}{\delta}+\frac{(1-\gamma)y}{\delta} \qquad (2.13)$$

with respect to y. The resulting expression

$$\frac{d\bar{e}}{dy}=-\phi+\frac{1-\gamma}{\delta}$$

may be positive or negative, since both terms to the right of the equality sign have opposite signs which are independent of each other. A rise in full-employment output, for example, because of an improved production technology, may cause the exchange rate to appreciate or to depreciate. Parameters that would make an appreciation more likely are a high income elasticity of the demand for money (ϕ), a high marginal propensity to consume (γ), or a high real exchange rate elasticity of the demand for domestic goods (δ).

PROBLEM 3.1

Explain the described negative association between $d\bar{e}/dy$ and the parameters ϕ, γ and δ in *economic terms*.

The impact response of the exchange rate follows from differentiating

$$e=\bar{e}+\frac{m-p-\phi y}{\lambda\theta}+\frac{i^{*}}{\theta} \qquad (2.16)$$

with respect to y. Taking (2.13) into account, this yields

$$\frac{de}{dy}=-\phi\left(1+\frac{1}{\lambda\theta}\right)+\frac{1-\gamma}{\delta}$$

Obviously, the impact response of the exchange rate may just as well be positive or negative. In any case, by making use of

$$\bar{p}=m-\phi y+\lambda i^{*} \qquad (2.12)$$

it follows

$$\frac{d\bar{p}}{dy}=-\phi<0$$

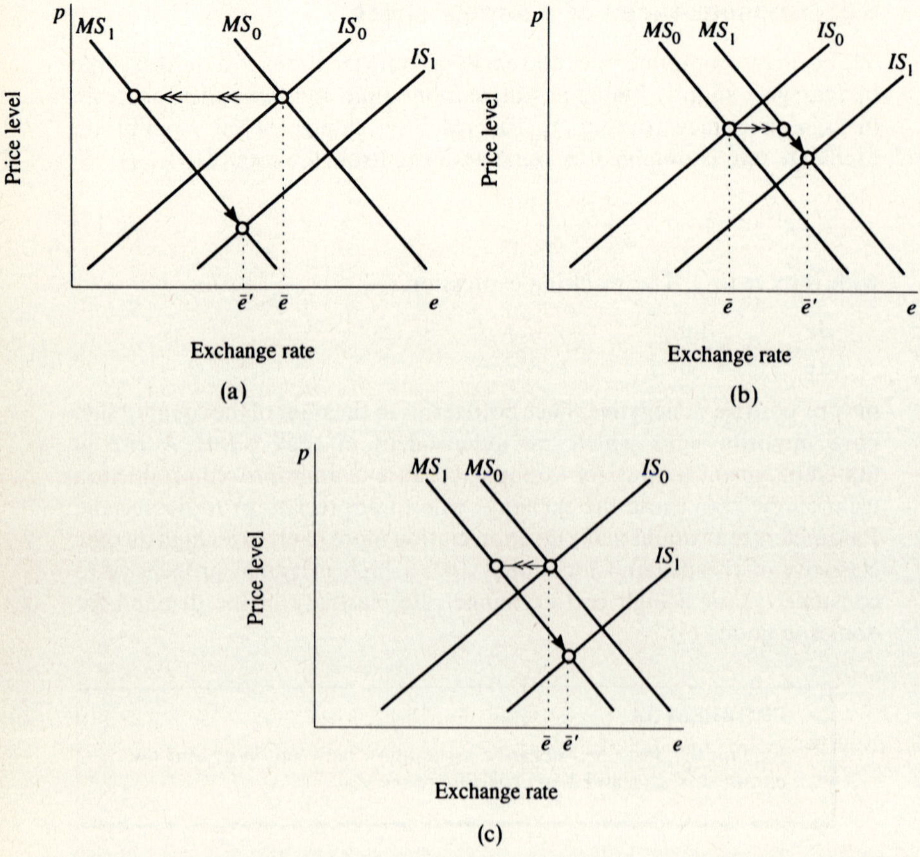

Figure 3.1 Consequences of a positive supply shock: (a) case study 1; (b) case study 2a; (c) case study 2b

which means that the price level falls *in the long run*. This eventual reduction of the price level may come about via three stylized paths, all indicating a different development of the exchange rate. Figure 3.1(a–c) depicts the three possible cases.

Case study 1 (see Figure 3.1a):
$A \equiv -\phi + (1-\gamma)/\delta < 0 \Rightarrow d\bar{e}/dy < 0$ and $de/dy < d\bar{e}/dy$. The exchange rate falls both in the short and in the long run, though the short-run response is stronger. Thus the exchange rate overshoots. The price level declines monotonically to its new equilibrium value. The real exchange rate initially falls (appreciation), then rises, and eventually settles for a value higher than the initial equilibrium value.

Case study 2a (see Figure 3.1b):
$A > \phi/(\lambda\theta) \Rightarrow d\bar{e}/dy > 0$ and $0 < de/dy < d\bar{e}/dy$. The exchange rate rises both in the short and in the long run, though more pronouncedly in the long run. Thus we have no overshooting of the exchange rate in this case. Here again the price level declines monotonically to its new equilibrium value. The real exchange rate also depreciates both in the short and in the long run.

Case study 2b (see Figure 3.1c):
$0 < A < \phi/(\lambda\theta) \Rightarrow d\bar{e}/dy > 0$ and $de/dy < 0$. The impact response of the exchange rate is to appreciate, that is, to fall. In the long run, however, it depreciates. Thus we do not have exchange rate overshooting in the traditional sense. As in the other cases, the price level declines monotonically. The real exchange rate declines initially but rises above its initial equilibrium value later on.

To summarize these results: we have learned that after a supply-side disturbance the exchange rate *may* overshoot, but that this does not *have to* be the case. This is in contrast to the results that we obtained when we analyzed demand-side disturbances above.

3.2 Demand-determined output

We now relax the assumption of a completely rigid exogenous supply of aggregate output. While the postulate of a fully employed economy is being retained, the production possibilities are now considered fully flexible in the short run.

Model 3.1
Model with demand-determined output

1	**Goods market**		
	$\dot{p} = \pi(y - \bar{y})$	Phillips curve	(3.1)
	$y = \delta(e - p) + \gamma y + g$	aggregate demand	(3.2)
2	**Money market**		
	$m^d = p + \phi y - \lambda i$	money demand	(3.3)
	$m^s = m^d = m = m$	money market equilibrium	(3.4)
3	**International asset market**		
	$i = i^* + E(\dot{e})$	asset market equilibrium	(3.5)
	$E(\dot{e}) = \theta(\bar{e} - e)$	expectations formation	(3.6)

Notes: Lower-case variables are in natural logarithms, an exception being the interest rate. A dot indicates the change of the respective variable over time.

Greek letters denote positive parameters. $E(.)$ is the expectations operator. Variables are defined as follows:

$\dot{p}$	domestic inflation rate	i	domestic interest rate
y	aggregate demand for domestic goods (equals aggregate output)	m	domestic money
		i^*	foreign interest rate (exogenous)
$\bar{y}$	natural output of domestic goods (exogenous)	$\dot{e}$	rate of depreciation
		$\bar{e}$	equilibrium exchange rate
e	exchange rate	m^s	domestic money supply
p	domestic price level	m^d	domestic money demand
g	government expenditure		

The difference between the model introduced at the beginning of Chapter 2 (Model 2.1) and the model with demand-determined output (Model 3.1) is hidden in the modified definition of variables in the goods market equations (3.1) and (3.2). While equation (3.2) is formally identical to the explanation of *desired* demand employed above, the use of *actual* output y as the left-hand variable indicates that supply always adjusts to demand. Equation (3.1) is another version of the Phillips curve, stating that inflation is proportional to the difference between actual output y and full-employment output $\bar{y}$.

While the structural equations of the monetary sector are left untouched, the endogenization of aggregate output leaves its marks in the monetary sector as well. Consider a money supply increase. In the original scenario with fixed output, interest rates fall, causing the exchange rate to overshoot. When output follows demand, however, the situation is more complex. Now the money supply increase does not only exert a downward pressure on the interest rate, *ceteris paribus*. To the extent that the exchange rate depreciates, this stimulates output, and, hence, the transactions demand for money. Thus, a money supply increase may generate its own transactions demand, leaving the effect on the interest rate open. Figure 3.2 illustrates the stylized possibilities.

If a money supply increase stimulates output by the exact amount necessary to generate the required money demand, the interest rate remains unchanged at the level of the world interest rate. The exchange rate jumps to where it is not expected to change any more – which is to its new long-run equilibrium value. This implies that the MS curve is vertical in this special case. The exchange rate does not overshoot.

Generally, the exchange rate is prevented from overshooting whenever the increase in the transactions demand for money equals or exceeds the money supply increase. In the latter case the slope of the MS curve even turns positive. As long as the transactions demand for money rises less than the money supply, the interest rate falls and the overshooting result obtains.

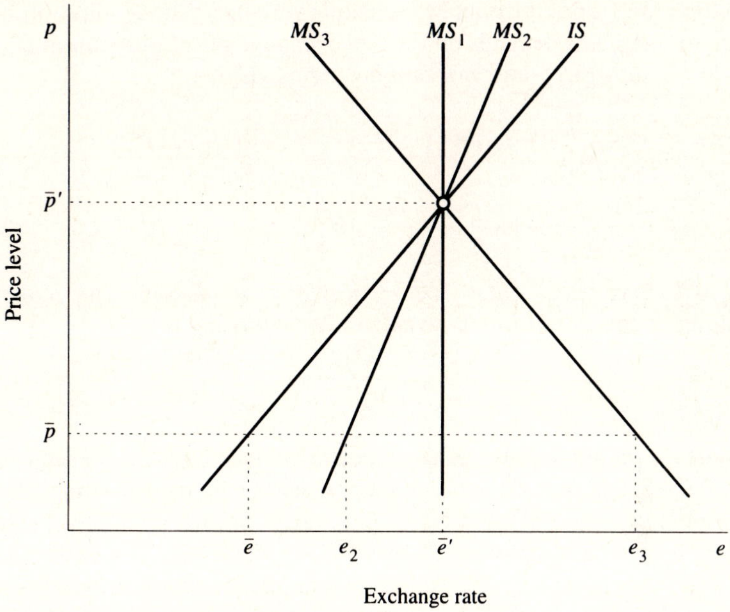

Figure 3.2 Feasible equilibrium schedules when output depends on demand

The goods market equilibrium schedule is obtained from (3.1) and (3.2) and assuming $\dot{p}=0$ (which implies $y=\bar{y}$):

$$p=e-\frac{1-\gamma}{\delta}\bar{y}+\frac{g}{\delta} \tag{3.7}$$

Solving (3.2) for y shows how output depends on the real exchange rate:

$$y=\frac{\delta}{1-\gamma}(e-p)+\frac{g}{1-\gamma} \tag{3.8}$$

A preliminary MS schedule is obtained by combining (3.3)–(3.6) and solving for p:

$$p=m-\phi y+\lambda i^*+\lambda\theta(\bar{e}-e) \tag{3.9}$$

Equilibrium values are obtained exactly as in the simplified Dornbusch model, and read:

$$\bar{p}=m-\phi\bar{y}+\lambda i^* \tag{3.10}$$

$$\bar{e}=m-\phi\bar{y}+\lambda i^*-\frac{g}{\delta}+\frac{1-\gamma}{\delta}\bar{y} \tag{3.11}$$

Equation (3.9) is not the final MS schedule yet, since endogenous output on the right-hand side depends on the real exchange rate. Substitution of (3.8) and (3.11) into (3.9), and rearranging terms yields

$$p=\frac{1-\gamma}{1-\gamma-\delta\phi}\left[(1+\theta\lambda)m-\left(\frac{\phi}{1-\gamma}+\frac{\theta\lambda}{\delta}\right)g+\lambda(1+\theta\lambda)\,i^{*}\right.$$
$$\left.+\frac{\theta\lambda(1-\gamma-\phi)}{\delta}\bar{y}-\left(\lambda\theta+\frac{\delta\phi}{1-\gamma}\right)e\right] \tag{3.12}$$

The MS curve turns out to be vertical if $1-\gamma-\delta\phi=0$. The economic meaning of this condition is revealed after rewriting it as

$$\frac{\delta\phi}{1-\gamma}=1 \tag{3.13}$$

Assume the money supply rises by one, the number given on the right-hand side: if the MS curve was vertical, there would be no overshooting, that is, the exchange rate also rises by 1. This raises output by $\delta/(1-\gamma)$, which pushes the demand for money up by $\delta\phi/(1-\gamma)$. Thus (3.13) states that if the equilibrium response of the exchange rate raises money demand just as much as the money supply was increased, the MS curve is vertical. Under the not very plausible assumption that $\delta\phi/(1-\gamma)>1$, the MS curve possesses a positive slope.

The same result is obtained by computing the impact response of the exchange rate. Solving (3.12) for e and differentiating with respect to m yields

$$\frac{\mathrm{d}e}{\mathrm{d}m}=\frac{1-\gamma+\lambda\theta(1-\gamma)}{\phi\delta+\lambda\theta(1-\gamma)}>0 \tag{3.14}$$

The exchange rate always increases, and it overshoots if $1-\gamma>\phi\delta$, which is and must be the same as the condition for a negatively sloped MS curve derived above. Since the exchange rate *must* depreciate after a money supply increase, output must rise, as can be directly read off equation (3.2).

To sum this up, if output is entirely determined by demand, the exchange rate may, but must not, overshoot. The condition that would prevent overshooting is a rather strong and unrealistic one, however. It would require output to be so elastic with respect to the real exchange rate, even in the short run, that a money supply increase has a perverse liquidity effect, that is, it produces an incipient excess demand for money.

3.3 A tariff on imports

The effects of a tariff on imports may be analyzed by means of Model 3.2. Compared with the basic Dornbusch model only equation (3.2′) has

Model 3.2
Model with a tariff on imports

1 Goods market		
$\dot{p}=\pi(y^d-y)$	Phillips curve	(3.1)
$y^d=\delta(e-p)+\beta z+\gamma y+g$	aggregate demand	(3.2′)
2 Money market		
$m^d=p+\phi y-\lambda i$	money demand	(3.3)
$m^s=m^d=m$	money market equilibrium	(3.4)
3 International asset market		
$i=i^*+E(\dot{e})$	asset market equilibrium	(3.5)
$E(\dot{e})=\theta(\bar{e}-e)$	expectations formation	(3.6)

Notes: The notes to Model 3.1 apply. Variables are defined as follows:

$\dot{p}$	domestic inflation rate	i	domestic interest rate
y^d	aggregate demand for domestic goods	m	domestic money
		i^*	foreign interest rate (exogenous)
y	aggregate supply of domestic goods (exogenous)	$\dot{e}$	rate of depreciation
		$\bar{e}$	equilibrium exchange rate
e	exchange rate	$\dot{m}$	money supply growth rate
p	domestic price level	g	government expenditure
z	tariff on imports		

changed. It now states that the demand for domestic goods also depends on the tariff rate t, which is a constitutive element of the relative price between domestic and foreign goods, just as the real exchange rate is. In order to simplify the notation, the tariff variable is defined as $Z=1+t$, so that free trade obtains when $Z=1$ and, hence, $\ln Z\equiv z=0$.

Just as the parameter δ, β is positive since an increase of z renders import goods more expensive compared to domestic goods, just as a real depreciation does. However, while a real depreciation makes domestic goods comparatively cheaper for both domestic *and* foreign customers, implementation of a tariff leaves relative prices unchanged for foreign customers. This is why it seems reasonable to assume that a change in $e-p$ has a greater impact on demand than an equivalent change in z. We therefore postulate $\beta<\delta$.

In analogy to our analysis of previous models, the *IS curve* results from combining (3.1) and (3.2′), postulating $\dot{p}=0$, and solving for the price level:

$$p=e+\frac{\beta}{\delta}z+\frac{\gamma-1}{\delta}y+\frac{g}{\delta} \tag{3.15}$$

An introduction or an increase of import tariffs thus shifts the IS schedule upwards. The higher the tariff for imports becomes, the higher domestic goods prices must be in order to keep the domestic goods market in equilibrium.

The MS curve is the same as in our basic model and reads

$$p = m - \phi y + \lambda i^* + \lambda\theta(\bar{e} - e) \tag{2.11}$$

While the tariff rate does not seem to play an explicit role in the monetary sector, it implicitly does so via its impact on the equilibrium exchange rate. To the extent that an increase of the tariff rate reduces the equilibrium exchange rate $\bar{e}$, the MS curve shifts to the left. It shifts just as far as the IS curve does. This follows directly from (2.11). Requiring $\bar{e} = e$, we obtain the long-term equilibrium price level

$$\bar{p} = m - \phi y + \lambda i^*$$

In the long run the price level only reflects the quantity theory of money and does not respond to tariff policies. In terms of our graphical presentation in Figure 3.3, this means that the MS curve shifts just as far to the left (from *MS* to *MS'*) as the IS curve does (from *IS* to *IS'*). Only then do both equilibrium schedules still intersect at the previous price level.

The long-run equilibrium exchange rate drops from $\bar{e}$ to $\bar{e}'$, whereas the equilibrium price level stays put at $\bar{p}$. Since goods prices are the only sticky variable in our model, which obviously does not even have to respond to

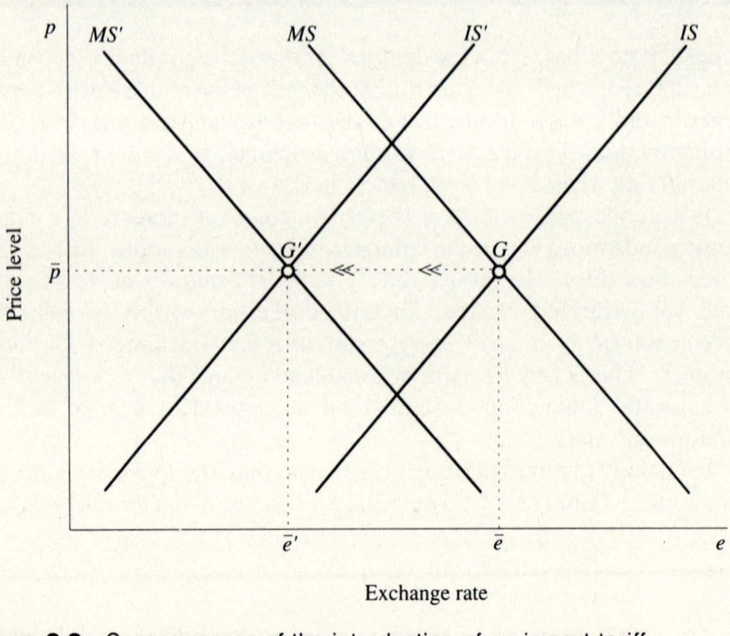

Figure 3.3 Consequences of the introduction of an import tariff

tariff changes, the economy immediately jumps from the initial equilibrium G to the new equilibrium G'. *The exchange rate* without any detour drops to $\bar{e}'$, and thus *does not overshoot.*

This result may be generalized: if an exogenous shock does not call for an adjustment of the price level, then the exchange rate does not overshoot. Actually, this already follows from the insight derived in previous sections that the exchange rate overshoots during the impact period because stickiness prevents goods prices from adjusting as required. In situations where goods prices do not have to adjust, price stickiness cannot possibly be a problem.

The conclusion that trade barriers do not affect the domestic price level at all is certainly surprising and quite contrary to intuition and conventional analyses. Responsible for this is the not quite appropriate choice of the price level for domestic goods, p, as a deflator for domestic money (see equation (3.3)).

When domestic agents not only hold domestic money for the purpose of buying domestic goods, but their consumption basket also contains foreign goods, then real balances fall not only as domestic goods become more expensive but also when foreign goods become more expensive *in terms of domestic currency*. In such a situation, $Q = P^{\alpha}(Z \cdot E \cdot P^*)^{1-\alpha}$ is a more appropriate deflator of domestic money.[1] While the key results of the Dornbusch model are robust against such a modification (see Dornbusch 1976: 1164, fn. 3), it allows for a more sophisticated analysis of the consequences of tariff changes.

Proceed from the modified model, Model 3.3. Equation (3.3a) results from taking the natural logarithm of $Q = P^{\alpha}(Z \cdot E \cdot P^*)^{1-\alpha}$ and letting $P^* = 1$.

The IS curve representing goods market equilibria is the same as in our previous model (repeated here):

$$p = e + \frac{\beta}{\delta} z + \frac{\gamma - 1}{\delta} y + \frac{g}{\delta} \tag{3.15}$$

The MS curve is obtained by combining equations (3.3′)–(3.6):

$$p = \frac{1}{\alpha}[m - (1-\alpha)e - (1-\alpha)z - \phi y + \lambda i^* + \lambda\theta(\bar{e} - e)] \tag{3.16}$$

Qualitatively, a tariff hike has the same effect in both sectors as in our previous model: the IS curve shifts to the left. This signals that an increase of the tariff rate must be accompanied by a real appreciation if the domestic goods market is to remain in equilibrium. The MS curve shifts to the left as well; but this time this is not only because the IS curve has shifted to the left and thus reduced the equilibrium exchange rate $\bar{e}$, but also because tariffs make imports more expensive and thus generate an additional demand for

Model 3.3
Model with import tariff and price index

1 Goods market

$\dot{p}=\pi(y^d-y)$	Phillips curve	(3.1)
$y^d=\delta(e-p)+\beta z+\gamma y+g$	aggregate demand	(3.2′)

2 Money market

$m^d=q+\phi y-\lambda i$	money demand	(3.3′)
$q=\alpha p+(1-\alpha)e+(1-\alpha)z$	domestic price index	(3.3a)
$m^s=m^d=m$	money demand equilibrium	(3.4)

3 International asset market

$i=i^*+E(\dot{e})$	asset market equilibrium	(3.5)
$E(\dot{e})=\theta(\bar{e}-e)$	expectations formation	(3.6)

Notes: The notes to Model 3.1 apply. Variables are defined as follows:

$\dot{p}$	domestic inflation rate	i	domestic interest rate
y^d	aggregate demand for domestic goods	m	domestic money
		i^*	foreign interest rate (exogenous)
y	aggregate supply of domestic goods (exogenous)	$\dot{e}$	rate of depreciation
		$\bar{e}$	equilibrium exchange rate
e	exchange rate	$\dot{m}$	money supply growth rate
p	domestic price level	z	tariff
g	government expenditure	q	domestic price index

domestic money. As long as the domestic money supply remains unchanged, money market equilibrium can only be achieved by reducing the price for domestic goods and/or an appreciation.

From the directions in which both curves move we already see that increased protection leads to an appreciation. An expression for the long-run equilibrium exchange rate is obtained by equating (3.15) and (3.16) and solving for $\bar{e}$:

$$\bar{e}=m-\left(1-\alpha+\frac{\alpha\beta}{\delta}\right)z-\left[\phi-\frac{\alpha(1-\gamma)}{\delta}\right]y-\frac{\alpha}{\delta}g+\lambda i^* \tag{3.17}$$

Since we have argued previously that the tariff elasticity of the demand for domestic goods falls short of the exchange rate elasticity of the demand for domestic goods, that is, $\beta<\delta$, differentiation of (3.17) with respect to z gives

$$\frac{d\bar{e}}{dz}=-\left(1-\alpha+\frac{\alpha\beta}{\delta}\right)>-1 \text{ and } \frac{d\bar{e}}{dz}<0$$

This means that a price increase for imported goods due to a higher tariff is in the long run partly compensated for by an appreciation, but not fully so.

The equilibrium price level follows from inserting (3.17) into (3.15). After a series of transformations we obtain

$$\bar{p}=m-\phi y+\lambda i^{*}-(1-\alpha)\left(1-\frac{\beta}{\delta}\right)z+\frac{1-\alpha}{\delta}[g-(1-\gamma)y] \tag{3.18}$$

The response of the equilibrium price level,

$$\frac{\mathrm{d}\bar{p}}{\mathrm{d}z}=-(1-\alpha)\left(1-\frac{\beta}{\delta}\right)<0$$

is negative because of $\beta<\delta$. At first sight it seems to contradict intuition that the price level should fall when tariff rates increase. Note, however, that p is only the price level for domestic goods. The price index comprising all goods consumed by domestic residents, q, is determined by the money demand function (3.3′). Since in a stationary, long-run equilibrium $i=i^*$ and i^*, y and m are all exogenous, tariff policies cannot possibly have an influence on the domestic price *index*. Thus the increase of effective imports goods prices described above must be compensated for by a reduction of domestic goods prices.

PROBLEM 3.2

Introduce perfect foresight into the present model and derive its dynamics by means of a phase diagram.

We may now proceed to demonstrate the consequences of import tariffs graphically. Let the economy be in long-run equilibrium point G (see Figure 3.4). *Ceteris paribus*, the introduction of a tariff on imports makes import goods more expensive and thus in a first step reduces domestic real balances. Since for a given nominal supply of money this has to be compensated for by a price reduction for domestic goods and/or an appreciation, the MS curve shifts downwards. This movement is reinforced by the fact that a downward movement of the MS schedule (and the IS schedule) reduces the equilibrium exchange rate, finally bringing the money market equilibrium schedule from MS to MS'.

Rising tariffs, *ceteris paribus*, change relative prices in favour of the domestically produced good. In order to bring the relative price back to its previous value and thus balance supply and demand again, the price level must rise and/or exchange rate must sink. This shifts the IS curve upward. How far the IS curve shifts upwards, relative to the downward shift of the

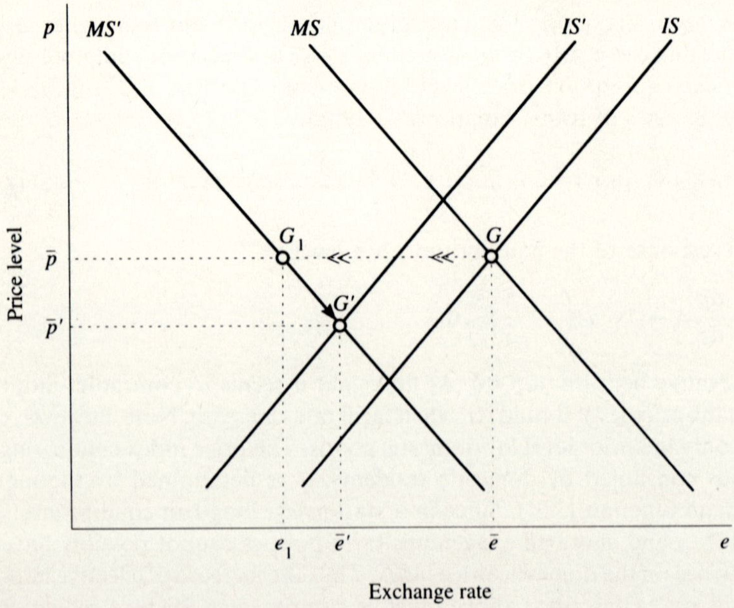

Figure 3.4 Consequences of the introduction of an import tariff if the domestic price index includes import goods

MS curve, determines whether the equilibrium price level increases or decreases. We may clarify this issue by means of the following line of argument, without having to take recourse to formulas.

If p were to remain constant, an appreciation alone would have to compensate for the tariff increase. Since the exchange rate elasticity of the demand for domestic goods exceeds the latter's tariff elasticity, the exchange rate does not have to fall by the same percentage as tariffs were increased in order to compensate for the tariff hike. Thus, after the adjustment of the exchange rate were completed, imported goods would still be more expensive in domestic currency than before the tariff hike. This situation – unchanged domestic goods prices and higher effective import goods prices – cannot possibly be a money market equilibrium, since with a given nominal supply of money the domestic price *index* must not change. This should make it perfectly clear that in the long run prices for domestic goods must sink.

If p were to rise, because of $q =$ constant, imports would have to become cheaper. Thus e would have to fall by more than z rises. This cannot be a goods market equilibrium, since we have argued in the previous paragraph that when p is unchanged the exchange rate must not change as much as z in order to restore goods market equilibrium. Under the present assumption of a risen price for domestic goods this would apply all the more.

Hence the goods market equilibrium schedule in Figure 3.4 shifts into a position like IS'. In the long run the price level and the exchange rate drop to $\bar{p}'$ and $\bar{e}'$, respectively. Since the price level is sticky, the exchange rate initially overshoots to e_1 and subsequently rises to $\bar{e}'$, simultaneously with falling imports goods prices.

3.4 Imperfect capital mobility

Up to now we have assumed foreign and domestic assets to be perfect substitutes, implying that capital is perfectly mobile (see also Frenkel and Rodriguez 1982). Under this assumption all capital will flow into the currency with the highest expected yield. Therefore, the balance of payments can only then be in equilibrium if expected yields at home and abroad are identical. Then investors are indifferent between investments in domestic or foreign currency and thus accommodate any current-account disequilibrium at the market interest rate.

Recall that the balance of payments BP comprises the current account CA and the capital account CP:

$$BP = CA + CP \tag{3.19}$$

If we ignore all determinants of the balance of payments which are of no interest in the present context and if we postulate that the current account depends linearly on the real exchange rate, $e-p$ and the capital account depends linearly on the expected excess yield of domestic assets, $i-i^*-\theta(\bar{e}-e)$, we obtain

$$BP = \xi(e-p) + \kappa[i-i^*-\theta(\bar{e}-e)] \tag{3.20}$$

In this formulation perfect capital mobility would imply $\kappa \to \infty$. As long as ξ is finite, the balance of payments can only be in equilibrium, $BP=0$, for $i-i^*-\theta(\bar{e}-e)=0$. In contrast, for finite values of κ, appropriate expected-yield differentials are needed to neutralize current-account surpluses and deficits.

Integration of this generalized condition for a balance of payments equilibrium into our previous model of a small open economy results in Model 3.4. The goods market is the same as in previous model variants.

■ **Model 3.4**
Model with less than perfectly mobile capital

---

1 **Goods market**

$\dot{p} = \pi(y^d - y)$	Phillips curve	(3.1)
$y^d = \delta(e-p) + \gamma y + g$	aggregate demand	(3.2)

2 Money market

$m^d = p + \phi y - \lambda i$	money demand	(3.3)
$m^s = m^d = m$	money market equilibrium	(3.4)

3 International asset market

$\xi(e-p) + \kappa[i - i^* - E(\dot{e})] = 0$	balance of payments equilibrium	(3.5′)
$E(\dot{e}) = \theta(\bar{e} - e)$	expectations formation	(3.6)

Notes: The notes to Model 3.1 apply. Variables are defined as follows:

$\dot{p}$	domestic inflation rate	i	domestic interest rate
y^d	aggregate demand for domestic goods	m	domestic money
		i^*	foreign interest rate (exogenous)
y	aggregate supply of domestic goods (exogenous)	$\dot{e}$	rate of depreciation
		$\bar{e}$	equilibrium exchange rate
e	exchange rate	$\dot{m}$	money supply growth rate
p	domestic price level		
g	government expenditure		

Again, the equilibrium condition is the IS curve with unity slope. The equilibrium condition for the monetary sector (including the balance of payments) results from equations (3.3)–(3.6) and reads

$$p = \frac{m - \phi y + \lambda i^*}{1 - \lambda\xi/\kappa} + \frac{\lambda\theta\bar{e}}{1 - \lambda\xi/\kappa} - \frac{\lambda\theta + \lambda\xi/\kappa}{1 - \lambda\xi/\kappa} e \qquad (3.21)$$

By the way, equation (3.21) simplifies to (2.11) for $\kappa \to \infty$. The slope of the new MS curve depends on the sign of the expression $-(1-\lambda\xi/\kappa)$. It can obviously be negative as in our previous model, but positive as well. A positive slope may be encountered if ξ/κ is very large, that is, if the current account responds strongly to movements of the real exchange rate, or if capital mobility is very small.

The direction into which parameter changes shift the MS curve also depends on the expression $1-\lambda\xi/\kappa$. If the slope of the curve is negative, a money supply increase shifts the curve upwards. If the slope is positive, a money supply increase shifts the curve downwards. This has the effect that the long-run consequences of a money supply increase are qualitatively independent of the slope of the MS curve.

PROBLEM 3.3

Demonstrate that with a positively sloped MS curve a given money supply increase not only shifts the equilibrium point in the same direction as with a negatively sloped MS curve, but exactly to the same point.

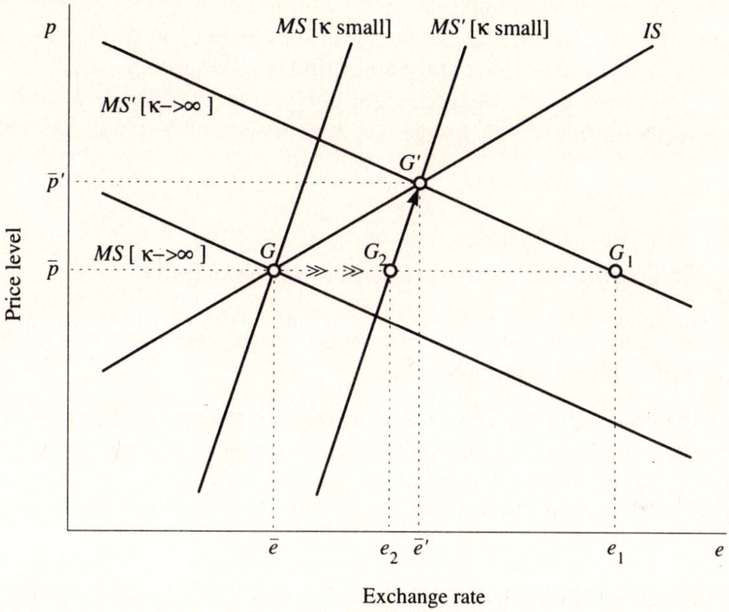

Figure 3.5 The consequences of imperfect capital mobility for exchange rate overshooting and the long-run properties of the model

Figure 3.5 illustrates that a given money supply expansion in the long run shifts the economy from G to G', no matter whether the MS curve is positively or negatively sloped.

For $\kappa \to \infty$ the present model is identical with the Dornbusch model. Therefore the exchange rate initially overshoots from $\bar{e}$ to e_1. If ξ/κ is large enough for the MS schedule to be positively sloped, the exchange rate no longer overshoots. During the impact period, it only jumps to e_2. Subsequently, it begins to rise towards $\bar{e}'$, with the pace being set by the simultaneously increasing price level.

In economic terms, the following occurs: in order to simplify the argument, let the current account be in equilibrium in G. The increased nominal money supply will only be demanded at a reduced domestic interest rate. Now if the exchange rate remained at $\bar{e}$, the current account would remain in equilibrium, but the capital account would move into deficit – since domestic assets pay lower interest and are expected to devalue. Thus the balance of payments would be in deficit. If the exchange rate were to rise to e_1, the capital account would remain in equilibrium, but the country would run a current-account surplus. Thus any exchange rate between $\bar{e}$ and e_1 generates a *current-account surplus* and a *capital-account deficit*. At some exchange rate larger than $\bar{e}$ and smaller than e_1 the current-account surplus and the capital-account deficit exactly balance. In Figure 3.5 the exchange rate elasticities of the current and capital accounts are such as to fix this short-run equilibrium exchange rate at e_2.

The key message of the preceding analysis reads that when capital is not perfectly mobile, the exchange rate may overshoot, but it does not have to.

3.5 Endogenous money supply expectations

Two very crucial assumptions are hidden in the treatment of monetary policy in the Dornbusch model:[2]

1. Any money supply increase is *unexpected*. If the money supply increase were expected,[3] it would not make sense to assume individuals believe that up until the money supply effectively increases the exchange rate would remain at its *old* equilibrium value.

2. Any observed money supply increase is considered permanent. Individuals do not expect any further changes of the money supply. Both these assumptions are plausible if the money supply follows a **random walk**,[4] that is,

$$m_t = m_{t-1} + \varepsilon_t \tag{3.22}$$

where ε_t represents 'white noise'. The random variable ε_t represents *white noise* if the expected value of ε_t is zero $[E(\varepsilon_t)=0]$ and ε is not autocorrelated $[E(\varepsilon_t, \varepsilon_{t-j})=0$ for $j \neq 0]$. The assumption that ε_t is white noise implies $E_{t-1}m_t = m_{t-1}$: rational individuals expect at time $t-1$ to observe the same money supply at time t which they have observed at $t-1$. Well in line with the assumption employed in the Dornbusch model, each change in the money supply comes as a *surprise* and is considered *permanent*. Thus today's observed money supply has no impact at all on expected future money supply changes.

Statistical analyses of money supply developments in industrial countries reveal that paths resembling the one described by equation (3.22) are more the exception than the rule. This should not come as a surprise, since (3.22) postulates very peculiar behaviour by the central bank. It implies (a) that the central bank never changes its course (for example, from a low-inflation to high-inflation policy, or vice versa) and (b) that nothing unforeseen disturbs the money supply process (that there is no unplanned change in the money supply) which the central bank might try to neutralize or correct.

Suppose the market does not believe in the money supply following a random walk. Rather, observed (unexpected) changes of the money supply are taken as a signal for further money supply movements to come. This is already the case if individuals are not perfectly sure whether an observed money supply increase is transitory or permanent. Now, an expected money supply increase in the next period also means a proportional increase of the equilibrium exchange rate in the next period. In this situation our devaluation expectations formation hypothesis (3.6) is incomplete, but has to be augmented by the term $E(\mathrm{d}\bar{e}/\mathrm{d}t)$:

$$E(\dot{e}) = \theta(\bar{e} - e) + E(\mathrm{d}\bar{e}/\mathrm{d}t) \qquad (3.6')$$

According to this augmented hypothesis the market believes, on the one hand, that existing exchange rate disequilibria tend to be eliminated and, on the other hand, that the exchange rate directly follows the anticipated course of its equilibrium value. It will now be demonstrated that with this simple generalization the exchange rate does not necessarily overshoot after an unexpected money supply increase.

Since it has been demonstrated in Chapter 2 (equation 2.14) that $\mathrm{d}m = \mathrm{d}\bar{e}$, we may assume that rational actors anticipate a one-to-one correlation between the equilibrium exchange rate and the money supply:

$$E(\mathrm{d}\bar{e}/\mathrm{d}t) = E(\dot{m})$$

Substituting this into (3.6′) yields

$$E(\dot{e}) = \theta(\bar{e} - e) + E(\dot{m}) \qquad (3.6'')$$

Combining (3.6″) with (3.3)–(3.5) gives a new monetary sector equilibrium condition which may be solved for e to obtain

$$e = \bar{e} + \frac{1}{\lambda\theta}[m - p - \phi y + \lambda i^* + \lambda E(\dot{m})] \qquad (3.23)$$

Now let time be measured in discrete increments. Suppose that money supply expectations are formed adaptively because agents do not know whether an observed change is permanent or transitory:[5]

$$E_t(m_{t+1}) = E_{t-1}(m_t) + \psi[m_t - E_{t-1}(m_t)] \qquad 0 \leq \psi \leq 1 \qquad (3.24)$$

After a one-time change of the money supply at time t the economy gradually adjusts the *expected* money supply to the new level. Hereby ψ per cent of the observed change is considered permanent, the rest, $1-\psi$, is considered transitory.

Example

Assume the economy has been in a long-run, stationary equilibrium [that is, $E(m) = m$] for some time. Now at time t the money supply increases from 100 to 110. Let $\psi = 0.5$. On the basis of (3.24) we obtain

$$E_t(m_{t+1}) = 100 + 0.5[110 - 100] = 105$$

For time $t+1$ the economy expects a *reduction* of the money supply by some 5 per cent from 110 to 105. The expected money supply for time $t+2$ is:

$$E_{t+1}(m_{t+2})=105+0.5[110-105]=107.5$$

Obviously, individuals have revised their initial interpretation made at time t. Now, one period later, they no longer believe that $100(1-\psi)=$ 50 per cent of the unexpected money supply change is transitory, but only $100(1-\psi)^2=100(1-0.5)^2=25$ per cent. One period later this share will have fallen even further to $100(1-\psi)^3=100(1-0.5)^3=12.5$ per cent.

When expectations are being formed on the basis of (3.24), actors believe n periods after an unexpected shock occurred that $100(1-\psi)^{n+1}$ per cent of the shock is transitory, that is, it will be removed during the following period.[6] This interpretation comprises the Dornbusch model as a special case for $\psi=1$.

The analysis of the impact response of the exchange rate to a money supply increase in the general case of adaptive money supply expectations is facilitated by treating time as a discrete variable, which we already have done in (3.24).[7] Subtracting m_t from both sides of (3.24) yields

$$E_t(m_{t+1})-m_t=E_{t-1}m_t-m_t+\psi[m_t-E_{t-1}(m_t)] \tag{3.25}$$

The difference on the left-hand side of the equality sign is the discrete time equivalent to $E(\dot{m})$ in (3.6″). It is nothing but the *change* of the money supply which individuals expect after they have learned of the money supply shock at time t. Thus we may rewrite (3.25) as

$$E_t(\dot{m}_{t+1})=(\psi-1)\,[m_t-E_{t-1}(m_t)] \tag{3.26}$$

To keep the exposition simple, assume that up to time $t-1$ the economy was in long-run equilibrium with a constant money supply at m^*, which implies $E_{t-1}(m_t)=m^*$. Denoting money supplied immediately after the shock (at time t) by m, (3.26) may be rewritten without time subscripts:

$$E(\dot{m})=(\psi-1)\,[m-m^*] \tag{3.27}$$

Substitution of (3.27) into (3.23) gives

$$e=\bar{e}+\frac{1}{\lambda\theta}[m-p-\phi y+\lambda i^*+\lambda(\psi-1)(m-m^*)] \tag{3.28}$$

Differentiating (3.28) with respect to m, we obtain the impact response of the exchange rate to an unexpected money supply increase (while recalling the homogeneity property $\mathrm{d}\bar{e}/\mathrm{d}m=1$):

$$\frac{\mathrm{d}e}{\mathrm{d}m}=1+\frac{1}{\lambda\theta}-\frac{1-\psi}{\theta} \tag{3.29}$$

The impact response of the exchange rate may obviously be smaller or larger than 1. Thus if the economy believes in an inherent stability of monetary policy in the sense postulated by (3.25), then the exchange rate does not necessarily overshoot after an unexpected money supply increase. The condition for an overshooting of the exchange rate is

$$1+\frac{1}{\lambda\theta}-\frac{1-\psi}{\theta}>1$$

which may be simplified to

$$1>\lambda(1-\psi)$$

Some coefficient estimates for Switzerland may help to assess the empirical relevance of this condition: the semi-interest-rate elasticity of the demand for money, $-\lambda$, is estimated at -6.6.[8] Making use of this in the overshooting condition above, we see that the exchange rate only overshoots if $\psi>0.85$; that is, the Swiss economy must be convinced that 85 per cent of an observed unexpected money supply change will be permanent. If more than 15 per cent of the unexpected money supply change is considered transitory, *the exchange rate does not overshoot.*

According to (3.29), the possibility even exists that the exchange rate initially falls after a money supply increase, that is, it *appreciates*. The condition for this to occur is

$$1+\frac{1}{\lambda\theta}-\frac{1-\psi}{\theta}<0$$

or

$$\lambda(1-\theta-\psi)>1$$

Making use of $\lambda=6.6$ again, this condition becomes $\theta+\psi<0.85$. There is no reason to believe that this parameter constellation could not occur in reality.

We now turn to the question of how this somewhat strange formal result – that a currency may respond to an unexpected money supply increase by appreciating – may be explained in economic terms.

Incorporating (3.6′) into uncovered interest parity $i=i^*+E(\dot{e})$, the equilibrium condition for the international asset market becomes

$$i=i^*+\theta(\bar{e}-e)+E(\mathrm{d}\bar{e}/\mathrm{d}t)$$

Recall that, because of the price stickiness assumed in our model, the additional liquidity will only be demanded at a lower interest rate. This domestic interest deficit must be compensated for by appreciation expectations if the international capital market is to remain in equilibrium. From (3.6′) we see that depreciation expectations are made up of two components: the expected change of the equilibrium exchange rate $[E(\mathrm{d}\bar{e}/\mathrm{d}t)]$, which equals the expected money supply change, and the expected correction of the current exchange rate disequilibrium $[\theta(\bar{e}-e)]$. According to our adaptive money supply expectations hypothesis, individuals expect after a sudden surge of the money supply that this will be reduced subsequently and that, therefore, the equilibrium exchange rate will also fall $[E(\mathrm{d}\bar{e}/\mathrm{d}t)<0]$.

The crucial question is whether this partial appreciation expectation due to the second component already suffices to compensate investors for the existing domestic interest deficit. Whether this is true or not determines the contribution required from the first component, $\theta(\bar{e}-e)$, in order to equate domestic and foreign yields. If $E(\dot{m})=E(\mathrm{d}\bar{e}/\mathrm{d}t)<i-i^*$, the exchange rate does not overshoot its present equilibrium. If $E(\dot{m})$ falls short of $i-i^*$ by a large enough amount, the exchange rate has to fall even below its pre-shock equilibrium value in order to maintain uncovered interest parity. The exchange rate appreciates.

This result fits into the graphical presentation of the model as follows (see Figure 3.6): let G be the long-run equilibrium point before the money supply increase. G is on the IS curve, which is identical with the one being

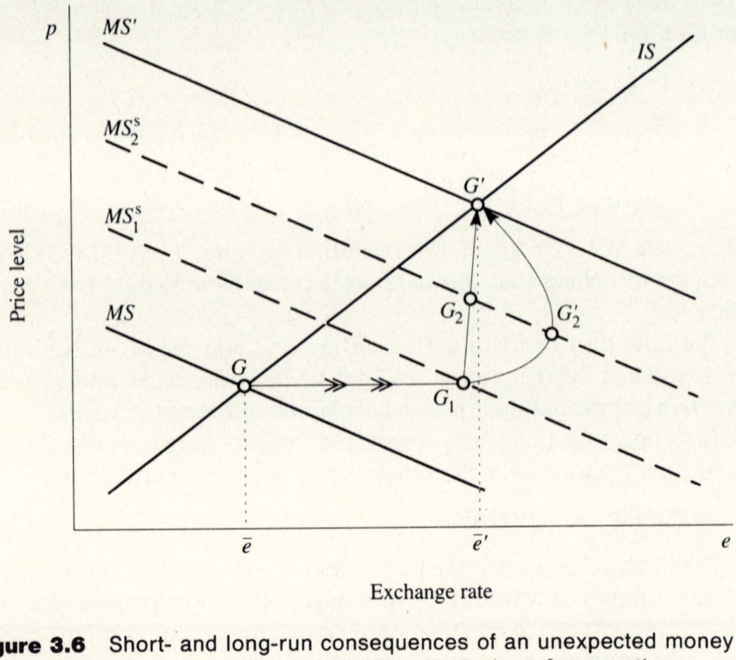

Figure 3.6 Short- and long-run consequences of an unexpected money supply increase, part of which is considered transitory [assumption: $\lambda(1-\psi)>1$]

used in our basic model. It is also on the MS curve, which is also identical with the one being used in the basic model, since G, being a static equilibrium, implies $E(\dot{m})=0$. We may therefore label this initial equilibrium schedule for the monetary sector a *long-run* MS curve. After an unexpected and permanent money supply increase, this long-run MS curve shifts to MS'. The point of intersection between MS' and IS marks the new long-run equilibrium point. Since immediately after the shock the economy expects that the money supply will be reduced again $[E(\dot{m})<0]$, the MS curve does not shift to MS' immediately but to a first short-run equilibrium position M_1^s. While the economy subsequently realizes that the money supply may have been raised permanently, the short-run MS curve shifts upwards to the right and comes to halt in MS'. The price level and the exchange rate without overshooting adjust to their new long-run equilibria via G_1 (impact effect) and G_2.[9]

Figure 3.7 illustrates the aforementioned possibility that the short-run MS curve initially moves to the left, and only subsequently shifts upwards towards MS'. The consequence is an initial appreciation of the exchange rate to e_1 followed by a continuous depreciation. The price level initially falls and then rises monotonically.

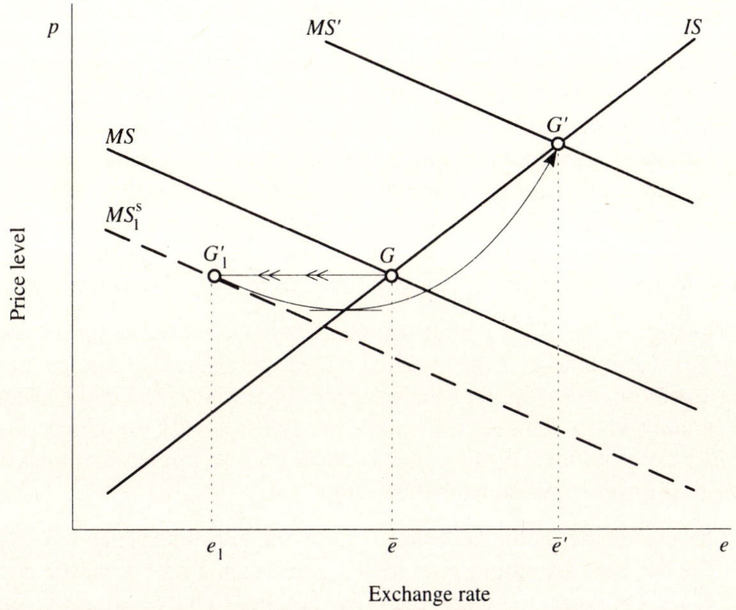

Figure 3.7 Short- and long-run consequences of an unexpected money supply increase, all of which is considered transitory [assumption: $\lambda(1-\theta-\psi)>1$]

PROBLEM 3.4

Assume the economy reads a one-time unexpected increase of the money supply as a signal of a permanent shift to a more inflationary monetary policy.

1. Sketch the responses of the price level and the exchange rate graphically.
2. Try to formalize this modification of the model and derive the impact response of the exchange rate.

3.6 Answers to the problems

Problem 3.1

Initially, an expansion of aggregate supply creates an excess supply of domestic goods. In the new long-run equilibrium the domestic currency must have depreciated just enough (in real terms) to generate additional demand to soak up the initial excess supply.

1. The higher the marginal propensity to consume (γ) is, the smaller is the excess supply generated by a given expansion of aggregate supply. The smaller the excess supply is, the smaller is the required real exchange rate depreciation. Since we know from the money market equilibrium condition that an increase of aggregate supply reduces the price level by a factor of $-\phi$, which is independent of γ, a smaller increase of the real exchange rate requires a smaller increase or a stronger reduction of the nominal exchange rate. To sum up: smaller values of γ result in a lower exchange rate.

2. The higher the real exchange rate elasticity of the demand for domestic goods (δ) is, the smaller is the required increase of the real exchange rate in order to eliminate the initial excess supply. The smaller the real exchange rate is allowed to remain, the smaller is the nominal exchange rate e (because the price level is independent of δ). To sum up: larger values of δ result in a lower nominal exchange rate e.

3. The higher the income elasticity of the demand for money (ϕ) is, the more the demand for money rises after a given increase of domestic goods supply, and the more, therefore, the price level has to fall in order to equate money supply and money demand. The lower the price level is, the lower the exchange rate has to be in order to produce the real exchange rate required for a goods market equilibrium. To sum up: higher values for ϕ result in a lower nominal exchange rate e.

Problem 3.2

In a first step we arrive at conditions under which the endogenous variables e and p do not change any more. From (3.1) and (3.2′) we obtain

$$\dot{p}=\pi[\delta(e-p)+\beta z+(\gamma-1)y+g] \tag{3.30}$$

and from (3.3′), (3.3a), (3.4), (3.5) and $E(\dot{e})=\dot{e}$

$$\dot{e}=\frac{1}{\lambda}[\alpha p+(1-\alpha)e+(1-\alpha)z+\phi y-m]-i^* \tag{3.31}$$

Setting $\dot{p}=0$ in (3.30) and $\dot{e}=0$ in (3.31), we obtain the following two demarcation lines:

$$p=e+\frac{\beta}{\delta}z+\frac{\gamma-1}{\delta}y+\frac{g}{\delta} \qquad [\dot{p}=0] \tag{3.32}$$

$$p=\frac{1-\alpha}{\alpha}e-\frac{1-\alpha}{\alpha}z-\frac{\phi}{\alpha}y+\frac{m}{\alpha}+\frac{\lambda}{\alpha}i^* \qquad [\dot{e}=0] \tag{3.33}$$

Since $0<\alpha<1$, the slopes of the two demarcation lines have opposite signs (see Figure 3.8). The dynamic properties of the model are revealed after differentiating (3.30) with respect to p,

$$\mathrm{d}\dot{p}/\mathrm{d}p=-\pi\delta<0$$

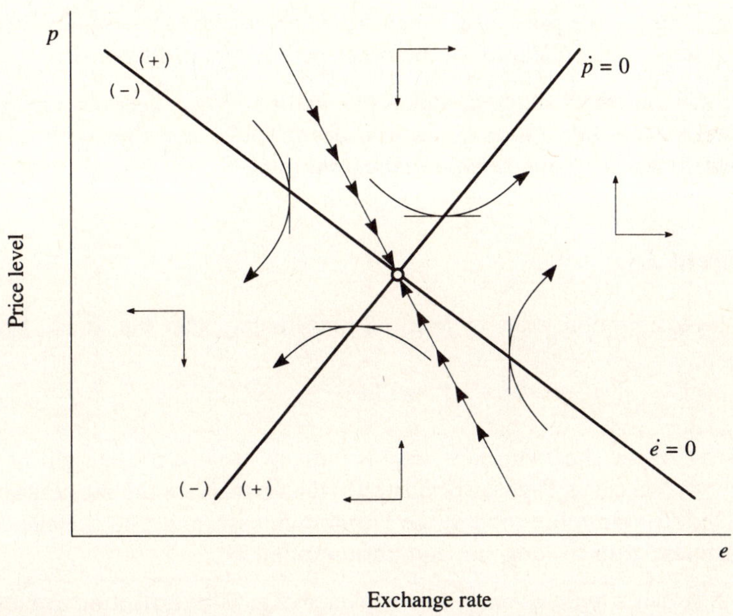

Figure 3.8 Perfect foresight paths in a model with import tariffs and price index

and by differentiating (3.31) with respect to p,

$$d\dot{e}/dp = \alpha/\lambda > 0$$

and by making use of this result in the phase diagram in Figure 3.8. Obviously we have another case of saddle-path stability.

Problem 3.3

The structural equations of the monetary sector can be combined to the following long-run (that is, we assume $e = \bar{e}$) relationship:

$$p = m - \phi y + \lambda i^* + \frac{\lambda \xi}{\kappa}(p - e) \tag{3.34}$$

The IS curve (see equation (3.7)) may be rewritten as

$$p - e = \frac{g - (1 - \gamma)y}{\delta} \tag{3.35}$$

Inserting (3.35) into (3.34) produces

$$p = m - \phi y + \lambda i^* + \frac{\lambda \xi}{\kappa \delta}[g - (1 - \gamma)y] \tag{3.36}$$

In the long run the price level changes proportionally to the money supply and does so independently of the other parameters of the model.

Hint: Of course, for different values of κ and/or ξ the exogenous variables must assume other initial values in order to make sure that both model variants start from the same initial equilibrium G.

Problem 3.4

1. By assumption we have $E(\dot{m}) > 0$ immediately after the shock. From

$$e = \bar{e} + \frac{1}{\lambda \theta}[m - p - \phi y + \lambda i^* + \lambda E(\dot{m})] \tag{3.23}$$

we see that the short-run MS curve is initially situated to the right of the long-run MS curve. Figure 3.9 illustrates that in this case the exchange rate overshoots even more than in the Dornbusch case, and also sketches the adjustment path to long-run equilibrium point G'.

2. A money supply increase is then taken to signal the transition to a more inflationary monetary policy; for example, if expectations are adaptive with regard to the money supply *growth rate*:

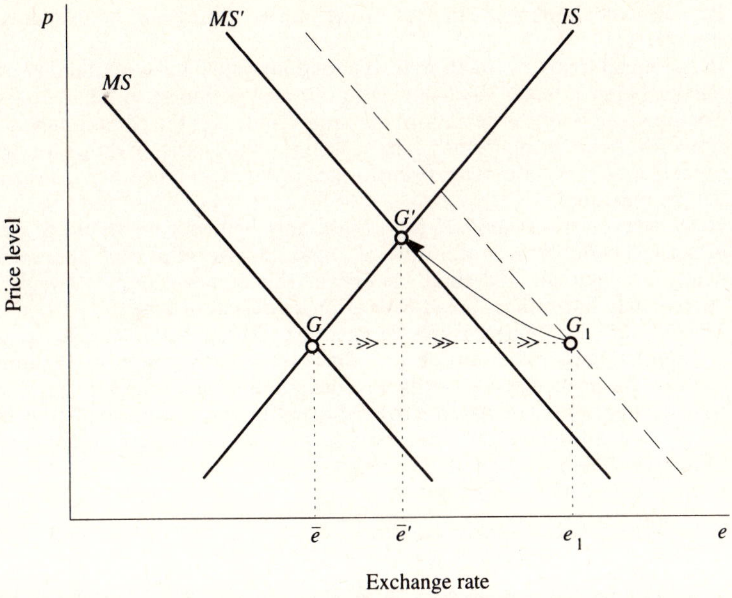

Figure 3.9 Overshooting when individuals expect a one-time money supply increase to signal more money growth tomorrow

$$E_t(\dot{m}_{t+1}) = E_{t-1}(\dot{m}_t) + \psi'[\dot{m}_t - E_{t-1}(\dot{m}_t)1] \qquad (3.37)$$
$$[0 \leq \psi' \leq 1]$$

Since, by assumption, the economy was in a stationary equilibrium before the shock, we have $E_{t-1}(\dot{m}_t) = 0$ and, therefore, $\dot{m}_t - E_{t-1}(\dot{m}_t) = m - m^*$ (m^* is the money supply before the shock, m the new money supply level after the shock). Dropping subscripts, this transforms (3.37) to

$$E(\dot{m}) = \psi'(m - m^*) \qquad (3.38)$$

Substitution of (3.38) into (3.23) and differentiation with respect to m yields

$$\frac{de}{dm} = 1 + \frac{1}{\lambda\theta} + \frac{\psi'}{\theta}$$

In line with the result of our graphical analysis, the exchange rate overshoots by a factor ψ'/θ more than in the Dornbusch model.

NOTES

1. α represents the weight of domestic goods in the consumption baskets of domestic residents. For $\alpha = 1$ the present version is identical with the model we have worked with so far.
2. The argument of this section draws on Gärtner (1983).

3. Expected or announced changes in the money supply will be examined in Chapter 4.
4. In colloquial terms a variable follows a random walk if it has no trend or other regular pattern, but is just as likely to rise next period as to fall.
5. The subscript on the expectations operator E indicates the point in time when expectations are being formed. The subscript on the variable shows for which point in time expectations are being formed or the exact time when the variable will be measured.
6. Here, the expression *transitory* is used in a short-sighted sense which only looks at the next period. It is conceivable, of course, that a central bank does want to neutralize fully an undesired change in the money supply, though not immediately but rather spread over a longer period of time.
7. The Dornbusch model measures time continuously so that $\dot{p}$ is the change over an infinitesimally small unit of time. Since we are now analyzing the impact effect on the exchange rate – which by definition occurs before the price level has time to react ($\dot{p}$ is equal to zero) and therefore can be derived directly from the permanently equilibrated monetary sector – the transition from continuous to discrete time is irrelevant.
8. For the period 1951–86 we arrive at

$$\underset{}{m-p=-6.10+1.03y-6.60Ri} \qquad \bar{R}^2=0.97$$
$$(4.12)\ (4.59)\ \ (6.48) \qquad \mathrm{DW}=1.65$$

where numbers in parentheses are absolute t-values, $\bar{R}^2$ is the coefficient of determination adjusted for degrees of freedom, and DW the Durbin–Watson statistic. For the error term first-order autocorrelation is assumed. The employed data series are M1, the consumer price index, GNP and Swiss federal government bond yields.
9. This result is not compulsory. If prices react very sluggishly or if agents quickly realize that the monetary expansion was not transitory after all, an adjustment path via G_2' with an overshooting exchange rate becomes feasible.

REFERENCES

Dornbusch, Rudiger (1976) 'Expectations and exchange rate dynamics', *Journal of Political Economy* 84, 1167–76.

Frenkel, Jacob A. and Carlos A. Rodriguez (1982) 'Exchange rate dynamics and the overshooting hypothesis', *IMF Staff Papers* 29, 1–30.

Gärtner, Manfred (1983) 'Asset market models of the small open economy with endogenous money supply expectations', *Journal of Institutional Economics* 139, 643–59.

Chapter 4

Policy anticipation, resource discovery and a structural real sector

This chapter modifies and extends the Dornbusch model in several respects. One purpose for doing this is to show that the model can be put to use on a host of questions. A second purpose is to demonstrate that key properties of the basic model are quite sensitive to changes in the structure of the model.

4.1 Anticipated changes in the money supply

As repeatedly emphasized in Chapters 2 and 3, Dornbusch (1976) examined (1) unexpected and (2) permanent changes in the money supply. Assumption (2) has already been abandoned in Chapter 3. Now we shall revive it, while dropping the assumption that the money supply increase occurs unexpectedly. Wilson's (1979) analysis of this case is formally demanding. Therefore, we settle for a verbal and graphical analysis of the issues involved.

Assume the following scenario: the central bank announces a doubling of the money supply exactly one year from today and economic agents believe this statement.[1] This tells economic agents that the price level will double in the long run and that the exchange rate, *ceteris paribus*, will more than double in one year – because of overshooting. As a consequence, domestic interest-bearing assets are going to lose half of their value relative to foreign assets. In these circumstances investors will try the following.

1. They will try to move from financial into real assets.[2] Some rationing will occur in the short run, as long as the price level is fixed. Another disadvantage of real assets is that yields will only begin to accrue in one year's time.

2. They will try to move from domestic into foreign interest-bearing assets. Ideally, this will take place 364 days from now, on the day before the

money supply doubles. Yet if all agents take this action, the exchange rate jumps one day prior to the monetary expansion. For agents being aware of this, it would be wise to move into foreign assets two days prior to the announced expansion, in order to take advantage of the still lower exchange rate. Yet, once again, if all agents act in this manner, the value of the domestic currency jumps two days before the money supply increase. This chain of reasoning links back to the moment the expansion is announced. As a consequence, domestic assets should be converted into foreign assets immediately after the central bank's announcement. This causes the domestic currency to depreciate right away.

As an interim result we may state that an announced, or for some other reason expected, disturbance triggers immediate responses of behaviour and of the exchange rate. The following arguments provide a first idea of the value to which the exchange rate jumps.

1. At the moment at which the future money supply increase is announced the domestic interest rate does not respond – y, p and m remain unchanged – and still equals the foreign interest rate. Consequently the exchange rate must jump to a value at which actors expect no immediate change. Assuming perfect foresight, the exchange rate must not change immediately after the jump. Since the initial depreciation has caused an undervaluation, the demand for domestic goods exceeds the supply, and prices begin to rise. In the Dornbusch diagram the economy moves upwards (see Figure 4.1). Rising prices reduce the real-money supply and drive the interest rate up. As the domestic interest rate becomes larger than the foreign interest rate agents must develop the expectation of a depreciating domestic currency in order to keep the international asset market in equilibrium. With perfect foresight this implies that the exchange rate actually depreciates. The economy moves to the north-east in Figure 4.1. Before the money supply is actually expanded, the continuously rising price level leads to a steady reduction of the real-money supply. The domestic interest rate advantage becomes larger and larger. Therefore the correctly anticipated depreciation must be accelerating. In graphical terms, this means that the adjustment path becomes flatter and flatter.

2. As soon as the money supply actually increases, we are back in the scenario of the initial Dornbusch model, since no further money supply changes are expected. Therefore, the adjustment path hits the MS' curve at the very moment of the money supply increase. Any further adjustment is on MS' towards G'. From one moment to the other the accelerating depreciation turns into an appreciation because of the kink in the adjustment path which occurs in G_3. The international capital market stays in permanent equilibrium, nevertheless, since at the same time domestic interest rates, which have been above foreign interest rates, fall below

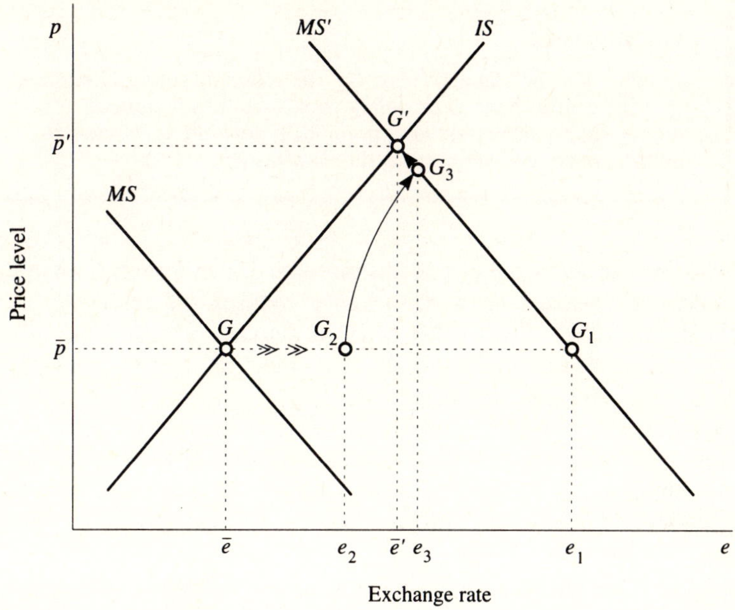

Figure 4.1 The case of an announced and, therefore, expected one-time money supply increase

foreign interest rates. This occurs because the price level has not yet reached its new equilibrium value (that is, it has not doubled yet). Therefore, the real-money supply exceeds the money supply that existed at the previous long-run equilibrium in G and the domestic interest rate now has to be smaller than the foreign one.

Let us summarize the *three phases* of adjustment following an announcement and the subsequent realization of a monetary expansion by drawing on Figure 4.1. Phase 1 is the initial impact period during which prices are fixed, while the exchange rate jumps to e_2 immediately. It *may* overshoot, but *must* not. The precise location of e_2 depends on the length of the 'announcement period', the time that elapses from when the money supply increase has been announced to when it is implemented. In the limiting case, when this period is zero, we are back in the Dornbusch scenario. The exchange rate overshoots from $\bar{e}$ to e_1. The longer the 'announcement period', the further G_2 (and e_2) moves leftwards.

Phase 2 comprises the period of time between the announcement and realization of the monetary expansion. During this announcement period we move on a curve which begins vertically in G_2 and then flattens as it moves towards G_3 on MS'. As we hit MS' we enter phase 3, during which we move from G_3 towards the new long-run equilibrium point G' along MS'.

PROBLEM 4.1

Assume that, having arrived at G_3, the economy suddenly realizes that the central bank is unwilling to initiate the announced money supply increase. Show graphically how the exchange rate and the price level respond to this new insight.

The most relevant policy conclusion to be drawn from this analysis is the following: *announcing* a disturbance reduces the response of the exchange rate to this disturbance when it actually occurs. This calls for steady policies. Abrupt shifts should be avoided, or, if they are necessary, ought to be announced well in advance.

Arguments against this policy conclusion exist. It can be shown, for example, that while the exchange rate response at the time of the money supply increase may be smaller when the increase has been announced ahead of time, the exchange rate now needs more time to adjust to its new long-run equilibrium (Gärtner 1986).

Figure 4.2 illustrates this problem using three different exchange rate

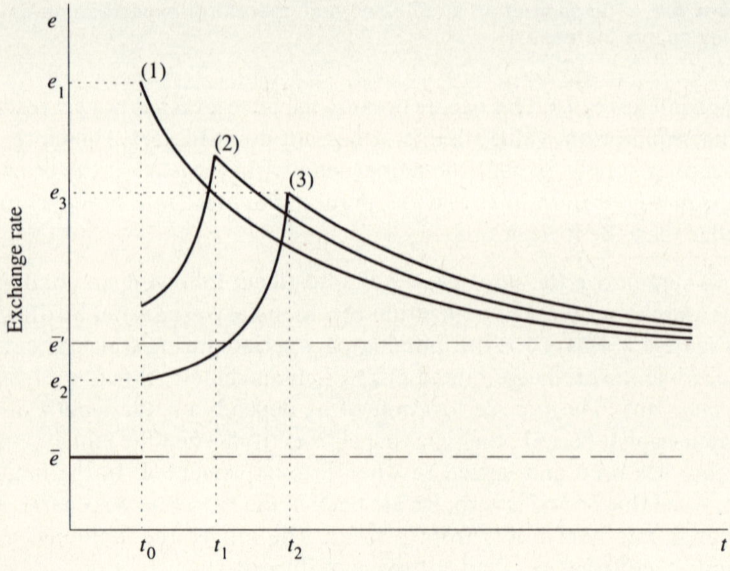

Figure 4.2 Exchange rate responses: (1) to an unexpected money supply increase in t_0; (2) to a money supply increase which is announced in t_0 and implemented in t_1; and (3) to a money supply increase which is announced in t_0 and implemented in t_2

adjustment paths: one which results after an unannounced money supply increase; one which results from a short announcement period; and one which results from a long announcement period. This confronts economic policymakers with a trade-off between large but short displacements of the exchange rate from equilibrium, on the one hand, and small but lasting ones, on the other hand.

PROBLEM 4.2

Replace the assumption of perfect foresight by $E(\dot{e})=\theta(\bar{e}-e)$ and examine the effects of an announced monetary supply increase.

4.2 The discovery of raw materials

The following sections analyze the consequences for a small open economy that derive from the discovery of new natural resources. Research in this area was, for the most part, stimulated by British oil discoveries in the North Sea during the 1970s. We proceed from the following Model 4.1.

Model 4.1
Model for analysis of resource discoveries

1	**Goods market**		
	$\dot{p}=\pi(y^d-y)$	Phillips curve	(4.1)
	$y^d=\delta(e-p)+\gamma y+g+\zeta y_p^r$	aggregate demand	(4.2)
2	**Money market**		
	$m^d=q+\phi y-\lambda i+\rho y^r$	money demand	(4.3′)
	$q=\alpha p+(1-\alpha)e$	domestic price index	(4.3a)
	$m^s=m^d=m$	money market equilibrium	(4.4)
3	**International asset market**		
	$i=i^*+E(\dot{e})$	asset market equilibrium	(4.5)
	$E(\dot{e})=\theta(\bar{e}-e)$	expectations formation	(4.6)

Notes: Lower-case variables are in natural logarithms, an exception being the interest rate. A dot indicates the change of the respective variable over time. Greek letters denote positive parameters. $E(.)$ is the expectations operator. Variables are defined as follows:

$\dot{p}$	domestic inflation rate	i	domestic interest rate
y^d	aggregate demand for domestic goods	m	domestic money (exogenous)
		i^*	foreign interest rate (exogenous)

y	aggregate supply of domestic goods (exogenous)	$\dot{e}$	rate of depreciation
e	exchange rate	$\bar{e}$	equilibrium exchange rate
p	price level of domestic goods	q	domestic price index
g	government expenditure	y^r	actual income from natural resources
y_p^r	permanent income from natural resources		

As has been done previously, we assume that nominal money balances are deflated by a weighted average of the prices for domestically produced goods and for imports. A discovery of new natural resources affects two markets directly. On the goods market we assume that consumption is a function of permanent income. This is why y_p^r in equation (4.2) is the *permanent* flow of income arising from the newly discovered resources. y^r in equation (4.3), however, represents *actual* income from newly discovered resources.

Following the standard procedure that we have employed time and again, the IS schedule is obtained from the goods market equations and the MS schedule from the equations comprising the money market and the international asset market:

$$p = e + \frac{\zeta}{\delta} y_p^r + \frac{\gamma - 1}{\delta} y + \frac{g}{\delta} \tag{4.7}$$

$$p = \frac{1}{\alpha}[m - (1-\alpha)e - \phi y + \lambda i^* - \rho y^r + \lambda\theta(\bar{e} - e)] \tag{4.8}$$

As usual, the IS curve (4.7) has a positive slope. The slope of the MS curve is negative, as long as domestically produced goods have any weight in the domestic price index ($\alpha > 0$) (see Model 4.1 and Figure 4.3).

From (4.7) and (4.8) we also see that both equilibrium schedules shift if the discovery of new raw materials raises domestic wealth. If this increase in wealth raises permanent income by Δy_p^r, the demand for domestically produced goods rises via the permanent income hypothesis by a factor $\zeta \Delta y_p^r$. Since our small open economy already operates at full employment, this additional demand can only be met if foreign demand for domestic products decreases and/or if domestic demand is redirected towards foreign goods for other reasons. This requires a change in relative prices $e - p$ in favour of foreign products, that is, an appreciation. Thus the IS schedule shifts upwards.

The equilibrium schedule for the monetary sector moves downwards for two reasons. For one thing, as we have argued, the additional demand for domestic goods, *ceteris paribus*, leads to an appreciation. Hence, assuming the money market equilibrium schedule to be given for the

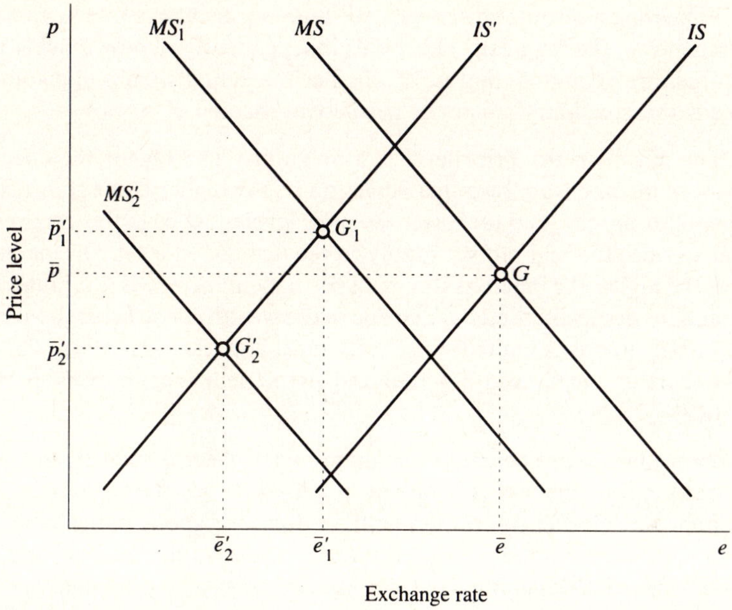

Figure 4.3 Consequences of a resource discovery in the short, medium, and long run

moment, the equilibrium exchange rate declines as well. Since the unchanged domestic money supply fixes the domestic price index q and, hence, the interest rate i in the long run, the exchange rate must fall along with the equilibrium exchange rate. This shifts the MS curve downwards to the left. This effect is reinforced by the income derived from the new resources, which leads to a higher transactions demand for real balances. *Ceteris paribus*, this must drive the price level down in order to raise the real-money supply.

From (4.7) and (4.8) we obtain the equilibrium exchange rate and the equilibrium price level:

$$\bar{e}=m-\left[\frac{(\gamma-1)\alpha}{\delta}+\phi\right]y-\frac{\alpha}{\delta}g+\lambda i^*-\frac{\alpha\zeta}{\delta}y_p^r-\rho y^r \tag{4.9}$$

$$\bar{p}=m+\left[\frac{(\gamma-1)(1-\alpha)}{\delta}-\phi\right]y+\frac{1-\alpha}{\delta}g+\lambda i^*$$
$$+\frac{(1-\alpha)\zeta}{\delta}y_p^r-\rho y^r \tag{4.10}$$

The formal results are in line with the verbal arguments presented above.

1. Following a resource discovery, the nominal exchange rate in any case appreciates in the long run. This holds independently of how quickly new resources are exploited, that is, of whether the actual stream of income y^r exceeds the imaginary stream of permanent income y^r_p or not.

2. The effect on the price level is ambiguous. The higher the effective stream of income from resource depletion is, the higher is the transaction demand for money, and the lower the price level must be in the long run in order to raise the real-money supply to the demanded level. On the other hand, the higher the inherent stream of permanent income is, the higher the demand for domestic goods will be due to the wealth effect. Since the supply of domestic goods is limited, their price must rise, *ceteris paribus*. The net effect remains open, even if actual and permanent income streams were identical ($y^r_p = y^r$).[3]

Holding other things constant, the inflationary effect is smaller, the more the transactions demand for money is raised by y^r; the higher the real exchange rate elasticity of the demand for domestic goods is, the larger the share of domestic goods in the domestic consumption basket, and the smaller the additional demand for domestic goods generated by the increase in wealth.

Figure 4.3 illustrates the two conceivable comparative-static results graphically. The cases distinguish between the possibilities of a very slow and a very speedy depletion of discovered resources. Note that the goods market is only affected by the sheer volume of discovered resources, not by how fast resources are exploited[4] (see equation (4.7)). Therefore the IS curve shifts to IS' in both cases. If new resources are only slowly exploited, or not at all, the MS curve only shifts to MS_1' and the price level rises to $\bar{p}_1'$ in the long run. A fast depletion of resources raises effective income enough to move the MS curve to MS_2', thus causing the prices of domestic goods to fall to $\bar{p}_2'$ in the long run.

We conclude by noting that the exchange rate overshoots if resources are being depleted quickly, but does not do so if resources are depleted at a more modest pace (see Figure 4.4).

4.3 A structural real sector

Our previous treatment of the goods market implies the assumption that the home country and the rest of the world produce one homogeneous good each. This has prevented us from distinguishing between tradable and nontradable goods, a distinction which the pertinent literature frequently makes when addressing specific questions.

Model 4.2 explicitly distinguishes between **tradable** and **nontradable**

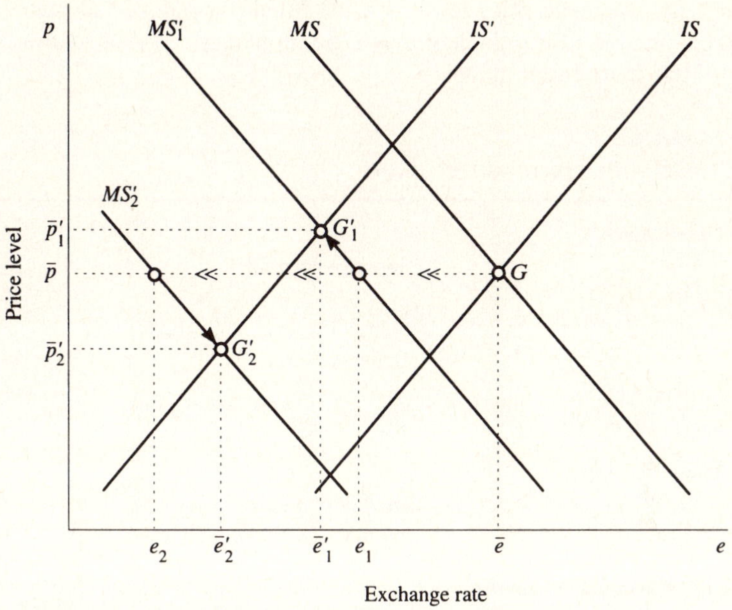

Figure 4.4 The speed of resource depletion and exchange rate overshooting

goods. These are produced in the **exposed** and in the **sheltered** sector, respectively. We further assume that wage and price movements in both sectors are not determined in neoclassically functioning markets, but via a centralized labour market with strong trade unions. The effect is that wage and profit shares remain constant over time in both sectors.

Equations (4.1a)–(4.1e) describe the proposed structural goods market. This part of the model is identical to what is known as the **Scandinavian inflation model**. Equation (4.1a) states that the law of one price holds for tradable goods. The price for domestically produced goods, p_T, cannot deviate from the world market price for tradable goods expressed in domestic currency, $p^* + e$. Collective wage formation in the exposed sector, where tradable goods are being produced, makes sure that the wage share (and thus, implicitly, the profit share) does not change. Nominal wages in the exposed sector, therefore, are calculated as the sum of sectoral goods prices and sectoral labour productivity (equation (4.1b)). Strong, centralized labour unions (or highly mobile labour) further ensure that real wages and therefore nominal wages in both sectors develop in a parallel fashion (equation (4.1c)). Prices in the sheltered sector are determined as a mark-up over wage costs per unit (equation (4.1d)). This leaves income shares of labour and capital unchanged in this sector as well. Finally, equation (4.1e) defines the domestic price level as a weighted average of the prices for tradable and for nontradable goods. The monetary sector is identical to that of the Dornbusch model.

■ Model 4.2
Model with structural real sector

1 Goods market

$p_T = p^* + e$	law of one price	(4.1a)
$w_T = p_T + x_T$		(4.1b)
$w_N = w_T$	structural wage and price determination	(4.1c)
$p_N = w_N - x_N$		(4.1d)
$p = (1-\alpha_N)p_T + \alpha_N p_N$	price index	(4.1e)

2 Money market

$m^d = p + \phi y - \lambda i$	money demand	(4.3)
$m^s = m^d = m$	money market equilibrium	(4.4)

3 International asset market

$i = i^* + E(\dot{e})$	asset market equilibrium	(4.5)
$E(\dot{e}) = \theta(\bar{e} - e)$	expectations formation	(4.6)

Notes: The notes of Model 4.1 apply. Variables are defined as follows:

i	domestic interest rate	m	domestic money (exogenous)
i^*	foreign interest rate (exogenous)	y	aggregate supply of domestic goods (exogenous)
m^d	demand for money		
$\bar{e}$	equilibrium exchange rate	e	exchange rate
$\dot{e}$	rate of depreciation	p	domestic price level
p^*	world market price level	p_T	price of tradables
w_T	wage in the exposed sector	p_N	price of nontradables
w_N	wage in the sheltered sector	x_T	productivity in the exposed sector
x_N	productivity in the sheltered sector	m^s	supply of money

Figure 4.5 visualizes in the form of a flow diagram the causal relationships of our model of a structural goods market and an exchange rate which is determined in the asset markets. Arrows indicate the direction in which causality is proposed to flow. Exogenous variables are given in squares, endogenous variables in circles.[5]

The equilibrium condition of the monetary sector is the same as in the Dornbusch model:

$$p = m - \phi y + \lambda[i^* + \theta(\bar{e} - e)] \tag{4.11}$$

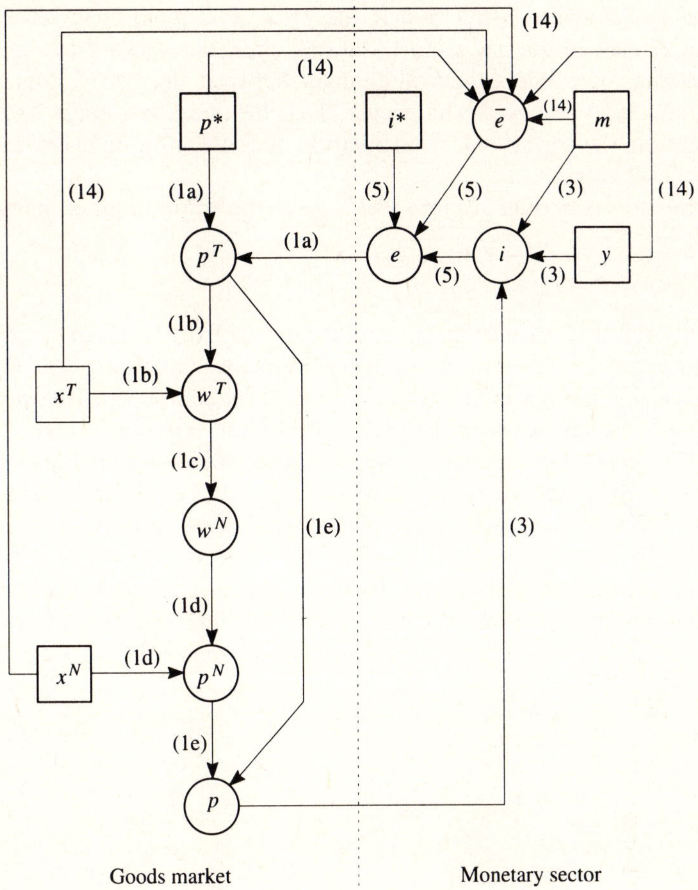

Figure 4.5 Causal relationships in the exchange rate model with a structural goods market

The equilibrium condition for the goods market follows from combining equations (4.1a)–(4.1e) and reads

$$p = p^* + e + \alpha_N(x_T - x_N) \tag{4.12}$$

If equations (4.1a)–(4.1e) hold at all points of time, equation (4.12) is not only an equilibrium condition but describes the actual relationship between prices and the exchange rate that holds in the goods market.

The equilibrium price level follows from (4.11) after letting $\bar{e} = e$:

$$\bar{p} = m - \phi y + \lambda i^* \tag{4.13}$$

What is quite interesting is that the price level in no way reflects our changed view of the real sector. Still only monetary factors determine the price level. Feasible structural changes between the two sectors of our economy play no role whatsoever. Despite structural wage and price formation, the import of foreign inflation does not show up in the domestic price level either.

Substitution of (4.13) into (4.12) gives the equilibrium exchange rate

$$\begin{aligned}\bar{e} &= m - \phi y + \lambda i^* - \alpha_N(x_T - x_N) - p^* \\ &= \bar{p} - p^* - \alpha_N(x_T - x_N)\end{aligned} \tag{4.14}$$

Equation (4.14) reveals that the equilibrium exchange rate comprises three components: a *domestic* component (domestic inflation), an *imported* component (foreign inflation) and a *structural* component (the weighted productivity gap between the sheltered and the exposed sector).

The effects of a money supply increase are shown in Figure 4.6: a money supply increase shifts the MS curve to MS'. This leads to identical price and exchange rate increases in the form of a movement from G to G'. If price and wage responses, as given by equations (4.1a)–(4.1e), occur instantaneously, the exchange rate immediately rises to $\bar{e}'$ and does not overshoot. Introduction of wage and price stickiness would imply that

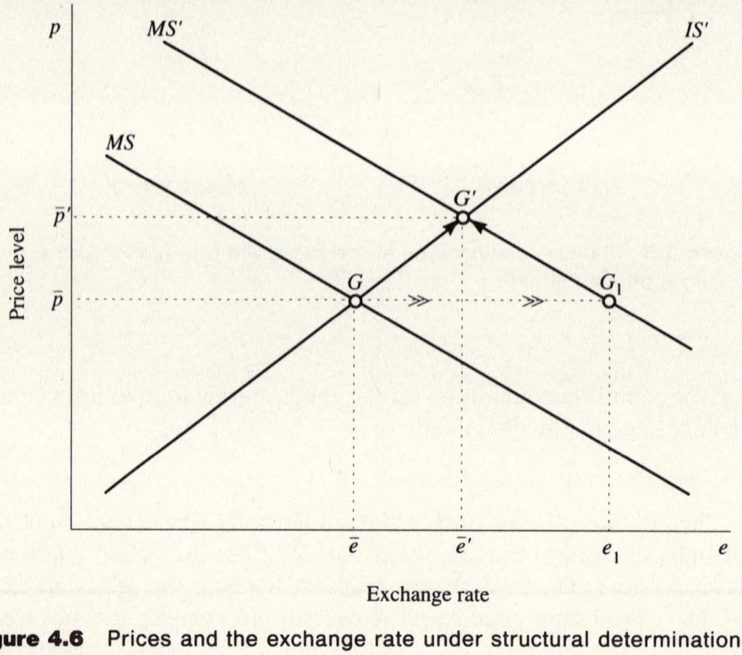

Figure 4.6 Prices and the exchange rate under structural determination of wages and prices

equations (4.1a)–(4.1e) only hold in the long run. Thus the price level is sticky, and the asymmetric adjustment speeds in the goods market versus the monetary sector cause the exchange rate to overshoot to e_1.

PROBLEM 4.3

In formal terms the analyzed structural model of an open economy under flexible exchange rates is an equilibrium model with perfectly flexible prices. The verbal discussion of Figure 4.6 also comprises the case that prices are sticky. Please state the idea that structural wage and price determination needs time mathematically.

4.4 Answers to the problems

Problem 4.1

Figure 4.7 shows how prices and the exchange rate continue to develop beyond G_3. If individuals *suddenly* realize in G_3 that the money supply will

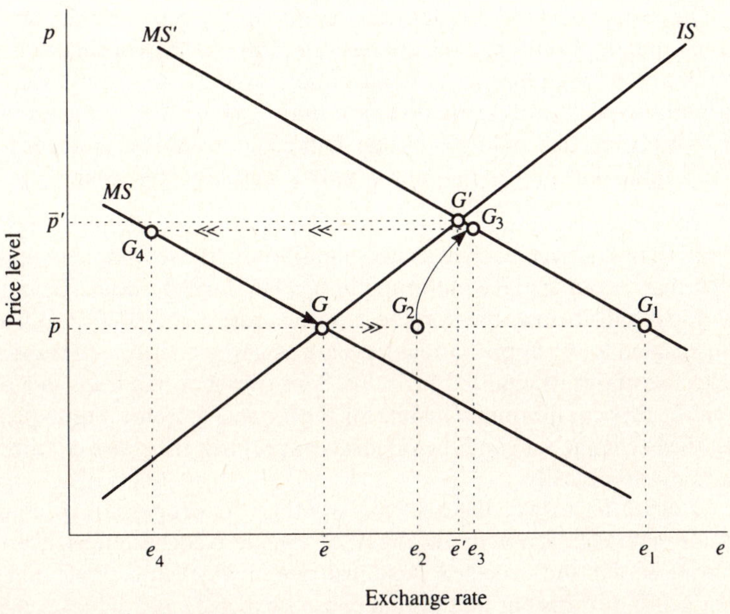

Figure 4.7 Prices and the exchange rate when individuals suddenly realize that monetary authorities renege on previous announcements

not be increased as announced, they also know that the equilibrium exchange rate is still at $\bar{e}$. This shifts the MS curve right back to MS. At the exaggerated price level given at $G_3(p_3 > \bar{p})$ a monetary-sector equilibrium requires that the exchange rate overshoots to e_4, and afterwards gradually rises back towards $\bar{e}$.

Problem 4.2

When assuming that the exchange rate is expected to adapt gradually to its equilibrium value, as in the Dornbusch model, it again proves useful to distinguish between the time period from the announcement until the money supply change, and the time after the money supply change.

1. Immediately after the announcement domestic and foreign interest rates are still equal. This is because domestic liquidity has not increased yet. Given this, the international capital market equilibrium requires that no further changes of the exchange rate are expected. This is the case if the exchange rate immediately jumps to its new equilibrium value (we suppose here that $\bar{e}'$ is the long-run equilibrium value which results after the announced money supply increase is implemented) (see Figure 4.8). We may note that the exchange rate does not overshoot in this scenario.

The excess demand for domestic goods in G_1 drives prices up. The real-money supply falls and the interest rate rises. To keep the international asset market in equilibrium, depreciation expectations must develop. Given our expectations formation assumption, this calls for the exchange rate to fall below its equilibrium value. Our economy moves upwards to the left in Figure 4.8 until the money supply is actually increased.

2. The money supply increase raises the real-money supply. Since the prive level has not yet reached its new equilibrium, the real-money supply is higher than in our initial equilibrium in G. Therefore, the domestic interest rate must fall below the foreign interest rate. This deficit must be compensated for by appreciation expectations, which require the exchange rate to rise above its equilibrium value. This overshooting leads to a point G_3 on the new equilibrium schedule for the monetary sector. Subsequently, both the exchange rate and the price level approach their new equilibrium values monotonically.

In order to answer the question whether the proposed expectations formation makes sense in the light of the derived reactions, we may confront actual and expected exchange rate changes in a single diagram (Figure 4.9). It turns out that during phase 1 expected and actual exchange rate changes point in just the opposite direction. Between the initial jump of the exchange rate at time t_0 and the eventual money supply increase at time

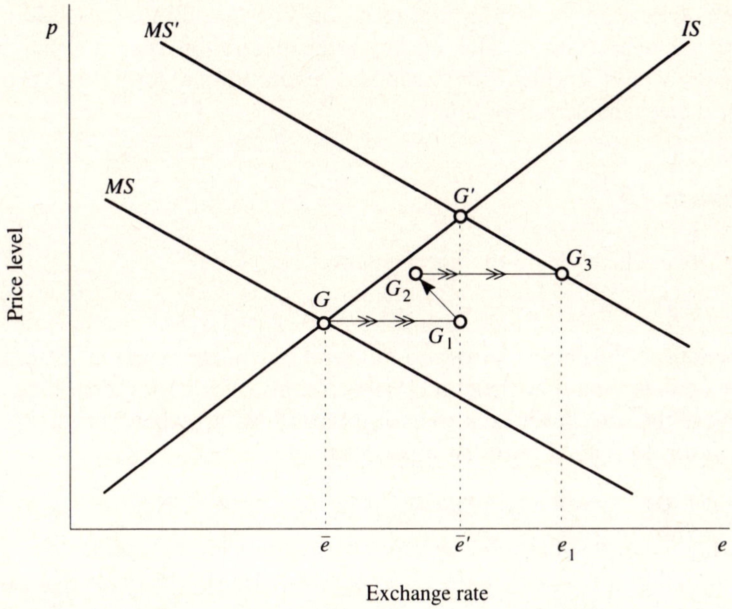

Figure 4.8 The case of an announced money supply increase when exchange rate expectations are adaptive

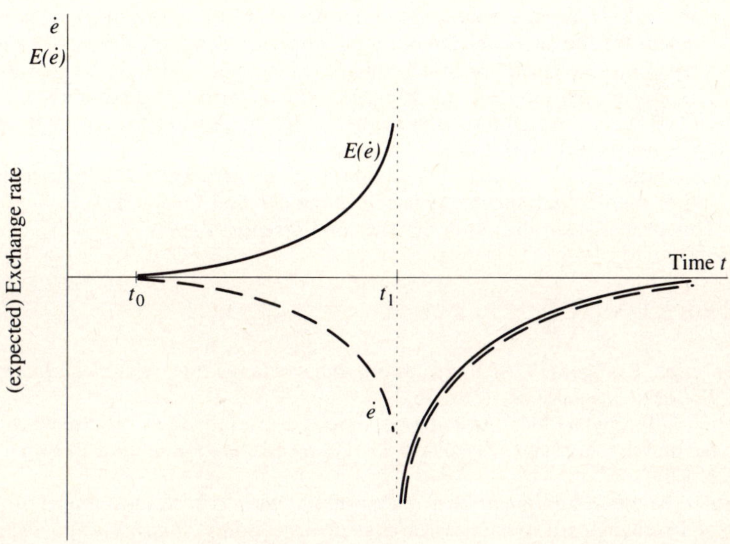

Figure 4.9 Actual and expected (adaptive) depreciation before and after an announced money supply increase

t_1, we observe an accelerating appreciation, but, in contrast, an accelerating expected depreciation. This excludes the possibility that rational individuals would employ the proposed expectations formation process over a relevant period of time.

Problem 4.3

The price which clears the goods market is

$$p = p^* + e + \alpha_N(x_T - x_N) \tag{4.12}$$

Whenever (4.12) holds, prices do not tend to change in any direction. We may now assume that structural wage and price formation processes tend to drive the price level back to its equilibrium value, whenever (4.12) does not hold. In formal terms we may postulate

$$\dot{p} = \pi[p^* + e + \alpha_N(x_T - x_N) - p]$$

Letting $\dot{p} = 0$, we obtain the *equilibrium condition* (4.12) represented by the IS line in Figure 4.4. Below the IS curve we have $\dot{p} > 0$, above the IS curve we have $\dot{p} < 0$.

NOTES

1. If individuals do not believe the announcement of the central bank, nothing happens for the next twelve months. In one year from now the money supply increases unexpectedly, with the consequences we have already derived above.
2. The Dornbusch model is not equipped to deal with this possibility.
3. Only if the discovered resources are being left untouched ($y^r = 0$) does the price level unequivocally rise in the long run.
4. Of course, this is a direct consequence of the assumption that permanent, rather than actual, income determines the demand for goods.
5. This presentation draws on Gärtner and Ursprung (1980).

REFERENCES

Dornbusch, Rudiger (1976) 'Expectations and exchange rate dynamics', *Journal of Political Economy* 84, 1167–76.

Gärtner, Manfred (1986) 'Anticipated shocks and exchange rate disequilibrium beyond the short run', *Zeitschrift für Wirtschafts- und Sozialwissenschaften* 106, 1–13.

Gärtner, Manfred and Heinrich W. Ursprung (1980) 'A structural model of price and exchange rate dynamics in a small open economy', *Journal of Economics* 40 (3–4), 321–42.

Wilson, Charles (1979) 'Anticipated shocks and exchange rate dynamics', *Journal of Political Economy* 87, 639–47.

Chapter 5

Monetarist exchange rate models

The monetarist approach to the exchange rate is linked to other standard models of the open economy in at least two ways. On the one hand, it follows from the monetarist approach to the balance of payments which in a system of fixed exchange rates explains balance of payments disequilibria and, thus, changes of central banks' currency reserves.[1] Under a system of flexible exchange rates the balance of payments is in permanent equilibrium, and the same theory explains movements of the exchange rate, that is, movements of that price which equilibrates the balance of payments in the short run. On the other hand, the monetarist exchange rate model directly follows by dropping the assumption of sticky prices from the Dornbusch model discussed at length in Chapters 2, 3 and 4 above.

With prices being sticky, the goods market needs time to equilibrate supply and demand after an exogenous disturbance. The gradual adjustment of the price level to its new equilibrium is described by the Phillips curve:

$$\dot{p}=\pi(y^d-y) \tag{5.1}$$

We obtain the monetarist exchange rate model in its simplest form by postulating **flexible prices** in (5.1), which clear the market *immediately*. Flexible prices may be introduced in two ways:

1. By postulating $\pi \to \infty$. Assuming this and dividing both sides by π, we obtain $y^d=y$. The goods market is in permanent equilibrium.

2. By augmenting the Phillips curve by expected inflation $E(\dot{p})$,

   $$\dot{p}=\pi(y^d-y)+E(\dot{p}) \tag{5.1'}$$

   and by postulating perfect foresight $E(\dot{p})=\dot{p}$. From (5.1') we also obtain permanent goods market equilibrium $y^d=y$.[2]

Now, if the demand for domestically produced goods,

$$y^d = \delta(e + p^* - p) + \gamma y + g \tag{5.2}$$

depends on a single endogenous variable, which is the real exchange rate, the goods market can only remain in permanent equilibrium if this very variable does not change, that is, if $e + p^* - p = [(1-\gamma)y - g]/\delta = \text{constant}$. Letting this constant be equal to zero for ease of exposition, the equilibrium condition for the goods market becomes $e + p^* - p = 0$.

5.1 The basic monetarist model

With this preliminary reflection we are all set to consider the basic monetarist exchange rate model, Model 5.1. Model 5.1 differs from the simplified Dornbusch model of Chapter 2 (Model 2.1) in two points: (1) the goods market is always in equilibrium; and (2) we have not yet decided how exchange rate expectations are being formed.

■ **Model 5.1**
Basic monetarist exchange rate model (continuous time)

1 **Goods market**

$p = e + p^*$ goods market equilibrium (5.3)

2 **Money market**

$m - p = \phi y - \lambda i$ money market equilibrium (5.4)

3 **Asset market**

$i = i^* + E(\dot{e})$ asset market equilibrium (5.5)

Notes: Lower-case letters are the natural logarithms of the respective variables (except for interest rates). Greek letters are positive parameters. $E(.)$ is the expectations operator. Variables are defined as follows:

i	domestic interest rate	m	domestic money supply (exogenous)
i^*	foreign interest rate (exogenous)	e	exchange rate
y	aggregate supply of domestic goods (exogenous)	$\dot{e}$	rate of depreciation
p	domestic price level	p^*	foreign price level (exogenous)

5.1.1 A stationary economy

In a **stationary** environment exchange rate expectations do not play a crucial role. All markets are in permanent equilibrium, and in equilibrium we have $E(\dot{e})=0$. The long-run properties of the Dornbusch model now also apply in the short run. In order to obtain an exchange rate equation we substitute (5.5) into (5.4) and the resulting equation into (5.3):

$$e=m-\phi y+\lambda i^*-p^* \tag{5.6}$$

At each point in time the exchange rate exactly reflects the difference between the domestic equilibrium price level[3] and the foreign price level. This directly corresponds to the respective long-run property of the Dornbusch model derived in Chapter 2. Quite generally, the monetarist exchange rate model may be considered a special case of the Dornbusch model with perfectly flexible goods prices, and its short-run behaviour is identical to the long-run behaviour of the Dornbusch model. This is not particularly exciting since the exchange rate and the price level are simply explained by the **purchasing-power parity hypothesis** and the **quantity theory of money**.

Figure 5.1 illustrates the key properties of the monetary exchange rate model graphically. The left-hand quadrant depicts the equilibrium locus for the monetary sector for a given (exogenous) goods supply in a stationary environment (see equations (5.4) and (5.5)). For given values of y and i^* the

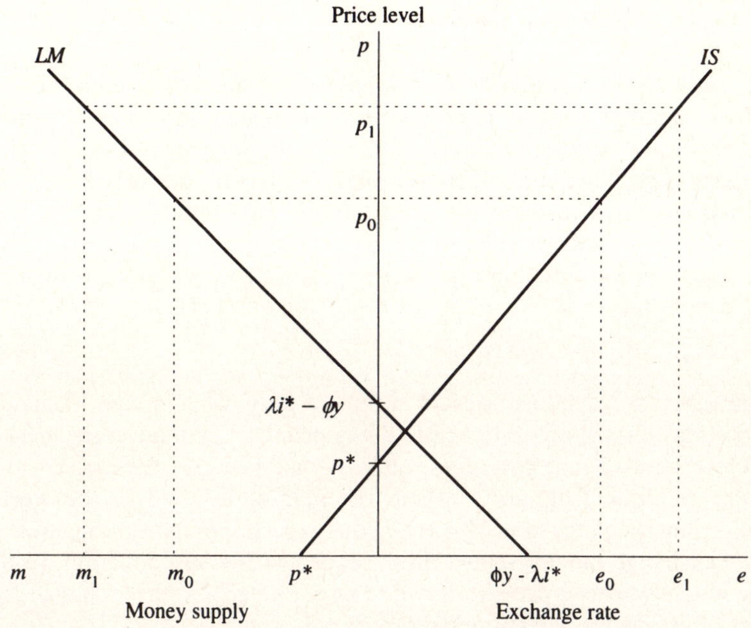

Figure 5.1 Basic monetarist exchange rate model in a stationary environment

monetary sector can only remain in equilibrium if the real-money supply remains constant. This condition is graphically represented by a straight line with unity slope. The right-hand quadrant depicts the equilibrium schedule for the goods market which results from equation (5.3). Equilibrium in the goods market requires a constant real exchange rate which, again, may be represented graphically by a straight line with unity slope.

A nominal domestic money supply of m_0 produces a domestic price level of p_0 and an exchange rate of e_0. Since both equilibrium conditions possess unity slope, the graph visualizes the extreme homogeneity properties of the monetarist exchange rate model. If the money supply increases from m_0 to m_1 the price level and the exchange rate rise by the same percentage rate from p_0 to p_1 and e_0 to e_1, respectively. Our graph also permits us to trace the consequences of exogenous shocks; for example, an increase of the foreign price level p^* moves the goods market equilibrium line to the left, thus lowering the exchange rate while leaving the price level unchanged. Choosing another example: if a money supply increase from m_0 to m_1 would at the same time stimulate domestic production, this would shift the money market equilibrium schedule to the left and the resulting price increase would fall short of the initial money supply increase.

5.1.2 An inflationary economy

The monetary exchange rate model produces some less straightforward and less familiar insights if we give up the assumption of a stationary economy and proceed to postulate an inflationary and/or growing economy. Even if we continue to postulate permanent market clearing, we nevertheless have to drop the assumption of stationary exchange rate expectations. Equations (5.3)–(5.5) may be combined to yield an exchange rate equation for this more general case – that is, without postulating $E(\dot{e})=0$:

$$e=m-\phi y+\lambda i^*+\lambda E(\dot{e})-p^* \tag{5.6'}$$

Equation (5.6′) demonstrates in a simple way why foreign exchange markets are characterized by self-fulfilling prophecy. Whatever the market expects, the exchange rate does, at least qualitatively. We arrived at a similar result in Chapter 3, where the market believed in the wrong equilibrium exchange rate. This erroneous expectation indeed triggered an initial exchange rate movement in the expected (wrong) direction. In the long run, however, expectations had to be corrected and the exchange rate effect of erroneous perceptions disappeared.

Suppose that money demand abroad is determined in the same way as money demand at home:

$$m^* - p^* = \phi y^* - \lambda i^* \tag{5.4'}$$

Then equations (5.4), (5.4′) and (5.3) yield the fundamental monetarist exchange rate equation

$$e = m - m^* - \phi(y - y^*) + \lambda(i - i^*) \tag{5.6''}$$

Equation (5.6″) shows that the exchange rate is not determined by how fundamental variables develop in absolute terms, but how they move relative to respective variables abroad. Thus the domestic currency may appreciate despite inflationary money growth, as long as the foreign central banks pursue an even more inflationary policy.

Of course, by drawing on (5.5) we may replace the interest differential by expected depreciation. This way we obtain another version of the monetarist exchange rate equation:

$$e = m - m^* - \phi(y - y^*) + \lambda E(\dot{e}) \tag{5.6'''}$$

If the market is aware of the fact that the real exchange rate must remain constant, expected depreciation must equal the expected inflation differential, and we obtain

$$e = m - m^* - \phi(y - y^*) + \lambda[E(\dot{p}) - E(\dot{p}^*)] \tag{5.7}$$

Finally, knowing that our economy remains in permanent equilibrium, and that in this equilibrium incomes are at their full-employment levels $\bar{y}$ and $\bar{y}^*$, and inflation equals money growth, we may replace expected inflation rates by expected money growth, and thus obtain

$$e = m - m^* - \phi(\bar{y} - \bar{y}^*) + \lambda[E(\dot{m}) - E(\dot{m}^*)] \tag{5.7'}$$

Interestingly, (5.7′) reveals that, despite flexible prices, the exchange rate may respond more than proportionally to a money supply increase; namely, if a money supply increase *today* generates expectations of another money supply increase *tomorrow*. If we postulate $\mathrm{d}E(\dot{m})/\mathrm{d}m > 0$, then in this spirit the exchange rate effect of a money supply increase in (5.7′) becomes

$$\frac{\mathrm{d}e}{\mathrm{d}m} = 1 + \lambda \frac{\mathrm{d}E(\dot{m})}{\mathrm{d}m} > 1 \tag{5.8}$$

This more than proportional response of the exchange rate has been coined **magnification effect** (see Bilson 1979) and must not be confused with the **overshooting effect**, which occurs in the sticky-price version of the monetary model. The term *overshooting* refers to a temporary overreaction of the nominal exchange rate as compared to its equilibrium value. It has its roots in the stickiness of goods prices and is accompanied by a temporary disequilibrium of the real exchange rate. In contrast, the *magnification effect* occurs with perfectly flexible goods prices. Nor does the exchange rate

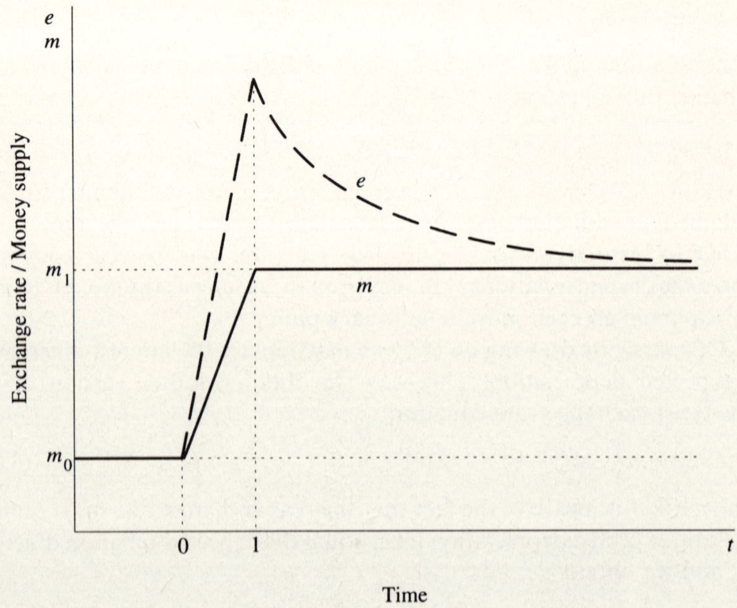

Figure 5.2 One-time money supply increase and exchange rate overshooting in discrete time

overshoot, since the equilibrium exchange rate also increases more than proportionally after we move to a steeper money supply growth path. All this happens with a constantly cleared goods market and a constant real exchange rate. The latter implies that the price level also responds more than proportionally. This is due to the **Fisher effect**, which says that in the long run, when all adjustments have occurred, an increase in inflation is reflected fully in nominal interest rates. This raises the opportunity cost of holding money, and actors will reduce the amount of real balances they choose to hold. This means, however, that during the period of adjustment to an increase in money growth, prices must rise faster than money.

Figures 5.2–5.4 compare overshooting and magnification effects. Figure 5.2 starts by depicting the overshooting of the exchange rate due to a one-time, permanent increase of the money supply. The reason for this overreaction of the exchange rate is sticky goods prices. This overreaction is a temporary phenomenon which disappears after the shock.

Figure 5.3 illustrates the magnification effect, which – even if goods prices are perfectly flexible – is generated by the transition from one money supply growth path to a steeper one. Here the central bank keep the money supply constant at m_0 until time 0. Beginning in period 1, the money supply grows at a constant positive rate. The exchange rate responds by a more

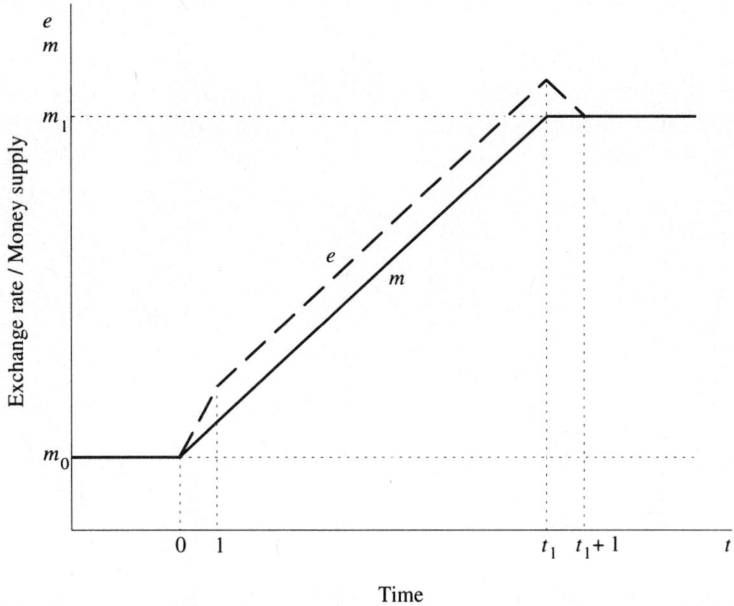

Figure 5.3 Magnification effect when money supply growth becomes more inflationary

than proportional increase in period 1. Afterwards the exchange rate grows at the same rate as the money supply. The magnification effect continues to exist as long as the money supply continues to grow along the chosen inflationary path. If at time $t_1 + 1$ the money supply is stabilized at m_1, the magnification effect disappears.

Since the scenario of the Dornbusch model assumes that goods prices are sticky in the short run, but nevertheless flexible in the long run, the equilibrium exchange rate must reflect the magnification effect. This follows from the assertion made at the beginning of this chapter that the monetarist exchange rate model may be considered a Dornbusch model with flexible prices or, by the same token, a long-run Dornbusch model. If, in the Dornbusch model, monetary policy unexpectedly becomes more inflationary, the magnification effect and the overshooting effect are superimposed on each other (see Figure 5.4). In period 1 the exchange rate overshoots its equilibrium value, which now comprises the magnification effect as well. As time passes, however, it asymptotically approaches this equilibrium value from above. Similarly, if the money supply is unexpectedly stabilized at time $t_1 + 1$, the exchange rate overreacts in the other direction and eventually approaches its new equilibrium value from below.

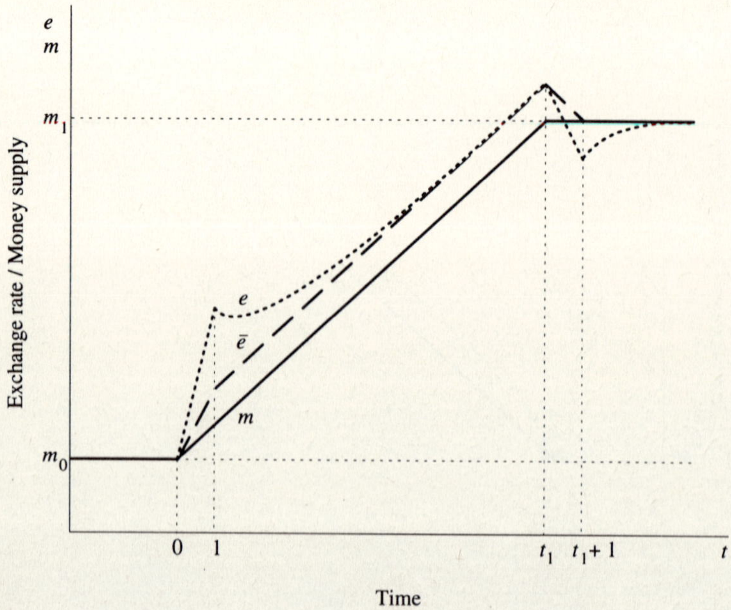

Figure 5.4 Magnification effect and overshooting with sticky prices when money supply growth becomes unexpectedly more inflationary

5.2 Magnification effect and information

We may clarify the relationship between money supply expectations and magnification effect by means of a model presented by Mussa (1976). In Mussa's view monetary policy, which we represent here by targeted money growth $\dot{m}'_t \equiv m'_t - m_{t-1}$, is subject to two sources of uncertainty. The targeted money growth rate evolves according to the following equation:

$$\dot{m}'_t = \dot{m}'_{t-1} + \varepsilon_t \tag{5.9}$$

where ε_t has an expected value of zero $[E(\varepsilon_t)=0]$, is not autocorrelated over time $[E(\varepsilon_t\varepsilon_{t-j})=0$ for $j \neq 0]$ and has constant variance $[E(\varepsilon_t\varepsilon_t)=\sigma^2_\varepsilon]$. A variable with the properties of ε_t is called **white noise**. The process described by equation (5.9) is called a **random walk**. In the context of our model, at any point in time the probability that the central bank selects a higher money growth target than it held during the previous period is just as high as the probability that it selects a lower one. In other words, the money growth target follows a *random walk*.

Assume further that the money supply is also subject to stochastic disturbances, which are not under the control of the central bank and which the central bank does not try to correct in subsequent periods:

$$m_t = m_{t-1} + \dot{m}'_t + \zeta_t \tag{5.10}$$

Again ζ_t represents white noise, which implies $E(\zeta_t)=0$, $E(\zeta_t\zeta_{t-j})=0$ for $j \neq 0$, and $E(\zeta_t\zeta_t)=\sigma_\zeta^2$.

Adding the stochastic money supply process described by equations (5.9) and (5.10) to a discrete-time version of our basic monetarist exchange rate model, we obtain the refined model, Model 5.2. Ignoring equations

Model 5.2
Model with stochastic money supply

1 Goods market

$p_t = e_t + p_t^*$	goods market equilibrium	(5.3)

2 Money market

$m_t - p_t = \phi y_t - \lambda i_t$	money market equilibrium	(5.4)
$m_t^* - p_t^* = \phi y_t^* - \lambda i_t^*$	money market equilibrium abroad	(5.4a)
$\dot{m}'_t = \dot{m}'_{t-1} + \varepsilon_t$	random walk of targeted money growth	(5.9)
$m_t = m_{t-1} + \dot{m}'_t + \zeta_t$	random walk of money supply with stochastic trend	(5.10)

3 Asset market

$i_t = i_t^* + E(\dot{e}_t)$	asset market equilibrium	(5.5)

Notes: Lower-case letters are the natural logarithms of the respective variables (except for interest rates). A dot indicates the derivative with respect to time. Greek letters are positive parameters, except for ε and ζ. $E(.)$ is the expectations operator. Foreign variables carry an asterisk. Variables are defined as follows:

y	domestic aggregate output (exogenous)	i	domestic interest rate
m	domestic money supply (exogenous)	e	exchange rate
$\dot{e}$	rate of depreciation	p	domestic price level
ε	random variable	$\dot{m}$	money growth rate
ζ	random variable	$\dot{m}'_t$	target rate for money growth

(5.9) and (5.10) for the time being, we may follow the above procedure to obtain an exchange rate equation which is identical to equation (5.7′):

$$e_t = m_t - m_t^* - \phi(y_t - y_t^*) + \lambda[E(\dot{m}_t) - E(\dot{m}_t^*)] \tag{5.7''}$$

The money growth expectations required in (5.7″) are obtained by combining equations (5.9) and (5.10). Substituting (5.9) into (5.10) yields

$$m_t = m_{t-1} + \dot{m}'_{t-1} + \varepsilon_t + \zeta_t \tag{5.11}$$

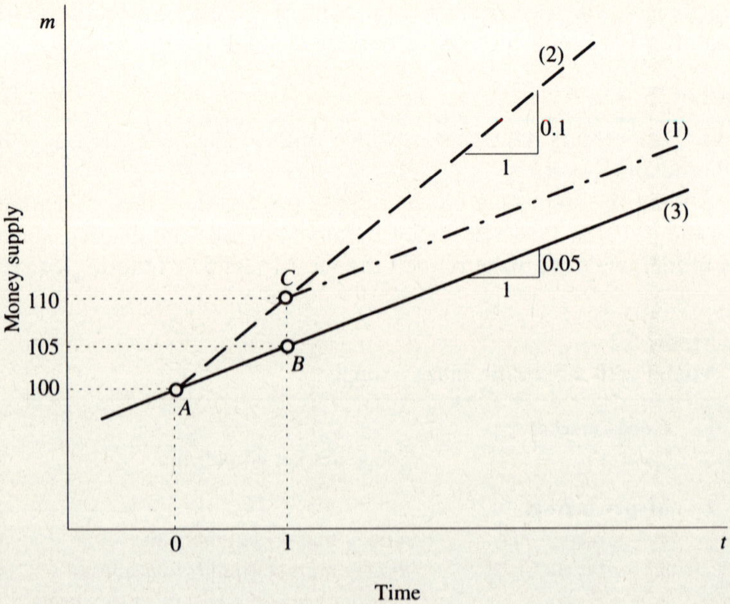

Figure 5.5 Some possible interpretations of an unexpected money supply increase

In order to form expectations on the basis of (5.11), the market must be aware of how the random variables ε_t and ζ_t have changed. The problem may be illustrated by means of a numerical example (see Figure 5.5).

Example
Let the money supply at time 0 be 100 units. Let the target rate for money supply growth, $\dot{m}_0'$, be 5 per cent. Further, let $\varepsilon_0 = \zeta_0 = 0$. Under this condition the money supply should grow along the solid line in Figure 5.5. Now assume that between 0 and 1 the money supply does not grow by 5 per cent, as had been expected, but by 10 per cent. In terms of our graph, the money supply does not move from *A* to *B*, as expected, but to *C*. If the market is convinced that the reason for this unexpected development is a one-time shock to the money supply, that is, $\zeta_1 = 5$, a further development along path (1) is expected. If, however, the market considers the unexpected money supply increase in period 1 as a signal for a permanent change of monetary policy, that is, $\varepsilon_1 = 5$, future money supply growth is expected to follow the steeper dashed line (2).

Actually, a third case is conceivable. The market might expect that the one-time shock to the money supply level will be corrected in the next period. Formally, this would change equation (5.10) to

$$m_t = m_{t-1} + \dot{m}'_t - \zeta_{t-1} + \zeta_t \tag{5.10'}$$

If the market considers the unexpected money supply increase in period 1 as a one-time mistake which will be corrected in the following period, the money supply is expected to continue to grow along the solid line (3) in Figure 5.5. It can easily be verified that in case (1) the money supply is expected to grow by 5 per cent in period 2, in case (2) it is expected to grow by 10 per cent and in case (3) it is expected to remain unchanged. This emphasizes the key role of the market's perceptions of the causes underlying the money supply increase.

Based on (5.11) the expected money supply for the next period is

$$E_t(m_{t+1}) = m_t + \dot{m}'_t \tag{5.12}$$

The subscript behind the expectations operator E indicates that expectations are being formed on the basis of information available at time t. Subtracting m_t from both sides of (5.12) yields the expected change of the money supply. Substituting this expected change into (5.7″) yields

$$e_t = m_t - m_t^* - \phi(y_t - y_t^*) + \lambda[\dot{m}'_t - E(\dot{m}_t^*)] \tag{5.13}$$

or, after making use of (5.9) and (5.10),

$$e_t = m_{t-1} + \dot{m}'_{t-1} + \varepsilon_t + \zeta_t - m_t^* - \phi(y_t - y_t^*) \\ + \lambda[\dot{m}'_{t-1} + \varepsilon_t - E(\dot{m}_t^*)] \tag{5.13'}$$

5.2.1 Perfect information

If market participants possess perfect information, they can distinguish between shocks to the money supply level and shocks to the money growth target. Money supply expectations are then formed on the basis of *all* information available at time t. Thus the response of the exchange rate to a one-time increase in the money supply (an increase in ζ_t) is

$$\left.\frac{de_t}{dm_t}\right|_{\varepsilon_t=0} = \frac{de_t}{d\zeta_t} = 1 \tag{5.14}$$

the response of the exchange rate to a one-time increase in the money supply growth rate (increase in ε_t) is

$$\left.\frac{de_t}{d\dot{m}_t}\right|_{\zeta_t=0} = \frac{de_t}{d\varepsilon_t} = 1 + \lambda \tag{5.14'}$$

With information being perfect, a more than proportional reaction of the exchange rate in terms of a magnification effect only results when monetary policy moves to a new, steeper expansion path.

5.2.2 Imperfect information

In a state of imperfect information at time t the market only observes the compound variable $\xi_t = \varepsilon_t + \zeta_t$, but is not in a position to break that up into its two components. Instead of the actual values of ε_t and ζ_t, expected or presumed values must be used when deriving an exchange rate equation like (5.13′) from equations (5.7″), (5.9), (5.10) and (5.12). If, for example, experience says that the share of ε_t in ξ_t is α, instead of (5.13′) we obtain

$$e_t = m_{t-1} + \dot{m}'_{t-1} + \alpha\xi_t + (1-\alpha)\xi_t + \lambda[\dot{m}'_{t-1} + \alpha\xi_t - E(\dot{m}_t^*)] - m_t^* - \phi(y_t - y_t^*) \tag{5.13″}$$

Differentiating this with respect to m_t gives the exchange rate effect of a money supply increase:

$$\frac{de_t}{dm_t} = \frac{de_t}{d\xi_t} = 1 + \alpha\lambda > 1 \tag{5.15}$$

Under imperfect information the exchange rate reaction reflects a magnification effect whenever the market, observing a money supply change, cannot positively exclude the possibility of a deliberate change of monetary policy ($1 \geq \alpha > 0$). The true nature of the observed shock is not relevant at this stage. In the medium and long run, however, α must be treated as an endogenous variable which changes if its presently perceived value produces systematic forecasting errors.[4]

Figure 5.6 illustrates this. Assume the money supply has moved from A to C because of a one-time shock to its level. Then the values assumed by the money supply in the following periods 2, 3 and 4 are indicated by points D, E and F, respectively. If the market mistakenly, because of imperfect information, believes in a 70 per cent probability that the unexpected increase from A to C has been caused by a shock to its level rather than a shock to its growth rate, we have $\alpha = 0.7$.

Under these circumstances, forecasts of one period ahead predict points D', E' and F' for periods 2, 3 and 4, respectively. Comparing these points with the actual development reveals that expectations are systematically off target. Rational actors must be expected to realize that they can reduce expectations errors by reducing α, and they will continue to do so until α has been reduced to its true value of zero.

When modelling exchange rate expectations, which play a central role for the short- and medium-run responses in open economies, we have two basically distinct options: we may postulate *rational expectations* directly; or we may make an effort to model how expectations are being formed.

Explicit modelling of expectation formation processes appears to be the appropriate procedure whenever economic agents have to deal with situations or structures with which they have no previous experience.

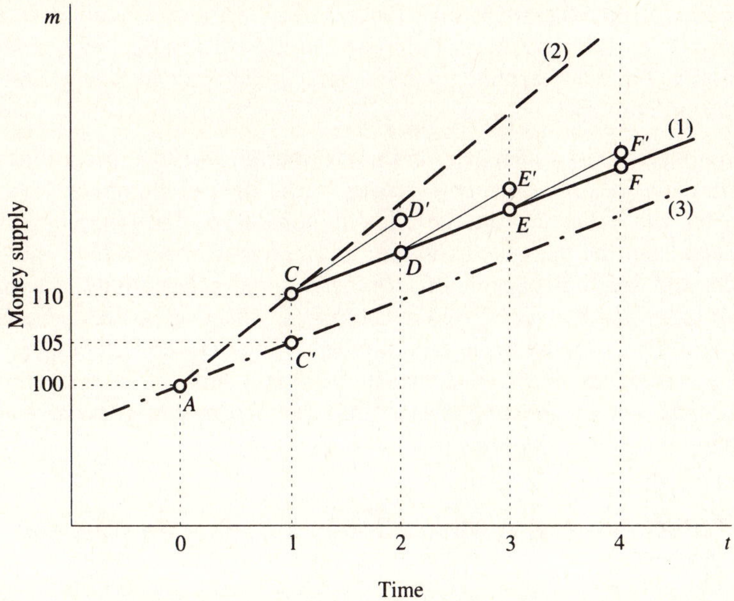

Figure 5.6 Expected and actual money supplies after a one-time shock to the money supply level when information is not perfect

1. Hyperinflations are thrilling but rare phenomena. Single countries have rarely suffered from them more than once within one generation's time. Since it appears that experience gathered by former generations is ignored or forgotten to a large extent, any generation hit by a hyperinflation must start from scratch when learning how to deal with this unfamiliar situation and how to understand the modified structural relationships. This means that any attempt to explain a country's macroeconomic development during a specific hyperinflationary period must include an effort to model learning processes.

2. If a political party, after being confined to the opposition for several decades, is elected to power, individuals need time to find out which elements of its political programme it actually wants, and is allowed, to implement and which it is not.

3. After the collapse of the Bretton Woods system of fixed exchange rates, actors had to build up a knowledge of how open economies operate under flexible exchange rates. Almost twenty years later this process is still in progress, as the present volume may document.

4. After one and a half decades of central planning and a worldwide war which completely changed institutional structures, the West German

economy during the 1950s and 1960s had to acquire a qualitative and quantitative understanding of the structural relationships of a market economy. Similar learning processes are under way in many Eastern European countries.

Many papers exist which expound model learning when expectations are not initially rational (see, for example, Lucas 1975 or Bernholz, Gärtner and Heri 1985). Throughout the following subsection of this chapter we will proceed from the opposite assumption: that agents are aware of the true model and are thus capable of forming rational expectations. A similar assumption had been employed in Chapter 2, where we postulated perfect foresight. By dropping the assumption held in the Dornbusch model, that actors consider an observed change in the money supply as permanent, we will obtain some interesting insights into the relationship between *today's* exchange rate and *tomorrow's* economic policy.

5.3 Rational expectations: today's exchange rate and the future

Assume that our model economy is not only driven by a set of structural relationships between macroeconomic variables but also by disturbances for which no structural explanation exists. Furthermore, assume that actors are aware of all structural relationships and draw on this knowledge when forming expectations. Since actors are rational and therefore make use of any available information when forming expectations, they also take into account any systematic component in the development of disturbances over time. The consequence of this is that expectations are correct on average. Expectations errors do occur, of course, but they are completely unsystematic, that is, random.

Postulating rational expectations in the sense that agents are perfectly aware of all structural relationships of our economic model overextends the knowledge of actors in real life. On the other hand, it does make sense to assume that agents will not permit themselves to be fooled in the same way time and again, but rather will respond by improving their understanding of how the economy works. Rational expectations macroeconomics takes this learning process to the limit and tries to distil those macroeconomic relationships and possibilities for economic policy that result after learning has led to complete knowledge. While there is legitimate disagreement over the question of how relevant this approach is for empirical macroeconomics, its usefulness as a *theoretical* counterposition to earlier Keynesian approaches with highly naive expectations formation is undisputed.

Let us begin by rewriting the basic monetaristic exchange rate model for discrete time (see Model 5.3). In order to simplify the exposition, the foreign variables p^* and i^* are both normalized to zero. We also ignore the possibility of stochastic disturbances, though the solution method proposed here can handle stochastic models as well.

■ **Model 5.3**
Basic monetarist exchange rate model (discrete time)

---

1 **Goods market**

$p_t = e_t$ goods market equilibrium (5.16)

2 **Money market**

$m_t - p_t = \phi y_t - \lambda i_t$ money market equilibrium (5.17)

3 **Asset market**

$i_t = E_t e_{t+1} - e_t$ asset market equilibrium (5.18)

Notes: Lower-case letters are the natural logarithms of the respective variables (except for the interest rate i). Greek letters are positive parameters. E is the expectations operator. $E_t e_{t+1}$ denotes the expectation of the exchange rate at time $t+1$ which individuals hold at time t. Variables are defined as follows:

i domestic interest rate
e exchange rate
p domestic price level
m domestic money supply (exogenous)
y aggregate supply of domestic goods (exogenous)

5.3.1 The rational expectations solution

In determining the exchange rate under rational expectations we employ the recipe which is applied in the appendix in more detail to an even simpler model.

Step 1: In a first step we solve the model for the variable we are interested in. For our present purposes this is the exchange rate. Thus we want to see the exchange rate on the left-hand side of the equation and nothing but exogenous or lagged endogenous variables on the right-hand side.[5] For the time being, expected variables are considered exogenous variables. We will return to this below. Inserting (5.16) and (5.18) into (5.17), we obtain

$$e_t = \frac{1}{1+\lambda}(m_t - \phi y_t + \lambda E_t e_{t+1}) \tag{5.19}$$

Step 2: Now we have to determine the expected exchange rate, which occurs on the right-hand side of (5.19). Recall our assumption that the economy knows our model, which means it knows equations (5.16), (5.17) and (5.18).

Then, of course, agents expect at time t that equations (5.16)–(5.18) will continue to hold at time $t+1$. We may therefore write these equations in their expected form:

$$E_t p_{t+1} = E_t e_{t+1} \tag{5.16e}$$

$$E_t m_{t+1} - E_t p_{t+1} = \phi E_t y_{t+1} - \lambda E_t i_{t+1} \tag{5.17e}$$

$$E_t i_{t+1} = E_t e_{t+2} - E_t e_{t+1} \tag{5.18e}$$

In fact, the first term on the right-hand side of (5.18e) should read $E_t E_{t+1} e_{t+2}$; that is, it indicates which expected exchange rate we expect at time t to have at time $t+1$. This, of course, is identical with the exchange rate we expect at the time t for $t+2$. Therefore we have $E_t E_{t+1} e_{t+2} = E_t e_{t+2}$.

Substituting (5.16e) and (5.18e) into (5.17e) and solving for $E_t e_{t+1}$ yields

$$E_t e_{t+1} = \frac{1}{1+\lambda}(E_t m_{t+1} - \phi E_t y_{t+1} + \lambda E_t e_{t+2}) \tag{5.20}$$

The exchange rate expected at t for $t+1$ is determined by the values expected for the exogenous variables for $t+1$ and by the exchange rate expected for $t+2$.

Step 3: In a process called **forward substitution**, we begin by substituting the expected exchange rate from (5.20) into the exchange rate equation (5.19) and rearrange terms to obtain

$$e_t = \frac{1}{1+\lambda}\left[m_t - \phi y_t + \frac{\lambda}{1+\lambda}(E_t m_{t+1} - \phi E_t y_{t+1})\right] + \left(\frac{\lambda}{1+\lambda}\right)^2 E_t e_{t+2} \tag{5.21}$$

While we have been able to eliminate the endogenous variable $E_t e_{t+1}$ from the right-hand side of (5.19), we now have another endogenous variable $E_t e_{t+2}$ in (5.21). In order to get rid of $E_t e_{t+2}$ as well, expectations in (5.20) are directed one period further into the future, that is to period $t+2$. Substituting the resulting equation into (5.21), we obtain

$$e_t = \frac{1}{1+\lambda}\left[m_t - \phi y_t + \frac{\lambda}{1+\lambda}(E_t m_{t+1} - \phi E_t y_{t+1}) + \left(\frac{\lambda}{1+\lambda}\right)^2 (E_t m_{t+2} - \phi E_t y_{t+2})\right] + \left(\frac{\lambda}{1+\lambda}\right)^3 E_t e_{t+3} \tag{5.22}$$

After collecting terms, we obtain

$$e_t = \frac{1}{1+\lambda}\left[m_t - \phi y_t + \sum_{j=1}^{2}\left(\frac{\lambda}{1+\lambda}\right)^j (E_t m_{t+j} - \phi E_t y_{t+j})\right] + \left(\frac{\lambda}{1+\lambda}\right)^3 E_t e_{t+3} \tag{5.22'}$$

Again, E_te_{t+2} has been eliminated as intended. Instead, another unknown expectation, E_te_{t+3}, appears on the right-hand side. Nevertheless, we recognize a pattern: the coefficient of the unknown expectation becomes smaller and smaller the further this expectation looks into the future. Obviously, the coefficient is $[\lambda/(1+\lambda)]^n$ if we have arrived at E_te_{t+n} by repeated substitution. As n approaches infinity, the coefficient approaches zero:

$$\lim_{n\to\infty}\left(\frac{\lambda}{1+\lambda}\right)^n=0$$

Combining this with the assumption that $\lim_{n\to\infty}E_te_{t+n}$ is finite, this finally gives us the exchange rate equation we were looking for:

$$e_t=\frac{1}{1+\lambda}\left\{m_t+\sum_{j=1}^{\infty}\left(\frac{\lambda}{1+\lambda}\right)^j E_tm_{t+j} -\phi\left[y_t+\sum_{j=1}^{\infty}\left(\frac{\lambda}{1+\lambda}\right)^j E_ty_{t+j}\right]\right\} \tag{5.23}$$

A number of important insights can be drawn from (5.23):

1. Today's exchange rate is determined by the entire expected future course of the exogenous variables.
2. The further away an expected variable lies in the future the smaller is its effect on today's exchange rate. This corresponds to the results from our analysis of announced money supply changes in Chapter 4.
3. If both the money supply and real output are expected to remain at their present levels, if $E_tm_{t+j}=m_t$ and $E_ty_{t+j}=y_t$ for all j, (5.23) simplifies to the familiar equation (5.23′)[6]

$$e_t=m_t-\phi y_t=p_t{}^{7} \tag{5.23′}$$

5.3.2 An announced money supply increase

We may draw on equation (5.23) to analyze the effect of an announced money supply increase.[7] Assume that the central bank announces at time t that at time $t+k$ it will permanently increase the money supply from its present level of m_t to m_{t+k}. If individuals fully believe this announcement, we have $E_tm_{t+j}=m_t$ for all $0<j<k$ and $E_tm_{t+j}=m_{t+k}$ for all $j\geq k$ in (5.24):[8]

$$e_t=\frac{1}{1+\lambda}\left[m_t+\frac{\lambda}{1+\lambda}m_t+\left(\frac{\lambda}{1+\lambda}\right)^2 m_t+\ldots+\left(\frac{\lambda}{1+\lambda}\right)^{k-1} m_t +\left(\frac{\lambda}{1+\lambda}\right)^k m_{t+k}+\left(\frac{\lambda}{1+\lambda}\right)^{k+1} m_{t+k}+\ldots\right] \tag{5.24}$$

Given this expected development of the money supply process, one period later the exchange rate is given by

$$e_{t+1}=\frac{1}{1+\lambda}\left[m_t+\frac{\lambda}{1+\lambda}m_t+\left(\frac{\lambda}{1+\lambda}\right)^2 m_t+\ldots+\left(\frac{\lambda}{1+\lambda}\right)^{k-2} m_t\right.$$
$$\left.+\left(\frac{\lambda}{1+\lambda}\right)^{k-1} m_{t+k}+\left(\frac{\lambda}{1+\lambda}\right)^{k} m_{t+k}+\ldots\right] \quad (5.25)$$

The rate of depreciation to be observed in the first period after the impact period is obtained by subtracting (5.24) from (5.25):

$$e_{t+1}-e_t=\frac{1}{1+\lambda}\left(\frac{\lambda}{1+\lambda}\right)^{k-1}(m_{t+k}-m_t) \quad (5.26)$$

In an analogous fashion we can draw on (5.24) to obtain the rate of depreciation at time $t+n$ (where $0<n\leq k$):

$$e_{t+n}-e_{t+n-1}=\frac{1}{1+\lambda}\left(\frac{\lambda}{1+\lambda}\right)^{k-n}(m_{t+k}-m_t) \quad (5.27)$$

Equation (5.27) reveals that exchange rate depreciation accelerates as the announced money supply increase draws closer, that is, as n approaches k. It culminates at $[1/(1+\lambda)]/(m_{t+k}-m_t)$ at time $t+k$.

PROBLEM 5.1

What is the rate of depreciation observed at time $t+k+1$?

The initial impact response of the exchange rate is obtained after differentiating (5.24) with respect to m_{t+k}. This yields

$$\frac{de_t}{dm_{t+k}}=\frac{1}{1+\lambda}\sum_{j=k}^{\infty}\left(\frac{\lambda}{1+\lambda}\right)^j$$

The impact effect on the exchange rate is always positive. Drawing on the result given in note 6, we also see that the effect is smaller than 1 if $k>0$, that is, if there is a lag between announcement and implementation.

In order to rationalize these results in economic terms, we may start by looking at the impact response of the exchange rate and the price level – which are identical because of equation (5.3). If prices did not respond when the announcement was made, the real money supply and the interest rate would not change. The exchange rate would be expected to, and actually would, remain at its pre-announcement level. From this initial reaction no perfect foresight path could lead to the higher post-implementation equilibrium price level.

Assume next that the price level initially responded by jumping to its prospective post-implementation equilibrium level. This would reduce the real-money supply and raise the interest rate above the foreign one. According to open interest parity, this must give rise to expected depreciation. If expectations are rational, there is actual depreciation too. Thus e and p fall below their post-implementation equilibrium levels. This downward movement could only come to a halt when e and p have reached pre-announcement levels, $i = i^*$, and $E_t e_{t+1} - e_t = 0$. But from this situation no perfect foresight path leads to the post-implementation equilibrium – by the same reasoning we employed above to rule out that e and p did *not* respond at the moment of impact.

So e and p must rise initially, but not to their post-implementation equilibrium levels. This generates a perfect foresight depreciation path which arrives at its new long-run equilibrium when the money supply actually rises. Since the real-money supply continues to fall along this path, the interest rate rises, and expected and actual depreciation accelerate. This development is stopped when m rises and the interest rate drops back to the level given by the foreign interest rate.

5.4 A neoclassical exchange rate model

A close relative of the monetarist approach is the **neoclassical view** (see Model 5.4), which dominated macroeconomics in the 1970s and 1980s.

■ Model 5.4
Neoclassical open-economy model

1 Goods market

$y_t = \pi(p_t - E_{t-1} p_t)$	aggregate supply	(5.28)
$y_t = \delta(e_t - p_t)$	aggregate demand	(5.29)

2 Monetary sector

$m_t - p_t = \phi y_t - \lambda i_t$	money market equilibrium	(5.4)
$i_t = E_t e_{t+1} - e_t$	asset market equilibrium	(5.5)

Notes: The notes to Model 5.3 apply. Variables are defined as follows:

- p domestic price level
- y aggregate supply for domestic goods
- m domestic money (exogenous)
- i domestic interest rate
- e exchange rate

Prices and wages are also fully flexible. Because of information asymmetries, however, the labour market may 'clear' below or above its perfect-information equilibrium level, causing output to deviate from its equilibrium level as well. This can be explained by reference to the **Lucas surprise supply curve** (5.28), which states that aggregate supply deviates from its natural level – which is normalized to zero – if the price level increases unexpectedly.

Information is asymmetric in the sense that firms observe the aggregate price level before workers do. Firms can base their calculations of the current real wage on the actual price level p_t, which they observe. Workers receive pertinent information with a lag of one period, and thus must derive their guess of the current real wage from a price expectation $E_{t-1}p_t$ based on the last period's information. Only if $p_t = E_{t-1}p_t$ do both parties perceive the same real wage and the labour market clears at full employment. If, for example, the price level rises unexpectedly, $p_t > E_{t-1}p_t$, there is a difference of view between workers and firms on what the current real wage is, which permits both labour demand and supply to rise. As a consequence, output increases.

Aggregate demand depends on the real exchange rate, an assumption already employed (equation (5.29)). The monetary sector is directly adopted from the monetary exchange rate model. In order to keep the equations below as compact as possible, full-employment output and the foreign interest rate have been set equal to zero, and δ includes the multiplier effect. It needs no elaboration that in stationary equilibrium $y = i = 0$ and $e = p = m$.

To acquire a feel for how this neoclassical open-economy model functions, we start with a graphical analysis (see Figure 5.7). We begin by solving (5.28) for the price level to obtain the aggregate supply (AS) curve

$$p_t = E_{t-1}p_t + \frac{1}{\pi} y_t \tag{5.30}$$

Equation (5.30) is a positively sloped line in a p/y diagram, and its position depends on price expectations.

The aggregate demand (AD) curve is obtained by combining equations (5.29), (5.4) and (5.5) and solving for prices:

$$p_t = \frac{1}{1+\lambda} m_t + \frac{\lambda}{1+\lambda} E_t e_{t+1} - \frac{\phi + \lambda/\delta}{1+\lambda} y_t \tag{5.31}$$

The AD curve is negatively sloped and shifts upwards as the money supply and/or the expected exchange rate rises. As we move down to the right on the AD curve the real exchange rate depreciates; otherwise demand would not increase to absorb rising output. The *position* of the AD curve

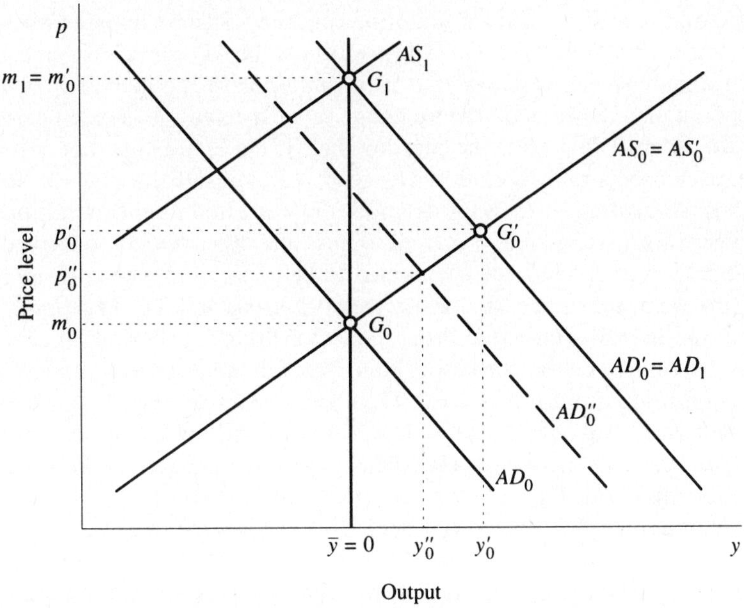

Figure 5.7 Neoclassical open-economy model

depends on today's money supply and on the exchange rate expected for next period. *Ceteris paribus*, a money supply increase requires an increase of the price level and/or aggregate output to eliminate incipient excess supply, thus shifting the AD curve to the right. If $E_t e_{t+1}$ rises, investors only continue to hold domestic assets if domestic interest rates rise. Again, this is accomplished by a rising price level and/or rising output, which shifts the AD curve to the right.[9]

What happens to the nominal exchange rate depends on where AS and AD intersect. As long as we rule out a negatively sloped AS curve, the exchange rate depreciates as a money supply increase shifts the AD curve to the right. This becomes obvious if we look at the limiting cases: if the AD curve is vertical, output remains constant and e must increase by the same amount as p to keep the real exchange rate constant. If the AD curve is horizontal, output rises and so must the real exchange rate. As p remains constant, this must be accomplished by a nominal depreciation. By the same argument, the nominal exchange rate rises whenever the AD curve possesses a positive slope.

Assume expectations are formed rationally, based on knowledge of the true model. Let the economy initially be in equilibrium at point G_0. In period 0 it is hit by an unexpected money supply increase from m_0 to m'_0. Since price-level expectations, which are relevant for aggregate supply, are based on the previous period's information, the AS curve remains where it was before the shock occurred. The position of the AD curve is not as easily determined. While we know that it moves up with the increased money supply, it also depends on the exchange rate expected for the next period.

In order to determine the effect on the AD curve, we note that nothing unexpected occurs in period 1. Hence $p_1 = E_0 p_1$, and thus, $y_1 = 0$ (from (5.28)). According to (5.29), this implies $e_1 = p_1$, and as this is rationally foreseen, $E_0 e_1 = E_0 p_1 = e_1 = p_1 = m_0'$. Thus, after the shock is observed in period 0, the exchange rate is expected to be in period 1 where the money supply went in period 0 unexpectedly. Letting $m_t = m_0'$ and $E_t e_{t+1} = E_0 e_1 = m_0'$ in (5.6), we see that the *post*-shock AD curve in period 0 intersects the long-run AS curve (the vertical line over full-employment output 0) at the equilibrium price level $p = m_0'$. Thus the price level in period 0, after the shock, is at p_0' and output is at y_0'. In period 1 the AS curve is at AS_1 and the AD curve stays at $AD_0' = AD_1$. The economy has settled at its new equilibrium point, G_1.

Now assume that the central bank does not increase the money supply unexpectedly, but credibly announces in period 0 that it will increase the money supply in period 1 from m_0 to m_1. As regards period 1, the argument of the preceding paragraph applies. Since nothing unexpected happens, AS_1 and AD_1 must intersect at G_1. In period 0 the AS curve is not affected by the announcement. The AD curve, however, is affected by the fact that individuals expect $E_0 e_1 = m_1 (> e_0 = m_0)$. This shifts the AD curve up, but only into a position between AD_0 and AD_1 [since $\lambda/(1+\lambda) < 1$]. Hence the immediate price and output effect of an announced policy change is smaller than that of an unexpected one.

On an intuitive level the announcement effect can be rationalized as follows. After the announcement individuals know that the exchange rate will depreciate tomorrow. This must be balanced by a higher interest rate. At a given money supply this calls for a price-level increase and a simultaneous increase in output.

A formal analysis of the behaviour of this model under rational price and exchange rate expectations may follow the procedure suggested in the appendix to this chapter.

Step 1: We begin by combining equations (5.28), (5.29), (5.4) and (5.5) to obtain a reduced form for the exchange rate (treating expectations as exogenous variables). This yields

$$e_t = \frac{1}{D}[(\pi+\delta)m_t + \lambda(\pi+\delta)E_t e_{t+1} - \pi(1-\phi\delta)E_{t-1}p_t] \tag{5.32}$$

where $D \equiv \delta + \lambda\delta + \pi\phi\delta + \pi\lambda > 0$.

Step 2: In order to pin down expectations, rewrite the model in expected form:

$$E_{t-1}y_t = \pi E_{t-1}p_t - \pi E_{t-1}p_t \tag{5.28e}$$

$$E_{t-1}y_t = \delta E_{t-1}e_t - \delta E_{t-1}p_t \tag{5.29e}$$

$$E_{t-1}m_t = E_{t-1}p_t + \phi E_{t-1}y_t - \lambda E_{t-1}i_t \tag{5.4e}$$

$$E_{t-1}i_t = E_{t-1}e_{t+1} - E_{t-1}e_t \tag{5.5e}$$

From (5.28e) we see that output is always expected to be in equilibrium,

$$E_{t-1}y_t = 0 \tag{5.28e$'$}$$

Combining this with (5.29e) suggests that the expected exchange rate always equals the expected price level:

$$E_{t-1}e_t = E_{t-1}p_t \tag{5.29e$'$}$$

Substituting (5.5e) into (5.4e) and making use of (5.28e′) and (5.29e′) gives, after rearranging terms

$$E_{t-1}e_t = \frac{1}{1+\lambda}E_{t-1}m_t + \frac{\lambda}{1+\lambda}E_{t-1}e_{t+1} \tag{5.33}$$

that is, the exchange rate expected for today is a weighted sum of the money supply expected for today and the exchange rate expected for tomorrow.

Step 3: After substituting (5.29e′) into (5.32) for $E_{t-1}p_t$ the exchange rate only depends on expected exchange rates and today's money supply. Forward (successive) substitution of (5.33) for expected exchange rates eventually yields

$$\begin{aligned} e_t = {} & \frac{\pi+\delta}{D}\left[m_t + \sum_{j=1}^{\infty}\left(\frac{\lambda}{1+\lambda}\right)^j E_t m_{t+j}\right] \\ & - \frac{\pi(1-\phi\delta)}{D(1+\lambda)}\sum_{j=0}^{\infty}\left(\frac{\lambda}{1+\lambda}\right)^j E_{t-1}m_{t+j} \end{aligned} \tag{5.34}$$

Equation (5.34) signals that the relationship between the exchange rate and monetary policy is more complex than in the monetarist model. This is because output responds to unexpected inflation, thereby interfering with the transmission process from monetary policy to currency prices. It may, therefore, prove worthwhile to analyse how output is determined in this neoclassical context.

Step 1: Inserting (5.5) into (5.4) and substituting the resulting equation for e_t in (5.29) gives, after solving for p_t,

$$p_t = \frac{\lambda}{1+\lambda}E_t e_{t+1} + \frac{1}{1+\lambda}m_t - \frac{\lambda+\delta\phi}{\delta(1+\lambda)}y_t \tag{5.35}$$

Now substitute (5.35) into (5.28) and solve for y_t to obtain the reduced form

$$y_t = \frac{\pi\delta(1+\lambda)}{\delta(1+\lambda)+\lambda\pi+\delta\pi\phi}\left[\frac{1}{1+\lambda}E_t e_{t+1} + \frac{1}{1+\lambda}m_t - E_{t-1}p_t\right] \tag{5.36}$$

Step 2: The required price and exchange rate expectations were derived above. See equations (5.29e′) and (5.33).

Step 3: Substitution of (5.29e′) for $E_{t-1}p_t$ in (5.36), followed by forward substitution of (5.33) gives, after collecting terms,

$$y_t = \frac{\pi\delta}{\delta(1+\lambda)+\lambda\pi+\delta\pi\phi}(m_t - E_{t-1}m_t) \tag{5.37}$$

Equation (5.37) states the core result from neoclassical macroeconomics that only unexpected policy matters. Whenever monetary policy differs from expectations, output differs from equilibrium output – which we had normalized to zero. Expected policy, no matter how inflationary, cannot move output away from equilibrium.

PROBLEM 5.2

1. Use equation (5.34) to determine the impact response of the exchange rate to a money supply increase which comes as a surprise and is considered permanent. Does the exchange rate overshoot?
2. Depict the model in the *p*/*e* plane (by means of IS and MS curves) and interpret the result derived under (1). (*Hint:* Assume $E_t e_{t+1} = \bar{e}_t$ – the exchange rate is expected to move into today's equilibrium in the next period – which is rational in the present context.)

5.5 Summary

The monetarist approach to the exchange rate emphasizes those factors which affect the exchange rate via national money markets. The way in which the approach was presented in Chapter 5 may blur this key premise, since for didactic reasons the monetarist approach was developed as a special case of the Dornbusch model. Under these circumstances the real exchange rate takes the form of an equilibrium condition for the goods market and then, of course, responds to supply shocks as well. Exchange rate models of the monetarist mould frequently omit this step and *assume* that purchasing-power parity holds. This amounts to postulating a constant real exchange rate. If we now postulate a stable money demand function, variables only influence the exchange rate to the extent that they change the real-money supply or the demand for real balances. Though supply-side shocks are omitted the monetarist approach explains empirical exchange rates rather well when monetary developments dominate. Thus, well-known and successful applications of the monetarist approach to the German hyperinflation of the 1920s exist (see Frenkel 1977). During hyperinflations the assumption of flexible goods prices is probably a much better description of reality than the assumption of sticky goods prices.

During normal times, such as the time between 1973 and the present, exchange rate movements can hardly be explained by movements of the real-money supply or real-money demand in a satisfactory way.[10] Thus Dornbusch (1989: 410) summarizes, referring to the basic monetarist exchange rate equation (5.6″): 'The empirical success of this equation has been so poor, and the PPP [purchasing-power parity] foundations so doubtful, that this approach is basically extinct.'

If, despite its failure as an empirical model, we have devoted an entire chapter to the monetarist exchange rate model, this has been for two reasons:

1. In order to present an exchange rate model for the long run.
2. By emphasizing the possible interpretation of the monetarist model as the long-run Dornbusch model, we could draw attention to phenomena and properties which are also present in the Dornbusch model but are either covered there by the dominating overshooting phenomenon or defined away by a number of simplifying assumptions.

Key results of our analysis are as follows.

1. If a money supply increase indicates the transition to a more inflationary policy, the initial devaluation exceeds the money supply increase. At first sight this *magnification effect* is confusingly similar to the overshooting phenomenon. What separates the two effects is that the magnification effect occurs at a constant real exchange rate and a cleared market for domestic goods and that it does not generate any **competitive advantage** for the domestic economy. By contrast, overshooting of the nominal exchange rate is always an overshooting of the real exchange rate and secures a temporary competitive advantage for the domestic economy.

2. All things we expect to happen in the future have a bearing on today's exchange rate. This statement not only refers to future monetary policies and output developments, which were the focus of our simplified model; it also refers to other policy instruments, to economic and political institutions, on the national and international level – in short, to everything that has the faintest economic relevance.

5.6 Answers to the problems

Problem 5.1

Evaluation of (5.24) at times $t+k$ and $t+k+1$ yields $e_{t+k}=e_{t+k+1}=m_{t+k}$. Hence the rate of depreciation we are looking for is zero. This is not surprising, of course, since the exchange rate reaches its new equilibrium level at time $t+k$.

Problem 5.2

1. The impact response of the exchange rate, $\mathrm{d}e_t/\mathrm{d}m_t$, is obtained by differentiating (5.34) with respect to m_t. The assumption that the increase came unexpectedly implies $\partial E_{t-1}m_{t+j}/\partial m_t=0$ for all $j\geq 0$ – the increase was not anticipated at time $t-1$. The assumption that the increase is considered permanent implies $\partial E_t m_{t+j}/\partial m_t=1$ for all $j>0$ – the money supply is expected to remain forever where it moved today. The impact response turns out to be

$$\frac{\mathrm{d}e_t}{\mathrm{d}m_t}=\frac{\pi+\delta}{D}\left[1+\sum_{j=1}^{\infty}\left(\frac{\lambda}{1+\lambda}\right)^j\right]$$

Making use of

$$\sum_{j=0}^{\infty}\left(\frac{\lambda}{1+\lambda}\right)^j=1+\lambda$$

which we have employed previously (see note 6), and writing out D in full, the impact response reads

$$\frac{\mathrm{d}e_t}{\mathrm{d}m_t}=\frac{\pi+\pi\lambda+\delta+\delta\lambda}{\delta\phi\pi+\pi\lambda+\delta+\delta\lambda}$$

The exchange rate may overshoot or not. Overshooting only occurs if $\delta\phi<1$.

2. Combining (5.28) and (5.29) and solving for p_t gives the IS curve

$$p_t=\frac{\delta}{\pi+\delta}e_t+\frac{\pi}{\pi+\delta}E_{t-1}p_t$$

which possesses unity slope when there is no inflation surprise ($E_{t-1}p_t=p_t$) and a positive slope of less than 1 in the case of surprise inflation.

Combining (5.29), (5.4) and (5.5), assuming $E_t e_{t+1}=\bar{e}_t$ as suggested, noting $\bar{e}_t=m_t$, and solving for p_t gives the MS curve

$$p_t=-\frac{\delta\phi+\lambda}{1-\delta\phi}e_t+\frac{1}{1-\delta\phi}m_t$$

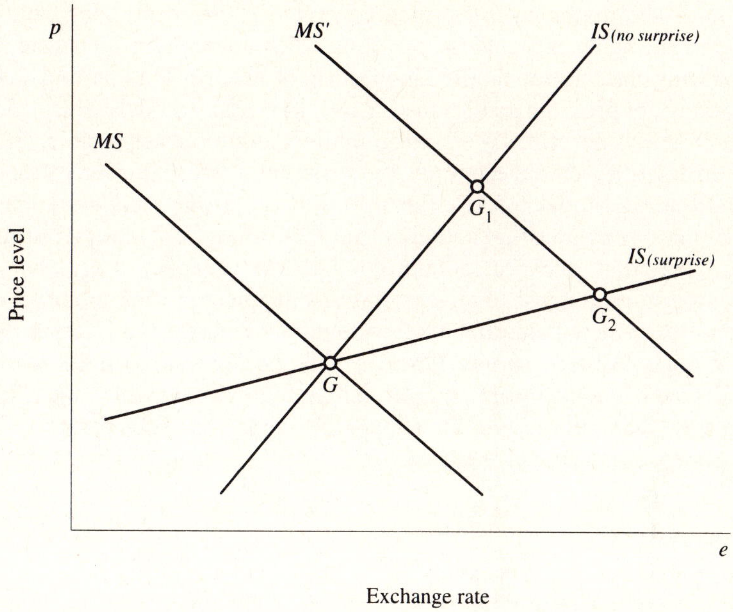

Figure 5.8 The neoclassical open-economy model in the *p*/*e*-plane

Figure 5.8 shows these equilibrium curves. Starting from point G, a money supply increase moves the economy into G_1 if it was expected, and into G_2 if it came unexpectedly. In the latter case the exchange rate obviously overshoots. Overshooting unambiguously occurs because by drawing the MS curve with a negative slope we implicitly assumed $\delta\phi < 1$, which is the overshooting condition derived above. To understand the economic meaning of this condition, assume that the money supply rises by 1, the number given on the right-hand side. If the MS curve was vertical, there would be no overshooting – and $\delta\phi = 0$, that is, the exchange rate also rises by 1. This raises output by δ, which pushes the demand for money up by $\delta\phi$. Thus overshooting occurs unless a money supply increase generates an excess *demand* for money. See also the discussion in Section 3.2.

APPENDIX

A method for solving rational expectations models

A host of methods for solving rational expectations models has been proposed. Each of them has its advantages, either because it is very general, or because it is particularly well suited to a certain type of model. For some methods the mathematical prerequisites are rather demanding and are beyond the skills expected in this book. This appendix is constrained to describing one solution method in the form of a recipe. This method has the advantage of providing solutions for certain types of models which can be interpreted rather directly. To keep matters as simple as possible, let our model describe a closed economy, the structure of which is given by the two equations in Model 5.5. In the tradition of the new classical macroeconomics we assume that actual output only differs from natural output to the extent that unexpected inflation hits the economy. Formally, this assumption is identical to an expectations-augmented Phillips curve.[11] In the context of new classical macroeconomics it is known as a Lucas surprise or Sargent–Wallace supply function. The equilibrium condition (5.39) results from a conventional money demand function in which the interest rate has been suppressed for simplicity, while the demand for money contains a stochastic element ε_t.

■ Model 5.5 Model of a closed economy

1 Goods market

$p_t = E_{t-1}p_t + \alpha(y_t - \bar{y})$	aggregate supply curve	(5.38)

2 Money market

$m_t - p_t = \phi y_t + \varepsilon_t$	money market equilibrium	(5.39)

Notes: Lower-case letters are the natural logarithms of the respective variables. Greek letters are positive parameters, except for ε. $E(.)$ is the expectations operator. Variables are defined as follows:

m	money supply (exogenous)	p	price level
y	aggregate output	$\bar{y}$	full-employment output
ε	random variable		

Basic solution method

The basic method for solving rational expectations is particularly simple if the model contains no expectations of future variables (see, for example, Minford and Peel 1983: 17ff.; Holden, Peel and Thompson 1985: 30ff.). This is why we choose to introduce the method by applying it to a model for a *closed* economy. As has been demonstrated time and again in this book, expectations of the future exchange rate play a key role in *open* economies.

Step 1: Solving for the reduced form. A reduced form is an equation derived from a model which has the selected endogenous variable on the left-hand side and either exogenous or lagged endogenous variables on the right-hand side. When performing this first step, expected variables are considered exogenous variables.

The model contains two endogenous variables, p_t and y_t. If we are interested in how y_t behaves under rational expectations, we must solve for the reduced form for y_t. Substituting (5.38) into (5.39) and solving for y_t yields

$$y_t = \frac{1}{\alpha+\phi}(m_t - E_{t-1}p_t + \alpha\bar{y} - \varepsilon_t) \tag{5.40}$$

Step 2: Taking expectations of the structural equations. Actors are assumed to be aware of the above model and form their expectations rationally. Then the model not only holds, but it is also expected to hold. Therefore we may write

$$E_{t-1}p_t = E_{t-1}p_t + \alpha E_{t-1}y_t - \alpha E_{t-1}\bar{y} \tag{5.41}$$

$$E_{t-1}m_t - E_{t-1}p_t = \phi E_{t-1}y_t + E_{t-1}\varepsilon_t \tag{5.42}$$

Step 3: Solving for the reduced form of that expected variable which occurs in the reduced form calculated in step 1. We need a reduced form equation for $E_{t-1}p_t$. Since $\bar{y}$ is a constant, which implies $E_{t-1}\bar{y}_t = \bar{y}$, (5.41) implies

$$E_{t-1}y_t = \bar{y} \tag{5.43}$$

Substituting (5.43) into (5.42) and making use of the assumption $E_{t-1}\varepsilon_t = 0$ yields the desired reduced form

$$E_{t-1}p_t = E_{t-1}m_t - \phi\bar{y} \tag{5.44}$$

Step 4: Substitution of the reduced form equation computed in step 3 into the reduced form computed in step 1. Substitution of (5.44) into (5.40) and rearranging terms yields

$$y_t = \bar{y} + \frac{m_t - E_{t-1}m_t}{\phi+\alpha} - \frac{\varepsilon_t}{\phi+\alpha} \tag{5.45}$$

The obtained solution says that, under rational expectations, output can only differ from full-employment output if either the money supply or money demand changes unexpectedly. If no further shocks occur during subsequent periods, y_t returns to its full-employment value $\bar{y}$ without delay. The income effect of a monetary shock is larger, the smaller the income elasticity of the demand for money ϕ is and the smaller α is.

NOTES

1. Any good macroeconomics textbook contains a presentation of the monetary approach to the balance of payments (see, for example, Dornbusch and Fischer 1990: Ch. 20, 762ff.), as does any serious textbook on international economics (examples are Gandolfo 1986 and Krugman and Obstfeld 1988).
2. Of course, $y^d = y$ holds permanently only in a deterministic model. If shocks hit the price level in a stochastic scenario with discrete time, (5.1′) permits temporary goods market disequilibria (though only for one period).
3. We obtain the equilibrium price level from (5.4) and $i = i^*$, which gives $\bar{p} = m - \phi y - \lambda i^*$.
4. Learning, which results in an eventual convergence of α to its true value, has been described in general terms for a stochastic environment in Lucas (1975). It has been employed by Bernholtz, Gärtner and Heri (1985) in the context of simulations of historical experiences with flexible exchange rates.
5. In technical terms we are trying to obtain a **reduced form** for the exchange rate. See Chiang (1984: 178).
6. This follows because

$$1 + \sum_{j=1}^{\infty}\left(\frac{\lambda}{1+\lambda}\right)^j = \sum_{j=0}^{\infty}\left(\frac{\lambda}{1+\lambda}\right)^j = \frac{1}{1-\lambda/(1+\lambda)} = 1 + \lambda$$

7. Chapter 4 has already provided a verbal discussion of the consequences of an announced money supply increase in the sticky price monetary model.
8. For notational convenience we let $y_t = E_t y_{t+j} = 0$.
9. In the complete model m_t and $E_t e_{t+1}$ will usually not be independent of each other, as will be demonstrated shortly.
10. This is documented in, for example, Dornbusch (1980).
11. The expectations-augmented Phillips curve reads $\dot{p}_t = E_{t-1}\dot{p}_t + \alpha(y_t - \bar{y})$. This may be rewritten as $p_t - p_{t-1} = E_{t-1}p_t - p_{t-1} + \alpha(y_t - \bar{y})$. Adding p_{t-1} to both sides gives (5.38).

REFERENCES

Bernholz, Peter, Manfred Gärtner and Erwin W. Heri (1985) 'Historical experiences with flexible rates: A simulation of common qualitative characteristics', *Journal of International Economics* 19, 21–45.

Bilson, John F. O. (1979) 'Recent developments in monetary models of exchange rate determination', *IMF Staff Papers* 26, 201–23.

Chiang, Alpha C. (1984) *Fundamental Methods of Mathematical Economics*, 3rd edn, Singapore: McGraw-Hill.

Dornbusch, Rudiger (1980) 'Exchange rate economics: Where do we stand?', *Brookings Papers on Economic Activity*, 143–85.

Dornbusch, Rudiger (1989) 'Real exchange rates and macroeconomics: A selective survey', *Scandinavian Journal of Economics* 91, 401–32.

Dornbusch, Rudiger and Stanley Fischer (1990) *Macroeconomics*, 5th edn, New York: McGraw-Hill.

Frenkel, Jacob A. (1977) 'A monetary approach to the exchange rate: Doctrinal aspects and empirical evidence', in J. Herin, Assar Lindbeck and Johan Myhrman (eds) *Flexible Exchange Rates and Stabilization Policy*, Boulder, CO: Westview Press, 68–92.

Gandolfo, Giancarlo (1986) *International Economics*. Berlin and Heidelberg: Springer.

Holden, K., D. A. Peel and J. L. Thompson (1985) *Expectations: Theory and evidence*, London: Macmillan.

Krugman, Paul R. and Maurice Obstfeld (1988) *International Economics: Theory and policy*, Glenview, IL: Scott Foresman.

Lucas, Robert E. (1975) 'An equilibrium model of the business cycle', *Journal of Political Economy* 83, 1113–44.

Minford, Patrick and David A. Peel (1983) *Rational Expectations and the New Macroeconomics*, Oxford: Martin Robertson.

Mussa, Michael (1976) 'The exchange rate, the balance of payments, and monetary policy under a regime of controlled floating', *Scandinavian Journal of Economics* 78, 229–48.

Chapter 6

The exchange rate under currency substitution

Modern exchange rate theory proceeds from the assumption that the exchange rate is not primarily determined by the demand for foreign currency generated by trade in goods and services, but rather by decisions on how to spread wealth over different available assets. Asset portfolios result from a two-step decision process which Figure 6.1 clarifies.

In a first step wealth is divided into liquid assets, that is, cash balances, and interest-bearing assets with reduced liquidity. The money demand function describes this decision by listing the relevant variables and by postulating hypotheses about the reaction of desired cash balances to changes of the right-hand variables.

In a second step we have to decide which part of cash balances and bonds to hold in domestic or in foreign currency. After this second decision has been made, total wealth is divided into four categories corresponding to the four fields of the matrix shown in Figure 6.1. The amount of foreign cash or bonds being held crucially depends on whether the foreign form of holding wealth is a close substitute for the domestic one. As regards money and bonds, we have so far employed two completely different assumptions.

As a rule, domestic and foreign *bonds* have been considered **perfect substitutes**. This means that in a situation of identical expected returns for domestic and foreign bonds risk-neutral investors do not care how big the share of foreign bonds is in relation to domestic bonds. The effective decision on how much domestic and foreign bonds are being held is made by exporters and importers and their net supply or demand of credit. In the next chapter we will give up this assumption that domestic and foreign bonds are perfect substitutes.

In the models discussed up to now *only domestic residents held domestic money*. The north-east element in our matrix in Figure 6.1 is always empty. This reflects the implicit assumption that domestic money under no circumstances can be substituted by foreign money, which seems to be at

		CHOICE OF CURRENCY	
		domestic currency	foreign currency
CHOICE OF ASSET	money		
	bonds		

Figure 6.1 Stylized portfolio choices in the portfolio balance approach

variance with the contemporaneous assumption that domestic and foreign bonds are perfect substitutes. These two assumptions are reconciled, however, by noting that bonds and money are held for quite different purposes. While *bonds* are primarily being held in an attempt to maximize expected *yields*, *money* has to serve as a *means of payment*, in addition to being a store of value. The extent to which foreign money can serve the same purposes as domestic money depends on how closely it approximates the ideal of being the good with the highest liquidity, as money is sometimes defined.

A number of situations are feasible in developed economies in which foreign money is almost as liquid as domestic money.

1. Along national borders individuals often acquire a major part of their demanded goods and services on the other side of the border. Since on the other side of the border foreign money is more liquid than domestic money, part of cash balances are being held in foreign currency.

2. Tourists typically hold cash balances in the form of a basket of currencies.

3. Firms which operate on the international level hold increasing shares of their means of payment in foreign currency. Whether these and other examples make **currency substitution** a quantitatively important phenomenon strongly depends on the smallness and the openness of an economy.[1] Also currency substitution seems to increase during phases of rapid inflation at home. For even if foreign money is a less than perfect substitute for domestic money when being used for purposes of payment, this may be overcompensated for by being a superior store of value. It does not come as a surprise, therefore, that a rather high degree of currency substitution can be observed during pronounced hyperinflations.

6.1 Currency substitution in the monetarist model

If, for the reasons given above, domestic residents only hold part of their demanded liquidity in domestic money, the money demand function has to be rewritten as

$$\frac{M}{P}=\Omega \cdot L(Y,i) \tag{6.1}$$

or, in order to stay with the functional form postulated in previous chapters,

$$\frac{M}{P}=\Omega \cdot Y^{\phi}\exp(-\lambda i) \qquad 0<\Omega\leq 1 \tag{6.1'}$$

Ω denotes the share of cash balances which domestic residents wish to hold in domestic currency. Thus $\Omega=1$ describes a world without currency substitution. Taking logs of (6.1′) and combining the resulting equation with the remaining part of the monetarist exchange rate model presented in Chapter 5, Model 6.1 obtains. Substituting (6.4) and (6.2) into (6.3) and solving for e yields the exchange rate equation

$$e=m-\phi y+\lambda E(\dot{e})-\omega \tag{6.5}$$

■ **Model 6.1**
Monetarist exchange rate model under currency substitution (1)

---

1 Goods market

$p=e$	goods market equilibrium	(6.2)

2 Money market

$m-p=\phi y-\lambda i+\omega$	money market equilibrium	(6.3)

3 Asset market

$i=E(\dot{e})$	asset market equilibrium	(6.4)

Notes: Lower-case letters are the natural logarithms of the respective variables (except for the interest rate i). A dot indicates the derivative with respect to time. Greek letters are positive parameters. $E(.)$ is the expectations operator. Variables are defined as follows:

p	domestic price level	i	domestic interest rate
y	aggregate supply of domestic goods (exogenous)	$\dot{e}$	rate of depreciation
		e	exchange rate
ω	share of domestic currency in total demand for real balances (logarithm)	m	domestic money supply (exogenous)

A change of preferences towards the domestic currency ($\Delta\omega > 0$) makes the domestic currency appreciate. This is not a very exciting result. More interesting insights result after specifying how exchange rate expectations are being formed and after noting that ω is not an exogenous parameter but rather an endogenous variable which, among others, depends on exchange rate expectations. This leads to the augmented model, Model 6.2, below.

Model 6.2
Monetarist exchange rate model under currency substitution (2)

1 Goods market

$p = e$	goods market equilibrium	(6.2)

2 Money market

$m - p = \phi y - \lambda i + \omega$	money market equilibrium	(6.3)
$\omega = -\alpha E(\dot{e}) - \beta var[E(\dot{e})]$	share of money demand directed towards domestic money	(6.3a)

3 Asset market

$i = E(\dot{e})$	asset market equilibrium	(6.4)
$E(\dot{e}) = E(\dot{m})$	depreciation expectations	(6.6)

Notes: Lower-case letters are the natural logarithms of the respective variables (except for the interest rate i). A dot indicates the derivative with respect to time. Greek letters are positive parameters. $E(.)$ is the expectations operator. Variables are defined as follows:

p	domestic price level	i	domestic interest rate
y	aggregate supply of domestic goods (exogenous)	$\dot{e}$	rate of depreciation
		e	exchange rate
ω	share of domestic currency in total demand for real balances (logarithm)	m	domestic money supply (exogenous)
		$\dot{m}$	money growth rate

Equation (6.3a) in Model 6.2 maintains that ω falls as depreciation expectations increase and as the variance of these expectations, which represents risk, becomes larger. Equation (6.6) says that expected devaluation always equals expected money growth. Substituting equations (6.3a) and (6.6) into the exchange rate equation (6.5), which had resulted from (6.2), (6.3) and (6.4), yields

$$e = m - \phi y + (\alpha + \lambda)E(\dot{m}) + \beta \text{var}[E(\dot{m})] \qquad (6.5')$$

Equation (6.5′) contains some by now familiar results and some new ones.

1. An unexpected and one-time increase of the money supply which may be characterized by $E(\dot{m}) = 0$ *before* and *after* the money supply increase,

causes money, the exchange rate and the price level to rise by the same percentage rates. Thus the quantity theory of money and purchasing-power parity hold permanently.

2. An unexpected shift of monetary policy to a more inflationary path initially triggers exchange rate and price level reactions which exceed the money supply increase. How pronounced this magnification effect is depends on the semi-interest elasticity of the demand for money (λ) and on how far $E(\dot{m})$ rises after an unexpected money supply increase.

3. This magnification effect is reinforced if domestic residents substitute foreign money for domestic money as inflation and depreciation expectations increase. Formally, this assumption means that ω is endogenous and that $\alpha > 0$. The larger α, the more a given depreciation shifts the demand for money away from the domestic currency and the more pronounced the depreciation eventually will be.

4. The magnification effect is even further reinforced if money growth rates become more volatile (their variance increases) as they grow bigger.

Since the goods market equilibrium condition $p = e$ holds permanently according to equation (6.2), it cannot be disturbed by more pronounced reactions of the exchange rate and of the price level due to currency substitution. Therefore currency substitution in the monetarist exchange rate model is apparently a monetary phenomenon and has no impact on the real part of the economy.

This is not a general result, however. If currency substitution occurs in a model with sticky goods prices it not only changes the volatility of the nominal exchange rate, but that of the real exchange rate as well.

PROBLEM 6.1

Augment the simplified Dornbusch model (Model 2.1) by the assumption of currency substitution. How does currency substitution affect the overshooting of the exchange rate during the impact period?

6.2 Currency substitution when money and goods demand depends on wealth

The models discussed in this chapter and in previous chapters neglect one aspect which is emphasized in modern consumer theory and monetary theory, namely that the demands for goods and money are less dependent on current income than on *permanent* income (see Model 6.3). The latter

Model 6.3
Currency substitution when money and goods demand depends on wealth

1 Goods market

1.1 Tradable goods

$Y^T = Y^T(E/P^N)$	$Y^T_{E/P^N} > 0$	domestic supply	(6.7)
$C^T = C^T(E/P^N, W)$	$C^T_{E/P^N} < 0, C^T_W > 0$	domestic demand	(6.8)
$M^* = Y^T - C^T$		trade balance	(6.9)

1.2 Nontradable goods

$Y^N = Y^N(E/P^N)$	$Y^N_{E/P^N} < 0$	domestic supply	(6.10)
$C^N = C^N(E/P^N, W)$	$C^N_{E/P^N} > 0, C^N_W > 0$	domestic demand	(6.11)
$Y^N = C^N$		equilibrium condition	(6.12)

2 Money market

$W = M' + M^*$		definition of wealth	(6.13)
$\frac{M'}{M^*} = L(\dot{e})$	$L_{\dot{e}} < 0$	wealth portfolio	(6.14)
$M' \equiv \frac{M}{E}$		definition	(6.15)

Notes: Lower-case letters are the natural logarithms of the respective variables. A dot indicates the derivative with respect to time. Subscripts indicate (partial) derivatives with respect to the given variable. Variables are defined as follows:

Y^T production of tradable goods in home country
C^T demand for tradable goods in home country
E exchange rate
P^N price of nontradable goods
M^* foreign money holdings of domestic residents
Y^N production of nontradable goods
C^N demand for nontradable goods
W domestic wealth (in foreign currency)
M domestic money supply
M' domestic money supply (in foreign currency)

variable may be approximated by wealth. If a key determinant of the demands for goods and for money is wealth, however, those solutions cannot possibly be of a long-run nature which comprise *current-account disequilibria*. This is because those disequilibria imply a permanent accumulation or decumulation of wealth. The model presented above is due to Calvo and Rodriguez (1977) and Frenkel and Rodriguez (1982). It focuses on the interaction between wealth and the exchange rate when currencies are perfect substitutes.

6.2.1 The money market

We begin the discussion of the model by looking at the monetary sector, which indeed is reduced to the **money market**. Since neither domestic nor foreign bonds exist, domestic residents have to hold their entire wealth W either in foreign money M^* or in domestic money M. Since M and M^* are denominated in different currencies, they do not simply add up to total wealth. Before we can do that, we must decide in which currency to express domestic wealth and then express both M and M^* in the same currency. Following Frenkel and Rodriguez (1982), W is measured in foreign currency. While this may appear strange, it is justified because foreign money is a substitute for domestic money by assumption. It simplifies the analysis because we can consider the foreign price level exogenous and constant. Then W represents a real claim on internationally traded goods.

Reflecting this assumption, domestic wealth expressed in foreign currency is computed according to equation (6.13), where $M' \equiv M/E$. Since domestic and foreign money are *imperfect* substitutes, domestic residents want to split their wealth into domestic and foreign money holdings in a specific way for a given set of exogenous variables. According to (6.14), this desired composition of wealth depends on expected depreciation, or, since we postulate perfect foresight, on actual depreciation. The faster the domestic currency depreciates, the smaller becomes the desired share of domestic currency of total wealth (see Figure 6.2), since domestic money becomes a more and more inferior means of storing wealth.

If portfolio adjustments to varying rates of depreciation are made instantly, the relationship depicted in Figure 6.2 holds at all points in time. Inverting the negative functional relationship between $\dot{e}$ and M'/M^* we may write

$$\dot{e} = \mathrm{l}(M'/M^*) \qquad \mathrm{l}_{M'/M^*} < 0 \tag{6.14'}$$

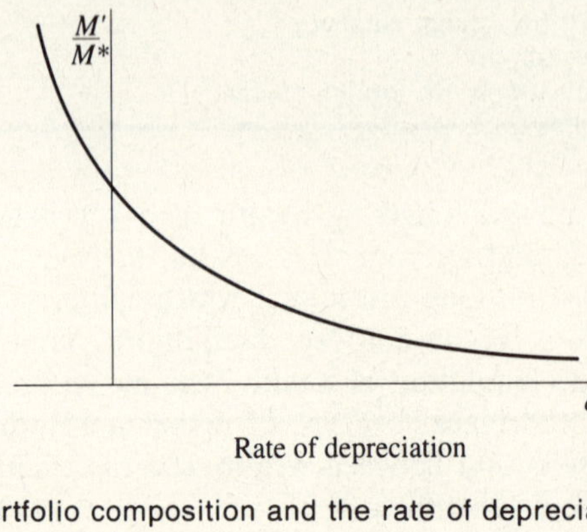

Figure 6.2 Portfolio composition and the rate of depreciation

6.2.2 The market for nontradables

Let us turn next to the domestic **market for nontradable goods**. For given factor endowments and production technology the *supply* of nontradable goods – which have to be produced at home – is determined by the relative price P^T/P^N. P^T and P^N are the prices for tradable and nontradable goods, respectively expressed in domestic currency. Since goods arbitrage prevents prices of tradable goods at home to deviate from prices for tradable goods abroad, we have $P^T = EP^{T*}$. After normalizing the price for tradable goods abroad, P^{T*}, to a value of 1, this condition becomes $P^T = E$. Thus the domestic currency price for tradable goods equals the exchange rate. This clarifies why the relative price between tradable and nontradable goods can be written as E/P^N, as we have done in (6.10). Now, if P^N increases relative to $E(=P^T)$, more nontradable goods are produced.

The *demand* for nontradable goods is also a function of the relative price, though it responds with the opposite sign. If nontradable goods become relatively more expensive, their consumption is reduced (equation (6.11)). In contrast to what we have postulated for supply, however, demand is also a function of wealth, reflecting the **permanent income hypothesis**. Without this assumption only *one* relative price exists which clears the market for nontradable goods. If the relative price E/P^N rises above this market clearing value, Y^N falls and C^N rises, which means that excess demand is increasing. With goods demand being dependent on wealth, this excess demand can only be compensated for by a reduction of wealth which reduces demand. This intuitively appealing **equilibrium condition** for the domestic market for nontradable goods is obtained formally by substituting (6.10) and (6.11) into (6.12). Since the conditions stated by the implicit function theorem hold, the resulting equation

$$Y^N(E/P^N) = C^N(E/P^N, W)$$

implies the functional relationship

$$E/P^N = f(W) \tag{6.16}$$

The implicit function rule, with which we have already become familiar in Chapter 1, determines the slope of (6.16) as

$$\frac{\mathrm{d}(E/P^N)}{\mathrm{d}W} = -\frac{-C^N_W}{Y^N_{E/P^N} - C^N_{E/P^N}} < 0 \tag{6.17}$$

6.2.3 The market for tradables

Equations (6.7) and (6.8) describe the supply of and demand for nontradable goods at home analogously to what we did in equations (6.10) and

(6.11) for nontradables. Of course, the derivatives with respect to the relative price E/P^N possess the reverse sign. An important difference between the market for tradable goods and the market for nontradable goods is that the former is an international market which does not have to be cleared *at home*. If the domestic production of tradable goods exceeds the domestic demand for tradable goods the difference can always be sold abroad at the world market price $P^T = E$. If domestic production falls short of domestic demand, the gap can be filled by imports.

The trade balance (6.9) reflects the monetary consequences of trade in goods. Since domestic residents neither give credit nor run into debt, and foreigners do not hold domestic money, balance of trade disequilibria must be financed in foreign currency. Thus trade imbalances directly affect foreign currency holdings of domestic residents. There is no other way to acquire foreign currency than by moving the balance of trade into a surplus.

6.2.4 Equilibria: graphical presentation

We begin by discussing the steady-state equilibria of our model. The discussion is based on the four quadrants of Figure 6.3. The north-west quadrant shows the two sectors comprising the goods market. *NG* is the

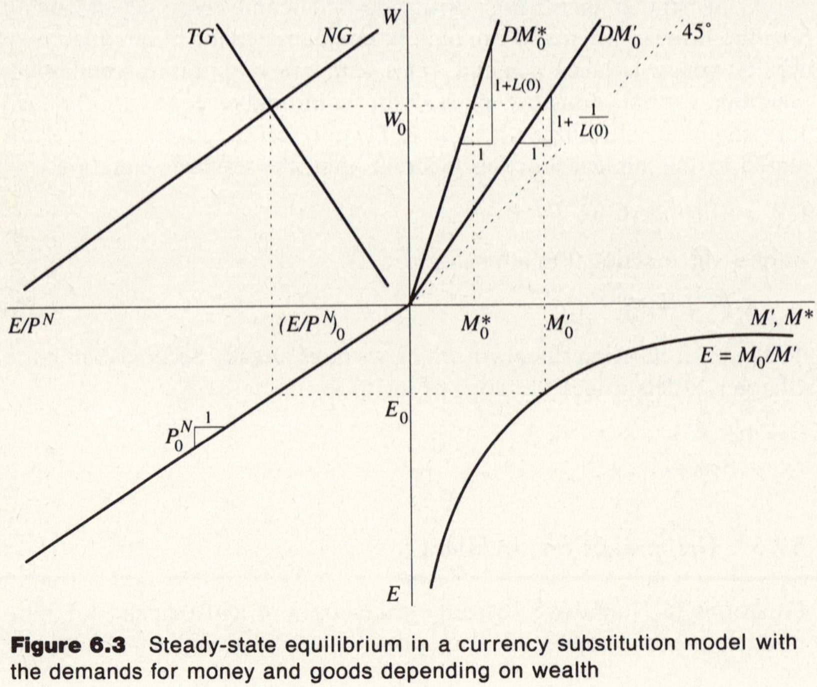

Figure 6.3 Steady-state equilibrium in a currency substitution model with the demands for money and goods depending on wealth

equilibrium condition for the domestic market for nontradable goods (equation (6.16)), which, according to (6.17), possesses a negative slope. Since prices are flexible by assumption we are *constantly* on NG.

Analogously, TG is the equilibrium condition for tradable goods. TG only holds in the long run. We obtain this condition by substituting (6.7) and (6.8) into (6.9) and letting $\dot{M}^*=0$, that is, requiring the balance of trade to be in equilibrium. Since the conditions stated by the implicit function theorem are met, the resulting relation implies the function

$$E/P^N = g(W) \tag{6.18}$$

which has a positive slope:

$$\frac{\partial(E/P^N)}{\partial W} = -\frac{-C_W^T}{Y_{E/P^N}^T - C_{E/P^N}^T} > 0 \tag{6.19}$$

Since (6.9) deliberately permits balance of trade disequilibria, these will be eliminated in the long run by appropriate market reactions.

The point of intersection between NG and TG determines the relative price $(E/P^N)_0$ and the level of wealth W_0, for which both sectors of the goods market are in equilibrium simultaneously. The north-east quadrant of Figure 6.3 shows which part of their nominal wealth domestic residents allot to foreign currency and how much to domestic currency in steady-equilibrium (that is, if $\dot{e}=0$). Letting $\dot{e}=0$ in (6.14), solving for M' and substituting the result into (6.13) yields

$$W = [1 + L(0)]M^* \tag{6.20}$$

Equation (6.20) describes domestic demand for foreign currency as function of wealth and as a function L of the rate of depreciation (which has been set equal to 0 in (6.20)). In Figure 6.4 this demand curve is denoted by DM_0^*. The point of intersection between this demand curve and the horizontal line through W_0 determines M_0^*. In a similar way we obtain

$$W = \left[1 + \frac{1}{L(0)}\right] M' \tag{6.21}$$

from (6.13) and (6.14), the demand for domestic currency (expressed in foreign currency). It is denoted by DM_0' in Figure 6.3 and serves to determine M_0'.

The south-east quadrant of Figure 6.3 makes use of the definition $M = E{\cdot}M'$ to determine the exchange rate E_0 for which the exogenous domestic money supply M_0 exactly corresponds to the foreign currency equivalent of domestic money, M_0', demanded in equilibrium. The hyperbola shown represents

$$E = \frac{M_0}{M'} \tag{6.22}$$

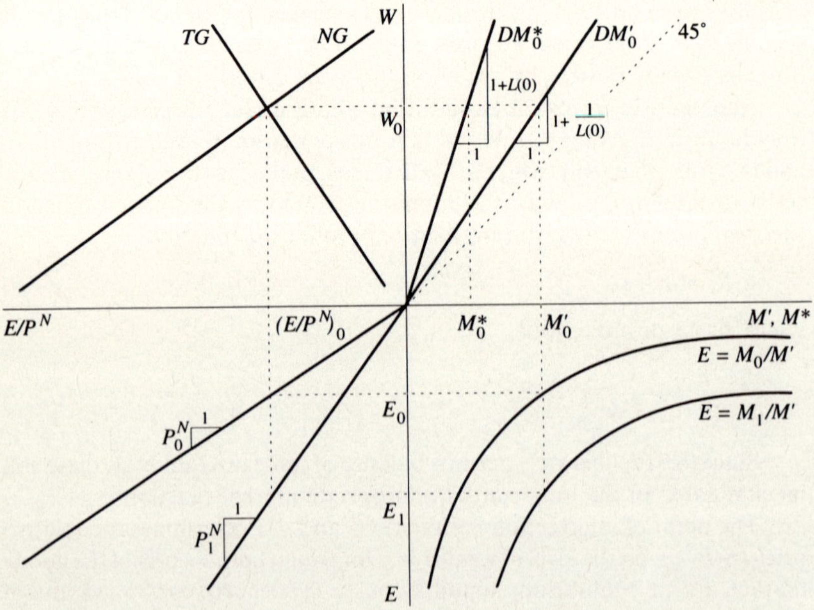

Figure 6.4 Comparative statics in a currency substitution model with the demands for money and goods depending on wealth

Finally, the south-west quadrant determines the price for nontradables which for a given nominal exchange rate E_0 produces the relative price $(E/P^N)_0 = E_0/P_0^N$ required for market clearing.

Consider Figure 6.4. An unexpected permanent increase of the money supply from M_0 to M_1 does not affect the goods market at all. Simultaneous equilibrium in both sectors still requires a relative price of $(E/P^N)_0$ and nominal wealth of W_0. Since in steady-state equilibrium we have $\dot{e} = 0$ as before the money supply increase, individuals hold the same amounts of foreign and domestic currency (expressed in foreign currency). Of course, M'_0, the desired amount of domestic money denominated in foreign currency, now must be made available at a domestic money supply which has increased from M_0 to M_1. Obviously, because of $M' = M/E$ this requires a depreciation. In technical terms this follows from the fact that the money supply increase shifts the south-east quadrant's hyperbola downwards. Now M' can only remain constant at M'_0 if the exchange rate rises from E_0 to E_1 *by the same percentage* as the money supply. In order to keep the relative price constant at $(E/P^N)_0$ as required by the goods market equilibrium condition, the price for nontraded goods also has to increase by the same percentage as the exchange rate (which is the price for tradables), so that finally $(E/P^N)_0 = E_1/P_1^N$.

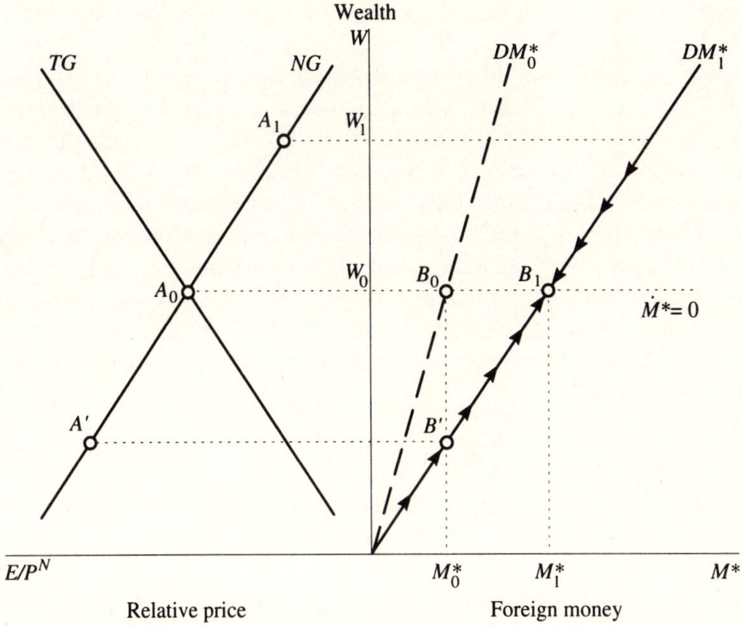

Figure 6.5 Consequences of an increase of money supply growth in a currency substitution model with the demands for money and goods depending on wealth

As an *intermediate result* we may note that our currency substitution model with nontradable goods possesses very conventional comparative static properties: the quantity theory of money holds just as purchasing-power parity does.

We now turn to an analysis of **inflationary equilibria** and their stability properties. Assume that our economy initially is in a static equilibrium with a constant money supply. Now the central bank begins to make the money supply grow at a constant rate.

Discussion

The following arguments may help to characterize the new inflationary equilibrium (see Figure 6.5).

1. Despite inflationary money growth the equilibrium level of domestic wealth remains at W_0. If the equilibrium level were higher, say at W_1, the economy would be in A_1 rather than in A_0, since the price for nontradables is perfectly flexible, leaving this market in permanent equilibrium. A_1 defines a trade balance in deficit. Therefore domestic holdings of foreign currency must begin to *fall*. This argument applies for all $W > W_0$ and, with

the opposite sign, for all $W < W_0$. Only $W = W_0$ equilibrates the balance of trade and renders $\dot{M}^* = 0$.

Now assume that in the situation of finite money growth $\dot{e}$ converges to a finite value in equilibrium,[2] then the demand curve for foreign money comes to rest at a fixed position (for example, DM_1^*) and the equilibrium point must be on this curve. For points north-east of B_1 on DM_1^* in Figure 6.5 we have $W > W_0$ and M^* falls because of the negative trade balance. *On* DM_1^*, however, this is only possible if we move downwards to the left, which at the same time decreases wealth. By analogous reasoning, it can be shown that from all points on DM_1^* south-west of B_1 we move in a north-easterly direction. Therefore, as soon as we have arrived at some constant rate of depreciation wealth converges to W_0, which equilibrates the trade balance.

2. If in inflationary equilibrium B_1 wealth W and foreign money holdings M^* are constant, so must M' be, because $W = M^* + M'$. Because $M' \equiv M/E$, this means that the exchange rate must rise at the same rate as the domestic money supply. Since DM_0^* was drawn for the case $\dot{e} = 0$, the new situation $\dot{e} = \dot{m} > 0$ must turn the demand for foreign money curve into a new, flatter position. This was anticipated in drawing Figure 6.5.

3. Just as before, goods market equilibrium is characterized by A_0, indicating the same relative price. This means that the price for non-tradables rises at the same speed as the exchange rate and just as fast as the money supply ($\dot{e} = \dot{p}^N = \dot{m}$).

4. We have shown that in equilibrium point B_1 we have $\dot{e} = \dot{m}$. Since in B_1 people hold *more* foreign money than in B_0 out of a constant level of wealth, they must hold *less* domestic money than in B_0. With this we see from $M_0/E_0 > M_1/E_1$ that during the transition process from B_0 to B_1 depreciation exceeds the money supply increase in percentage terms. This is the *magnification effect* introduced in Chapter 5. Again the reason for the observed *overreaction* of the exchange rate is that people reduce real balances during inflation. In Chapter 5 they implicitly had done so to the benefit of interest-bearing assets, here they do so to the benefit of foreign currency holdings.

6.2.5 Dynamics: graphical presentation

We proceed by describing the movement from B_0 to B_1 graphically. If B_1 is the new point of equilibrium, people hold too much domestic money (in real terms) and not enough foreign money when the money supply becomes more inflationary while they are still in B_0. We may get a picture of how the market responds in this situation by means of the following arguments.

Foreigners do not hold domestic money. Thus the initial domestic excess demand for M^* cannot be met by directly trading M for M^*. Foreign money can only be acquired by means of a balance of trade surplus. This requires time, however, and is not available in the short run. Domestic residents who possess too much domestic money and are in need of foreign money can only acquire foreign money from other domestic residents, paying with domestic money. Since this is what all domestic residents would like to do, there is an initial excess demand for M^*. The price at which people trade foreign money for domestic money, the exchange rate, begins to rise. With a rising exchange rate, however, domestic wealth and the demand for foreign currency fall. We can imagine that devaluation comes to a halt when we arrive at the temporary equilibrium in B'.

B' cannot be a long-run equilibrium point, since the goods market is in A'. With the balance of trade now being in surplus, domestic residents begin to accumulate foreign money. This leads to a slow movement, in the monetary sector along DM_1^* from B' to B_1, in the goods market from A' to A_0, until the economy eventually settles in the long-run equilibrium point B_1.

6.2.6 Formal analysis

This section backs the above informal description of the dynamic behaviour of our model by providing a formal analysis in the W/M^* diagram. Again we will draw on the familiar method of qualitatively analyzing the dynamic system by means of phase diagrams.

As a first step we have to determine the **demarcation lines**, that is, the graphical presentation of all points in which W and M^* do not change, respectively.

We have already derived the condition for constant foreign currency holdings verbally, based on the graphical presentation of the goods market above. The formal condition results after requiring the balance of trade to equal zero:

$$\dot{M}^* = 0 = Y^T - C^T \tag{6.9'}$$

subject to the condition that the market for nontradables must clear, that is:

$$E/P^N = f(W) \tag{6.16}$$

Substituting (6.7) and (6.8)

$$Y^T = Y^T(E/P^N) \tag{6.7}$$

$$C^T = C^T(E/P^N, W) \tag{6.8}$$

into (6.9′) and replacing the relative price E/P^N by the equilibrium condition (6.16) yields the first demarcation line:

$$\dot{M}^* = 0 = Y^T[f(W)] - C^T[f(W), W] \equiv h(W) \tag{6.23}$$

Since $\dot{M}^*$ depends on wealth only, it can only be zero for one particular level of wealth. Thus the demarcation line $\dot{M}^* = 0$ we are looking for is a horizontal line (see Figure 6.6). From

$$\frac{\partial \dot{M}^*}{\partial W} = Y_f^T f_W - C_f^T f_W - C_f^T < 0 \tag{6.24}$$

we can see that M^* falls in the area above the demarcation line and rises in the area below the demarcation line. This intertemporal movement of M^* is indicated by a set of directional arrows pointing to the left and to the right.

Trying to identify the second demarcation line $\dot{W} = 0$ is more complicated. Starting from the definition of wealth

$$W = M' + M^* \tag{6.13}$$

and differentiating with respect to time, we obtain

$$\dot{W} = \dot{M}' + \dot{M}^* \tag{6.25}$$

Substituting equation (6.23) for $\dot{M}^*$, we obtain

$$\dot{W} = \dot{M}' + h(W) \tag{6.26}$$

Because of $M' = M/E$, $\dot{M}'$ may be expressed as[3]

$$\dot{M}' \equiv M'(\dot{m} - \dot{e}) \tag{6.27}$$

Substitution of

$$\dot{e} = l(M'/M^*) \tag{6.14′}$$

into (6.27) and subsequent elimination of M' by making use of (6.13) gives

$$\dot{M}' = (W - M^*)\left[\dot{m} - l\left(\frac{W - M^*}{M^*}\right)\right] \tag{6.28}$$

By substituting (6.28) into (6.26) we finally obtain

$$\dot{W} = (W - M^*)\left[\dot{m} - l\left(\frac{W - M^*}{M^*}\right)\right] + h(W) \tag{6.29}$$

Equation (6.29) is a differential equation relating the two endogenous variables W and M^*, which are measured on the axes of the north-east quadrant in Figure 6.6.

The demarcation line $\dot{W} = 0$ results, though only in implicit form, after letting $\dot{W} = 0$ in (6.29):

$$\dot{W}=(W-M^*)\left[\dot{m}-l\left(\frac{W-M^*}{M^*}\right)\right]+h(W)=0=G(W,M^*) \tag{6.30}$$

According to the implicit function rule, the slope of the $\dot{W}=0$ curve is[4]

$$\frac{\partial W}{\partial M^*}=-\frac{G_{M^*}}{G_W}=\frac{\dot{m}+(W-M^*)l_{M^*}-l(W/M^*-1)}{\dot{m}-(W-M^*)l_W-l(W/M^*-1)+h'(W)} \tag{6.31}$$

and may either be positive or negative.

The intertemporal movement of W above and below the $\dot{W}=0$ curve is, after differentiating (6.30) with respect to W,

$$\frac{\partial \dot{W}}{\partial W}=\dot{m}-(W-M^*)l_W-l(W/M^*-1)+h'(W) \tag{6.32}$$

The sign of this derivative may also be positive or negative. We therefore have to distinguish two cases. We choose to discuss the case $\partial\dot{W}/\partial W>0$. This is the simpler one and the model has the same qualitative properties for the other case $\partial\dot{W}/\partial W<0$.[5]

Note that (6.32) equals the denominator of (6.31). Thus, by letting $\partial\dot{W}/\partial W>0$, we assume at the same time that the denominator of (6.31) is

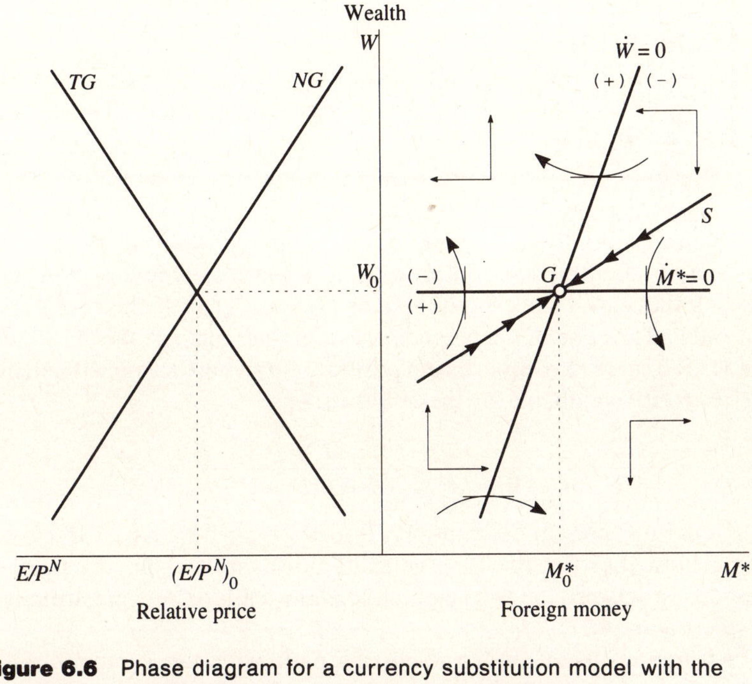

Figure 6.6 Phase diagram for a currency substitution model with the demands for money and goods depending on wealth

positive. The difference between the numerator and the denominator in (6.31) is, after dropping those terms which appear in both expressions,

$$(W-M^*)l_{M^*}+(W-M^*)l_w-h'(W)$$

Because of $W-M^*>0, l_{M^*}>0, l_W<0$ and $h'(W)<0$, a sufficient condition for the numerator in (6.31) to exceed the denominator is $l_{M^*}+l_W>0$. Applying the chain rule to $l(W/M^*-1)$ gives[6]

$$l_{M^*}+l_W=-l'W/M^{*2}+l'/M^*=\frac{l'}{M^*}\left(1-\frac{W}{M^*}\right)>0$$

So whenever the denominator in (6.31) is positive, which is the case since we assumed $\partial\dot{W}/\partial W>0$, the numerator is positive as well and the $\dot{W}=0$ curve has a positive slope. Figure 6.6 depicts this case. the vertical directional arrows indicate how domestic wealth changes in the four regions into which the phase space is divided by the two demarcation lines, for the case $\partial\dot{W}/\partial W>0$. The model displays saddle path stability, which is typical for models under perfect foresight. Only one pair of streamlines flow directly and consistently towards the equilibrium point G. From all other points which are not on S we move further and further away from G. This tendency is characterized by four curved streamlines.

PROBLEM 6.2

Make use of the phase diagram technique to analyze the dynamics of the present currency substitution model for the case $\partial\dot{W}/\partial W<0$.

The transition from one equilibrium to another may be described for the case of a central bank implementing a more inflationary monetary policy. If the central bank speeds up money supply growth, this rises $\dot{m}$, and thus only affects one of the two demarcation lines, namely the $\dot{W}=0$ line. The $\dot{M}^*=0$ curve remains in its old position. Applying the implicit function rule to (6.30), we obtain for the $\dot{W}=0$ curve

$$\frac{\partial W}{\partial\dot{m}}=-\frac{G_{M^*}}{G_W}=\frac{-(W-M^*)}{\dot{m}-(W-M^*)l_W-l(W/M^*-1)+h'(W)}$$

Under our present assumption $\partial\dot{W}/\partial W=G_W>0$ we have $\partial W/\partial\dot{m}<0$. This means, that the $\dot{W}=0$ curve shifts downwards. Thus the point of intersection between the two demarcation lines shifts to the right, from G to G_1 (see Figure 6.7).

Assume again that among all possible paths which are compatible with perfect foresight individuals choose the one which leads to equilibrium in

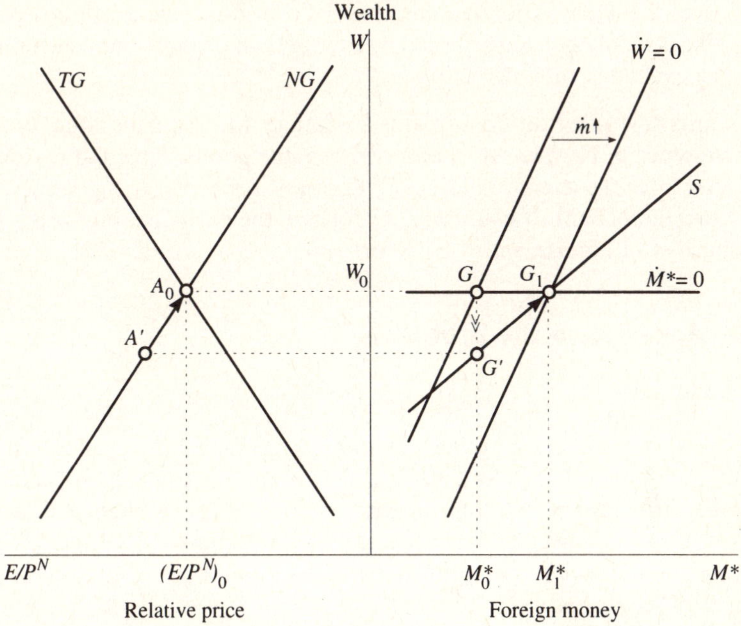

Figure 6.7 Consequences of an increase of the money supply growth rate in a currency substitution model with the demands for money and goods depending on wealth

the long run. Then the economy, after an initial jump of the exchange rate from G to G', converges along S to G_1.

6.3 Summary

The term *currency substitution* refers to a situation in which domestic residents hold both domestic and foreign currency. Key insights derived from currency substitution models of the exchange rate are the following:

1. In a more explicit way than its predecessors currency substitution models draw attention to the fact that unobserved preference changes may move the exchange rate.
2. Depending on expectations formation, the presence of currency substitution may enforce exchange rate phenomena such as overshooting or magnification, even if they have their roots elsewhere.
3. Currency substitution offers an explanation of its own for the magnification effect. As monetary policy adopts a more inflationary

pace, the share of foreign currency held in domestic portfolios rises. This can only be accomplished by a more than proportional reaction of the exchange rate and of prices.

4. Currency substitution explains exchange rate overshooting in the presence of flexible prices and nontradable goods. Here the reason is that foreign currency holdings by domestic residents change slowly via current account disequilibria. Therefore, the exchange rate bears the burden of adjustment in the short run.

6.4 Answers to the problems

Problem 6.1

We proceed from the simplified version of the Dornbusch model introduced in Chapter 2 (Model 2.1). In order to analyze the consequences of currency substitution for the impact reaction of the exchange rate we substitute the money demand function by equations (6.3) and (6.3a). Letting $\beta=0$, in order to simplify matters, the equilibrium condition for the monetary sector becomes

$$m+p=\phi y-\lambda\theta(\bar{e}-e)-\alpha\theta(\bar{e}-e)$$

Solving this for e, we obtain the exchange rate equation

$$e=\frac{m-p-\phi y}{\theta(\alpha+\lambda)}+\bar{e}$$

Keeping prices constant during the impact period, we obtain the impact reaction of the exchange rate to an unexpected money supply increase by differentiating with respect to m:

$$\frac{de}{dm}=1+\frac{1}{\theta(\alpha+\lambda)}$$

In this scenario currency substitution *reduces* overshooting tendencies and thus the volatility of the exchange rate. The reason for this is that the exchange rate must overshoot in the Dornbusch model in order to generate appreciation expectations which permit the domestic interest rate to fall below the foreign interest rate in order to raise the domestic money demand to the increased real money supply. Under currency substitution, appreciation expectations directly increase the demand for domestic money. Thus the contribution required from a lowering of the domestic interest rate becomes smaller. Since the interest rate does not have to fall as much as without currency substitution, the exchange rate also does not have to overshoot by the same amount.

Problem 6.2

Proceed from equation (6.31), which reads

$$\frac{\partial W}{\partial M^*} = -\frac{G_{M^*}}{G_W} = \frac{\dot{m} + (W - M^*)l_{M^*} - l(W/M^* - 1)}{\dot{m} - (W - M^*)l_W - l(W/M^* - 1) + h'(W)} \tag{6.31}$$

We have shown in the text, that $-G_{M^*} > G_W$ and that therefore $\partial W/\partial M^* > 0$ because $\partial \dot{W}/\partial W = G_W > 0$. If we now gradually reduce $\partial \dot{W}/\partial W$, we eventually arrive at a negatively sloped $\dot{W} = 0$ curve for $\partial \dot{W}/\partial W < 0$.

Figure 6.8 shows that this case displays the same sort of saddle path stability as did the case $\partial \dot{W}/\partial W > 0$.

As we have also demonstrated in the text, the direction into which the $\dot{W} = 0$ curve is shifted by an increase of the money supply growth rate,

$$\frac{\partial W}{\partial \dot{m}} = -\frac{G_{\dot{m}}}{G_W} = \frac{-(W - M^*)}{\dot{m} - (W - M^*)l_W - l(W/M^* - 1) + h'(W)}$$

directly depends on the sign of G_W. For $\partial \dot{W}/\partial W = G_w < 0$ we thus obtain $\partial W/\partial \dot{m} > 0$. Therefore, the equilibrium point shifts to the right on the $\dot{M}^* = 0$ curve, as it did under the alternative assumption $\partial \dot{W}/\partial W > 0$.

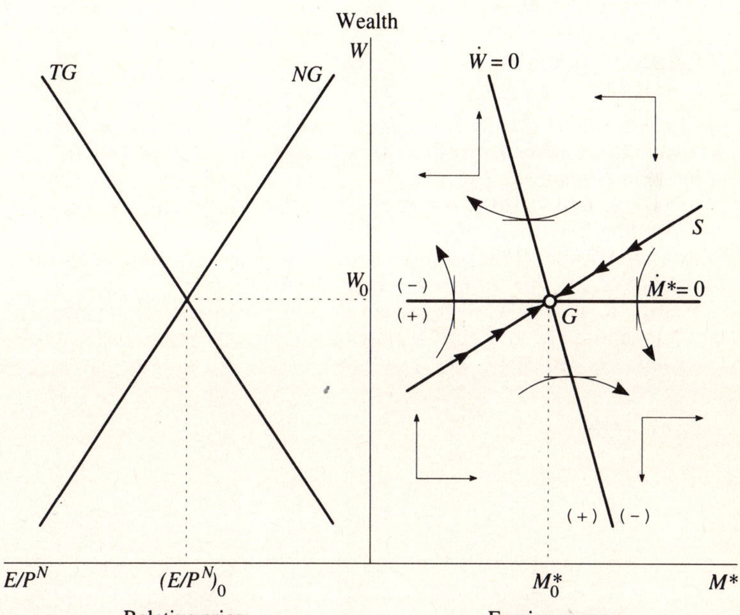

Figure 6.8 Phase diagram for a currency substitution model when $\partial W/\partial W < 0$

NOTES

1. The term *currency substitution* was introduced by Girton and Roper (1981) in the 1980s, though pertinent models had already been presented in the 1970s. Particularly well-known models are those by Kouri (1976) and Calvo and Rodriguez (1977). We will analyze the latter model below.
2. In principle, the case is feasible that $\dot{e}$ does not converge to a finite value after a change of the money growth rate. This case is hard to deal with verbally. We therefore return to this subject in the context of a formal analysis of the model below.
3. Differentiation of $M' = M/E$ with respect to time gives

$$\mathrm{d}M'/\mathrm{d}t = (l/E)\,\mathrm{d}M/\mathrm{d}t - (M/E^2)\,\mathrm{d}E/\mathrm{d}t$$

Dividing the left-hand side by M' and the right-hand side by M/E yields, after rearranging terms,

$$(\mathrm{d}M'/\mathrm{d}t)/M' = (\mathrm{d}M/\mathrm{d}t)/M - (\mathrm{d}E/\mathrm{d}t)/E$$

Multiplying both sides by M' gives equation (6.27).

4. l_{M^*} and l_W are the partial derivatives of $l(.)$ with respect to M^* and W.
5. A discussion of the case $\partial \dot{W}/\partial W < 0$ can be found at the end of this chapter as an answer to Problem 6.2.
6. l' is the derivative of $l(.)$ with respect to the entire expression given in parentheses. According to the chain rule, this has to be multiplied by the inner derivative with respect to the variable which changes.

REFERENCES

Calvo, Guillermo and Carlos A. Rodriguez (1977) 'A model of exchange rate determination under currency substitution and rational expectations', *Journal of Political Economy* 85, 261–78.

Frenkel, Jacob A. and Carlos Rodriguez (1982) 'Exchange rate dynamics and the overshooting hypothesis', *IMF Staff Papers* 29, 1–30.

Girton, L. and D. Roper (1981) 'Theory and implications of currency substitution', *Journal of Money, Credit and Banking* 13, 12–30.

Kouri, Penti J. K. (1976) 'The exchange rate and the balance of payments in the short run and in the long run: A monetary approach, *Scandinavian Journal of Economics* 78, 280–304.

Chapter 7

The portfolio balance approach

The introduction to Chapter 6 contained a stylized presentation of portfolio composition in the open economy. This presentation is repeated in Figure 7.1 in an effort to highlight the special assumptions underlying the portfolio balance approach to the exchange rate. This approach drops the key assumption of the previous chapter, namely that domestic and foreign money are perfect substitutes. Thus all money is being held in domestic currency, that is in M. Domestic and foreign interest-bearing assets, B and F respectively, are less than perfect substitutes, in particular because they carry different risk. Risk-averse individuals maximize utility by including both risk-free domestic bonds and risky foreign bonds in their portfolio. Of course, a necessary condition for the inclusion of foreign bonds is that their expected profit is higher than that of domestic bonds.

In this chapter, the demands for money, domestic bonds and foreign bonds will be modelled in an explicit fashion, then we will focus on the exchange rate effects resulting from the restrictions that each individual market must be in equilibrium permanently, and that total wealth equals the sum of assets demanded in the three markets. In a first step we work

		CHOICE OF CURRENCY	
		domestic currency	foreign currency
CHOICE OF ASSET	money	M	—
	bonds	B	F

Figure 7.1 Stylized portfolio choices in an open economy

with a **short-run model** in which wealth is exogenously given. In a second, **long-run model** we permit that changes of the real exchange rate produce current-account disequilibria. These must feed back to the exchange rate, since current-account deficits have to be financed by giving up domestic wealth, and current-account surpluses increase domestic wealth.

7.1 The model in the short run

The short-run portfolio balance approach to the exchange rate comprises the equations for the monetary sector of an open economy shown in Model 7.1.[1]

Model 7.1
Short-run portfolio balance approach

$W = M + B + EF$	wealth constraint	(7.1)
$M = m[i, i^* + E(\dot{e}), W]$	money market equilibrium	(7.2)
$m_i < 0; m_{i^*+E(\dot{e})} < 0; m_W > 0$		
$B = b[i, i^* + E(\dot{e}), W$	domestic bonds market	(7.3)
$b_i > 0; b_{i^*+E(\dot{e})} < 0; b_W > 0$	equilibrium	
$EF = f[i, i^* + E(\dot{e}), W]$	foreign bonds market equilibrium	(7.4)
$f_i < 0; f_{i^*+E(\dot{e})} > 0; f_W > 0$		

Notes: The signs of partial derivatives are given below behavioural equations. Variables are defined as follows:

M	domestic money supply	E	exchange rate
B	supply of domestic bonds	W	domestic wealth
F	supply of foreign bonds (in foreign currency) on the domestic market	i	interest rate
		i^*	foreign interest rate
		$E(\dot{e})$	expected depreciation

Equation (7.1) is the domestic wealth constraint. Equation (7.1) seems to suggest that in the *short run*, that is, with given wealth, domestic investors might acquire foreign bonds (F) by offering domestic bonds (B) or domestic money (M). Since we assume, however, that foreigners are prepared neither to hold domestic money nor to change their holdings of domestic bonds, the suggested substitution of wealth components is not really possible at the aggregate level. In the *long run*, however, foreign bonds may be accumulated via current-account surpluses.

Equation (7.2) postulates that the demand for money depends on wealth, and falls if expected yields of the two interest-bearing assets rise. Expected yields of domestic bonds equal the interest rate i. For foreign bonds they are equal to the sum of the foreign interest rate i^* and expected depreciation $E(\dot{e})$.

According to equation (7.3), the demand for domestic bonds also increases with wealth. If i rises, demand rises too. If returns expected for the competing foreign bonds increase, the demand for domestic bonds falls.

Since domestic and foreign bonds are considered substitutes by investors, equation (7.4) describes the demand for foreign bonds in a reciprocal way to the demand for domestic bonds described in (7.3). Some may be bothered by the assumption that the supply of foreign bonds in the home country cannot change in the short run. However, this assumption follows directly from the assumption that foreigners are interested in holding neither domestic money nor domestic bonds.

It deserves mention that the supply of foreign bonds in the home country is only fixed in foreign currency. The value of this physical supply in domestic currency, which must equal domestic demand, increases with the depreciation of the home currency. Thus a depreciation increases domestic wealth, since foreign bonds held by domestic residents increase in value.

7.1.1 Graphical presentation of the model

The equilibrium conditions for the three markets of the short-run portfolio balance approach may be represented graphically in a diagram with E and i on the axes. Again we proceed from the assumption of a small open economy with i^* being given exogenously. In order to simplify matters we further assume stationary exchange rate expectations $[E(\dot{e})=0]$. This permits us to concentrate on aspects which are typical for the portfolio balance approach.

The positively sloped curve in Figure 7.2 represents combinations of the exchange rate and the interest rate which clear the money market. Avoiding calculus, the positive slope may be justified as follows. Assume all markets are in equilibrium in A. If an increase in the interest rate moves us to the right to B, increased opportunity costs of holding money create an excess supply in the money market. At a given interest rate an additional demand for money could only result from a higher level of wealth. This, however, results from a devaluation of the domestic currency, that is, from an increase of the exchange rate. Thus the money market only remains in equilibrium if an increase in the interest rate is accompanied by an increase in the exchange rate.

By analogous reasoning we may demonstrate that the equilibrium condition for the market for domestic bonds BB is negatively sloped. Moving from A to B creates an excess demand for domestic bonds. In order to counterbalance this, wealth must fall.

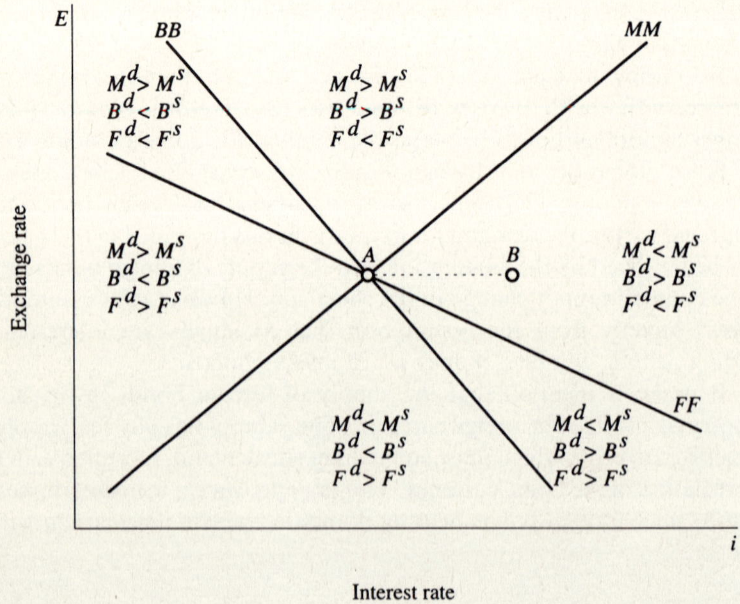

Figure 7.2 Equilibrium curves for the money market (*MM*) and the capital markets (*BB* and *FF*), and characterization of equilibria off the equilibrium curves

The argument regarding the FF curve, the equilibrium condition for the domestic market for foreign bonds, is more complicated. There is a temptation to argue analogously to the MM curve. Moving from *A* to *B* generates an excess supply, since a part of demand is redirected towards the substitute domestic bonds, which pay a higher interest rate. In contrast to the result obtained for the money market, this cannot be compensated for by a devaluation. While a devaluation would increase wealth and, therefore, the demand for foreign bonds, at the same time it would increase the *supply* of foreign bonds in the home country, expressed in domestic currency.

Table 7.1 explains this by means of a numerical example. Domestic wealth *W* equals £100 billion in period 1. Out of this £90 billion are being held in domestic assets (*M* and *B*), £10 billion in foreign assets (*F*).

Suppose now that all asset demands are homogenous in *W*, that is, *ceteris paribus*, all investors want to put constant shares of wealth into the three assets. In our example they desire to hold 10 per cent of wealth in foreign bonds. At an exchange rate of £2 per US dollar, in equilibrium foreign bonds to the amount of $5 billion are being held in period 1.

A devaluation of the exchange rate from £2 to £4 per dollar raises the

Table 7.1 Wealth portfolios and the exchange rate

Period	Wealth (in billion pounds sterling)						
	W	*M*+*B*	*EF* (actual)	*E* (£/$)	*F* (in $)	*EF* (desired)	*F* (desired)
1	100	90	10	2	5	10	5
2	110	90	20	4	5	11	2.75

pound value of domestically held foreign bonds and thus, for given M and B, raises wealth and also the demand for EF from £10 to £11. Expressed in dollars, however, the demanded value of foreign bonds declines from $5 to $2.75. Since the physical supply of F is constant in the short run at a value of $5 billion, a depreciation of the pound produces an excess supply of foreign bonds in the domestic market.

We may now make use of this result when depicting the FF curve in Figure 7.2. The decline in the demand for foreign bonds caused by the movement from A to B can only be neutralized by an appreciation. Therefore the FF curve has to have a negative slope, just like the BB curve. Which of the two curves is steeper depends on how strongly interest rate changes and exchange rate changes bear on demand in both markets. It is plausible to assume that interest rate changes rather bear on the demand for domestic bonds than on the demand for foreign bonds. On the other hand, exchange rate changes bear on the demand for foreign bonds rather than on the demand for domestic bonds. If this is true, the FF curve is flatter than the BB curve.[2]

PROBLEM 7.1

Show that the FF curve being steeper than the BB curve is a necessary condition for dynamic stability in the short-run portfolio balance approach. Proceed from the assumption that disequilibria in the market for domestic bonds give rise to interest rate changes, and disequilibria in the market for foreign bonds give rise to exchange rate changes.

An important property of our graphical model is that all three equilibrium curves always intersect at the same point. This follows from the wealth constraint. If two wealth components are being held exactly as desired, for example, money and domestic bonds, then the demand for the third component of wealth, here foreign bonds, must exactly equal given supply. This has the pleasant implication that it suffices to focus on two equilibrium curves when performing comparative static analyses. Work is facilitated if we always include the equilibrium curve which is not affected by the shock under consideration.

7.1.2 Comparative statics: graphical analysis

Let us start by clarifying how supply increases shift the equilibrium curves in each market. In doing this, we may draw on the relations between supply (characterized by the superscript s) and demand (characterized by the superscript d) given in the different sectors of Figure 7.2. Note that north-west of the MM curve there exists an excess demand for domestic money. Obviously, equilibrium in this area could only be obtained if the money supply were increased. Thus if the domestic money supply is increased, this shifts the equilibrium curve *MM* upwards and to the left (see Figure 7.3). By analogous reasoning it can be shown that increasing the supply of domestic bonds shifts the BB curve up to the right, and that an increase in the supply of foreign bonds in the home country shifts the FF curve down to the left.

We now turn to the analysis of the (short-run) comparative-static effects of a money supply increase. Figure 7.4 reveals that shifting the MM

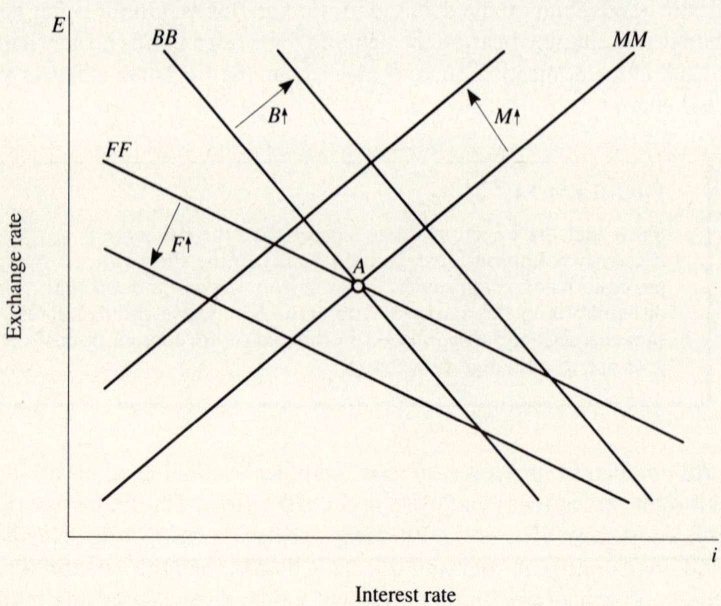

Figure 7.3 How an expansion of supply shifts equilibrium curves

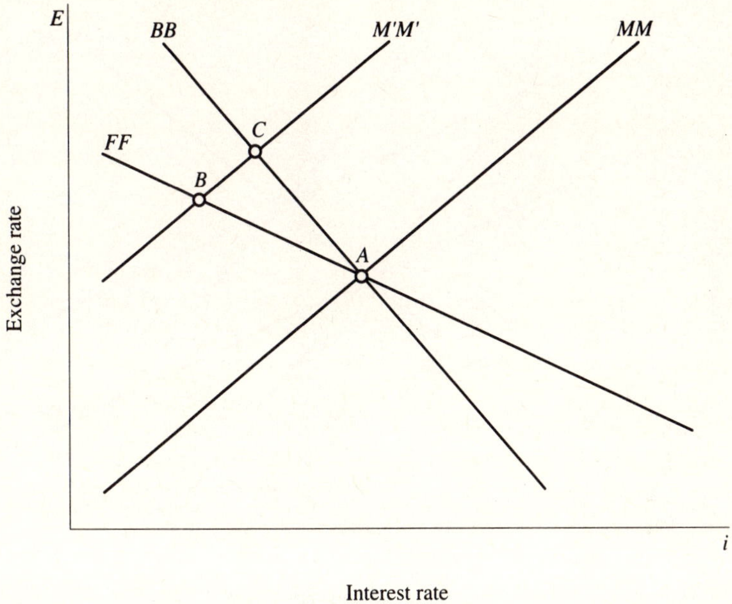

Figure 7.4 Interest rate and exchange rate effects of a money supply increase

curve to the north-west by raising the money supply leaves it open whether the economy moves from *A* to *B* or from *A* to *C*. An unambiguous result only obtains after we specify *how* the central bank has increased the money supply. *Creation of money by means of open-market operations* means that the central bank purchases domestic bonds with domestic money. Along with raising the domestic money supply, this simultaneously reduces the domestic bond supply. Thus not only the MM curve shifts upwards from *MM* to *M'M'*, but the BB curve shifts downwards at the same time. Since the physical supply of foreign bonds on the domestic market has not been affected, the FF curve rests in its old position. The new BB curve must intersect *M'M' on the FF curve*, that is, in *B*.

Creation of money by intervening in the foreign exchanges implies that the central bank buys foreign bonds with domestic money. This leaves the BB curve unchanged. The increase of the money supply and the concomitant reduction of the foreign bonds supply shift both the MM and the FF curve upwards, where they intersect on *BB* in *C*.

A key message of the portfolio balance approach is that the exchange rate not only depends on the aggregate money supply but also on the *composition* of domestic money as given in the central bank balance sheet. Increasing the money supply by foreign exchange market intervention (by

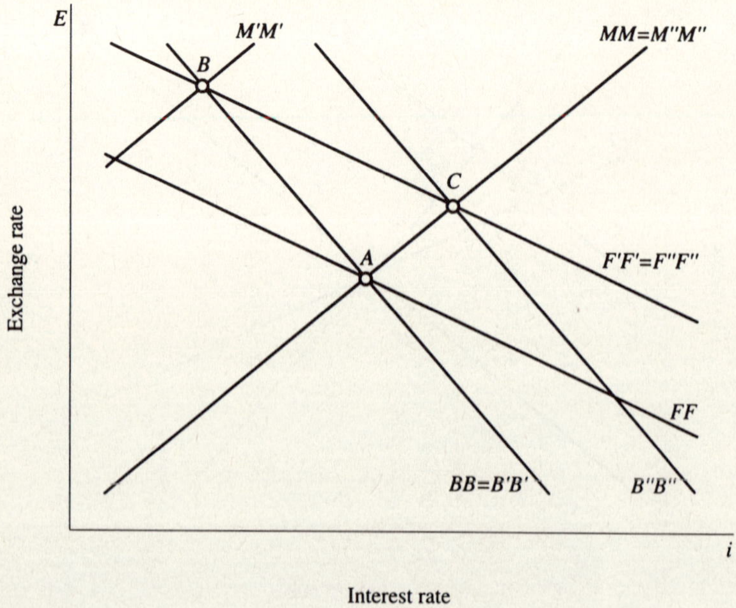

Figure 7.5 Interest rate and exchange rate effects of sterilized intervention in the foreign exchanges

buying foreign bonds) produces a more pronounced depreciation than a money supply increase by means of open-market operations (buying domestic bonds). This creates opportunities for the central bank which do not exist if domestic and foreign bonds are perfect substitutes. The portfolio balance approach permits manipulation of the exchange rate by means of sterilized intervention in the foreign exchanges, without creating inflation. For example, if the central bank goes for a depreciation of the domestic currency, it can purchase foreign bonds, thus shifting the FF curve to the north-east in Figure 7.5. In order to remove the added money supply (that is, sterilize), the central bank may now sell domestic bonds until the money supply is down to its initial level. This shifts the BB curve to the north-east. Since the MM curve stays put, the FF curve and the BB curve intersect on the MM curve at a higher exchange rate and a higher interest rate (Figure 7.5).

When analyzing the exchange rate and interest rate responses to a fiscal expansion we again have to distinguish two cases. This is due to the fact that a government budget deficit can be financed in two ways.

Assume *the budget deficit is financed by issuing debt to the private sector*. This raises the volume of domestic bonds and domestic wealth by the same amount.[3] *A* in Figure 7.6 would now reflect an excess supply of domestic

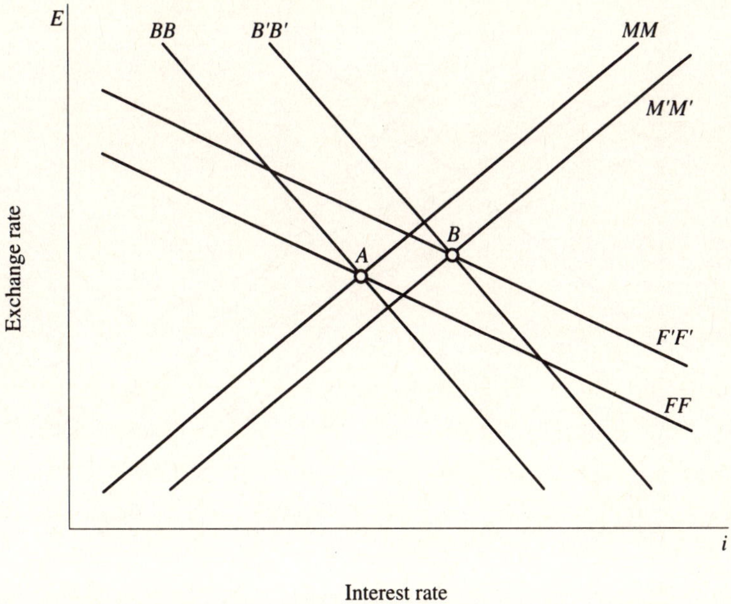

Figure 7.6 Interest rate and exchange rate effects of expansionary fiscal policy financed by issuing debt to the public

bonds, but excess demands for money and foreign bonds. In order to stimulate the demand for domestic bonds, interest rates must rise. Thus the BB curve moves to the right. In order to dampen the demand for foreign bonds, the domestic interest rate must rise. Thus the FF curve shifts to the right as well. Finally, this holds for the money market equilibrium schedule *MM*, since the existing excess demand for money can only be reduced by higher opportunity costs for holding money, that is, higher interest rates. All we can say without being more specific is that the new point of equilibrium must be to the right of *A*. Thus fiscal stimulation financed by issuing debt to the domestic private sector in any case raises interest rates, but may cause the domestic currency to appreciate or to depreciate.

Unambiguous effects are observed when *the government borrows from the central bank to finance its deficit* (Figure 7.7). In this case of **money financing** both *M* and *W* increase in the amount of the deficit. Since the supply of neither domestic bonds nor foreign bonds is increased, point *A* must now characterize the situation of excess demand in the markets for domestic and for foreign bonds. For a given exchange rate excess demand for domestic bonds can only be reduced if the interest rate drops and, thus, the BB curve shifts down to the left. In the market for foreign bonds, demand is reduced if the interest rate rises, that is, if the FF curve moves to

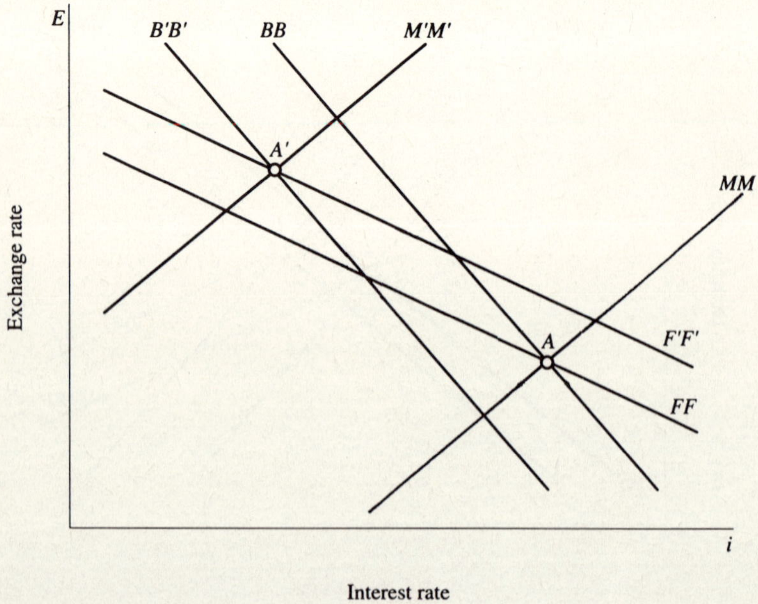

Figure 7.7 Interest rate and exchange rate effects of expansionary fiscal policy financed by printing money

the right. The simultaneous new equilibrium in both markets (and, therefore, in the money market as well!) obtains in *A'*, at a higher exchange rate and lower interest rate.

Our current assumption of a constant supply of foreign bonds on the domestic market calls for the current account to be in equilibrium during the period under consideration. Under a *current-account surplus* both the domestic supply of foreign bonds (expressed in foreign currency) and (for a given exchange rate) domestic wealth rise. Our initial equilibrium point *A* (see Figure 7.8) now reflects an excess supply of foreign bonds and an excess demand for domestic bonds and domestic money. Obviously, a change of the interest rate alone cannot possibly equilibrate both markets at the same time, since the interest rate would have to rise in order to equilibrate the money market, and would have to fall in order to equilibrate the market for domestic bonds. Since both cannot possibly occur at the same time, and since we have an excess supply of foreign assets and an excess demand for domestic assets in *A*, the exchange rate begins to fall. Thus foreign bonds lose value. Wealth falls and thus the demand for all three categories of assets. Since the supply of foreign bonds falls at an even faster rate than demand, the falling exchange rate reduces disequilibrium in all three markets.

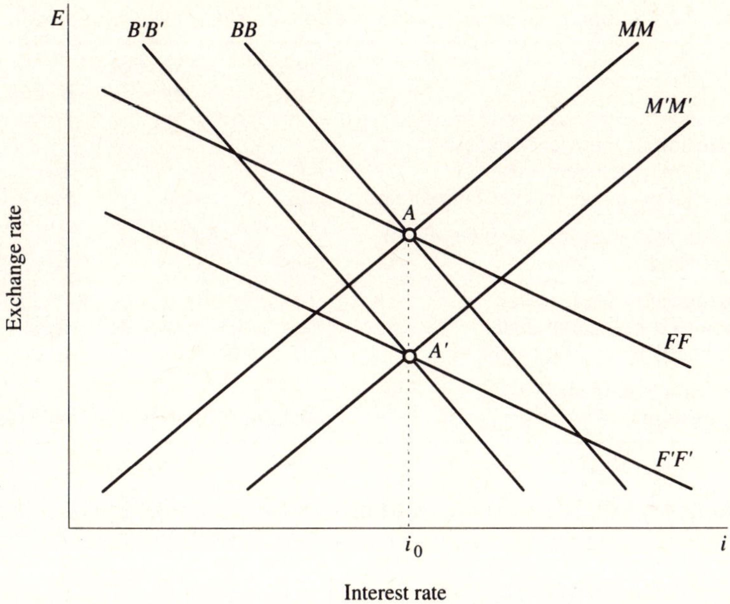

Figure 7.8 Interest and exchange rate reactions to a current account surplus

In order to establish a new general equilibrium, the exchange rate must fall to where the new BB curve and the new MM curve intersect. If this point of intersection produced an interest rate higher than i_0, wealth would have to be higher than in A in order to equilibrate the money market. It would have to be lower, however, in order to equilibrate the market for domestic bonds. Since these two equilibrium requirements are incompatible, $B'B'$ and $M'M'$ must intersect at the old interest rate. At the old interest rate i_0, however, general equilibrium is only possible if wealth is the same as in A. This is the case if the appreciation exactly eats up the increase in F produced by the current-account surplus, so that EF remains constant. Thus any imbalance of the current account leaves the interest rate and domestic wealth unchanged. However, it triggers an exchange rate reaction, which normally (that is, if the Marshall–Lerner condition holds) induces a reduction of the prevailing disequilibrium. Table 7.2 summarizes the comparative-static effects described in the previous sections.

7.1.3 Formal analysis of the model

Equations (7.2), (7.3) and (7.4) are equilibrium conditions for the three markets under consideration. The slope of each equilibrium condition is

Table 7.2 Summary of short-run effects of the portfolio balance approach

	Interest rate	*Exchange rate*	*Wealth*
Expansionary monetary policy			
open-market operations	falls	rises	rises
foreign exchange market intervention	falls	rises	rises
Foreign exchange market intervention			
sterilized	rises	rises	rises
Expansionary fiscal policy			
financed by issuing debt	rises	rises/falls	rises
financed by creating money	falls	rises	rises
Current-account surplus			
exogenous	unchanged	falls	unchanged

obtained by applying the implicit function rule. We start by rewriting the equilibrium conditions, making use of the wealth definition (7.1):

$$m[i, i^* + E(\dot{e}), M + B + EF] - M \equiv \Phi[i, i^* + E(\dot{e}), M + B + EF, M] = 0 \tag{7.2'}$$

$$b[i, i^* + E(\dot{e}), M + B + EF] - B \equiv \Psi[i, i^* + E(\dot{e}), M + B + EF, B] = 0 \tag{7.3'}$$

$$f[i, i^* + E(\dot{e}), M + B + EF] - EF \equiv \Omega[i, i^* + E(\dot{e}), M + B + EF, EF] = 0 \tag{7.4'}$$

Since $\Phi_E = m_W F$ is positive by assumption, (7.2′) postulates that the exchange rate is an implicit function of the interest rate i. Applying the implicit function rule, the *slope of the MM curve* turns out to be

$$\frac{\partial E}{\partial i} = \frac{-\Phi_i}{\Phi_E} = \frac{-m_i}{m_w F} > 0 \tag{7.5}$$

Analogously the *slope of the BB curve* is obtained from (7.3′):

$$\frac{\partial E}{\partial i} = \frac{-\Psi_i}{\Psi_E} = \frac{-b_i}{b_W F} < 0 \tag{7.6}$$

The *slope of the FF curve* is negative as well and is obtained from (7.4′):

$$\frac{\partial E}{\partial i} = \frac{-\Omega_i}{\Omega_E} = \frac{f_i}{(1 - f_w)F} < 0 \tag{7.7}$$

It has been argued above – and the answer to Problem 7.1 demonstrates this formally – that our present portfolio balance model is dynamically stable only if the BB curve is steeper than the FF curve. A comparison between (7.6) and (7.7) becomes possible if we work out the relationships between b_i and f_i, and between b_w and f_w.

We begin by substituting (7.2)–(7.4) into (7.1):

$$W = m[i, i^* + E(\dot{e}), W] + b[i, i^* + E(\dot{e}), W] + f[i, i^* + E(\dot{e}), W] \qquad (7.8)$$

All that equation (7.8) says is that actual wealth equals the sum of all demanded wealth components. Differentiating (7.8) with respect to W yields

$$\mathrm{d}W(1 - m_W - b_W - f_W) = 0 \qquad (7.9)$$

Following a wealth increase, the product on the left-hand side can only be zero if the expression given in parentheses is zero. This requires

$$m_W + b_W + f_W = 1 \qquad (7.10)$$

Equation (7.10) may be rewritten as $1 - f_W = m_W + b_W$. Because of $m_W > 0$, this implies

$$1 - f_W > b_W \qquad (7.11)$$

Equation (7.11) says that the denominator in (7.7) is larger than the denominator in (7.6).

Differentiation of (7.8) with respect to the interest rate yields

$$m_i + b_i + f_i = 0 \qquad (7.12)$$

Rewriting (7.12) as $-b_i = m_i + f_i$ and noting $m_i < 0$ gives

$$-b_i < f_i < 0 \qquad (7.13)$$

Equations (7.11) and (7.13) state *sufficient conditions* for

$$\frac{-b_i}{b_W F} < \frac{f_i}{(1 - f_W)F}$$

This means that, given the assumptions employed here, the BB curve is steeper than the FF curve. Hence, the model analyzed here is dynamically stable.

At the beginning of the graphical analysis of the model above it was emphasized that the model is overdetermined, in the sense that equilibrium values for three endogenous variables (i, W and E) are determined by means of four equations. According to **Walras' law**, given a budget restriction, only $n-1$ out of n markets are independent in general equilibrium. So we have one equilibrium condition too many, since it is implied by the two other equilibrium conditions and the budget constraint.

It is at our discretion which of the three markets we exclude. In what follows we only consider the markets for domestic and foreign bonds explicitly. This reduces the model to the following three equations:

$$b(i, W) = \mathrm{B} \tag{7.14}$$

$$f(i, W) = EF \tag{7.15}$$

$$W - b(i, W) - f(i, W) = M \tag{7.16}$$

Equation (7.16) is the money market equilibrium condition which results from the other two equilibrium conditions (7.14) and (7.15) and obeying the wealth constraint. In order to simplify the subsequent comparative-static analysis, expected yields of foreign bonds $[i^* + E(\dot{e})]$ are assumed constant and, in order to render a more compact notation, equal to zero.

The comparative-static effects of various policy measures are obtained after complete differentiation of equations (7.14)–(7.16). This produces the following system of equations:

$$b_i \mathrm{d}i + b_W \mathrm{d}W = \mathrm{d}B \tag{7.14'}$$

$$f_i \mathrm{d}i + f_W \mathrm{d}W - F\mathrm{d}E = E\mathrm{d}F \tag{7.15'}$$

$$-(b_i + f_i)\mathrm{d}i + (1 - b_W - f_W)\mathrm{d}W = \mathrm{d}M \tag{7.16'}$$

In matrix notation this system of linear equations may be expressed in the general form $Ax = d$. A is the coefficient matrix, which in the present case represents partial derivatives, x is the vector of changes of the endogenous variables and d is the vector of changes of the exogenous variables. Thus the system of equations reads

$$\begin{bmatrix} b_i & b_W & 0 \\ f_i & f_W & -F \\ -b_i - f_i & 1 - b_W - f_W & 0 \end{bmatrix} \begin{bmatrix} \mathrm{d}i \\ \mathrm{d}W \\ \mathrm{d}E \end{bmatrix} = \begin{bmatrix} \mathrm{d}B \\ E\mathrm{d}F \\ \mathrm{d}M \end{bmatrix} \tag{7.17}$$

Since we are interested in how the interest rate, wealth and the exchange rate respond to particular changes of the exogenous variables, we have to solve (7.17) for x, the vector of changes of the endogenous variables. That means we are looking for (see Chiang 1984: Chs 5, 6, 7 and esp. Ch. 8)

$$x = A^{-1}d = \frac{1}{|A|}\,\mathrm{adj}\,A\,d$$

where A^{-1} is the inverted coefficient matrix. A^{-1} is found by computing the adjoint matrix of A and dividing this by the determinant of A. After simplifying the presentation by making use of $m_W = 1 - b_W - f_W$ (from equation (7.10)) and $m_i = -b_i - f_i$ (from equation (7.12)) the solution vector for our system of equations reads

$$\begin{bmatrix} \mathrm{d}i \\ \mathrm{d}W \\ \mathrm{d}E \end{bmatrix} = \frac{1}{|A|} \begin{bmatrix} m_W F & 0 & -b_W F \\ -m_i F & 0 & b_i F \\ m_W f_i - m_i f_W & b_W m_i - b_i m_W & b_i f_W - b_W f_i \end{bmatrix} \begin{bmatrix} \mathrm{d}B \\ E\mathrm{d}F \\ \mathrm{d}M \end{bmatrix} \tag{7.18}$$

where $|A|=F(b_i m_W - b_W m_i)$. Equation (7.18) shows the reaction of each endogenous variable to changes of individual or groups of exogenous variables. For example, an analysis of the short-run consequences of cancelling third-world debt would require $dB=dM=0$ in the vector of changes of the exogenous variables. Thus only dF would have to remain in that vector with an appropriate negative value. We now turn to a formal analysis of the policy measures and shocks which we have already analyzed graphically above.

Creating money by open-market purchases

Creating money by purchasing domestic bonds from the public reduces the supply of domestic bonds by the same amount by which the domestic money supply increases. The supply of foreign bonds remains unaffected. Thus the transposed vector of exogenous changes is $d^T=(-dM, 0, dM)$.

Multiplying the inverted coefficient matrix A^{-1} by d yields the following reactions of the interest rate, of wealth and of the exchange rate, respectively:

$$\frac{di}{dM}=\frac{-F(m_W+b_W)}{|A|}<0$$

$$\frac{dW}{dM}=\frac{F(m_i+b_i)}{|A|}>0$$

$$\frac{dE}{dM}=\frac{-f_i(m_W+b_W)+f_W(m_i+b_i)}{|A|}>0$$

In qualitative terms the effects derived analytically are the same as those obtained from our graphical analysis above. When evaluating signs, note that $|A|=F(b_i m_W - b_W m_i)>0$ and $b_i>-m_i$ (from equation (7.12)).

Creating money by intervening in the foreign exchanges

Creating money by buying foreign bonds raises the supply of foreign bonds in the domestic market by the same amount by which the domestic money supply is increased. The supply of domestic bonds remains unchanged. We thus obtain $d^T=(0, -dM, dM)$ and arrive at the following results:

$$\frac{di}{dM}=\frac{Fb_W}{|A|}<0$$

$$\frac{dW}{dM}=\frac{Fb_i}{|A|}>0$$

$$\frac{dE}{dM}=\frac{b_i(m_W+f_W)-b_W(m_i+f_i)}{|A|}>0$$

Creating money by intervening in the foreign exchanges has the same qualitative effects on the endogenous variables as creating money by open-market operations. However, in the former case the exchange rate effect is stronger and the interest rate effect is weaker.

Sterilized foreign exchange market intervention

When intervention in the foreign exchanges is sterilized, the change in the domestic money supply which results from buying foreign bonds is neutralized by selling domestic bonds in the same amount. In this case the vector of changes of the exogenous variables is $d^T = (\mathrm{d}B, -\mathrm{d}B, 0)$. Multiplying the inverted coefficient matrix by d yields

$$\frac{\mathrm{d}i}{\mathrm{d}B} = \frac{-Fm_i}{|A|} > 0$$

$$\frac{\mathrm{d}W}{\mathrm{d}B} = \frac{Fm_i}{|A|} > 0$$

$$\frac{\mathrm{d}E}{\mathrm{d}B} = \frac{m_W(b_i + f_i) - m_i(b_W + f_W)}{|A|} > 0$$

Substitution between domestic and foreign bonds affects relative prices, that is, the interest rate and the exchange rate, since domestic and foreign bonds are not perfect substitutes. What is more, the appreciation generates an increase in wealth.

We now turn to an analysis of fiscal policy measures. Excess spending by the government may be financed either by issuing debt or by printing money.

Expansionary fiscal policy: debt financing

Deficit spending which is financed by issuing domestic bonds only affects the supply of domestic bonds. Thus $d^T = (\mathrm{d}B, 0, 0)$, and the multipliers for the three endogenous variables are

$$\frac{\mathrm{d}i}{\mathrm{d}B} = \frac{Fm_W}{|A|} > 0$$

$$\frac{\mathrm{d}W}{\mathrm{d}B} = \frac{-Fm_i}{|A|} > 0$$

$$\frac{\mathrm{d}E}{\mathrm{d}B} = \frac{m_W f_i - m_i f_W}{|A|} \gtreqless 0$$

The interest rate and wealth respond in exactly the same way as they did after sterilized intervention in the foreign exchanges. Now, however, the composition of wealth is different, since this time the wealth increase results from an additional supply of domestic bonds and not from an increased value of foreign bonds. The exchange rate effect is ambiguous.

Expansionary fiscal policy: money financing

Financing deficit spending by printing money only affects the domestic money supply: $d^T = (0, 0, \mathrm{d}M)$. In this case the multipliers are

$$\frac{\mathrm{d}i}{\mathrm{d}M} = \frac{-Fb_W}{|A|} < 0$$

$$\frac{\mathrm{d}W}{\mathrm{d}M} = \frac{Fb_i}{|A|} > 0$$

$$\frac{\mathrm{d}E}{\mathrm{d}M} = \frac{b_i f_W - b_W f_i}{|A|} > 0$$

The money supply increase drives down interest rates, raises wealth and depreciates the domestic currency.

A current-account surplus

A current-account surplus does not affect the money supply and the supply of foreign bonds. However, it raises the supply of foreign bonds in the domestic market. Therefore, we proceed from $d^T = (0, E\mathrm{d}F, 0)$ and compute the following multipliers:

$$\frac{\mathrm{d}i}{E\mathrm{d}F} = 0$$

$$\frac{\mathrm{d}W}{E\mathrm{d}F} = 0$$

$$\frac{\mathrm{d}E}{E\mathrm{d}F} = \frac{b_W m_i - b_i m_W}{|A|} < 0$$

Neither the interest rate nor wealth respond to a current-account surplus in the short run. The exchange rate falls. Expanding the third equation by $\mathrm{d}F$ and writing out $|A|$ in full shows by just how much the exchange rate falls:

$$\frac{\mathrm{d}E}{E} = \frac{-\mathrm{d}F(b_i m_W - b_W m_i)}{F(b_i m_W - b_W m_i)} = \frac{-\mathrm{d}F}{F}$$

The exchange rate appreciates by exactly the same percentage as that by which the current account surplus raises the domestic supply of foreign bonds, expressed in foreign currency. Thus the supply of foreign bonds expressed in domestic currency, EF, remains unchanged. Of course, this also follows from $\mathrm{d}W/E\mathrm{d}F = 0$.

More than anything else the comparative-static analysis of a current-account surplus reveals that the short-run perspective employed so far ignores interesting medium- and long-run consequences. For one thing, current-account disequilibria do not occur out of nowhere, but, among other things, reflect changes in relative prices. Thus our result that a current-account disequilibrium affects the exchange rate and, hence, relative prices, cannot be the end of the story. Rather, the exchange rate change must feed back to the current account. This gives rise to dynamic interactions, which are interesting enough to call for an analysis within a model with a long-run perspective.

7.2 The medium and long run

Model 7.2 below models the determinants of the current account and, hence, the goods market, in an attempt to endogenize the supply of foreign bonds in the domestic market.[4]

Model 7.2
Portfolio balance model beyond the short run

1 Monetary sector			
$W = M + B + EF$		wealth constraint	(7.19)
$M = m(i, W)$	$m_i < 0; m_w > 0$	money market	(7.20)
$B = b(i, W)$	$b_i > 0; b_w > 0$	domestic bonds market	(7.21)
$EF = f(i, W)$	$f_i < 0; f_w > 0$	foreign bonds market	(7.22)
2 Goods market			
$Y = C + I + NX$		equilibrium condition	(7.23)
$C = C(W/P)$	$C' > 0$	consumption	(7.24)
$NX = NX(E/P)$	$NX' > 0$	net exports	(7.25)
3 Balance of payments			
$BP = 0 = P \cdot NX/E + i^*F - T - \dot{F}$		balance of payments	(7.26)

Notes: Dots over variables denote derivatives with respect to time. Variables are defined as follows:

M	domestic money supply	E	exchange rate
B	supply of domestic bonds	W	domestic wealth
F	supply of foreign bonds	i	interest rate
Y	full-employment income	i^*	foreign interest rate
P	price level	NX	net exports (real, in domestic goods' equivalents)
C	consumption		
I	investment	BP	balance of payments (in foreign currency)
T	transfers abroad (in foreign currency)		

The monetary sector is identical to the short-run portfolio balance approach analyzed above. For notational convenience expected yields on foreign bonds are set equal to zero in equations (7.20)–(7.22).

Equilibrium in the goods market is defined by equation (7.23). Goods market equilibrium obtains permanently, since prices are perfectly flexible. Equation (7.24) says that consumption is a function of real wealth. According to (7.25) net exports rise when the real exchange rate rises. This implies the assumption that the Marshall–Lerner condition holds at all times, which excludes the possibility of a short-run perverse effect as suggested by the J-curve hypothesis.

Equation (7.26) notes that under flexible exchange rates the balance of payments is by definition in equilibrium . Thus the current account $(P{\cdot}NX/E+i^*F-T)$ and the capital account $(\dot{F})$ must add up to zero.[5] In a stationary equilibrium, that is, with the money supply and government debt being given, the amount of foreign bonds held by domestic residents must remain constant. In long-run equilibrium we therefore have $\dot{F}=0$, which implies $P{\cdot}NX/E=T-i^*F$ because of (7.26). The current account must balance: in other words, it must be in equilibrium.

7.2.1 Graphical analysis

The model outlined puts us in a position to analyze how policy measures or shocks feed back on to asset markets via the current account and capital account. Here we settle for an analysis of the long-run implication of the portfolio balance approach that results from a money supply increase due to open-market purchases.

The central building blocks of the model are depicted in Figure 7.9. The right-hand quadrant contains the familiar presentation of the asset markets. The left-hand quadrant shows net exports $NX(E/P)$ depending on the nominal exchange rate E. The lowest NX curve is drawn for a constant price level P_0. As the domestic price level increases, the NX curve shifts upwards.

Initially, let the economy be in a long-run equilibrium characterized by points A_0 and B_0, with the merchandize trade balance being in equilibrium. This implies i^*F equals T, that is, that invisible trade (services) and unilateral transfers balance. Wealth W is constant, since $\dot{F}$ equals zero.

Now the central bank expands the money supply by buying domestic bonds. The short-run reaction to this has already been analyzed above, both graphically and analytically. The excess supply of money and the excess demand for domestic bonds drive the interest rate down. This stimulates the demand for foreign bonds and causes the exchange rate to rise, until all asset markets clear at the new short-run equilibrium point A'.

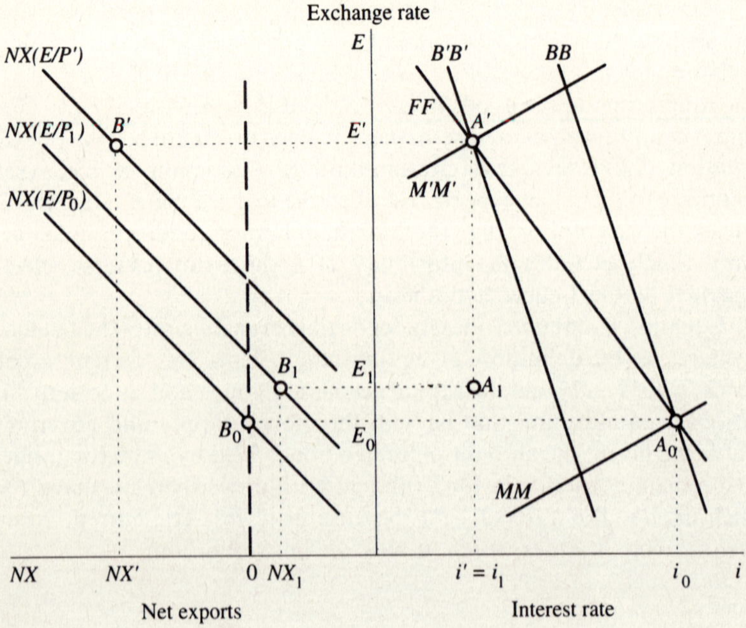

Figure 7.9 Short-, medium- and long-run consequences of a money-supply increase through open-market purchases in the portfolio balance approach

Initially, before prices have time to respond, the higher exchange rate E' has two consequences: (1) net exports are higher because of the implied real depreciation; (2) consumption demand is also higher due to the higher level of domestic wealth (because of the increase in EF). Thus, if the goods market was in equilibrium in A_0, there now is an excess demand for goods.

Suppose now prices are perfectly flexible, keeping the goods market in permanent equilibrium. Since at given prices we would observe an excess demand for goods, flexible prices *rise* immediately: this appreciates the domestic currency in real terms [compared to the hypothetical situation (E', P_0)] and reduces the current-account surplus. However, it also reduces real wealth and consumption demand. Therefore, a new, *higher price level* must exist which clears the market for domestic goods. We have arrived at the *intermediate result* that if prices are flexible a money supply increase via open-market purchases in the short run lowers the interest rate, but raises the exchange rate, nominal wealth and the price level. In the short run reactions of the interest rate, the exchange rate and (nominal) wealth are exclusively determined in the asset markets. What we do not know yet is how the real exchange rate E/P changes. Logically, three cases are possible.

The real exchange rate remains unaffected, that is, $E'/P'_a = E_0/P_0$. In this case the balance of trade remains in equilibrium ($NX' = NX_0 = 0$), but real wealth falls. Therefore consumption demand and, hence, aggregate demand would be smaller than in A_0. We would observe an excess supply of domestic goods ($Y^s > Y^d$). The economy would not be in equilibrium.

The real exchange rate moves up far enough to leave real wealth unchanged: $E'/P'_b > E_0/P_0$ and $W'/P'_b = W_0/P_0$. Now consumption demand would be unchanged ($C' = C_0$), but the balance of trade would be in surplus ($NX' > NX_0 = 0$). In this case we would observe an excess demand for domestic goods. Again the economy would not be in equilibrium.

The real exchange rate rises to E'/P'_c, where the goods market exactly clears ($Y^d = Y^s$). With E' being given, the argument advanced in (1) and (2) implies that the real exchange rate which clears the goods market requires a price level which is between P'_b and P'_a. Thus in the new (temporary) equilibrium we have $E_0/P_0 = E'/P'_a < E'/P'_c < E'/P'_b$. Thus the proposed money supply increase produces a real depreciation in the short run and thus a balance of trade in surplus and reduced consumption. In Figure 7.9 the balance of trade is characterized by B'. B' is on a higher NX curve, since the price level has risen.

B' cannot be a long-run equilibrium point. In a long-run equilibrium the current account must be balanced, and thus $\dot{F} = 0$:

$$\dot{F} = \frac{P}{E} NX(E/P) + i^*F - T = 0$$

Since $i^*F - T = 0$ is still holding and NX is positive because of the real depreciation, domestic residents accumulate foreign bonds ($\dot{F} > 0$). As has been demonstrated above, this leaves the interest rate unchanged but drives down the exchange rate. Starting in A' the economy moves vertically downwards. Just how far is determined by the restrictions that $\dot{F} > 0$ during the entire adjustment period, but that $\dot{F} = 0$ in the new long-run equilibrium. Thus $i^*F_1 > i^*F_0$, which means that the *balance of trade* must be *in deficit* in the new long-run equilibrium point B_1. This can only be the case, however, if the real exchange rate has fallen and is lower than in our initial long-run equilibrium ($E_1/P_1 < E_0/P_0$). As a consequence, moving from the temporary equilibrium points A' and B' to the respective new long-run equilibrium positions, the nominal exchange rate falls at a faster rate than the price level.

To sum up, an increase of the domestic money supply has the following consequences:

1. The home currency depreciates in the short run, but appreciates in the long run. This demonstrates that in the portfolio balance approach nominal shocks may have lasting consequences for the real economy.

2. The exchange rate overshoots its new equilibrium value. The reason for this is not *sticky prices*, but rather the fact that changes of wealth via balance of trade disequilibria need time.

3. While being in equilibrium initially, the balance of trade is brought into deficit in its new long-run equilibrium. This offers domestic residents the opportunity for permanently higher consumption, which is being financed out of permanently higher real wealth.

7.2.2 Formal derivation of equilibria

While the dynamic analysis of the model is a laborious task indeed, the short- and long-run comparative-static properties of the real exchange rate are obtained in a rather straightforward fashion. We focus on the real exchange rate, since the long-run non-neutrality of this variable is one of the most interesting and characteristic properties of the portfolio balance approach to the exchange rate.

Consider first how the *real* exchange rate changes between the initial point of general equilibrium A_0 and the new temporary equilibrium point A'. Since the goods market always clears in the light of perfectly flexible prices, we may compute the effect on the real exchange rate of a money supply increase via open-market purchases directly from the equilibrium condition for the goods market. Making use of the other structural equations of the model where appropriate, the total differential of the goods market equilibrium condition (7.23) is

$$\begin{aligned} \mathrm{d}Y = {} & C_w P^{-1}\mathrm{d}B + C_w P^{-1}\mathrm{d}M + C_w P^{-1}E\mathrm{d}F + C_w P^{-1}F\mathrm{d}E \\ & - C_w W P^{-2}\mathrm{d}P - NX_R E P^{-2}\mathrm{d}P + NX_R P^{-1}\mathrm{d}E \end{aligned} \tag{7.27}$$

To obtain a more compact notation, the definitions $w \equiv W/P$ and $R \equiv E/P$ are being used. We may simplify equation (7.27) by letting $\mathrm{d}Y = 0$, since income remains constant; $\mathrm{d}F = 0$, since the supply of foreign bonds does not change between A_0 and A'; and $\mathrm{d}M = -\mathrm{d}B$, which reflects the proposed policy measure:

$$0 = (C_w P^{-1}F + NX_R P^{-1})\mathrm{d}E - (C_w W P^{-2} + NX_R E P^{-2})\mathrm{d}P$$

Solving for $\mathrm{d}E/\mathrm{d}P$, we obtain

$$\frac{\mathrm{d}E}{\mathrm{d}P} = \frac{C_w W P^{-1} + NX_R E P^{-1}}{C_w F + NX_R} \tag{7.28}$$

Multiplication of (7.28) by P/E gives

$$\frac{\mathrm{d}E}{E}\frac{P}{\mathrm{d}P} = \frac{C_w W E^{-1} + NX_R}{C_w F + NX_R} > 1 \tag{7.29}$$

The > sign follows from the fact that all terms are positive and $W > EF$, that is, $WE^{-1} > F$. Equation (7.28) says that the real exchange rate increases while moving from A_0 to A', since the percentage rate of change in the exchange rate is higher than the percentage rate of change in the price level. While we already know that the exchange rate rises, we can see that the price level rises as well after rewriting (7.28):

$$\mathrm{d}P = \frac{P(C_w F + NX_R)}{C_w W + NX_R E}\mathrm{d}E$$

To sum up, we have demonstrated the following results:

$$E' > E_0$$
$$P' > P_0$$
$$E'/P' > E_0/P_0$$

Taking account of the net export function and the balance of payments identity, these results imply

$$NX' > NX_0$$
$$\dot{F}' > \dot{F}_0 = 0$$

We now turn to a comparison of points A' and A_1. The fact that the economy actually approaches a point such as A_1, which is characterized by $E_1 < E'$, follows from $\dot{F}' > 0$ and from the fact that a rising supply of foreign bonds drives the exchange rate down at a given interest rate. The concomitant movement of the price level follows from the goods market equilibrium condition, which holds permanently. Again we proceed from the total differential (7.27). This time we let $\mathrm{d}Y = \mathrm{d}M = \mathrm{d}B = 0$. We may draw on the insight gained on analyzing the consequences of a current-account surplus above, that when F rises, the product EF remains constant (see Section 7.1.3). In equation (7.27) this implies $C_w P^{-1} E\mathrm{d}F + C_w P^{-1} F\mathrm{d}E = 0$,[6] which simplifies (7.27) to

$$0 = P^{-1} NX_R \mathrm{d}E - (C_w W P^{-2} + NX_R E P^{-2})\mathrm{d}P$$

After multiplication by P^2 we obtain

$$\frac{\mathrm{d}E}{\mathrm{d}P} = \frac{C_w W + NX_R E}{P \cdot NX_R} > 0 \qquad (7.30)$$

Equation (7.30) says that the exchange rate and the price level always move in the same direction. Therefore, while moving from A' to A_1 the price level falls. The movement of the real exchange rate is obtained after multiplying (7.30) by P and dividing by E:

$$\frac{\mathrm{d}E}{E}\frac{P}{\mathrm{d}P} = \frac{C_w W E^{-1} + NX_R}{NX_R} > 1$$

The exchange rate falls at a faster pace than the price level. Therefore, the real exchange rate falls as well, and we may sum up the obtained results:

$$E_1 < E'$$
$$P_1 < P'$$
$$E_1/P_1 < E_0/P_0 < E'/P'$$
$$F_1 > F' = F_0$$
$$NX_1 < NX_0 < NX'$$

The preceding formal analysis has provided an understanding of the comparative-static properties of our model. Knowledge of how short- and long-run equilibria respond to changes of the exogenous variables is one thing, however; a quite different question, to which we turn in the next section, is whether the economy actually converges towards these equilibria, that is, whether the model is dynamically stable.

7.2.3 Is the model stable?

It is appropriate to move to a different graphical presentation of the model when analyzing its dynamic properties (Figure 7.10). In the left-hand quadrant prices are measured along the horizontal axis. The $\dot{P}=0$ curves depict those E/P combinations which, *ceteris paribus*, clear the goods market. The $\dot{F}=0$ curves combine all E/P combinations which balance the current account.

The slope of the $\dot{P}=0$ curve (the goods market equilibrium schedule) has already been computed as equation (7.28) above. The curve is obviously not linear. This follows from equation (7.29), which states that when moving along the $\dot{P}=0$ curve, the price elasticity of the exchange rate is greater than 1.

The slope of the $\dot{F}=0$ curve is obtained from the balance of payments identity, letting $\dot{F}=0$. The total differential[7] of this equation

$$\mathrm{d}P(NX(E/P)-EP^{-1}NX_R)+\mathrm{d}E(NX_R-PE^{-1}NX(E/P)) + i^*E\mathrm{d}F=0 \tag{7.31}$$

may be solved for $dF=0$, letting $\dot{F}=0$.

$$\frac{\mathrm{d}E}{\mathrm{d}P}=\frac{NX_R EP^{-1}-NX(E/P)}{i^*F+NX_R}$$

Multiplying by P/E yields the elasticity

$$\frac{\mathrm{d}E}{E}\frac{P}{\mathrm{d}P}=\frac{NX_R-PE^{-1}NX(E/P)}{i^*F+NX_R}=1$$

since on the $\dot{F}=0$ curve we have $i^*F=-PE^{-1}NX(E/P)$. On the $\dot{F}=0$

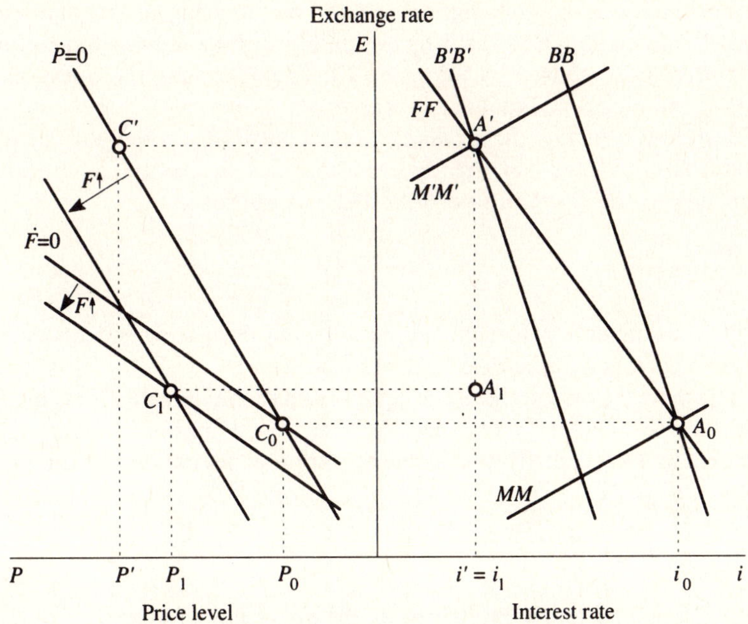

Figure 7.10 Interest rate and price effects of a money-supply increase via open-market purchases in the portfolio balance approach

curve the price elasticity of the exchange rate is constant at a value of 1 and, therefore, smaller than the price elasticity of the exchange rate on the $\dot{P}=0$ curve. Since the goods market is in equilibrium at all times the model instantaneously jumps from C_0 to C', where the balance of trade is positive, and F begins to rise. Since both equilibrium schedules are drawn for constant levels of F, we now have to ask how an increase in F shifts the equilibrium schedules.

The movement of the $\dot{P}=0$ curve is obtained from the total differential (7.27), this time letting $\mathrm{d}Y=\mathrm{d}B=\mathrm{d}M=\mathrm{d}P=0$:

$$\frac{\mathrm{d}E}{\mathrm{d}F}=\frac{-C_wE}{C_wF+NX_R}<0$$

The movement of the $\dot{F}=0$ curve is derived from the total differential of the balance of payments identity, letting $\mathrm{d}P=\dot{F}=\mathrm{d}i^*=0$:

$$\frac{\mathrm{d}E}{\mathrm{d}F}=\frac{-i^*E}{i^*F+NX_R}<0$$

An increase in the supply of foreign bonds shifts *both* equilibrium curves downwards. In C' the exchange rate is above the value which is required to equilibrate the balance of payments. This raises the question of whether the fall of the exchange rate caused by the rising supply of foreign bonds F is fast enough to catch up eventually with the downward shifting $\dot{F}=0$ curve (also caused by the rising F). This is exactly the question of whether the model is dynamically stable.

Just how quickly the exchange rate really falls when the current account is in surplus has already been analyzed in Section 7.1.3 above. According to the short-run portfolio balance approach

$$\frac{\mathrm{d}E}{E}\frac{F}{\mathrm{d}F}=-1$$

A 1 per cent increase of foreign debt holdings by domestic residents makes domestic currency appreciate by 1 per cent.

The model is only stable if the equilibrium exchange rate $\bar{E}$ falls by less than 1 per cent after foreign debt holdings by domestic residents have increased by 1 per cent. The exchange rate approaches its equilibrium value if

$$\frac{\mathrm{d}\bar{E}}{\bar{E}}\frac{F}{\mathrm{d}F}>-1$$

holds. $\bar{E}$ is the exchange rate given by the intersection between $\dot{P}=0$ and $\dot{F}=0$ curves.

After letting $\mathrm{d}Y=\mathrm{d}M=\mathrm{d}B=0$ the total differential (7.27) of the $\dot{P}=0$ curve yields

$$\mathrm{d}P=\frac{C_W F+NX_R}{C_W WP^{-1}+NX_R EP^{-1}}\mathrm{d}E+\frac{C_W E}{C_W WP^{-1}+NX_R EP^{-1}}\mathrm{d}F \quad (7.32)$$

The total differential (7.31) of the $\dot{F}=0$ curve yields

$$\mathrm{d}E=\frac{NX_R EP^{-1}-NX}{NX_R-EP^{-1}NX_R}\mathrm{d}P-\frac{i^*E}{NX_R-EP^{-1}NX_R}\mathrm{d}F \quad (7.33)$$

After substituting (7.32) into (7.33), rearranging terms, solving for $\mathrm{d}E/\mathrm{d}F$, and multiplying by F/E, we obtain the reaction of the equilibrium exchange rate to an increase of foreign bond holdings:

$$\frac{\mathrm{d}\bar{E}/\bar{E}}{\mathrm{d}F/F}=-\frac{NX\cdot PE^{-1}(C_W FE-C_W W)-NX_R C_W EF-P\cdot NX\cdot NX_R}{NXPE^{-1}(C_W FE-C_W W)-NX_R C_W EF+C_W W\cdot NX_R} \quad (7.34)$$

where the denominator is positive if the Marshall–Lerner condition holds. This can be seen after combining terms to yield $(NX_R-PE^{-1}NX)$ $C_W(W-EF)>0$. Comparing terms which differ between numerator and denominator in (7.34), it turns out that the model is stable (that is, $(\mathrm{d}\bar{E}/\bar{E})/(\mathrm{d}F/F)>-1$) *if and only if* $-P\cdot NX<C_W W$. Using $-PE^{-1}NX=i^*F$ in equilibrium, we obtain

$$i^*EF<C_W W \quad (7.35)$$

Equation (7.35) says that the present model is only then stable if domestic-currency income from holding foreign debt is smaller than total consumption (pretending that C_W is constant; the precise reference in our non-linear case is fictive consumption out of wealth at the current marginal propensity to consume).

7.3 Summary

The portfolio balance approach (PBA) may lack the elegance and transparency of the macroeconomic disequilibrium approach to the exchange rate. Studying this approach yields benefits in the form of insights, however, which other approaches do not deliver at all or do so in a less convincing fashion:

1. The PBA explains why and in what amounts both domestic and foreign residents hold domestic and foreign assets – even if all agents possess identical expectations.[9]
2. The PBA explains why central bank foreign exchange market intervention may work and may have lasting effects.
3. The PBA offers a rationale for exchange rate overshooting which does not rely on the somewhat disputed notion of sticky prices. Here overshooting is caused by the fact that the accumulation of wealth through current-account surpluses needs time.
4. Finally, the PBA discusses how policies may result in a redistribution of wealth between countries, in permanent changes of the real exchange rate, and in lasting current-account disequilibria.

7.4 Answer to the problem

Problem 7.1

If the market for domestic bonds determines the interest rate and the market for foreign bonds determines the exchange rate, the BB curve may be considered the $di/dt = 0$ locus and the FF curve may be considered the $\dot{e} = 0$ locus. Figures (7.11) and (7.12) show the short-run portfolio balance approach for different relative slopes of the BB and the FF curves. The plus and minus signs attached to the curves point to the interest rate and exchange rate movements which obtain above and below the respective curve. After constructing a phase diagram from this qualitative information, it becomes obvious that global stability only obtains if the BB curve is steeper than the FF curve.

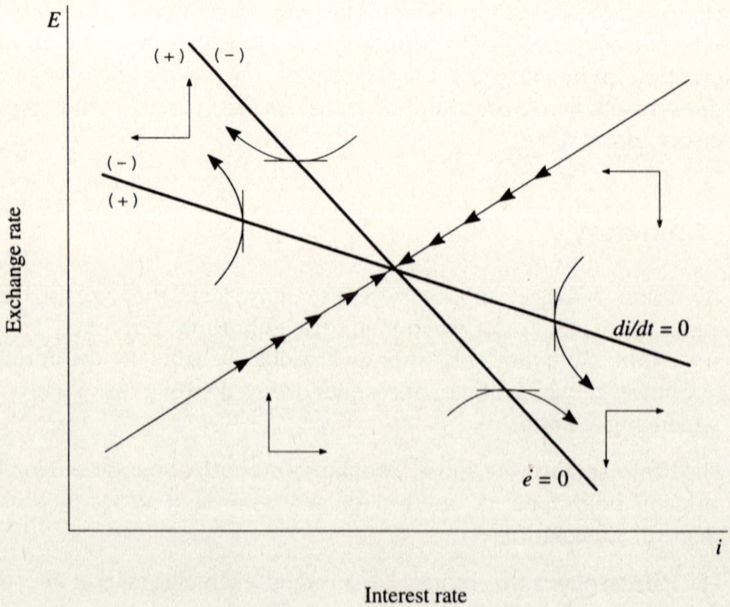

Figure 7.11 Saddle path stability in the portfolio balance approach when the *FF* curve is steeper than the *BB* curve

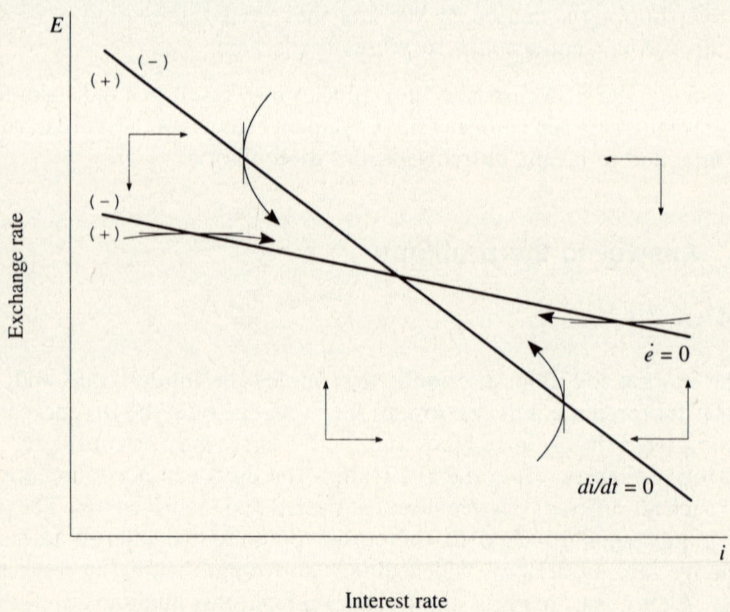

Figure 7.12 Global path stability in the portfolio balance approach when the *BB* curve is steeper than the *FF* curve

NOTES

1. The model presented here is due to Branson (1977).
2. It will be demonstrated in Section 7.1.3 that in our present model the BB curve is always steeper than the FF curve.
3. The view that private holdings of government debt are considered wealth is not undisputed. In particular, the **Ricardian equivalence theorem** revived by Barro (1974) takes strong issue with this view. According to this theorem rational actors know that when the government sells bonds to finance a budget deficit the private sector will at some time in the future face higher taxes to cover the interest payments and to eventually repay the debt. Thus government deficit spending by issuing debt to the public neither affects permanent income nor aggregate wealth. Tobin and Buiter (1978) argue, however, that government bonds are considered net wealth as long as economic agents discount future tax burdens to some degree. Up to this day, empirical evidence on the Ricardian equivalence theorem remains inconclusive (see Aschauer 1985).
4. The long-run model discussed here is deliberately kept simple. More complex models of a similar mould can be found in Allen and Kenen (1978), Genberg and Kierzkowski (1979) and Dornbusch and Fischer (1980).
5. In order to make the argument a little less awkward, exogenous transfers and services are combined into one account.
6. Collecting terms, this expression may be rewritten as $C_w P^{-1}(E\mathrm{d}F + F\mathrm{d}E) = 0$. Since we have shown $\mathrm{d}E/E = -\mathrm{d}F/F$ above, dividing both sides by EF yields $C_w P^{-1}(\mathrm{d}F/F + \mathrm{d}E/E) = 0$.
7. We also let $\mathrm{d}i^* = 0$ and $T = 0$. The assumption $T = 0$ implies that in equilibrium either we have $F = 0$ or the trade balance is not in equilibrium.
8. $Z > 0$ requires that the Marshall–Lerner conditions hold.
9. In the asset market approach a diversified portfolio of assets may result as a byproduct of the indifference of investors between domestic and foreign assets. In case of risk aversion the asset market approach only permits residents of one country to include foreign assets in their portfolio. This can only be overcome by introducing heterogeneous exchange rate expectations.

REFERENCES

Allen, P. R. and P. B. Kenen (1978) *Asset Markets, Exchange Rates and Economic Integration*, Cambridge: Cambridge University Press.

Aschauer, David A. (1985) 'Fiscal policy and aggregate demand', *American Economic Review* 75, 117–27.

Barro, Robert (1974) 'Are government bonds net wealth?', *Journal of Political Economy* 82, 1095–117.

Branson, William H. (1977) 'Asset markets and relative prices in exchange rate determination', *Sozialwissenschaftliche Annalen* 1, 69–89.

Chiang, Alpha C. (1984) *Fundamental Methods of Mathematical Economics*, 3rd edn, Singapore: McGraw-Hill.

Dornbusch, Rudiger and Stanley Fischer (1980) 'Exchange rates and the current account', *American Economic Review* 70, 960–71.

Genberg, Hans and Hendrik Kierzkowski (1979) 'Impact and long run effects of economic disturbances in a dynamic model of exchange rate determination', *Weltwirtschaftliches Archiv* 115, 605–27.

Tobin, James and Willem H. Buiter (1978) 'Debt neutrality: A brief review of evidence', in G. von Furstenberg (ed.) *Social Security versus Private Saving in Postindustrial Societies*, Chicago: American Council of Life Insurance, 1–27.

Chapter 8

Exchange rate economics today

Macroeconomic exchange rate models develop in response to the interaction between theoretical reflection and empirical insights. Two decades of recent experience with flexible exchange rates have produced a sufficient amount of data to permit meaningful empirical tests of central implications of our exchange rate models. Progress in exchange rate economics, therefore, is propelled by a constant interaction between theoretical and empirical research.

This chapter begins by providing a bird's eye perspective of the **econometric results** and **stylized facts** produced by empirical research on exchange rates. It will emphasize those stylized facts of flexible exchange rates which are not compatible with standard models of exchange rates and show how these deficiencies have stimulated new theoretical research. Recent developments which will be emphasized are **equilibrium exchange rate models** and approaches which model seemingly *excessive* exchange rate movements as **rational bubbles**.

8.1 Empirical exchange rate economics

At a very early stage after the collapse of the Bretton Woods system with fixed exchange rates, research into the behaviour of flexible exchange rates has also been of an empirical nature. Empirical studies fall into three categories:

1. Econometric estimates of exchange rate equations which are reduced forms of complete macroeconomic exchange rate models.
2. Econometric estimates of central structural equations of exchange rate models. Examples of such key relationships are the purchasing-power parity hypothesis or interest parity.

3. Confrontations of central implications of exchange rate models with the stylized facts observed for open economies under flexible exchange rates.

The categories are not exclusive, of course: for example, if statistical methods are used in category 3, the studies actually fall into category 2. Since we are not really concerned with statistical or methodological issues here, the following survey only differentiates between the econometric estimation of exchange rate equations and the results obtained from a confrontation of exchange rate models with the stylized facts of reality.

The main purpose of this brief sketch of the state of the art of empirical research on flexible exchange rates is to motivate recent theoretical developments as a reaction to insights gained from empirical research. Therefore, we will operate from an extreme bird's eye perspective and discuss neither methodological issues nor detailed results. Both would be interesting in a different context but would also occupy a lot of space if dealt with thoroughly.[1]

8.1.1 Estimation of exchange rate equations

All models presented in Chapters 2–6 contain structural and, implicitly, reduced-form exchange rate equations. Also, the comparative-static properties of the nonlinear portfolio balance approach presented in Chapter 7 may be used as a hypothesis in a simplified linear exchange rate equation.

Combining equations (2.5) and (2.6) yields an exchange rate equation, $e=\bar{e}-(i-i^*)/\theta$, for the sticky-price monetary model. Simplifying matters by letting $g=0$ and defining δ to include the multiplier effect, under real-world conditions – with foreign variables not constant – the equilibrium exchange rate is $\bar{e}=\bar{p}-\bar{p}^*$. Substituting this into the exchange rate equation and assuming that equilibrium price levels in the small home country and abroad are determined by identical money demand functions such as equation (2.3), we finally arrive at the exchange rate equation.

$$e_t=m_t-m_t^*-\phi(y_t-y_t^*)-\theta(i_t-i_t^*) \tag{8.1}$$

Equation (5.6″) determines the exchange rate in the monetarist model (the monetary model with flexible prices). This equation is repeated here with added time subscripts as equation (8.2):

$$e_t=m_t-m_t^*-\phi(y_t-y_t^*)+\lambda(i_t-i_t^*) \tag{8.2}$$

A comparison of equations (8.1) and (8.2) reveals that an increase of domestic interest rates relative to foreign interest rates produces an appreciation in the sticky price model, but a depreciation in the monetarist flexible price model. The reason for this is simply that in the short run interest rates under sticky prices respond differently from flexible prices. Under sticky prices the liquidity effect dominates. Rising interest rates, therefore, indicate restrictive monetary policy. If prices are flexible, rising interest rates signal the transition to a more inflationary monetary policy.

Exchange rate effects of interest rate increases under sticky prices become more similar to exchange rate effects under flexible prices if the Dornbusch model is analyzed in an inflationary context (see, for example, Frankel 1979; Bhandari and Turnovsky 1982; Gärtner 1983). Now economic agents not only expect a gradual movement of the exchange rate to its present equilibrium value, but also anticipate changes of this equilibrium value reflecting present inflationary tendencies. The nominal interest rate not only reflects (unexpected) liquidity changes but also inflation expectations. Though this approach operates with the assumption of sticky goods prices and is thus clearly in the tradition of the Mundell–Fleming and Dornbusch models, it is often treated as a model variant of its own and has been coined the RID (real interest differential) approach by Frankel (1979).

Equation (6.5′) explains exchange rates under currency substitution.[2] Modification of this equation to a two-country version which includes foreign variables and policy instruments along with the assumption that nominal interest rates reflect money growth expectations yields

$$e_t = m_t - m_t^* - \phi(y_t - y_t^*) + (\alpha + \lambda)(i_t - i_t^*) + \beta \mathrm{var}(i_t - i_t^*) \qquad (8.3)$$

Equation (8.3) very much resembles equation (8.2). What is new compared to the monetarist exchange rate model without currency substitution is that the domestic currency depreciates if the variance of the interest differential, $\mathrm{var}(i_t - i_t^*)$, increases. This, however, is not really a necessary ingredient within the currency substitution approach. Its influence would only then be quantitatively important if actors had strong risk aversion. The qualitative properties of the short-run portfolio balance approach derived in the previous chapter may be collected to yield an estimation equation linear in the logarithms of the included variables:

$$e_t = \alpha m_t - \alpha^* m_t^* + \beta b_t - \beta^* b_t^* + \gamma f_t - \gamma^* f_t^* \qquad (8.4)$$

Here b (b^*) and f (f^*) are domestic and foreign bonds, respectively, held by domestic agents (foreigners).

Numerous studies have tried to use equations (8.1)–(8.4) (and modifications of those equations) to test the potential of the models on which those equations are based to explain exchange rate developments. In a nutshell the results may be summarized as follows. For each approach presented estimation periods of sufficient length are found for which it is supported by the data. However, these results are not stable. Rather, they are very sensitive to changes of the estimation period or to the use of other currencies.

Going into more detail now, a number of authors find that the monetarist exchange rate model yields quite satisfactory results for the first five years, 1973–8, after Bretton Woods. For periods after 1978, however, the monetarist approach more or less breaks down. Frequently, the estimated exchange rate equations have a very poor fit and the wrong sign for crucial estimation coefficients. It is often argued that the main reason for this failure of the monetarist approach is the instability of money demand equations observed in the 1980s.

This problem affects all exchange rate models discussed in this book. Also, all approaches have difficulties in coming to grips with certain statistical problems, such as simultaneous equations bias, which results from the fact that the estimated exchange rate equations are not really reduced forms. Reduced forms should only have exogenous or lagged endogenous variables on the right-hand side. In fact, all exchange rate equations have explicitly or implicitly endogenous right-hand variables such as the interest differential (as a substitute for depreciation expectations) or differences in the money supply or in inflation rates. This endogenity may bias estimation coefficients. Therefore, and particularly if exchange rate expectations do not always follow the same simple pattern as in the original Dornbusch model, it does not come as a surprise that exchange rate equations based on the sticky price monetary model also produce mixed results.

One major problem with the currency substitution approach is that empirical studies can only produce evidence as to whether actors have substituted domestic money for something else or not. Available data usually do not permit us to answer the question of whether the exchange rate has risen because, in the light of rising inflation and rising interest rates, actors have substituted part of domestic money for foreign money, bonds or real estate. In the few cases when authors offer conclusions regarding the direction of substitution, the evidence suggests that during normal times in industrial countries currency substitution is a phenomenon of little quantitative importance.

A much smaller number of authors have subjected the portfolio balance approach to empirical scrutiny. The reason is probably the more difficult data situation. Since wealth variables are not covered in common statistical sources, they are either excluded from the estimation equation or approximated indirectly. For example, Branson, Haltunen and Masson (1979) drop domestic bonds from their estimation equation and proxy the volume of foreign bonds held by domestic residents by accumulated current-account surpluses. The obvious disadvantage of this procedure is that, for example, the exchange rate of the US dollar vs. the Japanese yen is also determined by Danish bonds held by American residents. Similar to the other approaches, the portfolio balance approach does not offer an empirically robust exchange rate equation.

A number of factors may explain this obviously rather disillusioning performance of empirical exchange rate equations, some of which have already been mentioned.

1. While models are built under the assumption of completely flexible exchange rates, they are confronted with data from the real world characterized by 'managed floating'. No central bank of any major industrial country has completely abstained from intervening in the foreign exchanges since the collapse of the Bretton Woods system. While periods of complete abstension have occurred, these have been interrupted time and again or followed by periods of massive intervention either by directly buying or selling currency, by publicizing exchange rate targets, by restricting capital mobility and so on.[3]

It can easily be demonstrated that those relationships which have been derived for flexible exchange rates need not necessarily hold for periods of 'dirty floating'. Consider the following example: under flexible exchange rates there is a positive relationship between the money supply and the exchange rate.[4] If the money supply increases, the exchange rate rises. Now, in periods of managed floating, central banks typically intervene in the foreign exchange market because they do not accept the result produced by the market. In order to fight market forces in our example of a rising exchange rate, however, the central bank has to buy domestic currency by giving up foreign exchange reserves. Thus the domestic money supply gets smaller as the exchange rate rises. *Ceteris paribus*, we expect a negative correlation between the exchange rate and the money supply. The relationship between the exchange rate and the money supply that results from the combined influence of both partial effects is not clear and is probably highly variable over time.

2. Not only monetary and foreign exchange policy and hence the flexibility of 'flexible' exchange rates have been very variable since 1973; but also changes have been observed for one key building block of exchange rate models, namely the money demand equation. If the money demand equation is not stable, as a number of authors concluded in the 1980s,[5] this must create problems for the empirical performance of exchange rate equations.

3. Though the central role of exchange rate expectations in determining the exchange rate is recognized, empirical work usually suffers from an inadequate treatment of expectations. Probably improvements can only be expected when data on exchange rate expectations derived from question-

naires cover periods which are long enough to permit inclusion in an estimation equation.

All these are serious reservations. They warn against naive transfers of implications derived from models of flexible exchange rates to real-world data from the 1970s and 1980s. Since econometric methods have difficulties in coping with the problems mentioned under (1)–(3), it should not come as a surprise that no single exchange rate model is continuously successful over the entire period of time since 1973. That individual models perform rather well for limited periods of time may suggest that the relevant model (and/or the model which the actors consider relevant in forming their expectations) changes. Further evidence in support of this interpretation will be presented below.

8.1.2 Stylized facts versus theory

There is another, softer way to evaluate the empirical performance of exchange rate theories. Here central implications of the model under consideration are compared with those stylized facts which periods of flexible exchange rates have produced according to the ruling consensus. This procedure avoids the danger of discarding an approach only because the available empirical methods are inadequate or because unobservable variables such as expectations or risk premiums can only be taken care of in an unsatisfactory way. On the other hand, of course, if a model is compatible with those stylized facts noted from a bird's eye perspective, this can only be considered weak evidence in favour of a specific exchange rate model. In particular, it is very difficult to discriminate between two competing models on the basis of this procedure.

Various authors have attempted to characterize empirically systems of flexible exchange rates.[6] While a host of other stylized facts has been discussed in the literature, only a few rather undisputed ones are presented here and will be used to evaluate the four basic exchange rate models presented in Chapters 2–7.

1. *Spot and forward exchange rates are highly correlated.* Figure 8.1 shows monthly spot and forward rates for the Deutschmark/dollar exchange rate from June 1973 to October 1991. The correlation coefficient between the two series is 0.9995. This stylized fact is compatible with all exchange rate models in which expectations play a central role. This happens to be the case for all models presented in Chapters 2–7. If today's exchange rate reflects expected future exchange rates, and if expected future exchange rates reflect expected future developments of all exogenous variables, then any new information about the development of these future exogenous

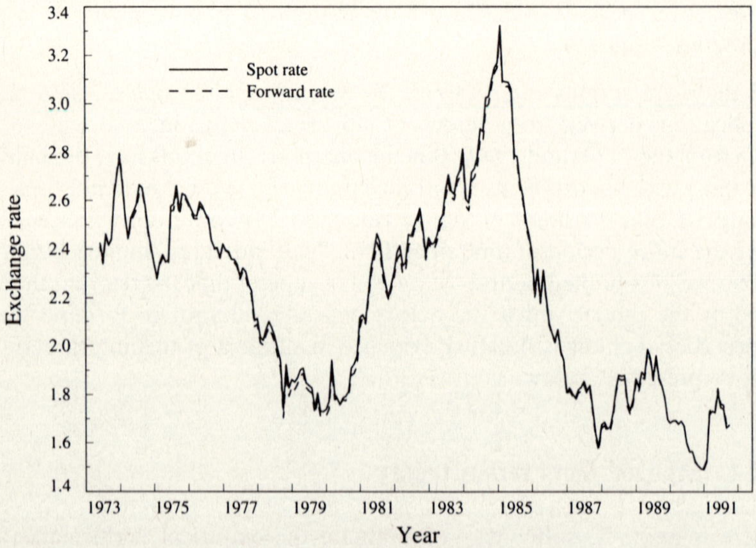

Figure 8.1 Spot and forward rates Deutschmark/dollar, monthly data (Source: IMF, International Financial Statistics, data tape)

variables influences both the expected exchange rate and today's actual exchange rate. Since the expected exchange rate determines the forward rate, this line of argument proposes a close correlation between today's spot rate and the forward rate. In an efficient foreign exchange market both rates should only then not move in synchrony if the interest differential changes.

2. *The forward rate is a poor predictor of the future spot rate*. This should not come as a surprise either. Since the spot rate more or less only changes because of unforeseen developments (news) which were not known at the time when the forward rate was determined, the forward rate cannot possibly be a good predictor of the future spot rate. Figure 8.2 illustrates this by confronting the depreciation forecast implied in the forward rate, which is equal to the interest differential, with the actual depreciation. This empirical regularity too is explained well by all standard models of exchange rate determination.

3. *Nominal and real exchange rates are highly correlated*; *in other words, nominal exchange rates are more volatile than goods prices*. Figure 8.3 illustrates this stylized fact by means of quarterly data for the Deutschmark/dollar exchange rate. For the time period from June 1973 to October 1991 the correlation coefficient is 0.68. This stylized fact of flexible exchange rates is easily compatible with the sticky price monetary model, but not so with the monetarist model assuming complete price flexibility.

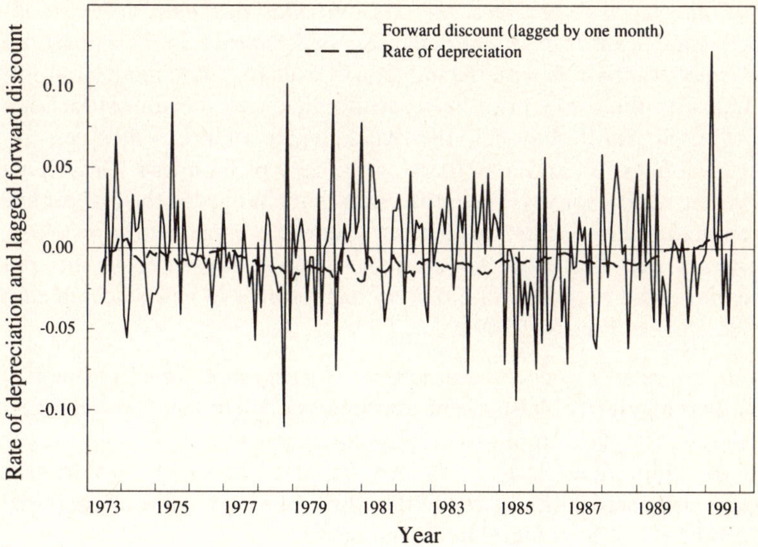

Figure 8.2 Forward premium (in per cent, lagged by one period) and actual rate of depreciation, monthly data
(Source: IMF, International Financial Statistics, data tape)

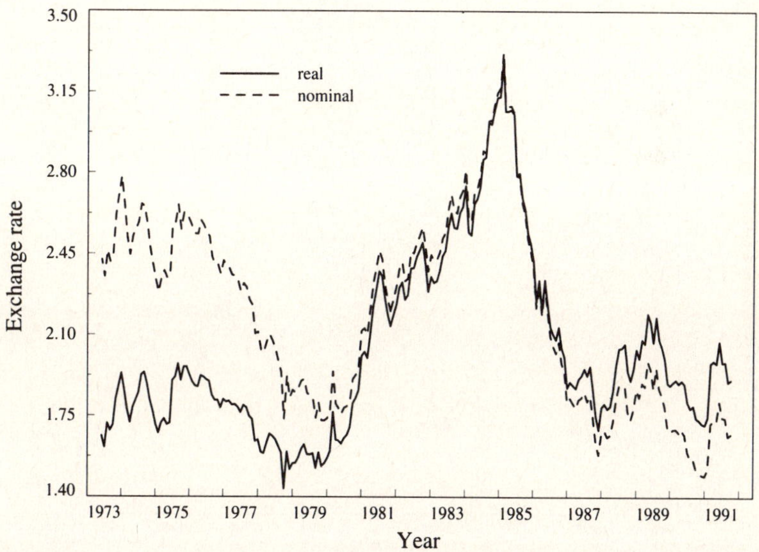

Figure 8.3 Nominal and real exchange rate Deutschmark/dollar, quarterly data
(Source: IMF, International Financial Statistics, data tape)

4. *Following a disturbance, the real exchange rate only slowly, if at all, moves back towards its equilibrium value* (*see Figure 8.3*). This observation too is not compatible with the monetarist exchange rate model, but is well in line with the sticky price macroeconomic disequilibrium model due to Dornbusch. In this model, the exact degree of price stickiness is an empirical question and may therefore be very pronounced. Occasionally, however, reality conveys the impression that changes in the real exchange rate remain permanent. This feature cannot be explained by recourse to monetary exchange rate models such as those presented in this book. Therefore, real exchange rate rigidity has resulted in new research efforts, which will be discussed below.

5. *Bilateral spot rates are characterized by very high volatility* (*see Figure 8.4*). This regularity is also a central property of all monetary exchange rate models which place emphasis on the role of new information for exchange rate determination. Particularly well suited is the sticky price monetary model, since here in the short run the whole burden of adjustment is on the exchange rate which therefore overshoots.

6. *There exist extended periods of time, during which the forecast error of the forward exchange rate is not random.* Indeed, as Figure 8.5 indicates, forecast errors of the forward rate appear to differ systematically from zero for extended periods of time. This raises doubts about the efficiency of the

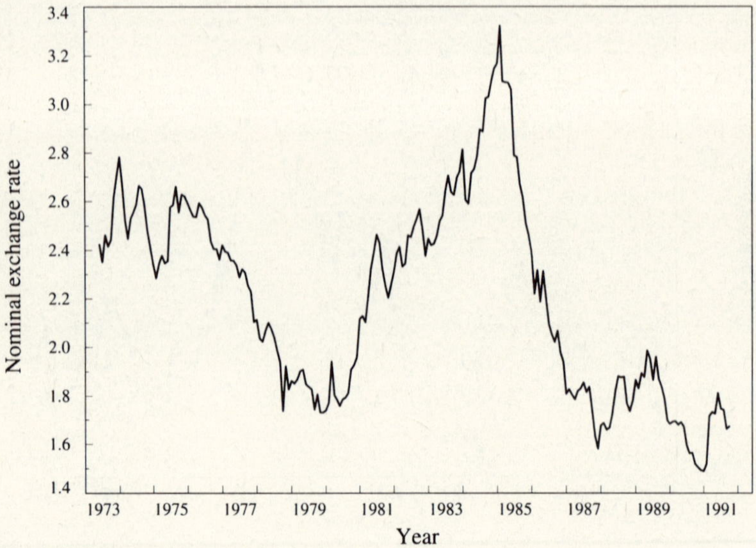

Figure 8.4 Nominal exchange rate Deutschmark/dollar, monthly data (Source: IMF, International Financial Statistics, data tape)

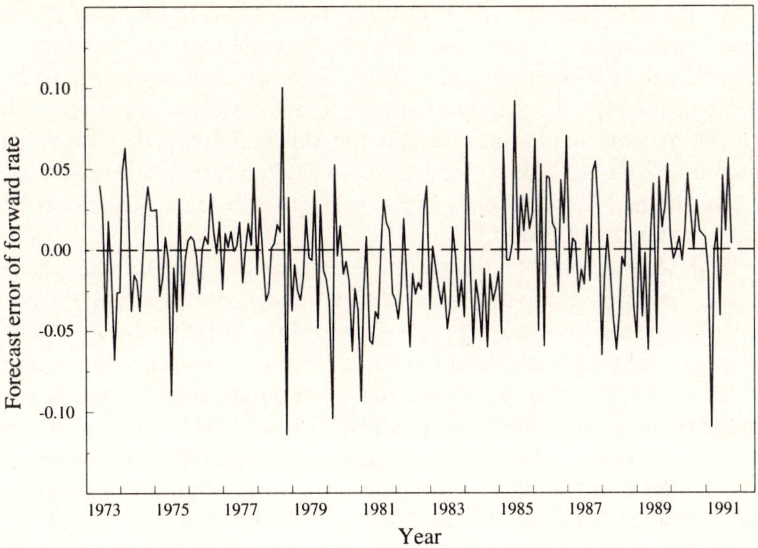

Figure 8.5 Forecasting error of the forward rate, monthly data (Source: IMF, International Financial Statistics, data tape)

foreign exchange market. As a number of researchers have found using sophisticated statistical methods, this bias of forward rate forecasts has been particularly pronounced during the rise of the US dollar between 1980 and 1985 (see, for example, Frankel and Froot 1987; Lewis 1989). This can be seen if we estimate a simple autoregressive specification for the forecast error of the forward rate for the Deutschmark/dollar exchange rate (estimation period: January 1980–February 1985). The estimated equation is

$$ {}_{t-1}f_t - e_t = \underset{(4.25)}{-0.021} + \underset{(0.37)}{0.048}({}_{t-2}f_{t-1} - e_{t-1}) \qquad \mathrm{DW}^7 = 1.976 $$

${}_{t-1}f_t$ is the dollar price in Deutschmarks offered at time $t-1$ for time t. Absolute t values are given in parentheses below the coefficient estimates. The estimated negative constant term says that during the boom period of the US dollar, which lasted some six years, the forward rate fell short of the eventual spot rate by two percentage points per month. This result suggests (a) and/or (b):

(a) Uncovered interest parity did not hold (dollars and Deutschmark are not perfect substitutes).

(b) Depreciation expectations were not rational but were systematically off target.

In the first case the constant term in the above estimation equation would represent a risk premium which the market requires for holding US dollars in the observed quantity. Since monthly data are being used, the estimated coefficient suggests a risk premium of 28 per cent per year. There is more or less unanimous consent that this is a completely implausible magnitude and that the systematically mistaken forward rate during the first half of the 1980s cannot be explained by the existence of a risk premium to any noteworthy extent.[8]

The second logical explanation for the observed empirical phenomenon is discussed along two lines. (a) It is conceded that during the period under consideration exchange rate expectations have not been rational to the extent that the actors were aware of the true macroeconomic model. Subsequently, however, it is shown that systematic expectations errors for a limited period of time can be compatible with rational behaviour – namely, if the true model has changed and if the actors, in a stochastic environment, have to become familiar with new structural relationships and new coefficients (as an example, see Lewis 1989). (b) It is demonstrated that systematic differences between the forward rate and the subsequent spot rate may nevertheless be compatible with rational expectations if agents are not sure whether the present movement away from equilibrium will continue in the next period or not.

7. *The volatility of the real exchange rate is much higher under systems of flexible exchange rates than under systems of fixed exchange rates.* Figure 8.6

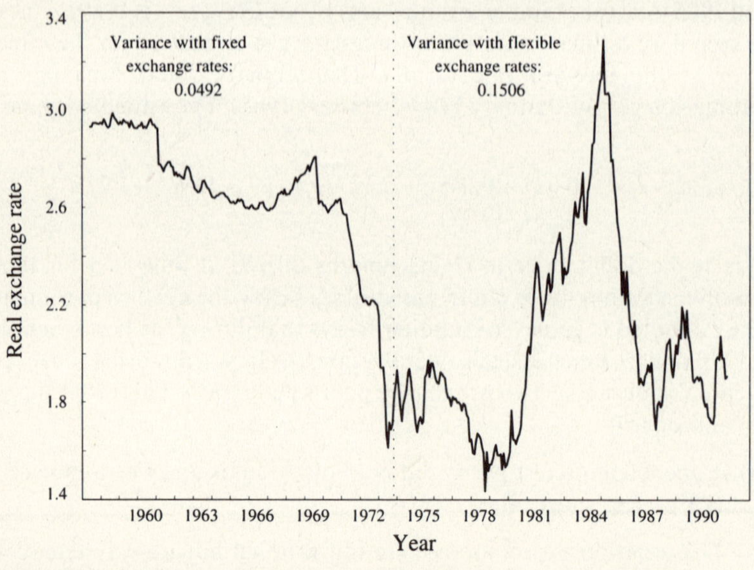

Figure 8.6 Real exchange rate Deutschmark/dollar, monthly data (Source: IMF, International Financial Statistics, data tape)

substantiates this assertion by means of monthly observations for the real Deutschmark/dollar rate from June 1957 to October 1991. Under the Bretton Woods system of fixed exchange rates up to May 1973, the variance of the real exchange rate is 0.0492. For the period of flexible exchange rates following the collapse of the Bretton Woods system the variance of the real exchange rate is as high as 0.1506. This empirical observation is not quite as trivial as it may seem at first glance. Recall that the monetarist exchange rate model assumes that goods prices are just as flexible as the exchange rate. With this assumption it is difficult to see why the real exchange rate EP^*/P should be less volatile when E is fixed than it is when E is determined in the market.

Table 8.1 repeats in concise form the stylized facts explained above and determines for each empirical regularity which of the models developed in this book are compatible with it and which are not. Apparently, the monetarist exchange rate model cannot adequately explain many of the stylized facts listed here, while the macroeconomic disequilibrium model (sticky-price monetary model) explains the majority of facts quite well.

Two empirical regularities remain, however, which no standard exchange rate model can explain: (1) that the real exchange rate occasionally shows no inclination at all to return to its former level after massive disturbances;[9] (2) that extended periods may occur, during which the forward rate misforecasts the spot rate to an extent which cannot be explained by the existence of a risk premium. Both these puzzles have stimulated new theoretical research. The next two subsections of this chapter will introduce important new developments.

Table 8.1 Exchange rate models vs. stylized facts of flexible exchange rates

Stylized fact	*Compatible models*	*Incompatible models*
1. Spot and forward exchange rates are highly correlated.	MSP, MFP, CS, PBA	—
2. The forward rate is a poor predictor of the future spot rate.	MSP, MFP, CS, PBA	—
3. Nominal and real exchange rates are highly correlated.	MSP, PBA	MFP, CS
4. After a disturbance, a real exchange rate does the following:		
(a) It only slowly moves back towards its equilibrium value.	MSP, PBA	MFP, CS
(b) It occasionally does not move towards its equilibrium value.	—	MSP, MFP, CS, PBA

Table 8.1 *cont.*

Stylized fact	*Compatible models*	*Incompatible models*
5. Bilateral spot rates are characterized by very high volatility.	MSP, MFP, CS, PBA	—
6. There exist extended periods of time, during which the forecast error of the forward exchange rate is not random:		
(a) To an extent that may be attributed to risk aversion.	CS, PBA	MSP, MFP
(b) To an extent that may not be attributed to risk aversion.	—	MSP, MFP, CS, PBA
7. The volatility of the real exchange rate is much higher under systems of flexible exchange rates than under systems of fixed exchange rates.	MSP, PBA	MFP, CS

Notes: The shorthand notation in columns 2 and 3 refers to the standard exchange rate models presented in Chapters 2, 5, 6 and 7. MSP denotes the monetary model with sticky prices (Dornbusch model), MFP the monetary model with flexible prices (monetarist model), CS the currency substitution model and PBA the portfolio balance approach.

8.2 Equilibrium exchange rates

The varying and overall rather modest empirical performance of monetary exchange rate models has led some authors to shift the focus from monetary to real disturbances. In principle, this shift of focus is possible in any one of the models presented in Chapters 2–7. However, in order to answer the question whether a careful modelling of the real economy suffices to explain the stylized facts of flexible exchange rates without having to take recourse to the assumption of sticky prices, real factors are introduced into a model with flexible prices such as the monetarist model. Other than in the monetarist exchange rate model, the models are strictly built on micro-economic foundation, within an intertemporal optimizing framework.[10] Models of this mould have been coined **equilibrium exchange rate models**.

The general idea underlying this approach is simple: changes in the supply of goods (for example, because of productivity shocks) and in the demand for goods (for example, because of preference shifts) or any expected change of future economic development have an impact on today's real variables, such as consumption, investment or the current account. But this changes relative prices in equilibrium. Therefore changes of the real exchange rate, which is a relative price, may well be a natural and necessary response to changing consumption, savings and investments plans.

Models tend to become very complicated as soon as these ideas are introduced into an intertemporal optimizing framework. Fortunately, the shift of emphasis characteristic of equilibrium exchange rate models as compared to monetary models may also be demonstrated within a simple static model. The discussion follows Stockman (1987).

Model 8.1 consists of a monetary sector and the goods market. The home country produces good Y while the world produces good X. Both goods are traded without transactions costs or any other restrictions. Real

Model 8.1
Equilibrium exchange rate model

1 Monetary sector

$\frac{M}{P} = Y^{\phi}$	domestic money demand	(8.5)
$\frac{M^*}{P^*} = X^{\phi}$	foreign money demand	(8.6)

2 Goods market

$Y = f(T, K, A)$	$f' > 0; f'' < 0$	production function for good Y	(8.7)
$X = g(T^*, K^*, A^*)$	$g' > 0; g'' < 0$	production function for good X	(8.8)
$U = U(x, y)$ $U_x, U_y > 0; U_{xx}, U_{yy} < 0$		utility function for representative individual	(8.9)
$\frac{U_x}{U_y} = R$		relative price	(8.10)
$R = \frac{EP^*}{P}$		real exchange rate	(8.11)

Notes: The signs of derivatives are given next to behavioural equations. An asterisk denotes the respective foreign variable. Variables are defined as follows:

M	domestic money supply	U_y	marginal utility of good Y
P	domestic price level	y	quantity of good Y per capita
Y	quantity of domestic good Y	x	quantity of good X per capita
X	quantity of foreign good X	K	capital
T	production technology	E	exchange rate
A	labour	U_x	marginal utility of good X
R	real exchange rate		

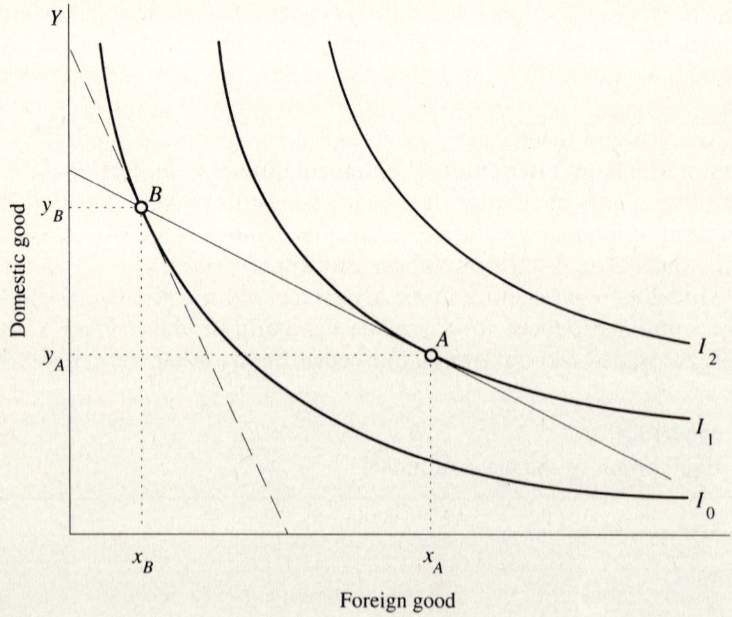

Figure 8.7 Individual utility maximization under a budget constraint

money demand at home is a function of domestic income, measured in Y. Equivalently, real money demand abroad is a function of foreign income, measured in X.

Equations (8.7) and (8.8) are production functions which state that quantities produced depend on factor inputs and the employed technology. Equation (8.9) is the utility function of a representative individual. To facilitate the graphical exposition below, assume that all individuals have the same utility function and the same income.[11] Since this implies that each individual can, and wants to, consume the same share of aggregate production, the utility level of each individual may be written as a function of per capita production, x and y. The indifference curves I_0, I_1 and I_2 depicted in Figure 8.7 characterize combinations of the two goods produced which lead to a constant utility level.

The consumption decisions each individual can make are constrained by his or her budget. Let the budget per head be b, the domestic price level P_A, the foreign price level P_A^* and the exchange rate E_A, then the choice set of our representative individual is given by the solid straight line. From a microeconomic perspective, prices and the exchange rate are given variables for each individual, who maximizes utility in the present case by consuming y_A and x_A. This puts the individual into point A, which is on the highest available indifference curve. If the budget constraint moves to the position indicated by the dashed line, because of price and/or income changes, the individual responds by changing his or her consumption basket maximizing utility in point B.

This microeconomic line of argument is not appropriate in our present macroeconomic context. Since the situation presented in Figure 8.7 equally applies to all individuals, we can no longer assume prices to be exogenous and quantities to respond. On the contrary, we now have to assume that the quantities produced (and consumed) per head are given according to production functions (8.7) and (8.8) and that prices respond in order to equate given supplies to desired demand.

As an example, assume the relative price were $R_A = (E_A P_A^*)/P_A$, so that our representative individual would desire to consume y_A and x_A. Based on the available factors of production and technology, however, x_B and y_B are produced per head. In this situation an aggregate excess demand for X in the amount $X_A - X_B$ and an excess supply of Y in the amount $Y_B - Y_A$ exists. Therefore, good X becomes more expensive compared to good Y. The relative price (that is, the real exchange rate) increases until it equals the (negative) slope of the budget constraint (the broken line on Figure 8.7). Only now demanded quantities equal supplied quantities for each of the two produced goods and our economy is equilibrium. If point A signals production possibilities given factor supplies and technologies, the terms of trade, or in our terminology the real exchange rate, equals the slope of indifference curve I_1 in A. Equation (8.10) states this equality between the real exchange rate and the (negative) marginal rate of substitution. Finally, the last equation of our model defines the real exchange rate in nominal prices. We have already made use of this equation in our example above.

Upon solving (8.5) and (8.6) for the price levels and substituting into (8.11), we arrive at the exchange rate equation

$$E = \frac{MX^{\phi}}{M^* Y^{\phi}} R \tag{8.12}$$

Note that (8.12) equals the exchange rate equation of the monetarist model if purchasing-power parity is assumed to hold at all times, $R = 1$ (with the implicit assumption that at home and abroad the same goods basket is consumed).[12] The innovation of equation (8.12) is that absolute purchasing-power parity is assumed to hold neither permanently nor in the long run. Rather, the real exchange rate, defined here as the real rate of the exchange between domestically produced good Y and the externally produced good X, is an *endogenous* variable. Figure 8.8 illustrates that this relative price is influenced by supply-side changes as well as by changes of the preferences determining demand.[13]

A reduction of domestic supply from Y_A to Y_D reduces the real exchange rate to the value indicated by the lesser slope of the indifference

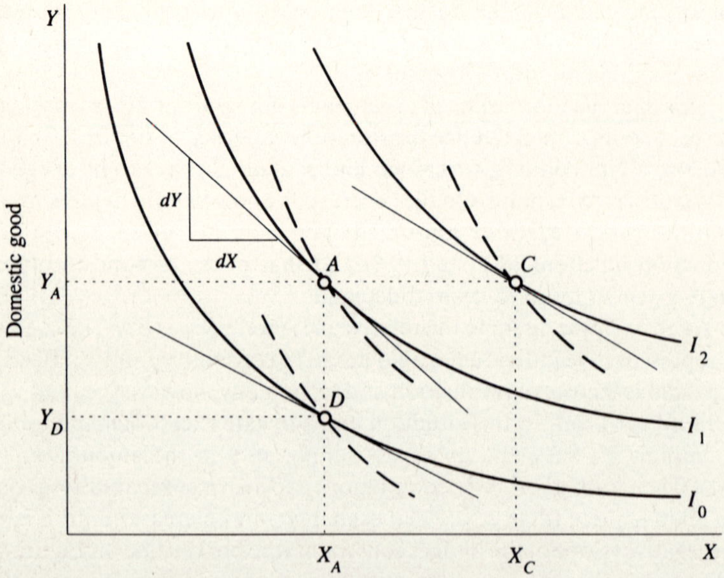

Figure 8.8 The real exchange rate as a macroeconomic response to preferences and the supply of goods

curve in D (we assume decreasing marginal utility). An expansion of supply abroad from X_A to X_C would have the same effect.

A change of preferences is identical to a change of the utility function and hence a movement of the indifference curves. A shift of preferences towards good X, for example, turns indifference curves steeper, with the effect that the real exchange rate is higher for any supply mix and equal to the steeper slopes of indifference curves through points A, C and D (the broken lines in Figure 8.8).

PROBLEM 8.1

If per capita income equals b, each individual faces the restriction

$$b = Py + EP^*x$$

This budget constraint meets the Y axis at b/P. Both b and P are obviously independent of preferences. Therefore, if preferences change – making indifference curves steeper – the budget constraint should nevertheless meet the Y axes at b/P. Given this argument, how can the real exchange rate change so as to make the budget constraint in A tangential to the new, steeper indifference curve?

Inserting (8.10) into (8.12), the exchange rate in general equilibrium is

$$E = \frac{MX^{\phi}U_x}{M^*Y^{\phi}U_y} \tag{8.13}$$

The new insight offered by this exchange rate equation is that any real shock which affects the marginal rate of substitution between goods in equilibrium changes the nominal and the real exchange rate. In contrast to monetary exchange rate models, nominal exchange rate changes do not *cause* real exchange rate changes; rather, both nominal and real exchange rate changes play their part in a macroeconomic equilibrium response to changing real factors such as production technology, preferences and factor supplies. This has rather far-reaching implications for monetary and exchange rate policies. A constant real exchange rate no longer carries any normative weight. Neither high exchange rate volatility nor massive changes of the real exchange rate are 'good' or 'bad'. Since both only reflect the endogenous emergence of new equilibria, they do not have to be fought by means of exchange rate management policies. Let us now turn to two examples purported to demonstrate the consequences of real supply and demand shocks for the exchange rate.

8.2.1 Technical progress at home

A one-time improvement of productivity in the home country increases the supply of good Y. This raises the real exchange rate, the price of X in terms of Y, and this, according to equation (8.12), also raises the nominal exchange rate E. With identical households at home and abroad this also raises the amount of good Y that is exported. Though we observe the already familiar positive correlation between the nominal exchange rate, the real exchange rate and real exports, the causal pattern is quite different from that encountered in monetary exchange rate models. The observed undervaluation and the increase in exports, due to the improved competitive position of the home country, are not *caused* by the observed depreciation. Rather, the productivity increase calls for a change of relative prices (the real exchange rate) and thus forces the nominal exchange rate to adapt.

Policy implications are radically different from those of monetary models: since the real exchange rate, which in our simple model is identical with the terms of trade, is only determined by preferences, technology and other real variables, any monetary measures designed to improve a country's competitive position are mistaken. Foreign exchange market intervention, for example, has no effect on the real exchange rate, despite the observed statistical correlation between the nominal and the real exchange rate (which is due to the response to real shocks).

8.2.2 Change of preferences

If consumer preferences shift from the domestically produced good *Y* to the foreign good *X*, this provokes a depreciation of the domestic currency. Graphically this shift of preferences from *Y* to *X* means that indifference curves become steeper (see dashed curves): for the utility level of our representative individual to remain constant a given reduction of *X* must be compensated for by a larger amount of *Y* than before. This holds for all possible combinations of *X* and *Y* and therefore, as shown in our graph (Figure 8.8), also for the bundles of goods represented by *A*, *C* and *D*.

If in Figure 8.8 supplied quantities were X_A and Y_A, *A* could not be an equilibrium, given relative prices which determine the slope of the budget constraint. Departing from *A*, each consumer could increase his or her own utility level by expanding the consumption of good *X* and reducing the consumption of good *Y*. Since this is impossible in the light of the constrained aggregate supply, the incipient disequilibrium changes relative prices. In terms of *Y*, *X* becomes more expensive. The real exchange rate rises.

The observed depreciation should not be mistaken as an improvement of the competitive position of the home country. While it is true that the domestically produced good is now comparatively cheaper, this is exactly matched by a reduced willingness to pay of those who demand the domestically produced good. Therefore, we observe the same consumption patterns in both countries and the same trade patterns internationally after the devaluation as we did before the devaluation. Here again it would be completely wrong to fight the observed nominal and real depreciation by means of monetary or exchange rate policies in order to restore competitiveness. Such policy measures are not necessary, nor would they bear the promise of success, since the observed exchange rate reaction is nothing but an equilibrium response to a demand shock.

PROBLEM 8.2

The home country places a tariff on the import of good *X*. How does this affect the exchange rate according to the equilibrium exchange rate model?

8.3 Exchange rate movements as bubbles

Foreign exchange markets occasionally have produced seemingly *unwarranted* and accelerating price movements away from their conceived equilibrium values, which cannot be explained by reference to the overshooting hypothesis alone. Recently, successful attempts have been made to model such price movements as bubbles which are compatible with rational behaviour.[14]

Whether a currency price is justified by fundamental variables such as the money supply, aggregate income, etc., depends on the exchange rate model employed. Generally, exchange rate bubbles may occur in any exchange rate model, and rationally so. We will demonstrate the possibility of rational exchange rate bubbles in the context of the monetarist model analyzed in Chapter 5 above. For convenience, the structural equations of the model are repeated in Model 8.2.

Model 8.2
Basic monetarist exchange rate model (discrete time)

1 Goods market

$p_t = e_t$	goods market equilibrium	(8.14)

2 Money market

$m_t - p_t = \phi y_t - \lambda i_t$	money market equilibrium	(8.15)

3 International asset market

$i_t = E_t e_{t+1} - e_t$	asset market equilibrium	(8.16)

Notes: Lower-case variables are in natural logarithms (except for the interest rate i). Greek letters denote positive parameters. E is the expectations operator. Variables are defined as follows:

- i domestic interest rate
- e exchange rate
- y aggregate supply of domestically produced goods (exogenous)
- m domestic money (exogenous)
- p domestic price level

8.3.1 Ever-expanding bubbles

From Chapter 5 we already know (equation (5.19)) that in the monetarist model today's exchange rate is a weighted *average* of today's fundamental variables and of the exchange rate expected for the next period:

$$e_t = \frac{1}{1+\lambda}(m_t - \phi y_t) + \frac{\lambda}{1+\lambda} E_t e_{t+1} \tag{8.17}$$

For our present purposes we may assume $m_t = \bar{m}$ and $y_t = \bar{y}$ for all t. Making use also of the definition $\alpha \equiv \lambda/(1+\lambda)$, this yields

$$e_t = (1-\alpha)(\bar{m} - \phi\bar{y}) + \alpha E_t e_{t+1} \tag{8.18}$$

If agents are aware of the structural relations governing our economy, rational actors, of course, also expect equation (8.18) to hold in the next period. Hence

$$E_t e_{t+1} = (1-\alpha)(\bar{m} - \phi\bar{y}) + \alpha E_t e_{t+2} \tag{8.19}$$

One way of solving our model, which has been employed in Chapter 5, is by forward substitution of (8.19) into (8.18). Forward substitution makes use of the fact that equation (8.19) must hold between any two successive periods of time.

Another way to obtain a solution is suggested by the fact that in the present deterministic context rational expectations are equivalent to perfect foresight. Hence exchange rates are always as expected and equation (8.19) therefore implies, after rearranging terms and shifting the equation back in time by one period,

$$e_{t+1} - \alpha^{-1} e_t = -\lambda^{-1}(\bar{m} - \phi y) \tag{8.20}$$

We see that the movement of the exchange rate over time is determined by a first-order linear difference equation with constant coefficients and constant inhomogeneity.[15] The general solution of (8.20) comprises a particular solution for this equation, $e_{t+1} = e_t = \bar{e} = \bar{m} - \phi\bar{y}$, and the so-called complementary solution of the homogeneous version of (8.20) (see Chiang 1984: 554–6). The homogeneous version of (8.20) is $e_{t+1} - \alpha^{-1} e_t = 0$ and has the solution $e_t = A\alpha^{-t}$, where A is an arbitrary constant. Thus the general solution of (8.20) is

$$e_t = \bar{e} + A\alpha^{-t} \tag{8.21}$$

Since (8.21) holds at any point in time, that is, at point $t=0$, A is given by (8.21) as

$$A = e_0 - \bar{e}$$

This is simply the deviation of the exchange rate at time 0 from its equilibrium value.[16] $A\alpha^{-t}$ in (8.21) denotes the deviation of the exchange rate from its equilibrium value at time t. Let us denote this deviation

$$s_t = A\alpha^{-t} \tag{8.22}$$

as a bubble s_t. Upon substituting (8.22) into (8.21), the exchange rate may be expressed as

$$e_t = \bar{e} + s_t \tag{8.23}$$

Figure 8.9 depicts exchange rate paths which may result from equation (8.23). Since $\alpha^{-1} > 1, s_0 \neq 0$, that is, any hint of a bubble at time 0 gives rise to an accelerating process which, despite rational expectations, moves the exchange rate further and further away from its stationary equilibrium

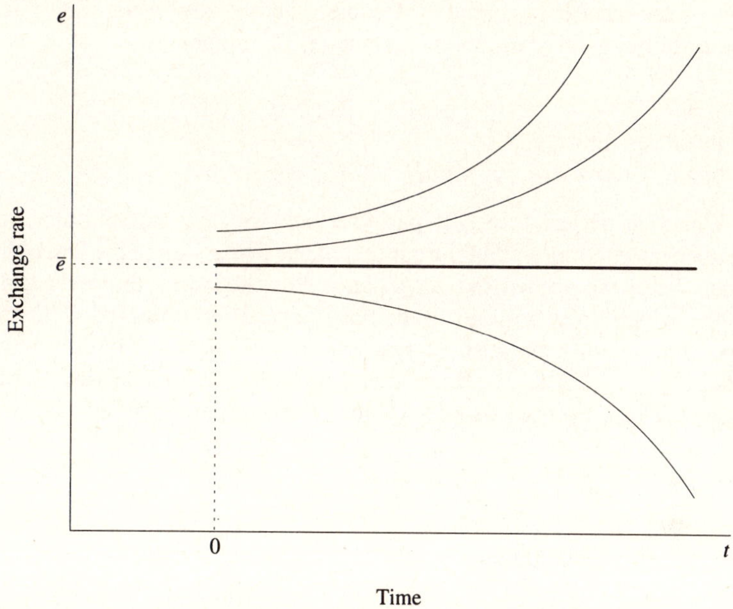

Figure 8.9 Possible exchange rate paths under rational expectations, including never-ending bubbles

value. Because actors expect the exchange rate to move away from its equilibrium value, the exchange rate indeed does so.

On the bubble time paths depicted in Figure 8.9 the following holds:

1. Actors have perfect foresight. Exchange rates are always as expected.
2. The exchange rate moves away from its equilibrium value at an accelerating pace.
3. Uncovered interest parity holds at all times. The foreign exchange market is efficient.
4. Market participants are always perfectly sure that the bubble will keep on growing.
5. Along bubble paths, market participants pay currency prices which are not justified by market fundamentals, only because the market counts on further exchange rate changes.

As we have seen, the monetarist exchange rate model (just as many other exchange rate models) may generate never-ending bubbles which grow at an accelerating pace. Of course, actors also recognize that an existing bubble will grow forever, since (8.23) implies:

$$\lim_{t\to\infty} E_0 s_t = \lim_{t\to\infty} s_0 \alpha^{-t} = \begin{cases} +\infty & \text{if } s_0 > 0 \\ 0 & \text{if } s_0 = 0 \\ -\infty & \text{if } s_0 < 0 \end{cases}$$

Unstable perfect foresight paths, which we now call bubbles, have already been encountered in the context of our discussion of the Dornbusch model. There we argued that experience tells the actors that ever-lasting bubbles which grow without limits have never been observed. Thus they know that, if only because of restrictions not included in our model, eventually $\lim_{t\to\infty} E_0 s_t = 0$. Since this implies $s_0 = 0$, ever-lasting bubbles cannot really come into existence. Among the time paths sketched in Figure 8.9 the economy automatically selects the horizontal equilibrium path $e_t = \bar{e}$.

8.3.2 Bursting bubbles

If ever-expanding bubbles are hard to justify, maybe temporary bubbles are not. Assume agents are not sure whether an existing bubble will keep on growing or whether it will burst in the next period. Define the bursting of a bubble as the sudden return of the exchange rate to its equilibrium value as defined by the fundamental variables. Hence, if a bubble bursts at time t^*, we have $s_{t^*} = 0$ and $e_{t^*} = \bar{e}$.

As a reference path, Figure 8.10 depicts a never-ending bubble, SS', which would result from the initial disequilibrium s_0. If at time 0 (in S) the market expects the bubble to burst in the next period with a probability smaller than 1, investors all change the currency today, making the bubble burst today, unless they expect a currency depreciation which not only compensates for lower interest rates abroad but also for the risk of a sudden loss of value of foreign bonds due to a bursting of the bubble.

Example

Assume that at point S in Figure 8.10 the domestic interest rate exceeds the foreign interest rate by 10 percentage points. Uncovered interest parity only holds in S if the domestic currency is expected to depreciate by 10 per cent. Under perfect foresight and the scenario of a never-ending bubble the domestic currency will indeed depreciate by 10 per cent, following the path SS'.

Things are different, however, if the market only expects the bubble to continue with a probability of 50 per cent. Now investors are only indifferent between both currencies if they expect the bubble to grow by more than 20 per cent in case it does not burst. This results from the equilibrium condition

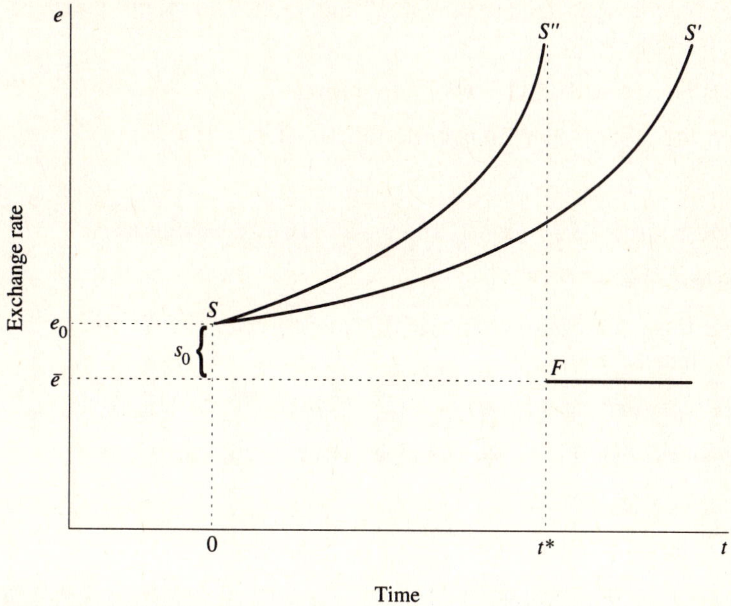

Figure 8.10 Comparison of a never-ending bubble (SS') and a bursting bubble ($SS''F$)

$$E_0e_1 - e_0 = i_0 \tag{8.24}$$

Note that $i_0 = 10$ and $E_0e_1 - e_0 = 0.5(e_1 - e_0) - 0.5(e_0 - \bar{e})$. Insertion of this into (8.24) yields:

$$e_1 - e_0 = 20 + (e_0 - \bar{e})$$

Thus a bubble about the continuation of which actors are not sure grows at a faster pace than a bubble which individuals consider never-ending. In the present example, the latter would grow at a rate of 10 per cent.

The time path SS'' in Figure 8.10 depicts one feasible path of a bursting bubble. Here the bubble bursts at time t^*. It is important to note that t^* is random and not known to the actors *ex ante*.

Generally, the equilibrium condition for the international capital market is

$$E_te_{t+1} - e_t = i_t \tag{8.25}$$

(where $i^* = 0$). If actors expect the bubble to continue in the next period with probability π (and thus to burst in the next period with probability $1 - \pi$), expected depreciation is

$$E_te_{t+1} - e_t = \pi(e_{t+1} - e_t) + (1 - \pi)(\bar{e} - e_t) \tag{8.26}$$

Equating the right-hand sides of (8.25) and (8.26) and solving for the rate of depreciation yields

$$e_{t+1}-e_t=\pi^{-1}i_t+(1-\pi)\pi^{-1}(e_t-\bar{e}) \tag{8.27}$$

From the money demand equation the interest rate is

$$i_t=\lambda^{-1}(p_t-\bar{m}+\phi y)$$

which, because of $\bar{e}=\bar{m}-\phi\bar{y}$ and $e_t=p_t$, may be written as

$$i_t=\lambda^{-1}(e_t-\bar{e})$$

Using this equation to eliminate the interest rate in (8.27) and collecting terms produces

$$e_{t+1}-(\alpha\pi)^{-1}e_t=[1-(\alpha\pi)^{-1}]\bar{e}$$

The solution of this first-order difference equation is

$$e_t=\bar{e}+(e_0-\bar{e})(\alpha\pi)^{-t}$$

or

$$e_t=\bar{m}-\phi\bar{y}+A(\alpha\pi)^{-t} \tag{8.28}$$

Equation (8.28) describes a bursting bubble which is compatible with rational expectations and a notion of an efficient foreign exchange market. Actors see both paths correctly, which the exchange rate may follow, and are also aware of the correct probability that the bubble may burst. A comparison of (8.28) and (8.21) reveals in general terms what has already been demonstrated by means of an example above: as long as they continue, bursting bubbles have to grow at a faster pace than ever-lasting bubbles.[17] This compensates market participants for the risk of losses that occur when the bubble bursts.

PROBLEM 8.3

The probability that an existing bubble bursts in the next period and the exchange rate returns to its equilibrium value is $1-\pi$. (1) What is the expected lifetime of the bubble? (2) Compute the rate of depreciation of the exchange rate.

Bursting bubbles in exchange rate development have one peculiar property: the forward exchange rate, which under the assumption of risk neutrality is identical to the expected exchange rate, is systematically smaller than the future spot rate for growing bubbles and larger than the future spot rate for falling bubbles, as long as the bubble does not burst.

Example

Depart from the working hypothesis that the booming dollar of the first half of the 1980s was generated by a bursting bubble of the kind analyzed above. This is tantamount to assuming that exchange rates, interest rates and the equilibrium exchange rate satisfy the following equation (obtained from (8.25) and (8.26)) at all times:

$$\pi(e_{t+1}-e_t)+(1-\pi)(\bar{e}_t-e_t)-(i_t-i_t^*)=0 \tag{8.29}$$

Between 1980 and 1985 the three differences given in parentheses on average equalled the following values:

$$\varnothing(e_{t+1}-e_t)=-0.13$$
$$\varnothing(\bar{e}_t-e_t)=0.33$$
$$\varnothing(i_t-i_t^*)=0.03$$

Upon substitution of this into (8.29) we arrive at $\pi=0.65$, which means that investors expected the bubble to continue in the next year with a probability of 65 per cent. In fact, the bubble continued to grow for five years. The probability for this to occur was only $\pi^5=(0.65)^5=0.12$, that is, 12 per cent. This is not a lot and signals that exchange rate bubbles of this intensity will not occur very frequently, but may well be observed on occasion.

In Figure 8.10 the bubble SS″F depicts an excessive development of the exchange rate that may result from the combination of the monetarist exchange rate model with a bursting bubble. Of course, exchange rates in reality do not appear to exhibit this very peculiar shape, with an accelerating movement away from, followed by a sudden return to, the equilibrium exchange rate.[18] More realistic looking bubbles result, however, from simple modifications of our model, which has been kept as simple as possible for expository purposes:

- The model can be put into a stochastic context, with unexpected changes of the fundamental variables or of the bubble.
- π may be considered a stochastic variable, following a random walk, for example.
- π may be endogenized, reflecting the age or the size of the bubble.
- The bubble may be introduced into the Dornbusch model with sticky prices. If a bubble bursts in this scenario, the exchange rate only slowly returns to its equilibrium value because of the slow movement of goods prices. In addition, the bubble does not have to grow as fast as in the context of the monetarist model, since losses that occur if the bubble bursts are smaller.

PROBLEM 8.4

Given the monetarist model of a bursting bubble presented above, define the bursting of the bubble as a stagnation of the exchange rate, not as an immediate return to the equilibrium value. Thus, if a bubble bursts, the exchange rate remains where it was in the last period. Discuss this case.

8.3.3 How do bubbles emerge?

The above discussion intimates that all we need for a bubble to emerge is some minimal displacement from the one stable rational expectations equilibrium path. While this appears easy to accomplish when information is imperfect, we will show that *bubble theories do not really explain what triggers the emergence of a bubble.*

The issues related to the genesis of a bubble are more or less the same for a never-ending and a bursting bubble. For the sake of simplicity we therefore proceed from Model 8.3, a model of a never-ending bubble, in which agents believe in a model different from the true model.

The movement of the exchange rate is determined by (8.14)–(8.16), which, after letting $m_t = \bar{m}$ and $y_t = \bar{y}$, can be combined to yield

$$e_t = \frac{1}{1+\lambda}(\bar{m} - \phi\bar{y}) + \frac{\lambda}{1+\lambda} E_t e_{t+1} \tag{8.17}$$

What differs from the above treatment of the model is that individuals derive their 'rational' expectations from the not quite correct model (8.14′)–(8.16′). In contrast to the true model, agents believe some arbitrary variable μ, which may stand for 'sunspots', to influence equilibrium in the goods market. If this perceived model were the true one, the exchange rate would follow

$$e_t = \frac{1}{1+\lambda}(m_t - \phi y_t - \mu_t) + \frac{\lambda}{1+\lambda} E_t e_{t+1} \tag{8.17′}$$

Since individuals believe (8.14′)–(8.16′) to be true, they *expect* the exchange rate to be driven by (8.17′):

$$E_t e_{t+1} = \frac{1}{1+\lambda}(\bar{m} - \phi\bar{y} - E_t\mu_{t+1}) + \frac{\lambda}{1+\lambda} E_t e_{t+2} \tag{8.30}$$

Here again, agents expect the exchange rate to follow a first-order difference equation, which now has the solution

■ Model 8.3 Monetarist exchange rate model with erroneous perceptions

True model

1 Goods market

$$p_t = e_t \tag{8.14}$$

2 Money market

$$m_t - p_t = \phi y_t - \lambda i_t \tag{8.15}$$

3 International asset market

$$i_t = E_t e_{t+1} - e_t \tag{8.16}$$

Perceived model

1 Goods market

$$p_t = e_t + \mu_t \tag{8.14'}$$

2 Money market

$$m_t - p_t = \phi y_t - \lambda i_t \tag{8.15'}$$

3 International asset market

$$i_t = E_t e_{t+1} - e_t \tag{8.16'}$$

Notes: Lower-case variables are in natural logarithms. Greek letters denote positive parameters. $E(.)$ is the expectations operator. Variables are defined as follows:

i	domestic interest rate	m	domestic money (exogenous)
e	exchange rate	p	domestic price level
y	aggregate supply of domestically produced goods (exogenous)	μ	'sunspot' variable

$$E_t e_{t+1} = \bar{m} - \phi\bar{y} - E_t\mu_{t+1} + A\left(\frac{1+\lambda}{\lambda}\right)^{t+1} \tag{8.31}$$

The involved constant A may conveniently be determined by letting $t = -1$ in (8.31):

$$A = E_{-1}e_0 - (\bar{m} - \phi\bar{y} - E_{-1}\mu_0) \tag{8.32}$$

Inserting (8.31) and (8.32) into (8.17) and combining terms yields

$$e_t = \bar{m} - \phi\bar{y} + \frac{\lambda}{1+\lambda}E_t\mu_{t+1} + [E_{-1}e_0 - (\bar{m} - \phi\bar{y} - E_{-1}\mu_0)]\left(\frac{1+\lambda}{\lambda}\right)^t \tag{8.33}$$

Equation (8.33) says that for a bubble to start growing in period 0 the expression in brackets must be different from zero. The economic meaning of this is revealed after noting $(\bar{m}-\phi\bar{y}-E_{-1}\mu_0)=E_{-1}\bar{e}_0$, which turns the expression given in brackets into $E_{-1}e_0-E_{-1}\bar{e}_0$. Thus a bubble is born if the market expects the exchange rate to differ from the *expected* equilibrium exchange rate in period 0. Whether this equilibrium is computed from the correct or from a completely wrong model is not really the issue.

But this is not all. Since flexible prices keep this monetarist model in equilibrium permanently, $E_{-1}\bar{e}_0$ is exactly the exchange rate which the agents' perceived model predicts in period -1 for period 0, given that the model was in its perceived equilibrium in period -1. So a bubble *begins* to develop in period 0 if, and only if, individuals anticipate the exchange rate to move to where it *cannot* move according to the model which they hold. As this would be completely irrational, the only remaining possibility is that the bubble already existed in period -1. But then we would have to explain what started the bubble in period -1. This line of reasoning eventually leads to the conclusion that an exchange rate bubble which we observe today must have existed from the very beginning.[19]

8.3.4 The peso problem

Another way to reconcile the existence of systematic forecast errors with rationality is by reference to the so-called **peso problem**. While the peso-problem hypothesis is an explanation in its own right, it bears some similarities to the reasoning behind bubble theories. This makes it appropriate to discuss the peso problem in the context of the present subsection.

Consider the basic monetarist exchange rate model (Model 8.2), letting $y_t=0$. Then the rational expectations solution (see Chapter 5) is

$$e_t=\frac{1}{1+\lambda}\left[m_t+\sum_{j=1}^{\infty}\left(\frac{\lambda}{1+\lambda}\right)^j E_t m_{t+j}\right] \tag{8.34}$$

Let the money supply follow the stochastic process

$$m_t=\begin{cases} m_{t-1} & \text{with probability } 1-\pi \\ 0 & \text{with probability } \pi \end{cases} \tag{8.35}$$

Equation (8.35) states that the possibility of an irreversible regime change (in monetary policy) exists whenever $m_t>0$. If $m_t>0$, the money supply remains at m_t in the next period with probability $1-\pi$, but may be reduced to zero with probability π. Once it is reduced to zero, it will remain there.

In order to obtain a more compact notation, we may assume without loss of generality that

$$m_t=1 \tag{8.36}$$

Now according to (8.35) the rational expectation of the money supply is $E_t m_{t+1} = 1 - \pi$ for $t+1$, $E_t m_{t+2} = (1-\pi)^2$ for $t+2$ and so on. In general, rational money supply expectations held at time t are

$$E_t m_{t+j} = (1-\pi)^j \tag{8.37}$$

Substituting (8.36) and (8.37) into (8.34) gives the exchange rate at time t:

$$\begin{aligned} e_t &= \frac{1}{1+\lambda}\left[1 + \frac{\lambda}{1+\lambda}(1-\pi) + \left(\frac{\lambda}{1+\lambda}\right)^2 (1-\pi)^2 + \dots\right] \\ &= \frac{1}{1+\lambda}\sum_{j=0}^{\infty}\left[\frac{\lambda}{1+\lambda}(1-\pi)\right]^j \end{aligned} \tag{8.38}$$

The expectations error to be observed at time $t+1$ depends on whether the regime change has already occurred or not. If it has occurred, no forecast error will be observed ever after, since $e_{t+j} = E_{t+j-1} e_{t+j} = 0$ for $j > 1$.[20] If the regime change has not taken place yet in period $t+1$, the observed expectations error is[21]

$$\begin{aligned} e_{t+1} - E_t e_{t+1} &= \frac{1}{1+\lambda}\left[1 + \frac{\lambda}{1+\lambda}(1-\pi) + \left(\frac{\lambda}{1+\lambda}\right)^2 (1-\pi)^2 + \dots\right] \\ &\quad -(1-\pi)\frac{1}{1+\lambda}\left[1 + (1-\pi)\frac{\lambda}{1+\lambda} + (1-\pi)^2 \right. \\ &\quad \left. \times \left(\frac{\lambda}{1+\lambda}\right)^2 + \dots\right] \\ &= \pi\frac{1}{1+\lambda}\sum_{j=0}^{\infty}\left[\frac{\lambda}{1+\lambda}(1-\pi)\right]^j \\ &= \pi e_{t+1} > 0 \end{aligned} \tag{8.39}$$

We might have arrived at the same result in a probably more straightforward fashion by noting $E_t e_{t+1} = (1-\pi)e_{t+1} + \pi \cdot 0$. Apparently, exchange rate expectations are systematically off target by consistently underestimating the eventual exchange rate as long as the possible change of regime does not occur.

Systematic expectations errors and forecast errors of the forward rate should be observed whenever there is a small but continuing chance of a regime change. Scenarios in which the peso problem might be at work are as follows:

- Hyperinflations, which agents know will eventually have to be stopped by an abrupt change of regime, economic and/or political.
- Generally, whenever the possibility of a revolution or of a more peaceful change of power exists.[22]

- When a country might enter a fixed-parity system such as the EMS.
- When some non-negligible probability exists of the outbreak of a war or of a major resource discovery.

Our mentioning of hyperinflations suggests that the peso problem might even interact with a bubble, if the bubble raises the likelihood of a regime change.

8.4 Summary

Numerous efforts to estimate exchange rate equations by means of econometric methods have produced rather sobering results. No explanation of empirical exchange rate movements seems to exist which is sufficiently stable over time. On the other hand, each of the models outlined in this book does fit the empirical data for limited periods of time. This conveys the impression that the institutional framework is not very stable, that the relevant exchange rate model changes from time to time. This is underlined by the empirical finding that opinion leaders alternate between different models on which they base their exchange rate expectations or forecasts.[23]

One way to respond to the observed structural instability of econometric exchange rate equations is to retreat to softer forms of empirical testing; for example, listing the recognized stylized facts of flexible exchange rates reveals that many of those facts correspond to central properties of standard exchange rate models. Standard models, though, are incapable of explaining two important empirical regularities which are frequently mentioned: the first observation is that real exchange rates are not only sticky, but occasionally show tendencies not to return at all to some previous equilibrium value. The second observation is that exchange rate forecasts implied by the forward rate may over long periods of time differ systematically from the eventual spot rate. The sheer size of this systematic expectations error cannot possibly be explained by the existence of a risk premium.

Theoretical research has responded to these two puzzling empirical regularities. *Equilibrium exchange rate models* focus on real factors behind exchange rate movements, such as preference changes or productivity shifts. Changes of the nominal or of the real exchange rates which are due to such causes are equilibrium responses and do not call for interference in the form of monetary, exchange rate or trade policy measures. It is a major weakness of this approach, however, that the proposed causes of permanent exchange rate changes are not readily observed and measured. But even without any, or without any precise, data, it appears more than daring to attribute the development of the Deutschmark/dollar exchange rate depicted in Figure 8.3 to preference changes and technology shocks alone. What is more, while the equilibrium exchange rate approach may explain an empirical regularity not readily explained by other models – the occasional persistence or finality of real exchange rate changes – it completely fails with regard to other stylized facts. Among those is the observation that the real exchange rate is much more volatile when nominal exchange rates are flexible than when they are fixed. These and other weaknesses take a huge bite out of the equilibrium exchange rate approach's claim to offer a complete explanation of exchange rate behaviour. The importance of its contribution to exchange rate theory remains undisputed, however, notably its pointing out that monetary exchange rate models do not pay proper attention to real variables.

Models of exchange rate *bubbles* and related approaches, such as the *peso problem*, show that systematically biased forecasts (*ex post*) of the forward rate do not necessarily mean that expectations were irrational *ex ante*. Biased forward rates may be due to destabilizing but insecure expectations which are self-fulfilling as long as the generated bubble does not burst and thus drive the exchange rate back to equilibrium at once. Similar to problems encountered with equilibrium exchange rate models, the existence of bubbles is difficult to verify empirically.[24] The main reason for this is that a bubble is defined in relation to some equilibrium, which has to be derived from some model. Therefore, empirical work on bubbles always tests a joint hypothesis: that the scrutinized data were not generated by a bubble and that the equilibrium model is correct. The obvious problem with this second part of the joint hypothesis is that, according to the econometric work reported above, no empirically satisfactory exchange rate model exists.[25]

Difficulties in explaining how bubbles emerge have shifted some of the focus of exchange rate theories back to the analysis and modelling of expectations formation processes. Recent and promising developments which move beyond the first-generation models sketched above drop the assumption that all actors have the same expectations. Departing from the survey results published in *Euromoney* referred to above, Frankel and Froot (1991), for example, postulate that the foreign exchange market is heterogeneous. A varying share of the market forms expectations by means of technical analysis, while the others believe in the exchange rate being determined by fundamental variables through a structural model.

On the basis of forceful empirical evidence Ito (1990) most convincingly pleads for further efforts to develop and improve models with heterogeneous exchange rate expectations. On the basis of survey data collected from forty-four Japanese enterprises over a period of two years, he concludes that expectations are pronouncedly heterogeneous and in many cases even reflect the wishful thinking of those who have been questioned.[26]

8.5 Answers to the problems

Problem 8.1

When answering this question, we must move from a microeconomic to a macroeconomic perspective.

The budget constraint for all domestic residents (denoted by the subscript D) is

$$PY = PY_D^d + EPX_D^d \rightarrow Y_D^d = Y - (EP^*/P)X_D^d$$

The budget constraint for all foreigners (denoted by the subscript F) is

$$P^*X = P^*X_F^d + PE^{-1}Y_F^d \rightarrow Y_F^d = (EP^*/P)X - (EP^*/P)X_F^d$$

The superscript d characterizes demanded quantities.

The budget constraint for the entire 'world' results from adding the domestic to the foreign budget constraint:

$$Y_D^d + Y_F^d = Y + (EP^*/P)X - (EP^*/P)(X_D^d + X_F^d)$$

Contrary to the microeconomic restriction formulated in the text, this aggregate restriction does not possess an exogenous constant term which is independent of monetary variables. Incipient disequilibria change both the slope and the constant term so as to equate the real exchange rate and the marginal rate of substitution.

Problem 8.2

A tariff changes neither preferences nor quantities produced. Therefore, the relative price does not change. Of course, now the relative price must include the tariff: $R = ZEP^*/P$. Since R, P and P^* do not change after the introduction of the tariff, the nominal exchange rate must sink in order to compensate exactly for the tariff (under free trade there is $Z = 1$).

Problem 8.3

1. The *a priori* probability that the bubble continues through the present period is π. Thus the expected lifetime of the bubble during the first period also equals π.

Should the bubbles still be alive at the beginning of the second period, the expected lifetime of the bubble during the second period would again equal π. Since the probability that the bubble has not already burst at the beginning of the next period also equals π, today's expectations of the bubble's lifetime during the second period alone equals π^2. By the same token, today's expectation of the bubble's lifetime during period 3 equals π^3, during period 4 equals π^4 and so on. Thus the expected total lifetime of a bubble which exists today is

$$\pi+\pi^2+\pi^3+\pi^4+\ldots+\pi^\infty=\pi/(1-\pi)$$

2. According to (8.28), a bursting bubble follows the path

$$e_t=\bar{e}+(e_0-\bar{e})(\alpha\pi)^{-t}$$

as long as it does not burst. We obtain the percentage rate of change of the exchange rate by shifting the equation forward by one period in time and then subtracting the old equation from this new equation. This yields

$$\begin{aligned} e_{t+1}-e_t&=(e_0-\bar{e})(\alpha\pi)^{-(t+1)}-(e_0-\bar{e})(\alpha\pi)^{-t} \\ &=(e_0-\bar{e})(1-\alpha\pi)(\alpha\pi)^{-(t+1)} \end{aligned}$$

The rate of depreciation increases with the probability that the bubble bursts and with the initial size of the bubble. Also, the bubble grows faster and faster in order to compensate for the steadily rising losses that would occur if the bubble bursts.

Problem 8.4

Common sense may suggest that such a bubble would not have to grow as fast as the one described in the text, since now the exchange rate is only stabilized when the bubble bursts. Recall, however, that an exchange rate on a bubble path is by definition not a stationary equilibrium and cannot possibly be. Also, on a bubble the real exchange rate remains constant just like the nominal money supply. Thus with rising prices the real money supply must sink and interest rates must rise. Therefore, excessive depreciation (which is an appreciation of the foreign currency) compensates not only for the risk that the bubble might burst but also for the steadily increasing interest rate deficit of the foreign currency.

Even after the bursting of the bubble the foreign interest rate would remain below the domestic interest rate as long as the exchange rate and flexible prices stagnate at their previous levels. An exchange rate, however, which actors expect to stagnate cannot compensate for the lower foreign interest rate any more. All actors would try to get rid of foreign assets in favour of domestic ones. The exchange rate starts to fall and this process continues until the exchange rate arrives at its equilibrium value.

The crucial point in this line of argument is that it would be irrational to define the bursting of a bubble as a stagnation of the exchange rate (at least as long as we assume flexible prices, as we did). Rational actors would anticipate that the exchange rate moves to its equilibrium value immediately, and would form expectations which are consistent with this knowledge. This means that they would define the bursting of a bubble as we did in the text.

NOTES

1. On a textbook level empirical estimates of exchange rate equations are surveyed in Ballie and McMahon (1987), Hacche (1983), MacDonald (1988) and MacDonald and Taylor (1989). More difficult reading are the research reports by Frankel (1983), Hoffman and Schlagenhauf (1985) and Meese and Rogoff (1983). For easy access many of the most influencial empirical studies are collected in MacDonald and Taylor (1992).
2. A different estimation equation results if currency substitution is introduced into the Dornbusch model or into the portfolio balance approach.
3. Gärtner (1987) reviews the econometric evidence on central bank intervention in the foreign exchanges. Gärtner (1990) proposes and tests a positive model of central bank intervention with data from six industrial countries.
4. Strictly speaking, this only holds for unexpected money supply changes. If money supply changes are partly expected and partly not, partly announced and partly not, this complicates matters further.
5. This is generally attributed to changes in payment procedures such as the widespread adoption of credit cards.
6. See, among others, Marrinan (1989) and Mussa (1979), who only draw on experience since 1973. Bernholz (1982) analyzes many earlier episodes of flexible exchange rates, some of which date back to the eighteenth and nineteenth centuries.
7. The Durbin–Watson test for autocorrelation of estimation errors is not really applicable when the lagged endogenous variable is among the regressors. It is shown here because the more appropriate Durbin-h test cannot be computed in the present example. The alternative test proposed by Durbin (see Pindyck and Rubinfeld 1981: 194–5), however, also does not reject the null hypothesis that estimation errors are not autocorrelated.
8. Frankel (1985) even concludes that risk premiums between currencies of industrial countries are negligibly small compared to interest differentials; and even interest differentials are rarely in double digits.
9. More recent work based on cointegration sheds some new light on this issue, however. For example, Kugler (1990) estimates error correction models with some success to identify purchasing-power parity as a centre of gravity for Deutschmark/Swiss franc and Deutschmark/French franc rates.
10. This is another reason for modelling the monetary part by means of the monetarist exchange rate model, which operates with flexible prices. There is still no satisfactory microeconomic explanation for the stickiness of nominal prices.
11. As has been said, this simplifies the exposition. Results do not change if we retreat to the assumption that utility functions are homothetic. This means that, for given price levels, all consumers want to consume goods X and Y in the same proportion.

12. Putting $X=Y^*, R=1$, and taking natural logarithms of both sides of (8.12) yields

$$e=m-m^*-\phi(y-y^*)$$

This is the same as equation (5.6″), neglecting interest rates.
13. Indifference curves and constraints now refer to the aggregates X and Y. We can do this since we assume that all individuals have identical utility functions and incomes.
14. Initially, bubble theories have been designed to explain excessive movements of stock prices. Santoni (1987) provides an application and references. In the meantime, these ideas have been fruitfully applied not only to the explanation of exchange rate movements (an early pertinent model has been proposed by Blanchard 1979, an early application has been offered by Dornbusch 1982), but also to the explanation of hyperinflations (see Obstfeld and Rogoff 1983). A compact but highly formal account of the present state of the art on the subject of bubbles and related topics is given in Blanchard and Fischer (1989: Ch. 5). Easier reading are the contributions to a symposium on 'Bubbles' published in the *Journal of Economic Perspectives*. See in particular Garber (1990), Shiller (1990) and Flood and Hodrick (1990).
15. See Chiang (1984: Ch. 16). Here constant inhomogeneity only results from the assumption that fundamental variables are constant, which has been made in order to simplify the exposition. This assumption is not crucial for the argument and results that follow.
16. Of course, the process described by equation (8.15) could start at any other point in time. Then A denotes exchange rate disequilibrium at this very point.
17. Since $0<\pi<1$ we have $(\alpha\pi)^{-t}>\pi^{-t}$ for $t>0$.
18. It seems that bubbles in goods prices, that is, hyperinflations, occasionally come to a sudden end.
19. Recent work tries to overcome this rather unsatisfactory result by postulating heterogeneous agents and focusing on learning processes. See Frankel and Froot (1991).
20. The reason is that the money supply has dropped to 0 at time $t+1$ and is known to remain at this level for good.
21. When forming expectations at time t, individuals expect the exchange rate to move to the level described by (8.38) with probability $1-\pi$ and to the level of zero with probability π.
22. An election is a different story, since the possibility of a change of power only exists at one particular date. This case will be analyzed in the next chapter.
23. According to Frankel and Froot (1990), in 1978, 83 per cent of the forecasting firms questioned by the periodical *Euromoney* formulated exchange rate forecasts on the basis of structural models of the kind presented in this book, while 13 per cent exclusively relied on technical analysis. In 1988, 23 per cent used structural models, while 58 per cent exclusively relied on technical analyses. In between, in 1984, not a single firm admitted the use of a structural model in order to generate exchange rate forecasts.
24. Flood and Hodrick (1990) provide a compact survey of the empirical tests for the existence of bubbles. Garber (1990) argues that the best-known examples of speculative excesses, such as the tulip mania in Holland in the seventeenth century, are often classified as bubbles prematurely.
25. It should be noted in this context, that the frequently cited results obtained by Meese and Rogoff (1983), which are not in support of orthodox exchange rate

models, cannot be rationalized as a consequence of the failure to take the possibility of bubbles into account. See Flood (1987).

26. This very result, that as a tendency exporters and importers tend to expect appreciations of the exchange rate, might just as well be a strategical response. Since those who are being questioned know that survey results are published as the opinion of experts, they may well hope that they can influence the expectations of the market and, hence, the exchange rate in the desired direction by giving strategical answers.

REFERENCES

Ballie, Richard T. and Patrick C. McMahon (1987) 'Empirical regularities in exchange rate behavior', in K. Alec Christal and Robert Sedgwick (eds) *Exchange Rates and the Open Economy*, Brighton: Wheatsheaf Books, 7–29.

Bernholz, Peter (1982) 'Flexible exchange rates in historical perspective', *Princeton Studies in International Finance*, 49 (July).

Bhandari, Jagdeep S. and Stephen J. Turnovsky (1982) 'Alternative monetary policies in an inflationary equilibrium model of the open economy', *Weltwirtschaftliches Archiv* 118, 1–18.

Blanchard, Olivier Jean (1979) 'Speculative bubbles, crashes and rational expectation', *Economic Letters* 3, 387–89.

Blanchard, Olivier Jean and Stanley Fischer (1989) *Lectures on Macroeconomics*, Cambridge, MA: MIT Press.

Branson, William H., H. Haltunen and P. Masson (1979) 'Exchange rates in the short run', *European Economic Review* 10, 309–41.

Chiang, Alpha C. (1984) *Fundamental Methods of Mathematical Economics*, 3rd edn, Singapore: McGraw-Hill.

Dornbusch, Rudiger (1982) 'Equilibrium and disequilibrium exchange rates', *Zeitschrift für Wirtschafts- und Sozialwissenschaften* 37, 573–99.

Flood, Robert P. (1987) 'Comments on speculation and the volatility of foreign currency exchange rates', in Karl Brunner and Allan H. Meltzer (eds) *Bubbles and other Essays* (Carnegie–Rochester Conference Series on Public Policy 26), Amsterdam: North-Holland, 57–62.

Flood, Robert P. and Robert J. Hodrick (1990) 'On testing for speculative bubbles', *Journal of Economic Perspectives* 4, 85–101.

Frankel, Jeffrey A. (1979) 'On the mark: A theory of floating exchange rates based on real interest differentials', *American Economic Review* 69, 601–22.

Frankel, Jeffrey A. (1983) 'Monetary and portfolio-balance models of exchange rate determination', in J. S. Bhandari and B. H. Putnam (eds) *Economic Interdependence and Flexible Exchange Rates*, Cambridge, MA: MIT Press, 84–115.

Frankel, Jeffrey A. (1985) 'The dazzling dollar, *Brookings Papers on Economic Activity* 1, 199–217.

Frankel, Jeffrey A. and Kenneth A. Froot (1987) 'Using survey data to test standard propositions regarding exchange rate expectations', *American Economic Review* 77, 133–53.

Frankel, Jeffrey A. and Kenneth A. Froot (1990) 'Chartists, fundamentalists, and trading in the foreign exchange market', *American Economic Review, Papers and Proceedings* 80, 181–5.

Frankel, Jeffrey A. and Kenneth A. Froot (1991) 'Chartists, fundamentalists, and the demand for dollars', in A. Courakis and M. Taylor (eds) *Policy Issues for Interdependent Economies*, Oxford: Clarendon Press, 73–126.

Garber, Peter M. (1990) 'Famous first bubbles', *Journal of Economic Perspectives* 4, 35–54.

Gärtner, Manfred (1983) 'Asset market models of the small open economy with endogenous money supply expectations', *Journal of Institutional Economics* 139, 643–59.

Gärtner, Manfred (1987) 'Intervention policy under floating exchange rates: An analysis of the Swiss case', *Economica* 54, 439–53.

Gärtner, Manfred (1990) 'Foreign exchange markets and central bank intervention', in Arye L. Hillman (ed.) *Markets and Politicians: Politicized economic choice*, Amsterdam: Kluwer Academic, 319–38.

Hacche, Graham (1983) 'The determinants of exchange rate movements', *Working Paper* 7, OECD Economics and Statistics Department.

Hoffman, Dennis L. and Don E. Schlagenhauf (1985) 'The impact of news and alternative theories of exchange rate determination', *Journal of Money, Credit, and Banking* 17, 328–46.

Ito, Takatoshi (1990) 'Foreign exchange rate expectations: Micro survey data', *American Economic Review* 80, 434–49.

Kuger, Peter (1990) 'The adjustment of exchange rates and prices to PPP', *Economic and Financial Prospects* 4, 4–6.

Lewis, Karen K. (1989) 'Can learning affect exchange rate behavior? The case of the dollar in the early 1980s', *Journal of Monetary Economics* 23, 79–100.

MacDonald, Ronald (1988) *Floating Exchange Rates: Theories and evidence*, London: Unwin Hyman.

MacDonald, Ronald and Mark P. Taylor (1989) (eds) *The Exchange Rate and Open Economy Macroeconomics*, Oxford: Basil Blackwell.

MacDonald, Ronald and Mark P. Taylor (eds) (1992) *Exchange Rate Economics*, vol. I, Aldershot: Edward Elgar.

Marrinan, Jane (1989) 'Exchange rate determination: Sorting out theory and evidence', *New England Economic Review*, November/December, 39–51.

Meese, Richard and Kenneth Rogoff (1983) 'Empirical exchange rate models of the seventies: Do they fit out of sample?' *Journal of International Economics* 14, 3–24.

Mussa, Michael (1979) 'Empirical regularities of exchange rates and the theory of foreign exchange markets', in Karl Brunner and Allan H. Meltzers (eds) *Politics for Employment, Prices and Exchange Rates* (Carnegie–Rochester Conference Series on Public Policy 11), Amsterdam: North-Holland, 9–51.

Obstfeld, Maurice and Kenneth Rogoff (1983) 'Speculative hyperinflations in macroeconomic models: Can we rule them out?' *Journal of Political Economy* 91, 675–87.

Pindyck, Robert S. and Daniel L. Rubinfeld (1981) *Econometric Models and Economic Forecasts*, 2nd edn, New York: McGraw-Hill.

Santoni, G. J. (1987) 'The great bull markets 1924–29 and 1982–87: Speculative bubbles or economic fundamentals?', *Federal Reserve Bank of St. Louis Review* 69 (9), 16–30.

Shiller, Robert J. (1990) 'Speculative prices and popular models', *Journal of Economic Perspectives* 4, 55–65.

Stockman, Alan C. (1987) 'The equilibrium approach to exchange rates', *Federal Reserve Bank of Richmond Economic Review*, March/April, 12–30.

Chapter 9

The political economy of flexible exchange rates

Our discussion of macroeconomic models under flexible exchange rates has covered a lot of ground. It remains incomplete, nevertheless, as long as we fail to understand how existing political institutions bear on economic dynamics, or how governments and central banks actually behave, given their objectives and the relevant economic and political constraints. This hardly needs motivation since notions of governments doing (almost) everything to win the next election are part of folklore. On the other hand, even these days academic and professional economists often are (or pretend to be) highly ignorant of these issues. For example, when the *Wall Street Journal* confronted one company president with his simply awful interest rate forecasts which he had volunteered one year earlier, he contended that his forecast would have been correct, had the Federal Reserve System behaved differently: 'I was wrong about the politics and right on the economics.'[1] Such an excuse is unacceptable, given what public choice scholars have accomplished over the past three decades, and in the light of the new insights and refinements recently acquired in the new theory of macroeconomic policy. In this work, policymakers are treated like any other agent. Therefore, policies are modelled as optimal choices, given an objective or utility function and a set of constraints.

Most of the mechanisms described in this chapter are not unique to an open economy under flexible exchange rates, but lurk under other international monetary arrangements as well. In fact, most of the issues were initially raised in the context of macroeconomic models of the closed economy. Nevertheless, studying these effects under alternative regimes is called for, as different regimes constrain utility maximizing policymakers in different ways.

The main body of this chapter consists of four sections, each of which focuses on a different link between the economy and the polity. Section 9.1 analyses the behaviour of a government whose main objective it is to get reelected. It is demonstrated that if voters are backward-looking and inflation expectations formation is adaptive, the government benefits from deliberately generating a **political business cycle**. It is also shown that as expectations turn rational the cycle in real variables disappears. While in this scenario a zero-inflation policy is optimal in the long run, it is not consistent with short-run incentives. As a result, the economy gets stuck in a suboptimal full-employment equilibrium with an inflationary bias.

Section 9.2 discards the disputable assumption of backward-looking voters and introduces the possibility that *competence* differs between governments. Again, governments prefer to get reelected. However, this time they not only face private economic agents forming rational expectations, but rational voters as well. Rational voters do not choose governments on the basis of observed *past* performance, but on the basis of expected *future* performance. Given some information asymmetries, an incompetent government may try to mimic the behaviour of a competent one, and a competent government may try to signal that it really is competent. Both efforts may generate election patterns reminiscent of a standard political business cycle.

In the third section different governments (or central banks[2]) have different policy preferences. These are implemented whenever the government is in power, no matter whether an election is coming up or not. Even if private agents are fully informed about these policies, the result of an uncertain election always conveys *news* about the future course of economic policy. This election surprise produces **blips** in the exchange rate which affect output. How long these real effects last depends on the flexibility of nominal variables such as wages.

The final section is much more tentative than the preceding three. It nevertheless serves an important purpose in putting these into perspective. Addressing issues which are at the core of today's theory of macroeconomic policy, Sections 9.1–9.3 stress the endogeny of economic policy. Accepting this, normative policy prescriptions appear futile. Instead, researchers have turned to look for institutional reforms that appropriately constrain policy makers. Section 9.4 goes one step further and argues that the choice of institutions is also endogenous. As regards the international monetary system, it is speculated that a regime of flexible exchange rates may not be a stable equilibrium in a democracy – for political rather than economic reasons.

9.1 The political business cycle and beyond

This section focuses on the assumption that all governments prefer winning an election to losing it. This may be due to a variety of reasons: because they derive utility from being in office *per se*; because being in office is a precondition for implementing preferred policies; because only time in office provides a proper place in the history books; and so on. Under proper assumptions, such as that we are dealing with close elections in an uncertain environment, such a government may be assumed to maximize votes V. Model 9.1 shows how this assumption bears on the course of the economy.[3]

■ Model 9.1
Model of the political business cycle

1 Goods market

$y_t=\pi(\dot{p}_t-E_{t-1}\dot{p}_t)$	aggregate supply	(9.1)
$E_{t-1}\dot{p}_t=\dot{p}_{t-1}$	inflation expectations	(9.2)
$y_t=\delta(e_t-p_t)$	aggregate demand	(9.3)

2 Monetary sector

$m_t=p_t+\phi y_t-\lambda i_t$	money market equilibrium	(9.4)
$i_t=E_te_{t+1}-e_t$	asset market equilibrium	(9.5)
$E_te_{t+1}-e_t=\theta(\bar{e}_t-e_t)$	exchange rate expectations	(9.6)

3 Political sector

$u_t=-\dot{p}_t^2/2+\xi y_t$	voters' period utility	(9.7)
$\max_m V_i=u_i \qquad i=2,4,6,\ldots$	government behaviour	(9.8)

4 Miscellaneous

$\dot{p}_t\equiv p_t-p_{t-1}$	definition	(9.9)

Notes: Lower-case variables are in natural logarithms, an exception being the interest rate. A dot indicates the derivative of the respective variable with respect to time. Greek letters denote positive parameters. Variables are defined as follows:

p	domestic price level	m	domestic money
y	aggregate output	i	domestic interest rate
u	voters' period utility	V	government vote share
e	exchange rate	$\dot{p}_t$	inflation rate
$\bar{e}$	equilibrium exchange rate		

The economy is identical to the neoclassical open-economy model discussed in Chapter 5, except for expectations formation and the fact that (9.1) makes output depend on unexpected inflation and not on erroneous expectations of the price *level*, as did equation (5.28) in Chapter 5.[4] There is stickiness in inflation expectations, which are adaptive (equation (9.2)). In a familiar way the exchange rate is expected to regress towards its equilibrium value (equation (9.6)). This coincides with rational expectations as long as no future policy changes are anticipated. Note that nominal shocks transmit variations of output through variations of the exchange rate. The functioning of the economic part of the model will not be discussed in any detail here, as it should be familiar from Section 5.4.

Equation (9.7) models voter behaviour by drawing on the stylized empirical fact that government popularity crucially depends on the country's economic performance. Here the government's share of the vote at a hypothetical election at time $t=i$ depends on current inflation and current output.[5] The implicit assumption in (9.7) is that voters are backward-looking and completely forget yesterday's state of the economy.[6] Equation (9.8) says that governments maximize votes during even-numbered periods, when elections are held. Non-election periods are odd-numbered. Equation (9.9) draws attention to the fact that the inflation rate equals the first difference in the natural logarithm of the price level. This links equations which include inflation with equations which include the price level.

9.1.1 The political business cycle

Figure 9.1 depicts the building blocks of our political business cycle model in a diagram with inflation and output on the axes. The political sector is

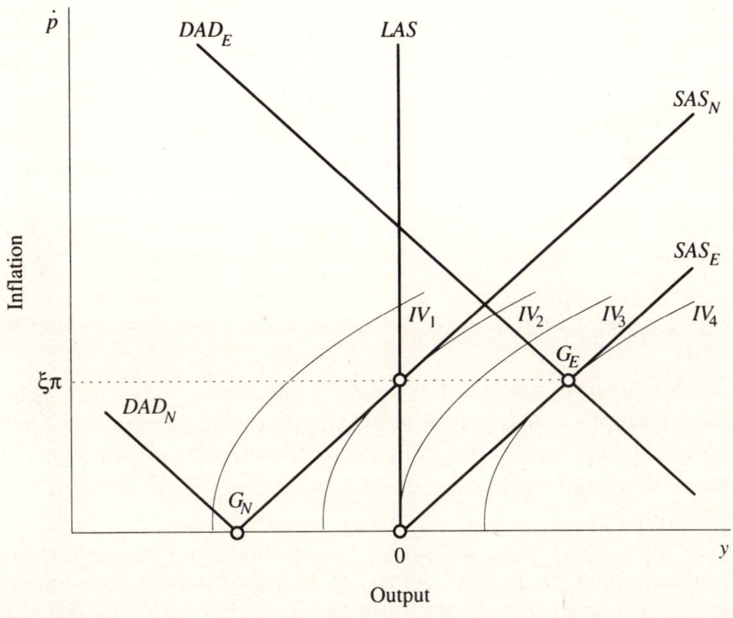

Figure 9.1 The political business cycle in the aggregate supply/aggregate demand framework

represented by a series of **iso-vote (IV) curves** representing combinations of $\dot{p}$ and y which yield given government vote shares, in (9.7). As we move to the right, higher vote shares obtain. Solving (9.7) for $\dot{p}_t$ gives the general equation for iso-vote curves:

$$\dot{p}_t=\sqrt{2(-V_t+\xi y_t)} \tag{9.10}$$

A dynamic aggregate demand (DAD) curve to be represented in the $\dot{p}/y$ plane is obtained as follows. Substitute (9.6) into (9.5), the resulting equation into (9.4) and solve for the exchange rate to obtain

$$e_t=\bar{e}_t-\frac{1}{\theta\lambda}(p_t+\phi y_t-m_t) \tag{9.11}$$

Substituting $y_t=\bar{y}_t=0$ into (9.3) and $y_t=\bar{y}_t=0$ and $\bar{i}=0$ into (9.4) gives

$$\bar{e}_t=\bar{p}_t=m_t \tag{9.12}$$

Inserting this into (9.11), substituting the resulting equation for e_t in (9.3), and then solving for p_t finally yields

$$p_t=m_t-\frac{\theta\lambda+\delta\phi}{\delta(1+\theta\lambda)}y_t \tag{9.13}$$

Taking first differences on both sides and making use of the definition, (9.9) gives the desired dynamic aggregate demand curve

$$\dot{p}_t=m_t-m_{t-1}-\frac{\theta\lambda+\delta\phi}{\delta(1+\theta\lambda)}(y_t-y_{t-1}) \tag{9.14}$$

which, *ceteris paribus*, shifts up and down one to one with changes in the money supply. The curve is dynamic in the sense that it shifts as long as output changes, that is, it is not in equilibrium.

A short-run or surprise aggregate supply (SAS) curve in the $\dot{p}/y$ plane results from substituting (9.2) into (9.1) and solving for $\dot{p}_t$:

$$\dot{p}_t=\dot{p}_{t-1}+\frac{1}{\pi}y_t \tag{9.15}$$

In equilibrium, when *DAD* and *SAS* intersect on *LAS* (the long-run aggregate supply schedule), inflation equals exchange rate depreciation. Output only increases – for example, as we move north-east on a given SAS curve – if depreciation exceeds inflation, that is, if there is a real depreciation.

The government is aware of how voters make their decision. Hence, it knows that when an election comes up at the end of an even numbered period, voters have completely forgotten (or discounted) the state of the economy that prevailed during the previous nonelection period. The government, therefore, does not really care how it rates with the voters during odd-numbered periods. During election periods it tries to reach the highest iso-vote curve possible.

Assume that there is zero inflation in the nonelection period 1.[7] Hence, the short-run aggregate supply curve for election period 2, SAS_E, intersects the y-axis at full-employment output $\bar{y}=0$. SAS_E represents the available options for the government in period 2. It is the *economic constraint* under which the government operates. The series of iso-vote curves depicts the *political constraint*. By appropriately changing the money supply, the government can move up or down on SAS_E so as to maximize votes. The highest possible vote share is obtained in G_E, the point of tangency between SAS_E and an iso-vote curve.

Since election period inflation $\dot{p}_E$ determines inflation expectations for the following nonelection period, the short-run aggregate supply curve shifts up to SAS_N. If the government were to keep the money supply expanding at the same pace as during the previous period, this would increase inflation again and shift the SAS curve up still further. The economic constraint would be much less favourable than during the previous election period, and, very likely, the government would be voted out of office. Hence, the government must 'invest' during nonelection periods; for example, in order to be able to maximize votes again in G_E during the next election period, nonelection period demand management must be restrictive enough to stop inflation. This is achieved in G_N. In this way vote-maximizing governments employ demand management policies which constantly shift the DAD curve from DAD_N to DAD_E and back, thus making the SAS curve alternate between SAS_N and SAS_E and the state of the economy between G_N and G_E.[8]

PROBLEM 9.1

Assume votes V are cast on the basis of the present and of the last period's state of the economy:

$$V=\sum_{i=0}^{1} \omega^i u_i \tag{9.8'}$$

ω measures the rate at which voters forget, and

$$u_i=-\dot{p}_i^2/2+\xi y_i \tag{9.7'}$$

Elections are being held in period 0; period 1 is a nonelection period. Given the other structural equations of this section, what are the optimal inflation rates in periods 0 and 1? *Hint:* Cycles must be linked in the sense that the inflation rate at the end of one cycle determines inflation expectations at the beginning of the next.

The optimal inflation rate during election periods is obtained by first solving (9.15) – the economic constraint which the government faces – for y_t. The resulting equation is substituted into the vote function (9.7) – the political constraint. Differentiation of the resulting equation with respect to $\dot{p}$ gives a first-order condition for a maximum vote share,

$$\frac{\mathrm{d}V_t}{\mathrm{d}\dot{p}_t} = -\dot{p}_t + \xi\pi = 0$$

which implies

$$\dot{p}_t = \xi\pi \tag{9.16}$$

Given the specific functional form of our vote function, vote-maximizing inflation does not depend on inflation expectations or last period's output. This does not necessarily hold for other feasible functional forms, but will come in handy to keep some of the arguments that follow as simple as possible.

If last period's inflation was zero, optimal output during the election period is obtained by substituting (9.18) and $\dot{p}_{t-1} = 0$ into (9.15). This yields

$$y_t = \xi\pi^2 \tag{9.17}$$

9.1.2 Vote maximization under rational expectations

Output levels which exceed full-employment output $\bar{y} = 0$ are only achieved by constantly fooling the economy by exploiting adaptive expectations formation. As private agents become aware of the cyclical nature of demand management, adaptive expectations turn into rational expectations. Since there are no more inflation surprises, we may substitute perfect foresight $\dot{p}_t = E_{t-1}\dot{p}_t$ into (9.1) to obtain the no-surprise aggregate supply function. This coincides with the long-run aggregate supply (LAS) curve, the vertical line through $\bar{y} = 0$ (see Figure 9.2).

Figure 9.2 introduces the concept of the *government reaction curve*. This is the locus of points at which a vote-maximizing government makes the DAD curve intersect a given SAS curve during election periods. According to (9.16) the vote-maximizing inflation rate is independent of inflation expectations (and, therefore, independent of output). Hence the government reaction curve during election periods, GR_E, is horizontal at $\dot{p} = \xi\pi$. If individuals form rational expectations, they correctly anticipate inflation to be at $\xi\pi$. $E_{t-1}\dot{p}_t = \xi\pi$, however, makes SAS_E intersect LAS exactly where LAS and GR_E intersect.

Under adaptive expectations the government is able to maximize votes at G_E'. Rational inflation expectations put this point out of reach. When

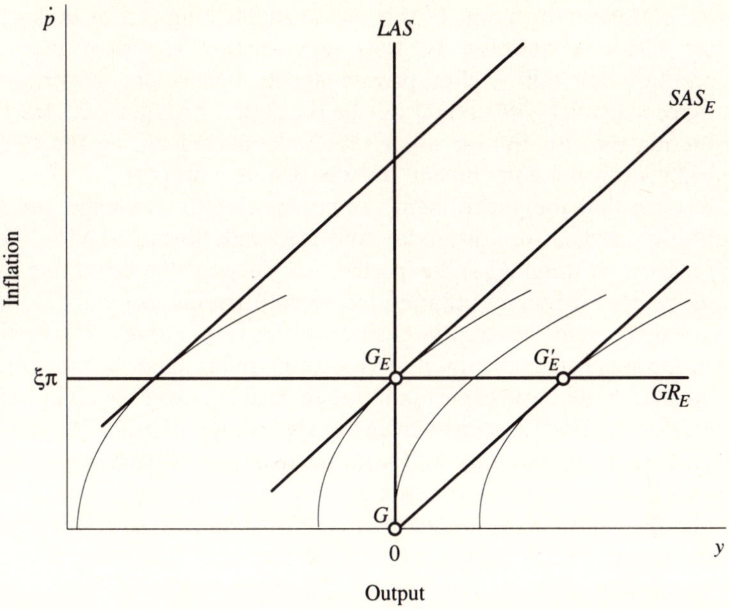

Figure 9.2 Vote maximization when inflation expectations are rational

individuals understand the incentives which rule government behaviour, the economic constraint moves into position SAS_E. With this new menu of options, votes are maximized in G_E. Given SAS_E, driving inflation above $\xi\pi$ and, even more so, driving it below $\xi\pi$, lowers the government's share of the vote.

From what is happening, a rational government eventually learns that inflation rates are anticipated and available choices are limited to points on the LAS curve. From all points on *LAS*, votes are maximized in *G*, where the economy is fully employed and there is no more inflation. Given this, it is tempting to conclude that rational expectations eventually take care of such rather nasty things as a political business cycles, and that the economy eventually settles at the socially optimal point *G*.

9.1.3 The credibility problem

Assume now that, in the light of the counterproductive effect of efforts to create a political business cycle, the government pledges to refrain from conducting discretionary monetary policy henceforth, but rather to stick to producing zero inflation during the upcoming election period.[9] Given that whatever inflation is generated will eventually be anticipated, the government's announcement is an *optimal plan* in the sense that it is intended to bring the economy to point G, the best available long-run or no-surprise choice. The key question is, however, whether the plan works. A precondition for this is that private agents believe the government's announcement. Why this might not be the case is brought out clearly by considering the situation as a *one-shot game* played during the election period between the government and the labour market.

Assume that the government can either stick to its pledge and keep inflation at zero, or use discretion and raise inflation to $\pi\xi$. The labour market must fix nominal and expected real wages at the beginning of the period, before it observes inflation (representing monetary policy). When fixing wages – and, hence, the position of the SAS curve – it can either believe the government pledge and expect zero inflation, or be prepared for discretionary policy and expect inflation to be at $\pi\xi$. Once wages have been negotiated and fixed the short-run aggregate supply curve at SAS_0 or $SAS_{\pi\xi}$ (see Figure 9.3), all that is left for the government to do is to choose between G_I and G_{II} in the first case, or between G_{III} and G_{IV} in the second case.

Figure 9.3 also gives the share of votes cast for the government in the four situations. Each is an outcome of the game for given moves of individual agents and the government. The point to note is that no matter what inflation rate the labour market expects – and, thus, what economic

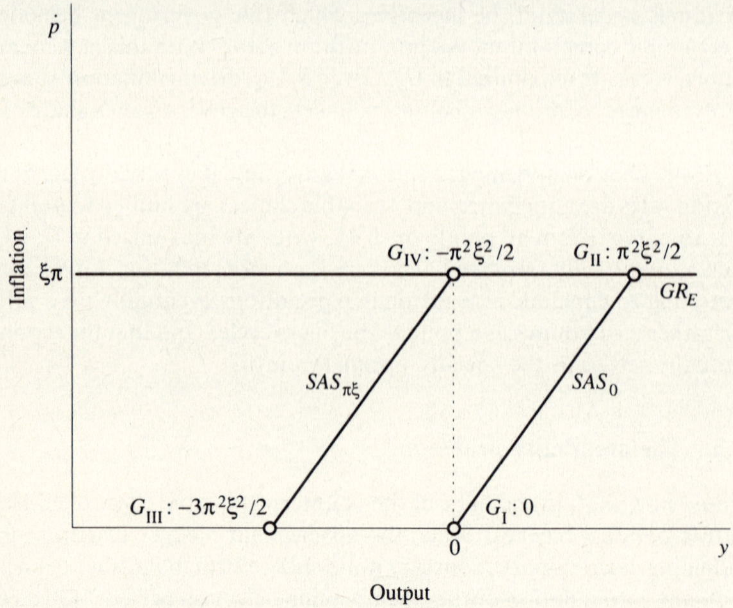

Figure 9.3 Vote shares in the four possible outcomes of the game between the government and the labour market

constraint the government faces, the government can always improve its vote share by reneging on its prior commitment to zero inflation. Inflating at a rate of $\pi\xi$ is the government's *dominant strategy*. Hence, announcement of a zero-inflation policy rule is *not credible* and rational labour market participants *always* expect inflation to equal $\pi\xi$. Despite the fact that the government would prefer G_{I} to any other perfect-foresight equilibrium, it finds the economy stuck at the suboptimal point G_{IV}. The literature has coined this sort of problem, which is also encountered in other policy areas, the **time inconsistency of optimal plans**. In the context of monetary policy it serves to rationalize the apparently obvious empirical phenomenon that democracies are subject to an inflationary bias.

We may restate the problem in more general terms by means of the concept of the **temptation curve**. The government's temptation to cheat, T, is defined for a given announced inflation rate $\dot{p}^a$, which private agents are assumed to believe ($E\dot{p}=\dot{p}^a$). Generally, the temptation to cheat can be defined as the utility increase that would result from cheating rather than playing it honest. In formal terms, temptation during the election period is the difference between the maximum share of the vote which the government can obtain by deviating from the announced inflation rate at its own discretion, and the share of the vote that results if the government sticks to its promise:

$$T(\dot{p}^a)=V(\dot{p}=\pi\xi;E\dot{p}=\dot{p}^a)-V(\dot{p}=E\dot{p}=\dot{p}^a) \tag{9.18}$$

Substituting the vote function (9.7) and afterwards the aggregate supply curve (9.1) into (9.18) gives a measure of temptation at different policy announcements:

$$T=(\dot{p}^a)^2/2-\pi\xi\dot{p}^a+\pi^2\xi^2/2 \tag{9.18$'$}$$

Differentiation of (9.18′) with respect to $\dot{p}^a$ gives

$$\frac{\mathrm{d}T}{\mathrm{d}\dot{p}^a}=\dot{p}^a-\pi\xi=0 \tag{9.19}$$

which is the first-order condition for minimum temptation to cheat. Since $\mathrm{d}^2T/\mathrm{d}(\dot{p}^a)^2=1>0$, (9.19) indeed defines a minimum. This minimum obtains at

$$\dot{p}^a=\xi\pi \tag{9.20}$$

Substitution of (9.20) into (9.18′) gives $T=0$, which says that when the government announces the inflation rate $\xi\pi$, there is no incentive to cheat.

Figure 9.4 depicts the temptation curve. It shows that for all policy announcements other than $\xi\pi$ the government is tempted to cheat. Hence, $\dot{p}^a=\xi\pi$ is the only *credible* policy announcement. Given any other policy announcement, the government would gain from breaking its promise.

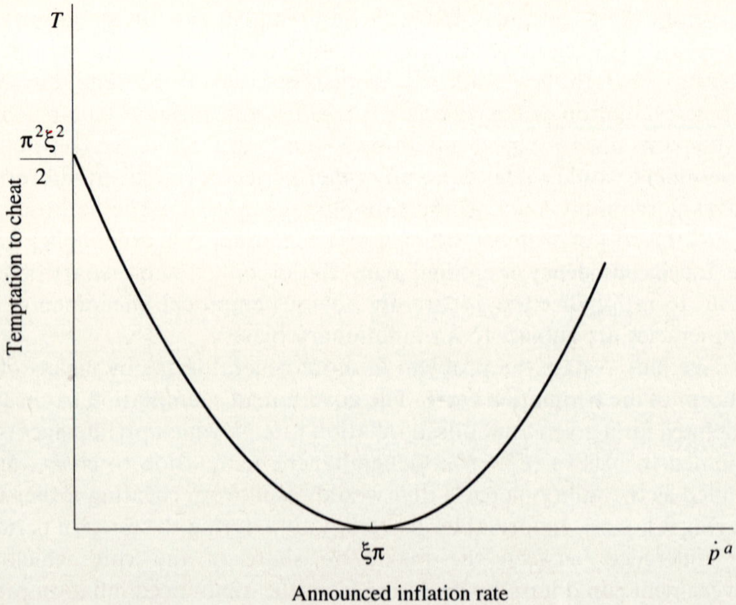

Figure 9.4 Government's temptation to renege on an announced inflation rate

Thus we arrive at the same result as above: namely, that democracies suffer from an inflationary bias of monetary policy. This bias need not be constant over an electoral term, though, but in models of the type discussed here it usually increases as the election draws nearer.

9.1.4 Reputation

The time inconsistency or credibility problem described in the previous section poses two related questions: (1) Did the lack of a long-run perspective not lead us to overstate the problem of time inconsistency? (2) How would institutions have to be redesigned in order to reduce the inflationary bias of democracies? The present section focuses on the first question, but also offers some concluding remarks on the second.

A major point of criticism of the analysis in Section 9.1.3 is that the interaction between the government and the labour market was modelled as a one-shot game.[10] This has led us to look only at the *benefits* from cheating during the current period. These benefits did not have to be balanced against any costs, since no such costs accrue in a one-shot game. This situation changes if the government anticipates playing the game again in the future. Then, whether the government cheats today determines whether it is expected to cheat tomorrow. Acquiring a bad reputation in this way has an impact on tomorrow's inflation expectations and, by intuition, should worsen the economic constraint facing the government. Thus, reneging on announced policy today not only creates benefits for the government, but also creates costs in the future. If these costs exceed today's benefits the government would not give in to the temptation to cheat. The present section looks into this argument in some detail.

The analysis of the role of reputation is facilitated if the phenomenon of an inflation bias is detached from the possibility of an election-cyclical movement of this bias.[11] The average inflation bias over an election term is obtained if we specify period length to equal the length of an election term, say four years. Hence, elections are held at the end of every period, and the temptation to cheat, which we have identified above for election periods, exists in every period.[12]

A finite time horizon

Assume for now that the game is replayed a finite number of times. Consider Model 9.2. To simplify things, the economy is condensed into a single equation. This implies that the government has direct control over the price level through monetary policy – an assumption we have already implicitly employed above and which is justified in the context of the neoclassical model. Working with the full model would not make any difference to the results to follow. Equation (9.7) is the familiar vote function. If so preferred, it may simply be considered the government utility stream per period, reflecting the same preferences which voters have.[13] Equation (9.8′) signals that the government intends to repeat the game T

■ **Model 9.2**
Reputation model: finite horizon

1 Economy

$y_t = \pi(\dot{p}_t - E_{t-1}\dot{p}_t)$ aggregate output (9.1)

2 Polity

$V_t = -\dot{p}_t^2/2 + \xi y_t$ vote function (period utility stream) (9.7′)

$\max_{p_0} U_0 = \sum_{t=0}^{T} \omega^t V_t$ government behaviour (9.8′)

Notes: The notes to Model 9.1 apply. Variables are defined as follows:

$\dot{p}$	inflation (policy instrument)	V	goverment's share of the vote
y	aggregate output	U	government utility
ω	government time preference		

times and maximizes the current value of the results from all $T+1$ rounds. Future utility is discounted at a rate ω', which we transform into $\omega = 1/(1+\omega')$.

To make it as simple as possible, let the game be played twice, in periods 0 and 1. The assumption is that if the government employs discretionary policy during period 0, it will be punished by the fact that individuals will expect the government to use discretion during period 1. Intuitively, that might work as an **enforcement** mechanism which prevents the government from cheating in period 0. Generally, enforcement is defined as the present value of all future losses caused by deviating from some announced policy today.

Unfortunately, there is no enforcement in our two-period game under rational expectations. This can be seen by working backwards from period 1 to period 0. Once we have arrived in period 1, the game is only played one more time. As we have seen above, optimal inflation in a one-shot game is $\pi\xi$, irrespective of what inflationary expectations are. If this is rationally anticipated by private agents, inflation in period 1 is $\dot{p}_1 = \pi\xi$, output is at its natural level, $y_1 = 0$, and the government's share of the vote is $V_1 = -\pi^2\xi^2/2$, *no matter what government policies are in period 0* – even if the government keeps its promise and selects $\dot{p}_a$! Hence, policies in period 0 have no effect on utility in period 1 and, also, are those which optimize the one-shot game, namely $\dot{p}_0 = \pi\xi$. Thus the temptation curve drawn in Figure 9.4 for the one-shot game also applies to period 0 and period 1 of the present two-period finite-horizon game. The only credible inflation target is $\pi\xi$ for both periods.

This result also applies when the game is repeated not only once, but a potentially large finite number of times. In the last period T a one-shot game is being played, hence $E_0\dot{p}_T = \dot{p}_T = \pi\xi$. Repeating the argument given above, this implies $E_0\dot{p}_{T-1} = \dot{p}_{T-1} = \pi\xi$. By continuous backward induction we eventually arrive at $\dot{p}_0 = \pi\xi$. Thus, even in this $T+1$ period policy game the only credible inflation rate is the one which we have already obtained in the one-shot game. No enforcement mechanism exists under a finite horizon which eliminates or reduces inflationary bias.

An infinite time horizon

Whenever the game is not expected to end in a deterministic way, there is no *last period* in the above sense. Then reputational forces controlling government discretion cannot be ruled out by backward induction. An infinite planning horizon applies whenever the termination of the game is decided stochastically, or when the government is not identified with an individual but with a collective body such as the ruling party. Then, even if each member of the party (or government) has a finite life or time in office, the overlapping of generations or office terms ensures that under reason-

Model 9.3
Reputation model: infinite horizon

1 Economy

$y_t = \pi(\dot{p}_t - E_{t-1}\dot{p}_t)$	aggregate output	(9.1)
$E_{t-1}\dot{p}_t = \begin{cases} \dot{p}_t^a \text{ if } \dot{p}_{t-1} = E_{t-2}\dot{p}_{t-1} \\ \pi\xi \text{ if } \dot{p}_{t-1} \neq E_{t-2}\dot{p}_{t-1} \end{cases}$	(rational) inflation expectations	(9.2′)

2 Polity

$V_t = -\dot{p}_t^2/2 + \xi y_t$	vote function	(9.10)
$\max_{p_0} U_0 = \sum_{t=0}^{\infty} \omega^t V_t$	government behaviour	(9.8″)

Notes: The notes to Model 9.1 apply. Variables are defined as follows:

$\dot{p}$	inflation (policy instrument)	V	government's share of the vote
y	aggregate output	U	government behaviour
ω	government time preference	$\dot{p}_a$	announced inflation

able decision procedures the government never enters into a final period (see Persson and Tabellini 1990: 42–3). In Model 9.3 we analyze the same structural model as in the previous section.

Now the horizon is infinite in (9.8″), and (9.2′) specifies an expectations mechanism which has the property of being a – though not the only – rational one. The mechanism is dichotomous in the sense that credibility can only assume two states: if the government is *credible*, individuals believe in the announced inflation rate. This is the case if the last period's inflation expectations were correct. If the government is *not credible*, individuals expect the discretionary inflation rate $\pi\xi$. This applies if individuals' inflation expectations proved wrong in the last period.

A credible government is punished for cheating by not being credible in the following period. Then according to (9.2′) the expected inflation rate is $\xi\pi$, which we have also shown to be the best government policy under discretion. Selecting $\dot{p} = \xi\pi$ also has the side effect of regaining credibility for the next period. Thus the punishment from violating an announced rule is fully received during the following period. Afterwards things carry on as if no cheating had ever occurred. The punishment consists of the difference between the utility level resulting from an anticipated inflation rate $\xi\pi$ and the utility level resulting from an anticipated inflation rate $\dot{p}^a$, discounted to its present value.

We now turn to the question of whether reputational forces in the infinite horizon model permit credible inflation announcements which are superior to (that is, below) the discretionary inflation bias $\xi\pi$, which also resulted from the finite-horizon reputation model. As long as parameters do not change, whatever is credible and optimal today is also credible and optimal tomorrow. Thus we are looking for a time-invariant, constant inflation announcement $\dot{p}^a$, to which we may refer as a **rule**.

The punishment that would result or the enforcement E that might prevent a government from violating a given rule $\dot{p}^a$ today (in period 0) is

$$E=\omega[V_1(\dot{p}_1=E_0\dot{p}_1=\dot{p}^a)-V_1(\dot{p}_1=E_0p_1=\xi\pi)] \tag{9.21}$$

Making use of (9.1) and (9.7′) and collecting terms yields

$$E=-\frac{\omega}{2}[(\dot{p}^a)^2-\pi^2\xi^2] \tag{9.21'}$$

Equation (9.21′) describes a parabola which is open from below, and intersects the ordinate at $\pi^2\xi^2/[2(1+\omega)]$ and the abscissa at $\pi\xi$. Figure 9.5 shows the enforcement curve along with the temptation curve introduced above.

The key to the interpretation of Figure 9.5 is that a rule is only credible if the government's gain from breaking it does not exceed the punishment to be received, $T\leq E$. Hence, given the present model, the ideal rule – which would maximize government utility at $U_0=0$ – is not credible, since temptation exceeds enforcement. However, a set of rules exists, $\dot{p}^a_b\leq\dot{p}^a<\xi\pi$,

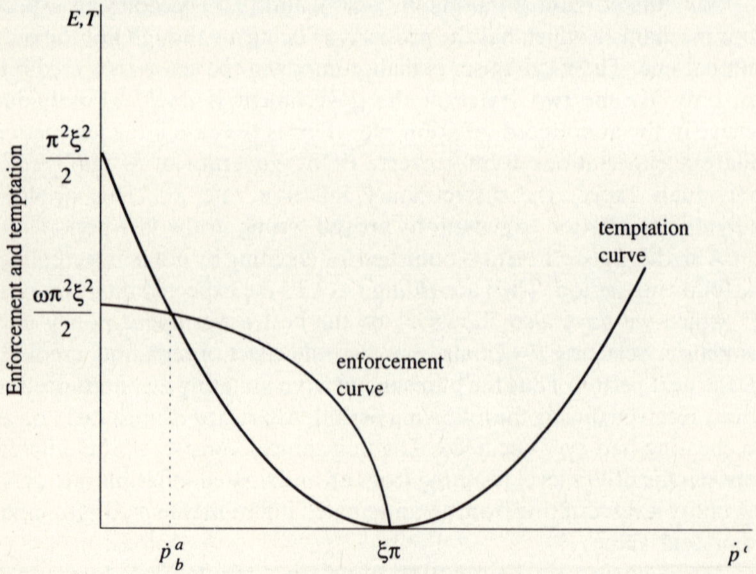

Figure 9.5 Benefits and costs of reneging on an announced inflation rate

which is both credible and superior to the discretionary solution. All of these rules are equilibrium outcomes of the game in the sense that the expectations formation process (9.2′) is rational, and the policymaker has no incentive to deviate from an announced rule. As regards the choice of rules, $\dot{p}_b^a = \pi\xi(1-\omega)/(1+\omega)$ is the best credible rule, since it maximizes utility.[14]

Some of the results obtained in this section are specific to the model. Other specifications of the vote function or of expectations formation, which also meet the requirement of rationality, may lead to somewhat different insights.

PROBLEM 9.2

Determine the enforcement curve and the set of credible rules when inflation expectations follow

$$E_{t-1}\dot{p}_t = \begin{cases} \dot{p}_t^a & \text{if } \dot{p}_{t-1} = E_{t-2}\dot{p}_{t-1} \text{ and } \dot{p}_{t-2} = E_{t-3}\dot{p}_{t-2} \\ \pi\xi & \text{otherwise} \end{cases}$$

Quite generally, though, reputation effects, even in the restricted sense employed here, tend to reduce the inflationary bias of democracies. A precondition is that policymakers maximize utility over an infinite horizon. Given this, chances that the socially optimal policy rule becomes feasible increase, the smaller the government's discount rate gets.

9.2 Equilibrium election cycles

The preceding analysis suffers from a not really satisfactory treatment of voters. Voters are backward-looking and base their voting decision on what governments do *before* elections. This makes it easy to fool them by doing something quite different after elections than before elections. Realizing this, rational voters should be forward-looking and base voting decisions on what they expect governments to do *after* the election.

Of course, as has been indicated above, a vote function such as equation (9.10) can also be looked upon as a government utility function, based on arguments completely unrelated to vote-maximization efforts. Then the result of an inflationary bias under discretionary policies still applies. The drawback is that we lose our explanation for the stylized empirical fact that governments vary policy instruments in the rhythm of elections. Equilibrium election cycle theories focus on explaining this phenomenon even with rational, forward-looking voters. In these models all actors involved behave entirely rationally, given the information which is available to them. The crux is that information is asymmetrical between actors, which makes policies geared at winning elections rational.

9.2.1 The model

Model 9.4 (from Persson and Tabellini 1990: Section 5.2) contains the key ingredients of an equilibrium election cycle model only, which should make it easier to take in the basic structure at a glance. Further assumptions are introduced in the text.

Model 9.4
Equilibrium election cycle model

1 Economy

$y_t = \pi(\dot{p}_t - E_{t-1}\dot{p}_t) + c_t^c$	aggregate output	(9.1′)
$c_t^c = s_t^c + s_{t-1}^c$	candidate competence	(9.22)
$s_t^c = \begin{cases} \bar{s} > 0 & \text{with probability } \rho \\ \underline{s} < 0 & \text{with probability } 1-\rho \end{cases}$	random shock to candidate competence	(9.23)

2 Polity

$U = E\left[\sum_{t=1}^{2} \omega^{t-1} u_t\right]$	voters' expected utility	(9.24)
$u_t = -\dot{p}_t^2/2 + \xi y_t$	period utility stream	(9.25)
$U^c = E^c\left[\sum_{t=1}^{2} \omega^{t-1} u_t + g_t^c G\right]$	candidate's expected utility	(9.26)

Notes: The notes to Model 9.1 apply. Variables are defined as follows:

y	aggregate output
p	price level (policy instrument)
ω	government time preference
c^c	competence of candidate c ($c = i, o$)
s^c	random shock to competence of candidate c
U	expected future utility of representative voter
U^c	expected future utility of candidate c
u	period utility stream
G	utility derived from being elected into government
g^c	government dummy variable; equals 1 if candidate is in office, equals zero otherwise
$0 < \rho < 1$	is an exogenous probability

Equation (9.1′) is the familiar surprise supply function. As a shortcut we continue to assume that governments have direct control over the inflation rate. The innovation here is that full-employment output depends on the competence of the candidate in office, c^c. Competence evolves stochastically over time. Equation (9.22) postulates a moving-average process of first order. Random shocks to competence are either positive or negative. They hit each candidate with the same probability and their effect lasts two periods. The rationale for all this is that whether a government is competent depends on the nature of current policy problems. Thus a candidate who displays extraordinary skills in convincing some other country to restrict exports voluntarily in order at least temporarily to remove pressure from competing domestic industries, need not be equally effective in convincing trade unions to freeze nominal wages after an oil price explosion. So while competence is partially lasting, it changes as new challenges for economic policy come up.

In the political sphere two periods are considered. Elections are held in period 1. Period 2 is a nonelection period. Voters decide how to cast their vote in period 1 on the basis of *expected* utility for the entire two-period electoral term as given in (9.24). Period utility streams in (9.25) are identical to the vote functions employed previously. Equation (9.26) describes expected utility of candidates. The first expression in brackets is the same as in (9.24). It simply states that candidates have the same basic preferences as other citizens. The second term in brackets shows what candidates expect to gain from being elected into office. This product equals G if the candidate is elected (since then $g_t^c = 1$), and zero if he or she fails (then $g_t^c = 0$). G is the additional value derived from being president for two periods after the upcoming election, discounted to its present value in period 1.

The following assumptions facilitate the exposition and discussion, without altering any substantial properties of the model.

$$s_0 = 0 \tag{9.27}$$

is the level of competence inherited from the previous nonelection period. $\bar{s}$ and $\underline{s}$ are normalized so as to yield an expected value of zero:

$$E_{t-1}s_t = \rho\bar{s} + (1-\rho)\underline{s} = 0 \tag{9.28}$$

As will be discussed in more detail below, voters maximize expected utility by choosing the most competent government. Since, according to (9.27), no competence is inherited from the past, candidates in period 1 are either competent, $s_1^c = \bar{s}$, or incompetent, $s_1^c = \underline{s}$.

The opponent's competence s_1^o is not observable to voters. Thus $E_0 s_1^o = 0$, which is the crucial value against which incumbent competence is measured. Voters prefer a competent incumbent to the opposition candidate, $s_1^i = \bar{s} > s_1^o = 0$. They prefer the opposition to an incompetent incum-

Table 9.1 The timing of events

Actors	*Period 1*			*Period 2*		
exogenous		shock to government competence s_1^i	election	new government assumes office	shock to government competence s_2^i	no election
government		observes s_1^i, sets $\dot{p}_1$			observes s_2^i, sets $\dot{p}_2$	
voters	observe $s_0^i = 0$		observe y_1	observe s_1^i, $\dot{p}_1$		observes y_2
labour market		sets $E_0\dot{p}_1$ (or wage)	observes $\dot{p}_1$, sets y_1		sets $E_1\dot{p}_2$ (or wage)	observes $\dot{p}_2$, sets y_2

bent, $s_1^o = 0 > s_1^i = \underline{s}$. If voters are fully informed, there is no mystery about what happens in this model. Things become more interesting and perhaps more realistic if we assume that voters only observe government competence with a lag of one period. Then a competent government might be expected to signal that it is competent indeed, while an incompetent government may try to mimic a competent one.

9.2.2 Timing of events and information structure

Optimal behaviour in this game between incumbent candidates and voters crucially depends on the assumed timing of events and on information asymmetries. Pertinent features of the model are laid out in Table 9.1.

For the most part, the succession of events *within* periods is not crucial, but should help to clarify the exposition. In period 1 there is a shock to government competence. This is only observed by the government, which subsequently sets the inflation rate to $\dot{p}_1$. Labour market participants have to form inflation expectations before they observe any period 1 information. With $E_0\dot{p}_1$ fixed, the labour market responds to actual inflation by setting y_1. Table 9.1 proposes that the labour market does so *as if* participants had observed $\dot{p}_1$. In fact, knowledge of the aggregate inflation rate may not be considered necessary. The 'as if' result could also be achieved if actors respond to sectoral stimuli. Then the following and crucial assumption is more plausible: voters only observe output y_1 in period 1, but do not observe p_1 until period 2. This is crucial, because if voters could observe both y_1 *and* p_1 before casting their vote, they could easily compute the full-employment output and, hence, government competence – we would be back to a game of symmetrical information. As it is, at election time voters have to guess to what extents currently observed output y_1 reflects government competence and surprise inflation. The described timing of events and information is repeated in period 2, but no elections are held.

9.2.3 Optimal government behaviour

Our next step is to derive optimal monetary policy, given that voters are rational but lack knowledge of current-period government competence. It will prove useful to start in period 2 and work back to period 1.

Period 2 is a convenient starting point. No election takes place, and this period's competence shock becomes known to voters before the next election. Hence, in period 2 no government of either type has an incentive to signal, but rather selects the optimal inflation rate under discretionary policy,

$$\dot{p}_2 = \pi\xi \tag{9.29}$$

In equilibrium, when expectations are rational, this implies the following:

$$E_1\dot{p}_2 = \pi\xi \tag{9.30}$$

$$y_2 = s_1^c + s_2^c \tag{9.31}$$

The same type of discretionary equilibrium would also apply in period 1 if incumbents did not care about reelection. Since incumbents do care about reelection, they have to compare the expected *net gain* from reelection that accrues in period 2 with the *cost* of any action which they decide to undertake in period 1 with an eye on improving reelection prospects.

Making use of $E_0 s_1^o = 0$, the incumbent's *net gain from reelection* may be expressed as

$$W(s_1^i) = u^i - u^o + G = \xi s_1^i + G \tag{9.32}$$

In principle, if the incumbent is incompetent ($s_1^i = \underline{s} < 0$), the possibility exists that he or she does not want to be reelected. Since then the incumbent would not run for reelection in the first place, we may postulate $G > -\xi\underline{s}$. A competent government is always more eager to be reelected than an incompetent one – $W(\bar{s}) > W(\underline{s}) > 0$. The reason is that an incompetent incumbent prefers the output level to be expected under the present opponent's rule to the employment level which he or she can deliver.

Consider next the *cost* which the incumbent incurs if he or she either attempts to signal his or her true identity, if competent, or tries to mimic a competent incumbent, if really incompetent. In both cases the incumbent increases output beyond the level that results from short-run discretionary policy at the cost of inflation.

According to (9.1), in order to produce an output level of y_1, the inflation rate must be set at

$$\dot{p}_1(y_1, s_1^i) = E_0\dot{p}_1 + \frac{1}{\pi}y_1 - \frac{1}{\pi}s_1^i \tag{9.33}$$

which, given inflation expectations, depends on the output target and on the competence level.

If short-run discretionary policy $\dot{p} = \pi\xi$ is pursued, output is

$$y_1(s_1^i) = \pi(\pi\xi - E_0\dot{p}_1) + s_1^i \tag{9.34}$$

We may now state the net costs (utility loss) which a candidate incurs who drives output to y_1 instead of settling for the short-run discretionary optimum. These *signalling costs* are

$$C(y_1, s_1^i) = u[\pi\xi, \pi(\pi\xi - E_0\dot{p}_1) + s_1^i] - u[\dot{p}(y_1, s_1^i), y_1] \tag{9.35}$$

where we make use of (9.33) and (9.34). Substituting (9.33) into (9.35) and writing out the utility levels according to (9.25) gives

$$C(y_1, s_1^i) = -\pi^2\xi^2/2 + \pi^2\xi^2 - \pi\xi E_0\dot{p}_1 + \xi s_1^i + \tfrac{1}{2}\left(E_0\dot{p}_1 + \frac{1}{\pi}y_1 - \frac{1}{\pi}s_1^i\right)^2 - \xi y_1 \tag{9.35$'$}$$

A look at the terms which involve y_1 shows that we are dealing with a U-shaped parabola, similar to the loss function employed in the previous section. Differentiation of (9.35′) with respect to y_1 gives the first-order condition for the minimum of the signalling-cost function:

$$\frac{\partial C}{\partial y_1} = [E_0\dot{p}_1 + (y_1 - s_1^i)/\pi]/\pi - \xi = 0 \tag{9.36}$$

Solving for y_1 gives

$$y_1 = \pi[\pi\xi - E_0\dot{p}_1] + s_1^i$$

It suffices for now to note that, given inflation expectations, the minimum of the cost function obtains at a higher output target under a competent government compared to an incompetent one. See Figure 9.6 for an illustration of the decision problem which a competent candidate (solid line) and an incompetent candidate (broken line) faces. The parabolas $C(\bar{s})$ and $C(\underline{s})$ indicate the costs incurred at various signalling or mimicking levels y_1. The horizontal lines $W(\bar{s})$ and $W(\underline{s})$ mark the net gain which a competent and an incompetent government, respectively, can expect from winning the election. Of course, this benefit only accrues in full if the selected output level positively convinces voters that the incumbent government is competent and thus must be reelected. $\bar{A}$ and $\underline{A}$, the points of intersection between the cost curve and the maximum benefit curve, mark the maximum output levels, $\bar{y}^{max}$ and $\underline{y}^{max}$, at which a government of the indicated type may aim to signal or mimic competence. If this cannot do the job of securing reelection, the government does not try to signal at all, but resorts to short-run discretion, where costs are minimized at $\bar{y}^{dis}$, and $\underline{y}^{dis}$, respectively. Note that since an incompetent government faces a lower benefit line and a cost curve located further to the left, its maximum mimicking level is always lower than the signalling level of a competent government.

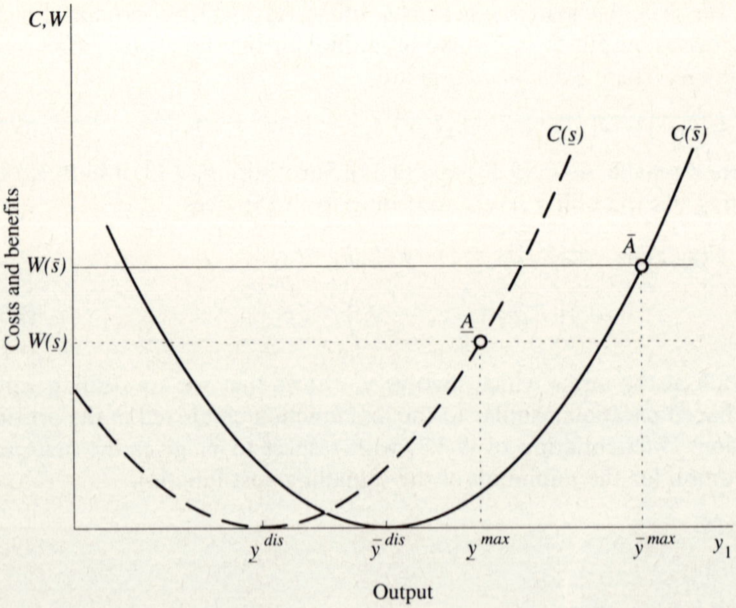

Figure 9.6 Signalling costs and benefits from reelection for competent and incompetent incumbents

The game outlined between voters and the government permits different types of equilibria. Below we will postulate two types and then proceed to demonstrate that they are so-called Nash equilibria indeed, in the sense that none of the actors involved has an incentive to deviate.

9.2.4 A separating equilibrium

An equilibrium is called **separating** if competent and incompetent governments select *different output levels*, and voters can positively infer from observing output in period 1 whether the incumbent is competent or not. Denote the posterior probability that the government is competent, given that y_1 is observed, by $\rho_1' = \text{prob}(s_1^i = \bar{s} : y_1)$. Then a separating equilibrium marks an appropriate threshold y^s, for which

$$\rho_1' = \begin{cases} 0 \text{ if } y_1 < y^s \\ 1 \text{ if } y_1 \geq y^s \end{cases} \tag{9.37}$$

Consider Figure 9.7. This threshold cannot be to the left of the incompetent type's maximum signalling level $\underline{y}^{max}$. Otherwise both types would benefit from sending the signal y^s, and (9.37) would not be rational. If

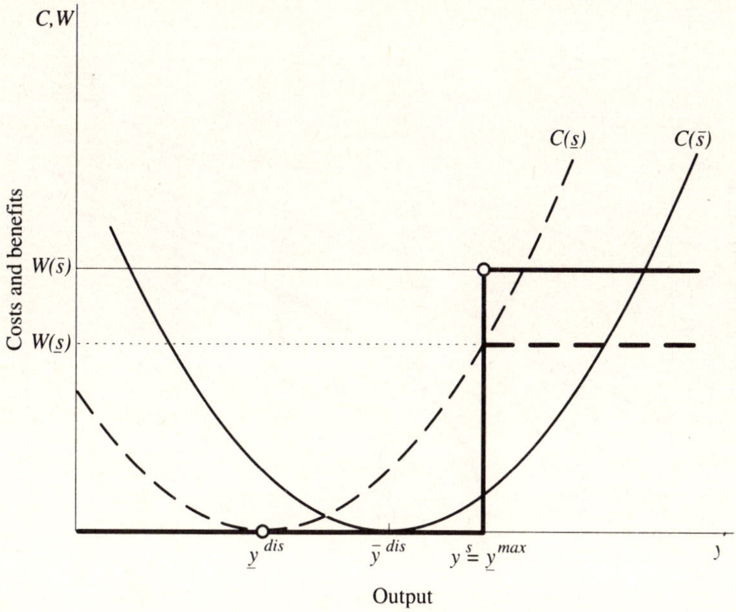

Figure 9.7 Costs and benefits in a separating equilibrium

y^s is at least equal to $\underline{y}^{max}$, an incompetent type has no incentive to mimic and settles for the discretionary optimum $\underline{y}^{dis}$ instead.[15] The competent type chooses the lowest output level which suffices to signal his or her true identity, $y^s = \underline{y}^{max}$, and which is just out of reach of the incompetent type.

> **PROBLEM 9.3**
>
> What policies do competent and incompetent incumbents employ if $\underline{y}^{max} < \bar{y}^{dis}$?

The situation just described is an equilibrium since neither type benefits from deviating, and the threshold selected by voters really works. Rational inflation expectations in this scenario are

$$E_0\dot{p}_1 = \rho\dot{p}(y^s, \bar{s}) + (1-\rho)\pi\xi \tag{9.38}$$

Substituting (9.33) into (9.38) and collecting terms, this turns into

$$E_0\dot{p}_1 = \pi\xi + \frac{\rho}{(1-\rho)\pi}(y^s - \bar{s}) \tag{9.38'}$$

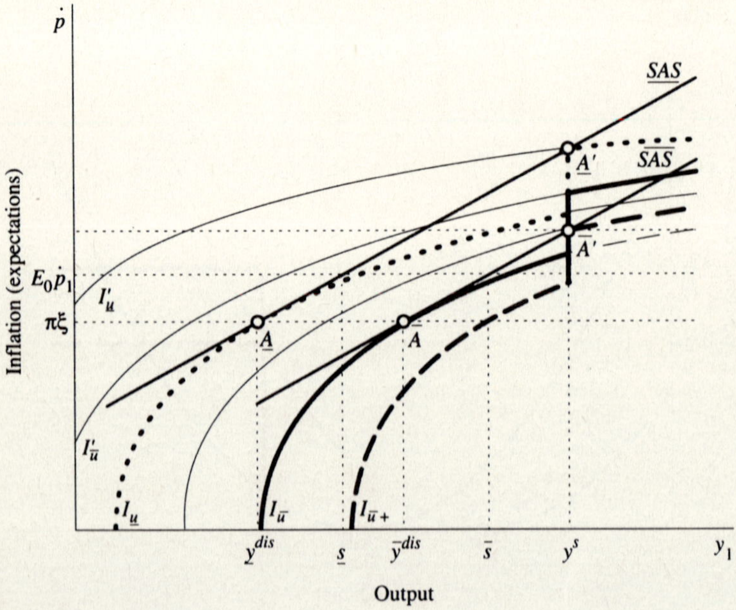

Figure 9.8 Separating equilibrium in an aggregate supply/aggregate demand framework

So in the nontrivial case $y^s > \bar{s}$ inflation expectations are higher than $\pi\xi$, the rate which an incompetent incumbent eventually chooses.[16] They are also smaller than $\pi\xi + (y^s - \bar{s})/\pi$, the rate which a signalling competent incumbent selects. Hence, an incompetent incumbent always creates unexpected deflation and a recession during election years – output is below the natural level associated with this candidate. The opposite holds for a competent incumbent. He or she inflates beyond expectations, creating a boom – output is above its natural level.

Figure 9.8 demonstrates how the separating equilibrium fits into the aggregate supply framework. $\underline{SAS}$ and $\overline{SAS}$ are the short-run aggregate supply curves of an incompetent and of a competent government, respectively. Their positions are determined by the points of intersection between the horizontal line at rational inflation expectations $E_0\dot{p}_1$ and the vertical lines at the respective natural output levels, $\underline{s}$ and $\bar{s}$. Given the options offered by the aggregate supply curve, each government maximizes utility (net of reelection considerations) by moving into the point of tangency between an indifference curve and the respective SAS curve. The indifference curves $I_{\underline{U}}$ and $I_{\bar{U}}$ depict all inflation output combinations which bring utility to $\underline{U}$ and $\bar{U}$, respectively.

$I'_{\underline{U}}(I'_{\bar{U}})$ gives inflation rates and output levels which yield the same utility level $\underline{U}(\bar{U})$ if the government is certain to be reelected. Since being reelected boosts utility by $\underline{W}\,(\bar{W})$, the utility level $\underline{U}(\bar{U})$, *ceteris paribus*, can now be achieved at lower output levels and/or higher inflation rates.

The separating equilibrium y^s signals the output level at which an incumbent correctly expects to turn from a sure loser into a sure winner. Hence, effective indifference curves display a discontinuity at y^s, as depicted for an incompetent incumbent by the bold dotted line, and for a competent incumbent by the bold solid line. As has been argued previously, y^s must be where the incompetent type becomes indifferent between $\underline{A}'$ and $\underline{A}$, that is, between mimicking and not. By assumption, he or she selects $\underline{A}$, and does so by disinflating unexpectedly, which drives output below its natural level of $\underline{s}$. The competent type inflates unexpectedly, pushing output beyond $\bar{s}$ to y^s. This brings him or her on to the indifference curve $I_{\bar{U}+}$ (the bold broken line in Figure 9.8). Again, moving away from $\bar{A}'$ along $\overline{SAS}$ to either side reduces utility. So the competent incumbent has no incentive to deviate, and $\bar{A}'$ qualifies as an equilibrium.

9.2.5 A pooling equilibrium

In a **pooling** equilibrium competent and incompetent governments select the *same output levels*. This makes it impossible for voters to conclude from observing output whether the incumbent is competent or not. In this case, posterior probabilities that the incumbent is competent may be described by

$$\rho_1' = \begin{cases} 0 & \text{if } y_1 < y^p \\ \rho & \text{if } y_1 \geq y^p \end{cases} \tag{9.39}$$

where y^p denotes the pooling equilibrium. In a pooling equilibrium both types produce the same output level. To arrive at y^p, the respective inflation rates to be generated by a competent and an incompetent incumbent are, according to (9.33),

$$\dot{p}_1(y^p, \bar{s}) = E_0\dot{p}_1 + \frac{1}{\pi}(y^p - \bar{s}) \tag{9.40}$$

$$\dot{p}_1(y^p, \underline{s}) = E_0\dot{p}_1 + \frac{1}{\pi}(y^p - \underline{s}) \tag{9.41}$$

For inflation expectations to be formed rationally, they must be a correctly weighted average of the inflation rates produced by each type:

$$E_0\dot{p}_1 = \rho\dot{p}_1(y^p, \bar{s}) + (1-\rho)\dot{p}_1(y^p, \underline{s}) \tag{9.42}$$

Substituting (9.40) and (9.41) into (9.42), and solving for y^p gives

$$\begin{aligned} y^p &= \rho\bar{s} + (1-\rho)\underline{s} \\ &= 0 \end{aligned} \tag{9.43}$$

The pooling equilibrium corresponds to the expected value of the competence shocks, which is zero. An intuitive rationalization is that if y^p exceeded $\bar{s}$ (fell short of $\underline{s}$), both types were required to inflate (deflate) unexpectedly. This could not be a rational expectations equilibrium. The equilibrium must, therefore, be between $\bar{s}$ and $\underline{s}$, with the incompetent type inflating and the competent type deflating unexpectedly. Substitution of (9.43) into (9.40) and (9.41), respectively, reveals that unexpected deflation under a competent government equals $\dot{p}_1(0, \bar{s}) - E_0\dot{p}_1 = -\bar{s}/\pi$, and unexpected inflation under an incompetent government equals $\dot{p}_1(0, \underline{s}) - E_0\dot{p}_1 = -\underline{s}/\pi$.

The fact that expected inflation dropped out of the solution of equations (9.40), (9.41) and (9.42) for y^p suggests that no unique inflation level exists in equilibrium. Figures 9.9 and 9.10 illustrate one such pooling equilibrium in which the competent incumbent selects the inflation rate $\pi\xi$.

Figure 9.9 depicts the equilibrium by means of aggregate supply curves and indifference curves. Since there is nothing that the competent

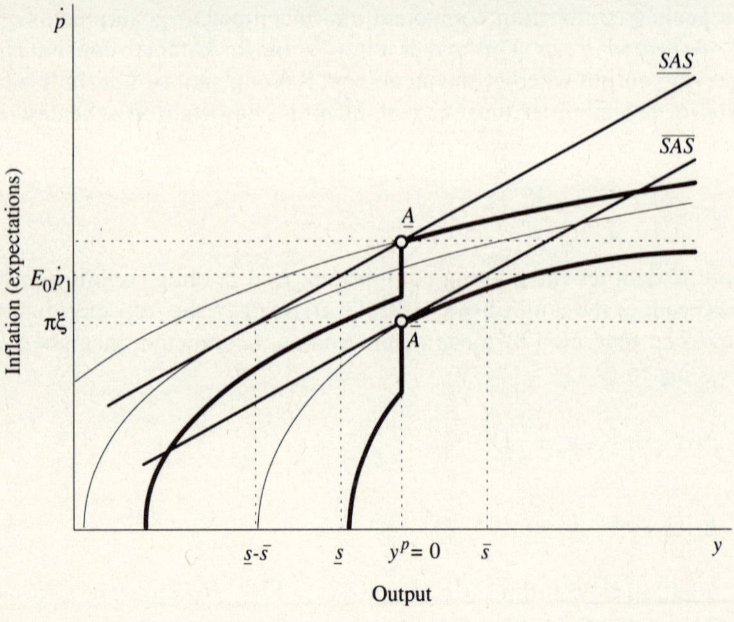

Figure 9.9 Pooling equilibrium in an aggregate supply/aggregate demand framework

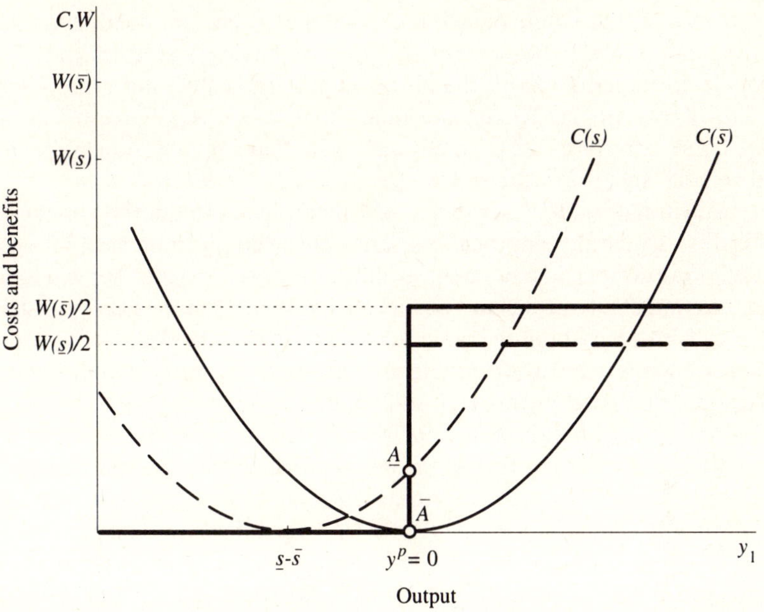

Figure 9.10 Costs and benefits in a pooling equilibrium

government can do to convince voters that it really is competent, it maximizes utility in $\bar{A}$ by choosing the inflation rate $\pi\xi$. The incompetent incumbent successfully mimics the competent one by unexpectedly inflating at $\pi\xi + (\bar{s} - \underline{s})/\pi$ and thus maximizing utility in $\underline{A}$. Given how voters read output levels, neither do incumbents face incentives to deviate from policies, nor do voters see any reason to adopt a new signalling interpretation. Figure 9.10 translates the pooling equilibrium into the cost benefit diagram.

9.2.6 Summary

Equilibrium election cycle models serve to demonstrate that even if all actors behave entirely rationally and are aware of each other's incentive structures, election patterns in policy instruments and other macroeconomic variables may be observed. These patterns may prove difficult to be distinguished from a traditional, naive political business cycle. In a separating equilibrium the competent incumbent inflates unexpectedly just before the election, and wins. This coincides with the optimal policy in a traditional political business cycle model. An incompetent incumbent deflates unexpectedly instead, and loses. The traditional explanation for this would be that voters punish the incompetent type for conducting bad policy, and reward the competent type for having raised output. The equilibrium explanation for the observed pattern is quite different. Voters do not reward (punish) an expansionary (contractionary) government for what it did in the past, but correctly *anticipate* that a pre-election expansion is a reliable signal for above-average output in the future.

Unfortunately, the possibility of other types of equilibria makes it difficult to gauge the empirical relevance of the equilibrium election cycle model; for example, in a pooling equilibrium the incompetent type inflates and the competent one deflates unexpectedly. What is more, the expansionary incumbent has about the same chance of winning the election as the one who produces a recession. So there may not exist too many patterns which the model discussed in this section could *not* explain.

Another weakness is that, while we have made voters entirely rational, we withhold current information from them which they possess in models of the naive type. It is not easy to accept that voters should learn about inflation much later than about output. Having difficulty in accepting this is no justification for discarding the entire approach, however. Originally, the model was devised to analyze fiscal policy. There the required information asymmetries are more plausible than in the context of monetary policy – the actual size of the budget deficit may not be revealed until the next fiscal year. Since under a set of plausible assumptions fiscal policy plays a minor role in open economics under flexible exchange rates – see Chapter 1 – equilibrium business cycles may be more important in relatively closed economies or under fixed exchange rates.

9.3 Elections and the exchange rate

This section demonstrates that election cycles in macroeconomic variables are bound to occur even if individuals are forward-looking and the government does not gear policy towards reelection. Assume that different policymakers have different preferences and, hence, set policy instruments at different levels.[17] In a competitive demoncracy with periodic elections this has two important implications. Assume there is an incumbent party (or candidate) and one opposition party (or candidate). Private agents are fully informed about each party's policy preferences. Then throughout the current electoral term policy is correctly anticipated to reflect the preferences of the incumbent. For the time following the next election it is expected to be a weighted average of the policies preferred by the incumbent and the opposition party, respectively, with the weights being the probabilities of the contenders to win the election. Looking at this from today, this amounts to an announced money supply change at the day after the next election.[18] As the election result is released, however, the money supply unexpectedly changes to the level attributed to the winner. There it is expected to stay for another, say, four years, right up to the next election, when again it is expected to change to a weighted average of both parties' choices. So even if no government resorts to discretionary monetary policy for stabilization (or other) purposes, and even though there is no uncertainty about the policy preferences of parties, exchange rates are driven by a succession of anticipated and unanticipated monetary policy changes.

For a graphical illustration of this **rational partisan theory** in Figure 9.11, assume that the present incumbent party sets the money supply at m^i, whenever in power. The present opposition party sets the money supply at $m^o > m^i$ when in power. Let prob^i be the exogenous probability that the present incumbent party will win the next election. Figure 9.11 measures time in years where elections are held every four years. The winning party takes office and implements policy in the election period. After the election in period 0 the expected future course of monetary policy is given by the solid line. As time elapses during the current term of office expectations remain based on the solid line. At the next election the money supply is expected to change to $m^w = \text{prob}^i \cdot m^i + (1 - \text{prob}^i)m^o$. It actually changes to either m^i or m^o, however, depending on who wins. In any case the money supply changes unexpectedly as long as $0 < \text{prob}^i < 1$. After the election

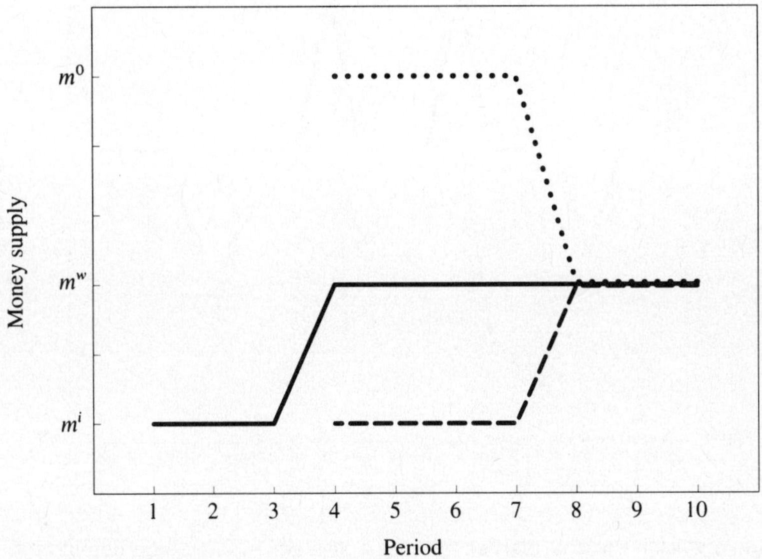

Figure 9.11 Partisan effects on the expected money supply

result is published the money supply is expected to follow either the broken line if the incumbent succeeded or otherwise the dotted line. The same kind of uncertainty applies and similar surprise effects occur at all future elections.

Exchange rate jumps at election dates and movements between elections can be derived by substituting the anticipated money supply patterns into equation (5.34), the rational-expectations solution of the neoclassical open-economy model derived in Chapter 5:

$$e_t = \frac{\pi+\delta}{D}\left[m_t + \sum_{j=1}^{\infty}\left(\frac{\lambda}{1+\lambda}\right)^j E_t m_{t+j}\right] - \frac{\pi(1-\phi\delta)}{D(1+\lambda)}\sum_{j=0}^{\infty}\left(\frac{\lambda}{1+\lambda}\right)^j E_{t-1} m_{t+j} \tag{5.34}$$

This may prove cumbersome and not very illuminating. A better understanding of how democratic elections may affect exchange rates and output according to rational partisan theory is probably acquired by looking at Figure 9.12.

Figure 9.12 shows simulated exchange rate and output movements over some four electoral terms. The initial incumbent's policy preference is $m^i = 1$, while the initial opposition prefers $m^o = 1.1$. Party i wins the elections

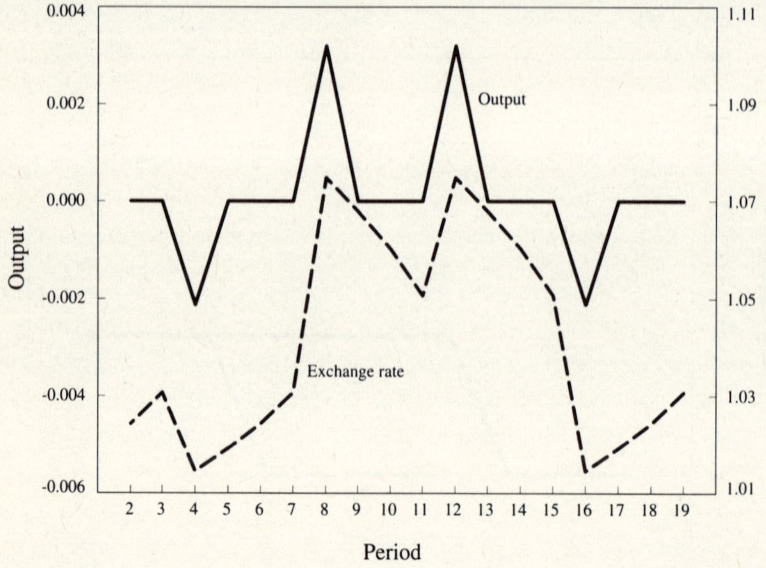

Figure 9.12 Rational partisan theory and election effects on output and the exchange rate (parameter values for simulation: $\delta=0.5$, $\pi=0.5$, $\phi=0.8$ and $\lambda=4$)

in periods 4 and 16, while party o wins in periods 8 and 12. Parameter values are given in the caption to Figure 9.12.

The simulation visualizes that though neither party deliberately attempts to generate movements in nominal and real variables, or to design policy with an eye on elections, there is a distinct election pattern both in the exchange rate and in real output. While we would expect such effects whenever there is a change of government, it is interesting to note that they occur just the same when one government serves several terms in office and policy never changes.

9.4 Choice of exchange rate regimes

The central message of the preceding sections is that institutional arrangements and utility maximization of policymakers may destabilize open economies under flexible exchange rates. This raises many questions regarding institutional reform. How often should elections take place? Should the number of times an incumbent can run for reelection be restricted? What is the optimal design for a central bank, regarding autonomy, etc.? What are the social benefits from accumulating and disseminating statistical information rapidly? Should monetary and/or fiscal policy be constrained by rules on the constitutional level? Or is it recommended to dump the system of flexible exchange rates in favour of some fixed-rate system?

In a way, questions such as the last one suffer from a similar weakness as did those which were posed by the traditional (apolitical) theory of economic policy. Traditionally, the theory of economic policy has searched for things like *optimal* monetary policy. The previous sections have shown that monetary policy may not be expected to be very receptive to scholarly advice. Rather, policymakers base decisions on cost–benefit calculations of their own, which makes *monetary policy endogenous*. Similarly, the choice and the evolution of institutions reflect optimizing behaviour on the part of all individuals involved, rendering *institutions endogenous* too. This insight has provoked a new view of institutions. Recent work includes efforts to model how exchange rate regimes evolve over time.[19] We now turn to a discussion of one such model, in which the evolution of the exchange rate system reflects the interaction between interest groups, voters and the government.

As a general framework for the analysis, picture a democracy with information costs. Both the government and voters deliberately choose not to be fully informed. In this scenario interest groups acquire an amount of influence on political decisions which goes far beyond the represented voting power.[20] The country is small and open, and its competitive position relative to the rest of the world depends on the (real) exchange rate and on trade protection, which may come in the form of tariffs and of nontariff barriers to trade. The three actors of our model are assumed to behave as follows.

Interest groups. Many groups in society have common interests. Because of the free-rider problem, only those which actually organize as an interest group, however, are those offering potentially large benefits to each individual member and/or which are not too large.[21] As a consequence, *producers* tend to be better organized and much more active and influential than *consumers*. As a first approximation, therefore, we pay attention to the interest of producers only.

With the classification employed here, the term 'producers' must comprise both capital owners and workers. If workers characteristically possess sector-specific skills, their welfare is linked qualitatively in the same way to changes in their sector's competitive position as is the welfare of capital owners.[22] So there is no need to distinguish between the two subgroups here.

A distinction which must be made is the one between exporting and import-competing industries. The latter is the traditional beneficiary of import restrictions. If anything, exporting industries may expect to be negatively affected by domestic tariffs, as foreign countries tend to retort by raising their tariffs too. Both sectors are affected by so-called exchange rate protection, which tries to reduce real exchange rate disequilibria and variability.

Voters. Voters want the government to provide high income. Given a presumed negative relationship between protection and efficiency (income), this implies that voters implicitly want low protection. Since all voters are also producers in the above sense, and since voters may be ready to sacrifice some efficiency for protection of certain sectors like agriculture, the optimal level of trade protection desired by voters probably exceeds zero. We assume that voters have no particular preference regarding the exchange rate regime or exchange rate protection.

Government. The government takes into account its own preferences, but also the demands of interest groups and the preferences of voters. As regards its own preferences: it is indifferent to the level of trade protection. But it wants to retain some control over monetary policy. So the exchange rate regime desired by the government does not have completely fixed rates.

With this general outline, consider Model 9.5. Equation (9.44) explains trade protection policies. The first argument, the variance of the exchange rate var(E), reflects the pressures of import-competing industries. If the domestic currency appreciates, the competitive position of such industries

■ Model 9.5
Evolution of exchange rate system and protectionism

$\dot{\pi}_T = \Phi[\text{var}(E), \pi_T - \pi_T^V]$ $\partial\Phi/\partial\text{var}(E) > 0, \partial\Phi/\partial\pi_T < 0$	protection dynamics	(9.44)
$\dot{\pi}_E = \Psi[\text{var}(E), \pi_T, \pi_E - \pi_E^G]$ $\partial\Psi/\partial\text{var}(E) > 0, \partial\Psi/\partial\delta\pi_T > 0, \partial\Psi/\partial\pi_E < 0$	exchange rate protection	(9.45)
$\text{var}(E) = \Omega(\pi_E)$ $d\Omega/d\pi_E < 0$	exchange rate variance	(9.46)

Notes: The signs of (partial) derivatives are given next to structural equations. Variables are defined as follows:

π_T	trade protection (tariffs, nontariff barriers)
π_E	exchange rate protection (intervention, capital controls, exchange rate targets, crawling pegs, pegged rates)
π_T^V	trade protection desired by voters
π_E^G	exchange rate protection desired by government
var(E)	variance of the exchange rate

Φ, Ψ and Ω denote functions

deteriorates. As a response, their efforts to obtain protection will intensify. If, later on, the real exchange rate depreciates back towards its former level, import-competing industries do not lobby for a removal of import barriers. Because of this asymmetry, a high *variance* of the exchange rate must be expected to push up trade barriers. To capture this in formal terms, we postulate that the *change* in trade protection (and not its *level*) is positively related to var(E).

The second argument in (9.44), $\pi_T - \pi_T^V$, reflects voters' demand for protection. Voters want protection to fall if it exceeds some potentially very small desired level π_T^V, and to rise in the opposite case.

By analogy with the above argument, equation (9.45) postulates that a variable exchange rate will push up the exporting industries' demand for exchange rate protection. As this cannot bring about any lasting improvements of the competitive position, it should at least reduce short-, medium- and long-run variations of the exchange rate, which may threaten to drive industries out of foreign markets. Demand for exchange rate protection also rises as exporters face trade barriers abroad. Assuming some foreign reaction to rising domestic trade barriers, (9.45) postulates that domestic trade barriers push up exchange rate protection. The third term in brackets, $\pi_E - \pi_E^G$, shows the government's preference for less than perfect exchange rate protection.

Equation (9.46) postulates that exchange rate protection successfully reduces exchange rate variability. Substituting (9.46) into (9.44) and (9.45) gives us a system of two differential equations:

$$\dot{\pi}_T = \Phi[\Omega(\pi_E), \pi_T - \pi_T^V] \qquad \partial\Phi/\partial\pi_E < 0, \partial\Phi/\partial\pi_T < 0 \tag{9.47}$$

$$\dot{\pi}_E = \Psi[\Omega(\pi_E), \pi_T, \pi_E - \pi_E^G] \qquad \partial\Psi/\partial\pi_E < 0, \partial\Psi/\partial\pi_T > 0, \partial\Psi/\partial\pi_E < 0 \tag{9.48}$$

It is convenient to analyze the dynamics of this system by means of the phase diagram approach introduced in previous chapters (Figure 9.13). The first demarcation line, $\dot{\pi}_T = 0$, follows from (9.47). According to the implicit function rule, its slope is

$$\left.\frac{d\pi_T}{d\pi_E}\right|_{\dot{\pi}_T=0} = -\frac{\partial\Phi/\partial\pi_E}{\partial\Phi/\partial\pi_T} < 0 \tag{9.49}$$

The second demarcation line, $\dot{\pi}_E = 0$, follows from (9.48) and possesses the slope

$$\left.\frac{d\pi_T}{d\pi_E}\right|_{\dot{\pi}_E=0} = -\frac{\partial\Psi/\partial\pi_E}{\partial\Psi/\partial\pi_T} > 0 \tag{9.50}$$

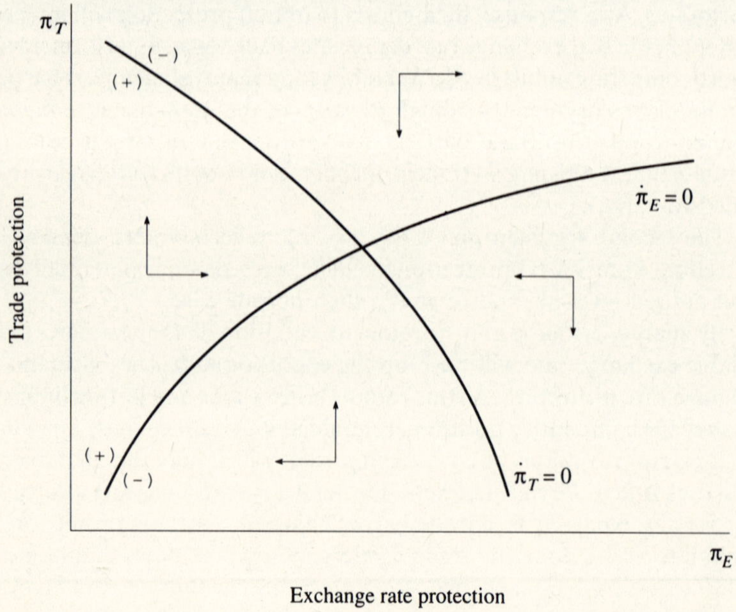

Figure 9.13 Exchange rate regimes and trade policies in the long run

Possessing negative and positive slopes, respectively, the two demarcation lines divide the phase space into four distinct regions. In order to determine the forces of motion that operate in each of the four regions, we simply refer back to (9.47) and compute $d\dot{\pi}_T/d\pi_E = \delta\Phi/\delta\pi_E < 0$. This tells us that north of $\dot{\pi}_T = 0$ trade protection falls; in the area to the south, it rises. From (9.48) we compute $d\dot{\pi}_T/d\pi_E = \delta\Psi/\delta\pi_E < 0$, which says that exchange rate protection moves back towards this demarcation line from either side. A set of directional arrows indicates the cyclical nature of the intertemporal movement of trade and exchange rate protection.

Given the long-run perspective of our model, the completion of one such cycle would need decades, if not generations. Over such a long time the social, political, economic and even military background, against which we have modelled the evolution of trade and exchange rate regimes, undergoes possibly dramatic changes: demographic changes, new international organizations or treaties, a new balance of political and military power – possibly wars, technical innovations, nations which are born or fall apart. All this would shift the demarcation lines and thus keep the cycle moving, even though the model is inherently stable.

Exchange rate protection is a heterogeneous variable. It reflects how the regime is outlined on paper – in particular whether rates are fixed or flexible – but also how it is operated in real life. Thus a regime of flexible exchange rates may well continue to exist on paper while exchange rate protection already increases due to increasing central bank intervention in the foreign exchanges. A regime of fixed exchange rates may be upheld formally, while frequent parity adjustments or widening intervention bands signal that protection falls. So if exchange rate protection is measured by how the regime is specified on paper, as we do along the abscissa in Figure 9.14, horizontal movements will be observed as sudden shifts from one regime to the other.

Despite its very high level of abstraction, the model yields refutable hypotheses, such as the following (see Figure 9.14):

1. Under a regime of flexible exchange rates trade policies become more and more protectionist.
2. Trade barriers only continue to be removed if the level of exchange rate protection is high, as under a fixed-rate system.
3. Countries tend to switch from flexible to fixed exchange rates only when trade protection is high.
4. Countries tend to introduce flexible exchange rates when trade protection is low.

This set of hypotheses seems well in line with what has happened since the Second World War on the international level. Starting in the north-east

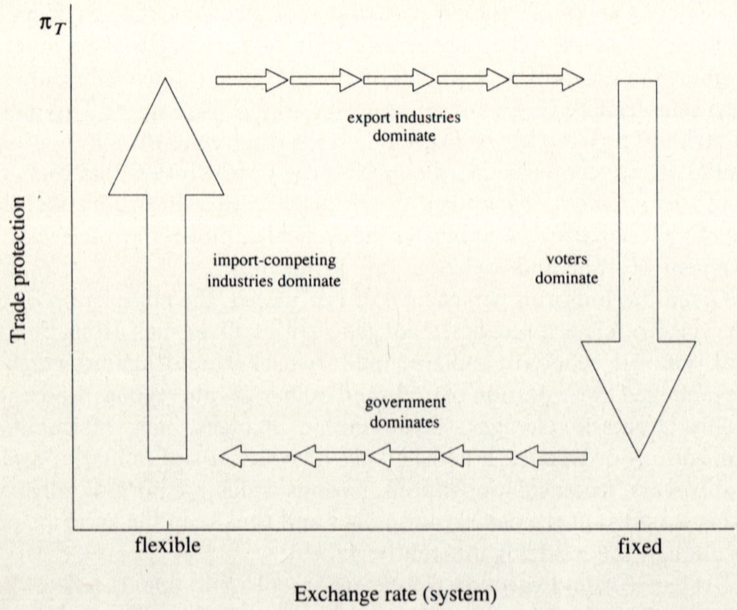

Figure 9.14 The protection–liberalization cycle in international trade and monetary relations

corner of Figure 9.14, the Bretton Woods system has permitted the worldwide reduction of tariff rates. After the collapse of this system, the volatility of flexible exchange rates led to the introduction of new forms of nontariff trade barriers.[23] By now, most countries are probably located somewhere in the north-west corner.[24]

9.5 Summary

This chapter has carried us beyond orthodox analyses of open economies under flexible exchange rates, which prevailed through the rest of the book. Major insights are the following.

1. If contenders for political offices have differing positions on economic policy issues, democratic elections introduce discontinuities into the course of the economy. This happens for two reasons: first, throughout any presidential term policy is expected to change after the next election; second, after the next election policies are different from what is expected.

2. If voters are backward-looking and inflation expectations are adaptive (or some other nominal rigidities exist), governments which want to win

elections may deliberately design economic policy so as to generate a political business cycle – and they may succeed in doing so.

3. If inflation expectations are rational (and no other nominal rigidities exist), government efforts to create a political business cycle fail. However, an election cycle in inflation rates or an inflationary bias must be expected to remain.

4. While the government may prefer to get rid of this inflationary bias, such attempts may not succeed because of time inconsistency. Announcements of noninflationary policies are never credible when the underlying game between the government and the labour market is repeated only a finite number of times. If the game is repeated an infinite number of times (or if the final round is determined stochastically), the punishment expected from acquiring the bad reputation of a cheating government may reduce or even eliminate the inflationary bias.

5. Even if voters are completely rational, that is, informed about the structure of the economy and forward-looking, election patterns in economic policy may nevertheless occur. A precondition is that voters lack the information that is necessary to judge the competence of the incumbent. Then signalling and mimicking efforts of competent and incompetent incumbents may give rise to deliberately generated surprise expansions, but also to surprise contractions at election dates.

6. The choice of exchange rate regimes also reflects optimizing behaviour of the government, in interaction with voters, interest groups and the economy. In particular, the volatility of exchange rates, which is high under regimes of flexible exchange rates and low under regimes of fixed exchange rates and which has been a central theme of this book, must be seen as a driving force behind evolutionary cycles in international trade and monetary relations.

The time inconsistency problem discussed here is of a very general nature. It is not only likely to haunt monetary and exchange rate policy, but also fields like fiscal policy, trade policy, or the credibility of institutional arrangements. Exciting research is going on in this area which applies a game-theoretic perspective to a host of policy problems. One such strand analyzes the advantages of tying one's hand by entering a free-trade agreement such as GATT or a fixed-rate system such as the EMS (on the latter, see Giavazzi and Pagano 1988). Another important line of research deals with the credibility problems involved in international policy coordination (see Canzoneri 1985). This latter issue derives from the special nature of political cycles in the open economy. These involve improvements in a country's competitive position which occur at the expense of other countries. Rational responses of foreign governments expand many of the games analyzed in this chapter into a multi-player setting.

9.6 Answers to the problems

Problem 9.1

Since we are looking for the optimal stable cycle, that is, a cycle which keeps repeating itself, all election periods ($i=0$) and nonelection periods ($i=1$) must be identical. According to (9.2) we have

$$\begin{aligned} E_1\dot{p}_0 &= \dot{p}_1 \\ E_0\dot{p}_1 &= \dot{p}_0 \end{aligned} \tag{9.51}$$

Substituting this into (9.1) gives

$$\begin{aligned} y_0 &= \pi(\dot{p}_0 - \dot{p}_1) \\ y_1 &= \pi(\dot{p}_1 - \dot{p}_0) \end{aligned} \tag{9.52}$$

Inserting (9.7′) into (9.8′), making use of (9.51) and (9.52), and differentiating with respect to $\dot{p}_0$ and $\dot{p}_1$ gives the first-order conditions for a vote maximum:

$$\begin{aligned} \partial V/\partial\dot{p}_0 &= -\dot{p}_0 + \xi\pi - \omega\xi\pi = 0 \\ \partial V/\partial\dot{p}_1 &= -\xi\pi - \omega\dot{p}_1 + \omega\xi\pi = 0 \end{aligned}$$

Thus the optimal cycle is given by the inflation rates below:

$$\dot{p}_0 = (1-\omega)\xi\pi$$

$$\dot{p}_1 = -\frac{1-\omega}{\omega}\xi\pi$$

Problem 9.2

Under the new expectations mechanism a government which has cheated is punished for two periods. Only after inflation was as expected for two subsequent periods does the government regain its reputation, and individuals believe in the announced rule again. In this scenario enforcement is given by

$$\begin{aligned} E = {} & \omega[V_1(\dot{p}_1 = E_0 p_1 = \xi\pi) - V_1(\dot{p}_1 = E_0\dot{p}_1 = \dot{p}^a)] \\ & + \omega^2[V_2(\dot{p}_2 = E_1 p_2 = \xi\pi) - V_2(\dot{p}_2 = E_1\dot{p}_2 = \dot{p}^a)] \end{aligned}$$

Making use of (9.1) and (9.7) and collecting terms gives

$$E = (\omega + \omega^2)[\pi^2\xi^2 - (\dot{p}^a)^2]/2$$

Figure 9.15 graphs this new enforcement curve against the familiar temptation curve. The new result is that the optimal rule $\dot{p}^a = 0$ may be

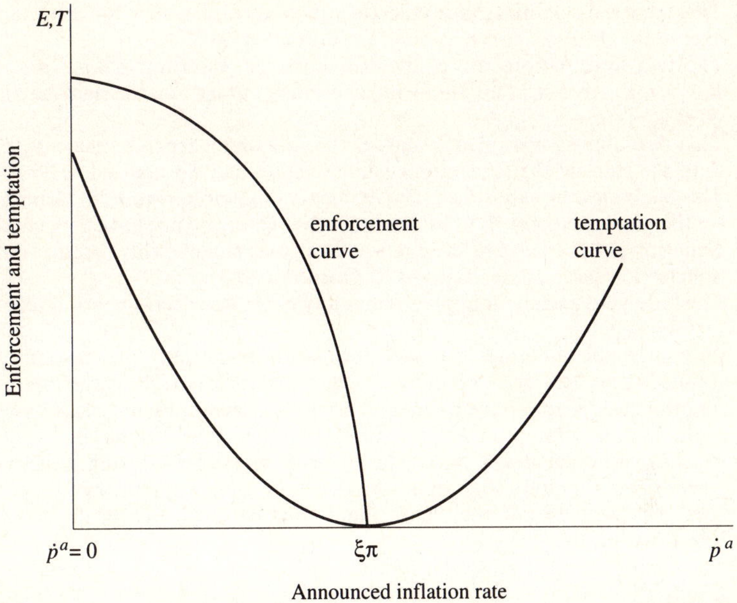

Figure 9.15 Possible benefits and costs of reneging on an announced inflation rate when the government loses credibility for two periods

credible, the condition being

$$\omega \geq \sqrt{5}/2 - 1/2 \approx 0.618$$

Problem 9.3

As in the case which is discussed in the text, for the competent incumbent it would suffice to raise output to y^{max} to signal his or her competence. However, in the present situation the incumbent will raise output further to his or her preferred level $\bar{y}^{dis}$, thus increasing net benefits. Therefore, in general terms, the signalling equilibrium is given by

$$y^s = \max[\underline{y}^{max}, \underline{y}^{dis}]$$

NOTES

1. The *Wall Street Journal Europe*, 2 January 1992, p. 13.
2. Throughout this chapter it is assumed that governments control monetary policy. So some of the results would not apply to countries with a highly independent central bank.

3. This theory of a **political business cycle**, originally discussed in the context of an exploitable Phillips curve, is due to Nordhaus (1975).
4. The two formulations are equivalent, however. Inserting $\dot{p}_t \equiv p_t - p_{t-1}$ and $E_{t-1}\dot{p}_t \equiv E_{t-1}p_t - p_{t-1}$ into (9.1) and cancelling out p_{t-1} on the right-hand side gives $y_t = \pi(p_t - E_{t-1}p_t)$.
5. That part of the government's share of the vote which depends on factors other than the state of the economy is kept constant and normalized to zero.
6. This facilitates the exposition. The necessary (and more plausible) assumption for the qualitative results to be derived is that voters do not have perfect recall. Equation (9.8) can also be rationalized as a government utility function during nonelection periods. See Barro and Gordon (1983).
7. The following argument applies under any other nonelection period inflation rate as well.
8. Of course, all our graphic model does is illustrate that vote maximization results in a political business cycle. The depicted cycle is arbitrarily chosen. The optimal cycle would have to be, and could be, derived by means of dynamic optimization techniques. What is more, the optimal cycle in the context of our expository model is *not finite*: the optimal investment during nonelection periods is an infinitely large recession. However, a *finite* optimal cycle results as soon as voters do not completely ignore last period's state of the economy when casting their vote.
9. The ideas presented in Sections 9.1.3 and 9.1.4 are mostly due to Barro and Gordon (1983).
10. On second thoughts, though, assuming a one-shot game may not be so unrealistic after all. Consider the US president, who is restricted to run for re-election but once – which is a one-shot game. Even then, however, he or she may be forced to take into account reputational effects spreading out over the vice-president and the party.
11. This could also be achieved by interpreting equation (9.10) as a government utility function, as done by Barro and Gordon (1983).
12. Since periods are longer, the SAS curve should be steeper. This leaves qualitative results unaffected.
13. Wishing output to rise above its 'natural' level of zero may appear implausible. It would make sense when 'natural' output is distorted, say due to trade union monopoly power or an inefficient tax system. Then voters and the government may prefer a reduction of individually involuntary unemployment risk.
14. The best credible rule is given by the point of intersection between the temptation curve and the enforcement curve. Equating (9.18′) and (9.21′) yields

$$\frac{1}{2}(\pi\xi - \dot{p}^a)^2 = \frac{\omega}{2}(\pi\xi - \dot{p}^a)(\pi\xi + \dot{p}^a)$$

Dividing both sides by $\pi\xi - \dot{p}^a$ and solving for $\dot{p}^a$ gives $\dot{p}^a = \pi\xi(1-\omega)/(1+\omega)$

15. Strictly speaking, the incompetent incumbent is indifferent between y^{dis} and y^{max}. So y^s really must be an infinitesimally small amount larger than $\bar{y}^{max}$. As this might make the language awkward and overload graphs, simply assume that an indifferent candidate always applies short-run discretion.

Recall that cost curves in Figures 9.6 and 9.7 are drawn for given inflation expectations. While Figure 9.6 holds for any arbitrary inflation expectation, Figure 9.7 requires rational expectations which adequately reflect the separating equilibrium. Because of this, labels such as y^{dis} generally do not refer to the same output levels in the two graphs. Since in Figure 9.7 the position of the curve determines the separating equilibrium, and the separating equilibrium via rational inflation expectations determines the position of the curve, both have to be determined simultaneously. For now the graphical analysis simply *assumes* that the equilibrium has been computed and that the position of the cost curve reflects inflation expectations which are compatible with this equilibrium. Details on rational inflation expectations are given below.

16. The trivial case is $y^s = \bar{s}$. Then, according to (9.38′) $E_0\dot{p}_1 = \pi\xi$, which is also the inflation rate which incumbents of both types will actually select. As there are no inflation surprises, output is either $\underline{s}$ or $\bar{s}$.
17. The assumption is that, for example, left-wing and right-wing parties want to favour their core constituencies which derive from different segments of the social spectrum. In its initial form, this **partisan theory** was introduced by Hibbs (1977). A second-generation version, the **rational partisan theory**, on which we draw here, was launched by Alesina (1987) and Alesina and Sachs (1988).
18. In some countries, like the United States, there is a considerable lag between the election and the inauguration of a new president. This complicates matters compared to the case discussed here. See Gärtner (1986).
19. See Flood, Bhandari and Horne (1989), and Gärtner and Ursprung (1989). In the first paper the exchange rate regime changes as an optimal response to changes of the underlying economic structure over time. The second paper employs more of a politico-economic perspective and contains an econometric illustration of the model to be presented below.
20. Given that the government and voters lack perfect information, interest groups may share selectively their information advantage which they derive from their field of specialization, or they may actively conduct information policy, by choosing to bring information to the public or not, but putting the blame on or giving credit to politicians for certain developments, justified or not.
21. Of course, this only holds as a rule of thumb. For a more differentiating discussion see Olson's (1965) classic work.
22. This is also supported by empirical work. See Magee (1980).
23. This has been noted by many observers. See Corden (1987).
24. EC member countries are located in the north-west of Figure 9.14, as regards their external relations, and in the south-east, as far as intracommunity relations are concerned.

REFERENCES

Alesina, A. (1987) 'Macroeconomic policy in a two-party system as a repeated game', *Quarterly Journal of Economics* 102, 651–78.

Alesina, A. and J. Sachs (1988) 'Political parties and the business cycle in the US, 1948–1984', *Journal of Money, Credit, and Banking* 20, 63–82.

Barro, R. J. and D. Gordon (1983) 'Rules, discretion, and reputation in a model of monetary policy', *Journal of Monetary Economics* 12, 101–21.

Canzoneri, Mathew B. (1985) 'Monetary policy games and the role of private information', *American Economic Review* 75, 1056–70.

Corden, W. M. (1987) 'The revival of protectionism in developed countries', in D. Salvatore (ed.) *The New Protectionist Threat to World Welfare*, New York: North-Holland, 45–68.

Flood, R. P., J. S. Bhandari and J. P. Horne (1989) 'Evolution of exchange rate regimes', *IMF Staff Papers* 36, 810–35.

Gärtner, M. (1986) 'Some political economy of flexible exchange rates', *European Journal of Political Economy* 2, 153–68.

Gärtner, M. and H. W. Ursprung (1989) 'Politische und ökonomische Gesetze für flexible Wechselkurse', *Jahrbuch für Neue Politische Ökonomie* 8, 109–25.

Giavazzi, F. and M. Pagano (1988) 'The advantage of tying one's hand: EMS discipline and central bank credibility', *European Economic Review* 32, 1055–75.

Hibbs, D. A. (1977) 'Political parties and macroeconomic policy', *American Political Science Review* 71, 1467–87.

Magee, S. P. (1980) 'Three simple tests of the Stolper–Samuelson theorem', in P. Oppenheimer (ed.) *Issues in International Economics*. London: 138–55.

Nordhaus, W. D. (1975) 'The political business cycle', *Review of Economic Studies* 42, 169–90.

Olson, M. (1965) *The Logic of Collective Action*, Cambridge, MA: Harvard University Press.

Persson, T. and G. Tabellini (1990) *Macroeconomic Policy, Credibility and Politics*, Chur: Harwood Academic.

Index